PONZI SCHEMES,
INVADERS FROM MARS
& MORE
EXTRAORDINARY
POPULAR DELUSIONS
AND THE
MADNESS OF CROWDS

Ghy heden van Malleghem wilt nu wel fyn gefint   Om v te genesen ben ick gecommen hier   Compt vry den meesten met den minsten sonder verhoyen
Ick Vrou Hexe wil hier oock wel worden bekrant   Tiouwen dienst met myn onder masterssen fier   Hebdy de werp int hooft oft luteren v de keyen

The Witch of Malleghem *(La Sorcière de Malleghem)*

This engraving by the Flemish artist Pieter Bruegel the Elder purports to show how the residents of a village proverbially known among the Flemings as a kind of "Suckerville" or "Foolstown" were treated for their disability. In that time (Bruegel lived from c. 1525 to 1569) madness was believed to result from bumps or "stones" on the head or the brain. The itinerant witch casually restores sanity by removing the "stones" surgically. From the expressions of most of the Malleghemians it can be seen that they are anxious to undergo the rude treatment. The abundance of stones may also say something about the extent of madness there.

PONZI SCHEMES, INVADERS FROM MARS & MORE EXTRAORDINARY POPULAR DELUSIONS AND THE MADNESS OF CROWDS

•

JOSEPH BULGATZ

HARMONY BOOKS/NEW YORK

Excerpt from 1984 by George Orwell, copyright 1949 by Harcourt Brace Jovanovich, Inc., and renewed 1977 by Sonia Brownell Orwell. Reprinted by permission of the publisher.

Copyright © 1992 by Joseph Bulgatz

Published by Harmony Books, a division of Crown Publishers, Inc., 201 East 50th Street, New York, New York 10022. Member of the Crown Publishing Group.

HARMONY and colophon are trademarks of Crown Publishers, Inc.

Manufactured in the United States of America

Library of Congress Cataloging-in-Publication Data

Bulgatz, Joseph.
    Ponzi schemes, invaders from Mars & other extraordinary popular
delusions / by Joseph Bulgatz. — 1st ed.
        p.   cm.
    Includes bibliographical references and index.
    1. Errors, Popular.   I. Title.
    AZ999.B85   1992
    001.9'6—dc20   91-39585
                                                               CIP

ISBN 0-517-58830-7

10   9   8   7   6   5   4   3   2   1

First Edition

CONTENTS

CONTENTS

ILLUSTRATIONS

PONZI SCHEMES, INVADERS FROM MARS & MORE EXTRAORDINARY POPULAR DELUSIONS AND THE MADNESS OF CROWDS

INTRODUCTION

To many readers enchanted by Charles Mackay's *Extraordinary Popular Delusions and the Madness of Crowds* the book glitters with the powerful appeal of a treasure map. Calling it an underground classic is too shallow an explanation, for while that may describe the manner in which its reputation grew on both sides of the Atlantic for a century and a half, it fails to convey the special feeling the book engenders. The most important secrets of the way in which the world operates are found in its pages. That a chapter is devoted to the delusion of alchemy hardly blunts the book's own alchemy: seemingly it continues to suggest, in the slightly antique style of the mid nineteenth century, magic formulas for success, or at least for avoiding failure.

For much of this we must thank Bernard Baruch, the legendary investor and public figure of the twentieth century who brought the book into the modern world and gave it its present idiosyncratic gloss. It was Baruch, around 1932, who claimed that the book had enabled him to save millions of dollars, an observation the publisher cannily included in the first of what would become eight editions, the last of which was issued in 1956. It was the same Baruch who wrote the foreword to that first edition. Forty-eight years later Andrew Tobias, in the foreword to a later edition, counseled readers: "If you read no more of this book than the first hundred pages—on money mania—it will be worth many times its purchase." Tobias's view followed what I call the "Baruch Gloss" on the book, in which the first three chapters on financial aberrations were deemed the heart of the work. It became a tradition that new Wall Street employees were routinely started off with copies of the book, further reinforcing the impression that it contained essential advice on making money.

* * *

Mackay was twenty-seven when the book was first published in 1841 under the title *Memoirs of Extraordinary Popular Delusions*. It included two chapters that were omitted in subsequent editions—"The Thuggee of India" and what Mackay called the "O.P. Mania" at Covent-Garden Theatre in London. With the second edition, brought out in 1852 by another publisher, the title was changed by deleting the words *Memoirs of* and adding the phrase *and the Madness of Crowds,* and chapters were added on "The Alchymists" and "The Magnetisers." In that form the book continued to be popular, and a third and fourth edition were published, the latter in 1892.

This success is in itself rather unusual, for the book was received without much enthusiasm by the press in 1841. *The Times* of London felt that the work promised more than it delivered. An anonymous reviewer for that newspaper thought the title a very attractive one, but was disappointed that Mackay merely chronicled a series of strange episodes, chiding him for failing

> to extract some addition to our knowledge of man, in his individual and in his social capacity, from the study of his weaknesses. The epidemical character of popular delusions; the classes most susceptible of such diseases; the laws (if there be any) which regulate their operations; the modifications they receive from education, government, manners, temperament, climate, as well as the proper mode of treating them, would furnish subjects for a highly useful as well as curious and interesting treatise.
>
> Mr. Mackay's work does not profess to be one of this kind.

The reviewer also took issue with Mackay's choice of subjects, contending that the "O.P. Mania at Covent-Garden Theatre" and the "Thuggee of India," as well as the "Popular Admiration or Great Thieves" and "Popular Follies of Great Cities" really were not delusions, concluding that only some eight or nine of the sixteen subjects fell properly into that category. As for the others, he found the subject of "Relics" treated in a "dry and meager manner," "Modern Prophecies" "very imperfectly treated," and "Duels and Ordeals" and "Haunted Houses" too well known. The opening chapters "Mississippi Land Scheme," "South Sea Bubble," and "Tulipomania," however, were better received, the reviewer commenting that the first two, "showing the ridiculous lengths to which an inordinate appetite for gain will hurry entire nations, may be beneficial at this time, when there is a proneness to the same species of epidemy," and the last was "a good burlesque upon stockjobbing." In his comments, virtually dividing the book in two between the first three chapters, which deal with the commercial world, and the remaining chapters, the 1841 reviewer foreshadowed the manner in which the book would be viewed by later generations and even provides a clue to the book's enduring success.

Who was Charles Mackay? A Scotsman by birth, he was educated there and in Brussels and was first employed as private secretary by William Cockerill, an inventor and manufacturer of spinning and weaving machinery. For ten years he was an editor of the *Morning Chronicle,* joining, in 1834, a staff that included a young reporter named Charles Dickens, and later was an editor of the *Glasgow Argus* and the *Illustrated London News.* A poet and writer of songs as well as a journalist and author, he published numerous songs, one of which, "The Good Time Coming," sold some 400,000 copies. It is some indication of his reputation as a songwriter that the title page of the 1852 edition of *Extraordinary Popular Delusions and the Madness of Crowds* identifies Mackay as the author of two songs, "Egeria" and "The Salamandrine." From October 1857 to May 1858 he lectured on poetry and song in the United States and Canada and was the London *Times* correspondent in New York from March 1862 to December 1865. In addition to *Extraordinary,* he produced, among other works, *A History of London, The Thames and its Tributaries, A History of the Mormons, Life and Liberty in America, The Founders of the American Republic,* memoirs, fiction, poetry, and several volumes on the English, Gaelic, and Celtic languages. Nothing in this body of work suggests the kind of quirky mind that conceived and executed *Extraordinary*'s unique tour of miscellaneous delusions, with the possible exception of one of the language books, *Lost Beauties of the English Language,* a survey of quaint phrases that were no longer in use.

Extraordinary was still in circulation at Mackay's death in 1889 and would be issued in a fourth edition three years later, but the truly remarkable phase of the book's life lay ahead awaiting the magical touch of Bernard Baruch.

Although he may have faded from the public mind, Baruch was an important personality in finance and in government until his death in 1965. Born in South Carolina in 1870, his long life had contacts with the Civil War, the closing of the frontier and the industrial growth of the nation, the era of the financial giants, World Wars I and II, and the nuclear age. As a child he experienced the bitterness of the South's defeat in the Civil War; as a young man he knew Diamond Jim Brady, Lillian Russell, Bet-a-Million Gates, and Edward H. Harriman; in his later years he was a close friend of Winston Churchill and remained active in public affairs for decades in the postwar period.

Starting out as a clerk in a Wall Street brokerage firm, Baruch became a partner at twenty-five and in 1902 had amassed a cash fortune of more than three million dollars by shrewd speculation. In those days the stock market was subject to far fewer regulations than today, was operated in a clublike atmosphere, and was dominated by such titans of finance as Morgan, Harriman, Rockefeller, and Thomas Fortune Ryan. Baruch became a regular at the Waldorf-Astoria, where it was customary for many of the Wall Street traders to gather after the market closed, exchange information, and arrange deals.

It was the great reputation of Baruch as a man with peerless insight into financial affairs that brought Mackay's book to life in this country. In his autobiography, *Baruch: My Own Story,* he describes how he discovered the work. While returning from Europe by ship in the early 1900s he was being interviewed by John Dater, a financial reporter for the old New York *Herald* when the talk turned to panics. Dater mentioned the Mackay book and urged Baruch to read it. Back in New York, Baruch and Dater searched through the secondhand bookstores until they found an old copy. It must have impressed him deeply, for thirty years later he told another interviewer that the book saved him millions of dollars. That reporter described it this way: "As we sat in Mr. Baruch's library, renewing an old friendship, he reached from a book-shelf a battered calf-skin volume the perusal of which he said had saved him millions of dollars. The name of the book is Mackay's *Memoirs of Extraordinary Popular Delusions.*" The scene is skeletal but compelling. There is the famous financier, already the confidant of presidents and an international figure, now some sixty years old with a characteristically kind look on his face, his eyes expressing a shrewd smile through pince-nez glasses, his hair parted in the center. He rises from his chair, astonishing us by his height, and goes to one wall of his richly wood-paneled library, reaching for a book he has taken down hundreds of times before. It is old and its leather cover is cracked and discolored, but the reverent way in which Baruch handles it makes plain to the reporter that it is something special.

In *My Own Story* as well as in his foreword to the first American edition of *Extraordinary* in 1932, Baruch discusses the book almost as if it consisted only of its first three chapters and encompassed nothing but the subject of financial manias. That limited response was obviously shaped by Baruch's years of financial experience, and, in turn, it gave the book in this country the same imprint as a source of valuable financial counsel, which I refer to as the Baruch Gloss. Writing later in 1957, Baruch extrapolated from the Mississippi Scheme, the South Sea Bubble, and the Tulipomania to include the Florida land boom of the 1920s and the stock market speculation that led to the crash of 1929. He saw clearly that Mackay was a narrator, not a diagnostician, but also saw as the work's outstanding value the message that in times of both speculative frenzy and ensuing despair there will be an inevitable return to normal conditions.

It seems likely that Baruch's intense admiration for the book was due to his realization that for years he had independently been applying its wisdom. In many of his financial successes we find him consciously separating himself from the crowd and its excesses. Repeatedly he tells with satisfaction how he sold before the top and bought above the bottom, insisting that the search for the absolute high and absolute low is unwise. In August 1929, for example, he was grouse hunting in Scotland when his personal antennae began picking up disturbing signals. He cabled three important businessmen in the United States asking for their judgment as to what was happening. Two replied in a noncommittal fashion, but the third, who occupied one of the highest financial positions in American finance, cabled back describing the situation as being "like a weathervane pointing into a gale of prosperity." Wizard Baruch acted on this stout advice in good contrarian fashion by commencing to sell and, upon returning to New York, sold everything he could weeks before the crash.

The word *speculator,* Baruch points out, has taken on the negative connotation of one who gambles, while it really derives from the Latin *speculari,* meaning to spy out and observe. In Baruch's view, a spectator is one who observes the future and acts before it occurs. To do that one must learn the facts, form a judgment as to their meaning, and then act in time. Such a simple set of rules may mask a very complicated task, but it obviously emphasizes the kind of common sense and recognition of the inevitable return to normalcy after upheavals that is one of the implied lessons of Mackay's book.

Baruch was not around to witness the financial excesses of the 1980s, but we might imagine his reaction, and based on his uncanny record, we can be sure that he would have made a great deal of money then. He would have compared the period to the years leading up to the crash of 1929, no doubt—both times of greed in which normal judgment became warped. We might imagine Baruch in the audience at the graduation ceremony in California listening in dismay to Ivan Boesky, explaining how "Greed is good," but too polite to express out loud the strong disapproval he felt.

The deflection that occurs in the minds of men during such periods of financial excess is difficult to capture. For an approach to the thoughts and feelings that flow through the inner consciousness of people caught up in such situations, we might follow in the satirical footsteps of John Kenneth Galbraith, who, under the pseudonym "Mark Epernay," published a slim book entitled *The McLandress Dimension* in 1963. In that book, "Dr. Herschel McLandress," described as a former professor of Psychiatric Measurement at the Harvard Medical School, revealed a new line of mensuration in the assessment of behavioral tendencies. The Dimension was that of the individual's relation to self, and the unit of measurement, called the McLandress Coefficient, or McL-C (pronounced "Mack-el-see"), reflected the intensity of the individual's identification with his own personality. In essence, the McL-C was the average of the intervals of time during which a subject's thoughts remained centered on some substantive phenomenon other than his own personality. The McL-C is usually established by interviewing the subject and, using a stopwatch surreptitiously, measuring the intervals of thought distraction between such indicators as substantive references to the first person singular. The interviews are supplemented by "secondary communications research," which consisted of studying the subject's books, articles, speeches, etc.

Theater people in general were found to have uniformly low McL-C's. Playwright Arthur Miller had a rating of thirty-five minutes, but Elizabeth Taylor's was only three minutes. The Reverend Martin Luther King, Jr., had a coefficient of four hours, but those of the Reverends Dr. Norman Vincent Peale and Billy Graham were in the middle range of three or four minutes. Among political leaders, President Kennedy scored twenty-nine minutes and Winston Churchill eight minutes. The highest McL-C in the U.S. government was recorded for the chief justice of the United States Supreme Court, and the lowest for Professor J. K. Galbraith, then the ambassador to India, who scored a (self-deprecating) one minute and fifteen seconds. The McL-C for Bernard Baruch came in at two minutes.

Amusing as it is, the McLandress Dimension may be relevant here to our further consideration of the Baruch Gloss of the Mackay book in that it might suggest a similar standard to measure the period of time in which an individual can think of something other than the acquisition of wealth—a psychological measurement we might call the Greed Quotient (GQ). As with the McLandress Dimension, the Greed Quotient would be determined by field research in the form of an interview conducted with a stopwatch. But where McLandress timed intervals between references to the first person singular, we would time intervals between references to wealth in its many forms.

There will, of course, be considerable fluctuation in the Greed reading from person to person, just as the McLandress Dimension yielded such variations. We might expect the Greed rating of an Ebenezer Scrooge to be in the low second range, and the second hand, would hardly move when the subject becomes one of today's aggressive young stockbrokers. On the other hand, readings of considerable duration might be recorded when we examined Mother Teresa or

Albert Schweitzer. To a greater degree than the McLandress Dimension, the GQ would tend to fluctuate with the times, and the circumstances. We can imagine, for example, that it must have been extremely high among many people in the Netherlands during the Tulipmania and in the United States before 1929 and in the 1980s, while it would have declined during times of war. This fluctuation, which we can identify as the Crowd Factor in our new psychometric equation, is, in fact, the theme of the first three chapters of Mackay's book.

Conceived in frivolity, the McLandress Dimension—and our derivative, the Greed Quotient—may actually have been overtaken by progress and brought within hailing distance of legitimacy. Real scientists have determined the frequency with which sexual thoughts arise in the minds of men and women, a measurement similar in form to those we have been discussing, if related to a different subject matter.

But if the Baruch Gloss accounts for the later success of Mackay's book, it has also served to narrow the work and cut off many readers from what should be appreciated as its larger meaning. This is not simply an account of money manias with clues between the lines as to how to become wealthy. The bulk of the work deals with many other areas of human activity, and the unifying theme is immeasurably more important. The initial difficulty we might have in coping with the two subjects in Mackay's title—a difficulty with which the anonymous *Times* reviewer also struggled—disappears when we begin to think of these chapters as tales with a moral. That single moral, which is really the theme of the whole book, is the lesson of history. In Santayana's graceful and compelling, but elusive, phrase, those who cannot remember the past are doomed to repeat it.

We all know the truth of that idea, but often seem helpless in applying it. Consider, for one thing, that when the rescuers arrived at Jonestown in the jungle clearing in Guyana they saw Santayana's dictum on a sign prominently displayed in the pavilion in the center of some nine hundred bodies. The old philosopher would no doubt have been stunned by such an interpretation.

In grappling with the meaning of prior events for purposes of present decision making, the problem becomes one of scale or complexity. In a relatively simple example, we feel confident that the pattern of the past, if applied to the present situation, will be a good guide. But if even the smallest child will not put her hand in a flame twice, what of the Dutch who, one hundred years after their tulipmania, suffered an almost equally virulent attack of hyacinth-mania? We inch along holding the Santayana dictum in front of us like a magical scepter, but it is tricky going in the confusing welter of experience. The United States confronted Iraq over the occupation of Kuwait, pointing to the painful lessons learned when Hitler was appeased, but was this the controlling historical model, or should we have looked instead to our frustrating experience in Vietnam? Where individual experience is a confusion of facts and feelings in which it is difficult to perceive a pattern the national experience is even more complex.

It is precisely for this reason that Mackay's work seems especially useful on a higher plane than that on which the Baruch Gloss has placed it. The aberrations may not be representative, or even fairly chosen, but they do show the potential for irrational acts in important areas of human behavior, and in doing so they counsel us against intolerance (the witch mania), quackery (the alchymysts, fortunetelling, the magnetisers), and other follies. That is no small achievement, and this book, a continuation of Mackay's, will attempt to reach that higher plane.

The Santayana dictum is an injunction to avoid the errors of the past, but it may also be seen as an implied prescription for success. We may be doomed if we repeat earlier mistakes, but what about repeating past successes? Won't that, by force of the same logic, improve our chances for success in our current endeavors? It is such thinking, no doubt, that has contributed to making ours an age of sequels and revivals. In support of this proposition we need look no further than recent trends in Hollywood and Broadway. What drives the filmmakers who pile up the Roman numerals after such movies as *Rocky* and *Nightmare on Elm Street* and the theatrical producers who revive *Fiddler on the Roof* and the Rodgers and Hammerstein musicals over and over is the fear that they will misapply Santayana's dictum. Rather than dare the uncertain future with the dauntingly complex pattern of the past, they choose to repeat a successful portion of the past or, in the case of a sequel, extend it. Such a cautious tiptoeing among yesterday's successes may be unimaginative, but it is commercially sound, and, albeit in a small way, it evidences an awareness of history.

This sequel to Mackay's work looks in similar directions. In some ways it follows patterns he established, but it also may contain a more conscious reaching for the moral of the tale. I would like to think that he would be pleased by the inclusion of chapters on Dowsing, and Lotteries, and that he would appreciate the parallels drawn between the Cargo Cults in Melanesia and modern cults in the United States, as well as the ironic juxtaposition of the British reaction to the Xhosa catastrophe with the nearly contemporaneous coming due of a centuries-old prophecy of the destruction of London.

Finally, for all its qualities, there is a troubling geographical imbalance about Mackay's book. It is a European study in the main, although delusions and crowd madness are hardly peculiar to that continent. To add cultural diversity as well as to demonstrate that self-evident proposition, I have reached out around the world to include material from Oceania, and South Africa. Still, some might say that, those chapters notwithstanding, the book has a decidedly American focus whereas Mackay's was European. This should not be interpreted to mean that delusions and crowd madness are more common here than elsewhere.

In prefaces to both the 1841 and 1852 editions Mackay refers to his work as "a chapter only in the great and awful book of human folly which yet remains to be written, and which Porson once jestingly said he would write in five hundred volumes."

Here is the second chapter.

PONZI AND COMPANY

The man whose name was to become the eponym for one of the greatest modern investment frauds, Charles Ponzi, emigrated from Italy to the United States in 1903 at the age of twenty-one. Born in Parma, he had been sent to school in Rome where he led the life of a dilettante, visiting theaters and cafes at night and sleeping during the day. It was a lifestyle that quickly exhausted his allowance and ended his career as a scholar. Taking the advice of an uncle, he set out for America equipped with $200 in cash and the assurances of his family that a fortune could easily be made in the new land. While at sea Ponzi lost all but $2.50 of the cash playing cards, but in time he would prove the family prescient about the fortune.

Landing in Boston, he began a series of travels that would take him around the country and Canada working at a variety of unskilled and semiskilled jobs. In a mining camp in Blocton, Alabama, he may have given a clue to the grandeur of his vision when, as a part-time book-keeper, interpreter, and male nurse, he unsuccessfully attempted to organize a water, power, and light company.

In the spring of 1919 he was back in Boston, recently married, and so discontented with his progress that he gave up his clerical job with a local produce company at which he earned $16 a week to gamble his small savings in a business enterprise. He rented a dingy little office on the fifth floor of the Niles Building on School Street, announcing on the front door that Charles Ponzi was an importer and exporter. Lacking both connections and capital, he conceived of a publication to be called *The Trader's Guide*, a free, loose-leaf service that would be supported by advertising. When he was unable to raise money for the venture either by selling an interest in it or by borrowing, he reluctantly turned his back on it, but not before he found what he always later claimed was the key to his fortune.

From Spain had come an inquiry about *The Trader's Guide* with an international postal reply coupon pinned to the letter. Curious, Ponzi studied these coupons, which were intended to facilitate prepayment of the return postage, and soon found that because of currency exchange rate imbalances they could be redeemed in the United States for significantly more than their cost in Europe. In the hectic months to come he would insist that this was the cornerstone of his investment strategy and fortune.

To exploit his discovery, Ponzi organized the Securities Exchange Company and circulated among acquaintances an offer to issue the company's promissory notes in amounts as little as $10, payable in 90 days with 50 percent interest. The name, suggestive of finance on the highest level, and antedating by fourteen years the Securities Act of the first Roosevelt administration, which established the federal Securities and Exchange Commission, may have been an inspired choice. However, the key to his success was the phenomenal rate of return, which worked out to more than 200 percent a year, and since Ponzi adopted the practice of taking up the notes 45 days after issuance, the annual interest rate was actually 400 percent. In addition, he hired agents who received a 10 percent commission on investments they procured.

At first there were only a few tentative investors who, although they disbelieved the promised return, were still willing to throw a $10 bill on the smoldering embers of their greed. When they received $15 back after 45 days, a fire began to rage. Not only did early investors reinvest, they told their friends, and word spread quickly throughout the city. Although just 18 people had invested money by January 1, 1920, seven months later no fewer than 30,219 people held notes totaling almost $15,000,000. By then the operations had spread out of Boston into other areas of New England and elsewhere, and the ranks of investors, originally limited to the poorer Italian immigrants, now included businessmen, policemen, and professionals.

Day by day the scheme expanded. Every morning at eight o'clock Ponzi would arrive at his office in a limousine to the cheers of the ever larger crowds. Police cleared the way for his car; office girls blew him kisses. In the offices of the Securities Exchange Company sixteen clerks were needed to handle the business. The tidal wave of incoming cash was so great that the cashiers just stuffed it into drawers or into their pockets. The bookkeeping system was nothing more than a series of cards arranged chronologically in order of the notes' maturities, a system so crude that a federal auditor later was unable to come within one million dollars of a state auditor's estimate of the firm's liabilities.

Although word of mouth was powerfully effective, remarkably the press took no notice of Ponzi's operations until July 4, 1920, when the *Post* ran a story that Ponzi was being sued by a furniture dealer for one million dollars. The dealer claimed that Ponzi had transferred to him an interest in the profits of the Securities Exchange Company, and reference was made to the firm's payment of 50 percent profits. The newspaper silence during the spring months was astonishing for several reasons. The city had been alive with talk about the new moneymaking miracle, a circumstance of which the press could hardly have been unaware. Moreover, Ponzi had expanded his offices into Pi Alley near Newspaper Row, and the crowds waiting outside Ponzi's office not only interfered with traffic but presented a daily physical barrier to Boston journalists on the way to their offices.

When he was interviewed in connection with the story about the suit, Ponzi blithely asserted that if the furniture dealer's claim was just he would have no difficulty in paying it because he had two million dollars in this country alone over and above all claims of investors. He also asserted that the plaintiff's attachment of his accounts in five banks affected no more than $100,000, leaving accounts in thirty other banks unaffected.

The stage was set for a publicity spectacle, which played out during the summer of 1920. It featured Ponzi, the *Boston Post,* assorted law enforcement personalities, politicians, and others. Center stage was almost always occupied by Ponzi, invariably described as a dapper, nattily dressed, small man with a straw hat and a walking stick, who smiled broadly, unperturbed by the swirl of events, and who demonstrated considerable skill at self-promotion. In his coat pocket, conspicuously displayed, was a certified check for one million dollars, all he needed for the rest of his life he said; anything beyond that amount would be used to "do good in the world."

At this time his operation extended throughout New England and into New York, New Jersey, and Pennsylvania. He claimed to be taking in $250,000 a day in Boston and a like amount in his other offices. He purchased a controlling interest in the Hanover Trust Company, held stock in other companies, owned a large home in Lexington as well as other real estate and securities, and was said to be worth $8,500,000.

The belated attention of the press served at first to encourage investment. Although newspaper accounts revealed that Ponzi was under investigation by the post office, the state attorney general and the Boston police, the fact that by the end of July nothing illegal had been disclosed was interpreted by the public as a kind of testimonial. Of three police inspectors assigned to investigate, two decided to give Ponzi some of their money. In time, most of the Boston police were found to have joined the lists of his investors, and members of the force often acted as his agents. Adding to the appearance of solidity, the Bradstreet Agency, a reputable firm engaged in credit analysis, pronounced him financially sound. The idea that this engaging man had actually discovered a way to make a lot of money easily began to gain credence in financial circles and to spread even further throughout society.

Saturday, July 24, 1920, seems to have been typical. Droves of people flocked to School Street to climb to Ponzi's humble offices and fight among themselves—men, women and children—to gain entrance. The crowd soon overflowed into the hallway, becoming packed solidly on the stairs and overflowing again into the street. Early in the day it was necessary to call the police. A woman with her baby waiting in the crowd to redeem a note caught Ponzi's eye. With his usual gallantry he spoke to her in Italian, took her note, and personally redeemed it. On the same day, competition appeared in the form of the Old Colony Foreign Exchange Company, which operated out of rooms adjacent to those of the Security Exchange Company and offered, through a bally-hoo man at the door, the same return of 50 percent in 45 days through international reply coupons. Ponzi's reaction was one of outrage. He declared the competitor a cheap imitator of his idea but without his moneymaking ability and threatened to call the police.

A reporter observing the crowd entering Ponzi's office noted that it consisted mostly of working people, but that all strata of society were represented. Notable were the number of young boys, including a fourteen-year-old who told the reporter he was employed as an errand boy at $7.20 a week and assured him that the $10 he used to purchase one of Ponzi's $15 notes was his own. Judge Frank Leveroni, of the Boston Juvenile Court, a respected lawyer, declared that Ponzi was honest and that he had invested money with him. When asked whether he thought it proper for a concern like Ponzi's to accept loans from fourteen-year-old boys, the judge stated that he considered it perfectly proper for Ponzi to accept loans from anyone.

Confidence in Ponzi grew to the point where he was hailed in the street as a hero. William S. MacNary, a former congressman and the treasurer of the Hanover Trust Company, publicly acclaimed Ponzi as the greatest financier America had ever produced. The *Boston Traveler* carried a front-page story under a headline claiming that Wall Street acknowledged Ponzi to be a real financial wizard and that there was no mystery in his great profits, following that up with an expert's explanation of how the Ponzi system worked.

A special correspondent for the *New York Evening World* sent up to investigate reported back that

> All Boston is get-rich-quick mad. At every corner, on the street-cars, behind the department-store counters, from luxurious parlor to humble kitchen, to the very outskirts of New England, Ponzi is making more hope, more anxiety, than any conquering general of old. . . . So tremendous has been the withdrawal of funds from savings banks that it is rumored there is consternation in high financial circles. . . .
>
> In narrow corridors, up the stairways, at the doorways, with the air hot and dense from the crowds who have gathered day by day, handsome women with jewels in their ears and the money-mad fever in their eyes, touch unkempt women with babies in their arms and children tugging at their skirts.

There's a terrible tenseness in the air and excitement runs high, the hands of big men are trembling and some women stutter as they talk. Lifetime savings are given away as if under the touch of an unseen hypnotist. Gaunt old maids give their money away as if it were pest-ridden, boys in knickerbockers gladly turn over all their wealth. Widows in long black veils, stenographers, fruit-peddlers in their overalls, all kinds. . . .

In the offices of the *Boston Post,* however, one man was not persuaded. Richard Grozier, the young assistant editor and acting publisher, was convinced that Ponzi's explanation about postal reply coupons was false and that he was actually paying early investors with later receipts. Grozier was thirty-five, a serious man with a square face and a level gaze. The son of E. A. Grozier, the *Post's* longtime editor and publisher, he graduated from Harvard and worked his way up in the newspaper. Together with the advantages of family and education he apparently had perception and courage. Unable to consult with his father, who was on an extended vacation, young Grozier determined to reveal Ponzi for what he was. It could not have been an easy decision, since sentiment now ran heavily in favor of Ponzi throughout the city and even into the offices of the *Post,* where more than sixty members of the mechanical staff, the police reporter and his family, and the day foreman of the press room had all invested with him. But Grozier absolved all members of the newspaper of responsibility, which he personally assumed, and instructed them to go to the limit in unmasking the financier. Thus began one of the prouder episodes in American journalism, an effort which would lead the *Post* to the Pulitzer Prize the next year.

On Monday, July 26, 1920, the *Post* began its campaign with a story by Clarence W. Barron, a highly regarded financier and publisher of the financial daily the *Boston News Bureau* (later *Barron's Weekly*), which sought to demonstrate the impossibility of the Ponzi scheme. While Barron admitted it was possible to make a little money by trading in international postal reply coupons, it was ridiculous to talk of running the profit into millions; the supply of such coupons was limited. Furthermore, it was certainly odd for Ponzi to deposit his money in banks

paying 5 percent interest when he claimed to know how to earn much
more. No one with wide financial or investment experience would look
twice at Ponzi's proposition. In short, said Barron, "the whole transaction looks to me like an immoral one."

Ponzi answered aggressively by starting an action for libel against
Barron for $5 million and attaching his property. He also announced to
the flocks of reporters who followed him around that he had "forgotten
more about international finance than Barron ever knew."

The authorities, perhaps prompted by the *Post*'s campaign, moved
belatedly into action. After a conference with Ponzi, District Attorney
Pelletier issued a statement that Ponzi had agreed to discontinue
receiving any more funds from the public until an auditor had reviewed
his books. Pelletier seemed cautious or unsure and stressed that this
action was not a closing and was done not because of any statutory
violation but only because it seemed proper as a matter of public
interest. Amiable throughout, Ponzi placed a notice in the *Post* affirm-
ing the agreement and promising to pay all maturing notes when
presented. He went even further, stating that all noteholders could
receive back their investment if they so desired.

On the previous day, the largest crowds yet developed at the
School Street offices, again spilling out into the street. Once again the
police had to be called to maintain order. Members of the crowd fought
with each other and with the police to get to the cashiers where they
exchanged their cash for notes. Following the Pelletier statement and
Ponzi's notice, however, it was different. The huge crowd was largely
made up of those who wanted to act on Ponzi's offer to return their
principal, as well as those who held matured notes. Many were visibly
frightened. The *Post* reported that throughout the day the office was
stormed by thousands who fought desperately with each other to get
into the two little rooms where the money was being paid. All day there
were sporadic riots. Women fainted and from time to time a group
would form a flying wedge and seek to take the office by force. The
glass-paneled entrance door was destroyed. Police, who had been on
the scene controlling the crowds every other day, did not appear until
just before the office closed. At noon Ponzi appeared and ordered
coffee, doughnuts, and frankfurters for the crowd. Circulating in the

crowd were agents of a newly formed syndicate who offered to buy Ponzi's notes at a discount. They found many willing to sell and bought up large quantities of Ponzi's paper. When it was all over, Ponzi had paid out more than $1 million to his panic-stricken investors, but the run seemed to have been stopped.

That evening Ponzi was calm and joked with reporters. Among other things, he discussed a proposed Ponzi Foundation, complained about the absence of police protection at the office, insisted he was solvent, and warned his investors about the syndicate buying up his notes, criticizing the money sharks who were gambling on the public's nervous tension.

In the state capital, Governor Calvin Coolidge, when asked what he intended to do about the Ponzi case, said he would direct the attorney general to make an investigation. At the federal level, United States Attorney Daniel J. Gallagher stepped in, joining District Attorney Pelletier in what had become a three-part inquiry.

On July 30 another dark cloud appeared. The New York postmaster declared that the entire world's supply of international postal reply coupons was not enough to enable Ponzi to accumulate his fortune. According to the postmaster, 160 million coupons would have been required, and in the prior three months only $360 worth of coupons were sold and only $370.50 was paid to redeem coupons. While the three governmental investigations remained inconclusive, Ponzi announced that he had received an offer of $10 million to buy his business.

A crowd again formed in School Street, but it was noticeably smaller and the run was over by 2 P.M. The syndicate was again present offering to buy up notes at a discount. A total of $250,000 was paid out, mostly to holders of matured notes, according to Ponzi, and it appeared as if confidence had been restored.

Despite a rising chorus of voices from the post office and other agencies arguing the impossibility of the coupon scheme, there was still support or at least a willingness to believe. The *Boston Traveler* front-paged an expert's explanation of how big profits could be made without cashing the reply coupons here.

Among the three prosecutors some friction may have developed, for District Attorney Pelletier retired from the case claiming that "too many cooks spoil the broth" and deferred to Attorney General Allen, who would now conduct a statewide probe. Later Pelletier would publicly criticize Allen.

Always cooperative, Ponzi called on United States Attorney Gallagher and spent time with Edwin L. Pride, the auditor designated by Gallagher. Even at this point the *Post* reporter assigned to the story could not conceal his admiration for Ponzi, noting that in his conversations with Pride, Ponzi "displayed a wonderful knowledge of accounting—of every known system of accounting. Not a question asked him by Mr. Pride but what he could answer; nothing that he could not explain."

In New York City foreign exchange agencies were swamped with inquiries by those who sought to emulate Ponzi, and hundreds of employees in the financial district studied foreign exchange rates with intense interest.

But by August 2 the events that would bring Ponzi down were taking shape. Ponzi had hired one of Boston's leading publicity experts, William H. McMasters, in July. McMasters was initially a believer, but gradually realized that Ponzi was not what he claimed to be. His suspicions were aroused when Ponzi, the self-styled expert in foreign exchange, seemed to have no contacts to rely on when he sent for his mother in Italy, but simply bought traveler's checks. McMasters was also puzzled when Ponzi dropped everything to go to a shoe store that offered him a free pair of shoes. Looking further, McMasters convinced himself not only that Ponzi could not pay all his obligations but that he was clearly a swindler and probably even crazy. Believing that his first duty as a publicity man was to the public, and seeing Ponzi-type operations springing up everywhere, he decided that the only way to correct the situation was to stop Ponzi. In a prominent story in the *Post* under his byline, McMasters declared Ponzi hopelessly insolvent. He demonstrated how the sale of notes had increased, that the money for redemptions was coming from new investors, and how Ponzi was able to make payment after the Pelletier agreement and would be able to continue to do so for a limited time. Furthermore, Ponzi had never issued or received a foreign draft. McMasters also recounted the visits he and Ponzi made to District Attorney Pelletier and Attorney General Allen. During one visit Pelletier was quoted as saying, "See here,

Ponzi, I think your scheme is crooked." In Allen's office Ponzi was, in McMaster's phrase, "in the fourth dimension of finance and romance." When they left Allen's office after more than three hours, Ponzi asked McMasters how he thought it went and McMasters said that he thought Ponzi needed a good lawyer and needed one badly. The McMasters story seemed to be a mortal blow to Ponzi, but the strength of confidence in him was astonishing.

The unflappable little financier retaliated in the evening papers. He ridiculed the McMasters story, denied being insolvent, claiming his assets were double his liabilities, and boldly called on the public to come get its money. According to Ponzi, a malicious attempt was being made to prevent him from working for the benefit of the general public. This was adroit, since there was a feeling among the people that Ponzi was their financier. In contrast to the wealthy elite whose financial methods were secret and who were identified as the oppressors, Ponzi represented the little men and women of the working class. Whether this feeling arose spontaneously or was engendered by Ponzi is unclear, but it accounted for the continuing momentum of the Ponzi phenomenon in spite of a series of negative developments. Years later, after he had been convicted and was in jail, many of Ponzi's noteholders remained loyal, still believing that if only he had been permitted to continue he would have paid everyone.

The McMasters story had its effect, nevertheless, and what may have been the greatest crowds yet gathered in School Street, driven by the frenzied desire to recover their investments. In the summer heat it was sweltering in the alley, and a river of straw hats worn by most of the men could be seen flowing out of the Niles Building. In addition to the foot patrolmen assigned to keep order, two officers with field glasses were posted on nearby roofs to look for pickpockets. Complaints were heard that some of the guards were charging as much as ten dollars for a place in the line. When Ponzi appeared at the office there was no hostility, and when he later strolled over to the State House he was followed by admiring crowds. Someone shouted out, "You're the greatest Italian of them all!" "No," said Ponzi, "Columbus and Marconi. Columbus discovered America. Marconi discovered the wireless." "You discovered money!" came the answering shout. When "Three cheers for Ponzi" was called for, they were given with a roar,

and Ponzi then shouted back, "Three groans for the *Post!*" A handbill
was distributed by a Cohasset Alderman defending Ponzi under the
headline " 'Ponzi, stop thief!' is the real thief's cry." It so aroused the
crowd's sympathies for Ponzi that mounted policemen were called to
the scene, and several people were knocked down in the confusion.
The run ended only when the office closed at 3 P.M. Since only forty to
fifty people per hour were able to get up to the cashiers' windows,
many waited in vain, and the total amount of redemptions was not as
large as it might otherwise have been.

That evening Ponzi took his wife and mother to the movies and
acted as if he had no problems at all. When pictures of him appeared on
the screen there were cheers, and he was quoted as saying that he
might try acting in the future. He had already let it be known that he
might seek public office. James J. Corbett, a former heavyweight
boxing champion who performed a vaudeville act at the same theater,
asked to be introduced to Ponzi and offered his protection when Ponzi
reflected about his lonely battles.

In time, a poet was put on the payroll of the Securities Exchange
Company. James Frances Morelli, a vaudevillian with a knack for
rhymes, was given a desk in the office and a weekly salary of three
hundred dollars. In return he produced verses such as this:

> *If they should ask you to sell your notes,*
> *Step forward and exclaim:*
> *"No indeed, I'm sorry, lad,*
> *'Cause my notes bear Ponzi's name."*
> *Just step in line, and wait with ease,*
> *And avoid all sorts of commotion*
> *For Ponzi has as many dollars as*
> *There are ripples in the ocean.*

Growing official criticism notwithstanding, the run originally started
by the Pelletier statement and accelerated by McMasters's revelations
was almost over by August 5. Among those who appeared at the office
of the Security Exchange Company, few were there to demand a
return of their principal and many came to inquire about investing.
Even more numerous were the speculators, but they were not particularly successful, as confidence in Ponzi, regularly falling and rising, was

again on the increase. The public was apparently persuaded that Ponzi would continue to be able to meet his obligations as they fell due.

The slow pace of the multiple governmental investigations elicited sharp criticism from Barron. Under the headline "Why Not Stop the Farce!" his *Boston News Bureau* railed at the authorities for not stopping Ponzi and posed this rhetorical question: "Suppose a policeman finds a suspicious-looking character at midnight trying to force a back window of a house which is closed for the summer. The stranger tells the policeman that the owner of the house invited him to spend the night. Should the policeman allow the stranger to continue his operation while he writes to the owner of the house in the mountains to see if the stranger's story is true?"

Soon Ponzi was heard from with a new scheme. He proposed a new firm, the Charles Ponzi Company, in which he would surround himself with experts, each of whom would receive a salary greater than that of the president of the United States. Every shareholder would receive 12 percent on his investment plus extra dividends of 25 percent, 50 percent, and even 100 percent. It was to be a profit-sharing operation. This was only proper since bankers, Ponzi claimed, unfairly paid 4½ to 5 percent to their depositors while making 100 percent on the deposits. Even the *Post,* locked in a fight to the finish with Ponzi, reported the details of this plan and explained how the new company was to operate out of a chain of offices from coast to coast.

A certain derangement prevailed that seemed to affect everyone. It was solemnly reported in the *Post* that a story, originally treated as more or less of a joke, had been under serious consideration by the assistant United States attorney working on the matter. In this story Ponzi was said to be acting for Lenin and Trotsky in a gigantic plan both to finance Soviet Russia and to disrupt banks and financial institutions in the United States.

With all of these activities, real and imagined, Ponzi still had time to attend to his image. He made an unannounced visit to the offices of the *Post,* where he appeared in the best of spirits, laughing and joking and talking to one of the editors for half an hour. At home he posed with his wife and his mother for a professional photographer, impressing the man with his willingness to enter into the make-believe of posing and the quickness of his mind and thoroughly enjoying himself.

But on the night of August 9 Ponzi was forced to announce that he would cease making payments on his notes. When he sought to make payment by checks drawn on his personal accounts at the Hanover Trust Company, the state banking commissioner froze those accounts. No longer smiling, Ponzi now appeared agitated and complained that the actions of the authorities were close to persecution.

Then, on the morning of August 11 the *Post* delivered a killing blow by revealing that Ponzi was a convicted forger who had served two and a half years in a Canadian jail. When confronted, Ponzi first denied the story but then admitted that it was true and that he had also been convicted of smuggling aliens into this country from Canada, another crime for which he served a sentence in the Atlanta federal prison. At the same time, the state bank commissioner closed the Hanover Trust Company, of which Ponzi was part owner, declaring that it had exhausted its reserves, impaired its capital, issued illegal and unsafe loans, and permitted Ponzi to overdraw almost half a million dollars. The *Post* congratulated itself editorially, stating that the end of the greatest money sensation in recent years was at hand, and reminded its readers that two weeks earlier it had predicted that the Ponzi phenomenon could not last.

It remained only for the investigators to unlock the secret of Ponzi's financial manipulation, a development slow in coming that finally occurred on August 17. As the *Post* reported it, the moneymaking secret was only a dream. Ponzi's dealings in international postal coupons were limited to a few hundred dollars. There was no scheme for manipulating foreign exchange and he had neither vast amounts of money in Europe nor an army of foreign agents. Those who received a profit from Ponzi got it only through the swindle of robbing Peter to pay Paul. As long as gullible Peters poured cash into Ponzi's lap he could pay the early-bird Pauls. In just eight short months Ponzi had taken in $15 million. But despite these enormous revenues the auditors found that he now had liabilities of $7 million, but assets of only $4 million.

Ponzi was arrested.

The *Post* unleashed its rhetorical fury. "Of all the get-rich-quick magnates that have operated, Ponzi is the king. He was ignorant of business, knew little or nothing of banking, his knowledge of foreign exchange was ludicrous, his statements to newspapers and business clubs were grotesque in their absurdity." And yet, even now, the *Post* could not resist commenting on the man's "bubbling vivacity, his boundless imagination, his smooth and ready tongue, coupled with a remarkable and winning charm of manner, his astute pretence of secrecy and mysterious hints of corrupt European governments ready to yield millions." The self-congratulation of the *Post* rose to a crescendo: "May this newspaper always have the good sense to see through such a palpable fraud, and the nerve and courage to pursue its exposure relentlessly until at last justice is done."

A more balanced, if sardonic, view was expressed by *The New Republic.* Contemplating the list of "respectabilities" who had been drawn in by Ponzi, that magazine concluded that the morality of the speculator had not changed over the three hundred years since the pious regent of France, having listened to John Law explain how paper money would make the state and the people rich, exclaimed, "If you are sent by God, I welcome you; but if you come from the Devil, don't go away." In the view of *The New Republic,* Ponzi's operation was really not that far removed from the business operations of other recent immigrants which had achieved remarkable success, and the main failure of the "respectabilities" may have been the inability to foresee the government's intervention.

Attorney General Allen placed a notice in the papers asking noteholders to come to his office. The throngs that began to show up were quite different in demeanor from those that had been seen in School Street. These were quiet people, sobered by the revelations and realizing that they had been taken in.

Brought down with Ponzi was State Treasurer Burrell who, it was discovered, had improperly used the influence of his office. In exchange for bank advertising for his private company, he deposited state funds in the now-closed Hanover Trust Company. The authorities also closed down Ponzi's competitor, the Old Colony Foreign Exchange Company, and jailed its officers. The president of that firm, which had followed Ponzi closely, now tried to distance itself, insisting that its operations were not like Ponzi's and that Old Colony offered big returns, "but not without first knowing full well what we are doing."

Day after day for several weeks the *Post* published lists of those who had invested with Ponzi, together with individual stories, tragic and otherwise. A printer's life savings of $4,600, earmarked to buy a house, was lost, as was a couple's $2,600 intended to pay for a trip back to Italy. A mother and daughter had loaned Ponzi $600, withdrawn it when there were rumors of his insolvency, and then reinvested it in a note that was now worthless. A wounded war veteran, saving up to go to Arizona where the climate held out the only hope for his damaged lungs, lost everything. The owner of a mortgage-free house borrowed $8,000 against a new mortgage, the proceeds of which were now gone.

As the lists of Ponzi's noteholders were made public there were more surprises. At first, it was believed that the notes averaged between $200 and $500 in amount, but now it was plain that larger amounts were involved. Thousands of people had invested much more substantial sums, going as high as a $33,000 investment received from a Quincy woman who had liquidated all her real estate for the purpose. The broker who sold Ponzi his Lexington house was listed for $20,000. There were many who had invested on a weekly basis, and women appeared to be the heaviest plungers. The middle and even wealthier classes were well represented. Judge Leveroni, who had publicly given his opinion that it was proper for Ponzi to accept the money of a fourteen-year-old boy, was down for $5,400 together with twenty-seven other Leveronis and eleven Leverones. Included were three police inspectors, the vanguard of no less than three-fourths of the Boston police force who had invested with Ponzi.

The Hanover Trust Company never reopened and five other banks eventually collapsed, including one that had loaned money to Ponzi.

A welter of legal actions now began that would continue for years. Ponzi was first prosecuted in 1920 in federal court on charges of using the mail to defraud. His guilty plea, he later said, was made on the advice of counsel that he would receive a light sentence. Instead, he was sentenced to five years. Two years later, while still serving the federal sentence, he was tried in state court on larceny charges, and, after ably conducting his own defense, he was acquitted on all counts. Testifying in his own behalf, he reaffirmed his belief that his business was legitimate from beginning to end and declared that neither he nor his wife kept any of the money entrusted to the Securities Exchange

Company. In 1925 he was tried again by the Commonwealth of Massa-chusetts on a new set of charges, convicted as a "common and notorious thief," and sentenced to seven to nine years. In the years that followed he jumped bail several times, emerged at various times in Florida, Texas, and Louisiana, and eventually served the seven-year sentence. When he was released in 1934 at age fifty-two, he was deported to Italy. With the rise of Mussolini he was offered a job in Brazil with Italy's new airline, but that lasted only a few years. In 1949 he died in the charity ward of a Rio de Janeiro hospital.

The practice of paying profits out of new investment proceeds has ever since borne the indelible name of the little Boston financier, but such a simple scheme was not without antecedents. In Montreal, about the time Ponzi was there, an individual by the name of C. D. Sheldon, also known variously as Wilson, Washburn, and Hoyt, took money from thousands of investors by promising huge profits. When it was dis-covered he was using the money of later investors to pay earlier investors, the authorities stepped in and found an enormous deficit. Sheldon was sent to jail, the same jail in which Ponzi served time for forgery in his early years, but after Ponzi had been released. It may well be that Ponzi was aware of the episode.

An even more notable predecessor was William Franklin Miller. When the ship bringing the young Ponzi to this country arrived in Boston, the echoes of the story of "520 Percent Miller" were still reverberating, and Miller himself was serving a jail sentence in Sing Sing. Given the publicity that attended Miller's rise and fall, it is likely that Ponzi knew of these events.

In early 1899 Miller was twenty, married with a baby, and em-ployed as a clerk on Wall Street. From a religious home, he regularly attended Sunday school in the Williamsburgh section of Brooklyn. One day he approached several of the young men in his Bible study group and suggested that he was in a position to exploit inside information and thus make large profits. In the end he was able to persuade each to lend him ten dollars against his written receipt, promising weekly dividends of one dollar, or a 10 percent weekly return which, on an annualized basis, became 520 percent. The receipt also contained the statement "The principal guaranteed against loss." Miller did not invest the proceeds and probably lacked the alleged inside information. Like Ponzi, he merely paid profits to earlier investors from the receipts of later investors.

The business was promising even at the beginning, so Miller left his job and spent the days going from house to house in Brooklyn soliciting clients. A small man, about five feet six inches tall, blond, with a bristly mustache, he could be seen walking the streets of Ridgewood and Williamsburgh wearing a black derby.

So rapidly did the business grow that in a month he was able to move from the desk space he occupied in a store to the entire top floor of 144 Floyd Street, a two-story frame building in a residential section, and eventually occupied the entire building. With his sudden prosperity he gave up his daily rounds and announced to the world that investors were required to come to him on Floyd Street to invest.

Like Ponzi, Miller early on offered a 5 percent commission to people who brought in new business, an arrangement that continued throughout the operation.

As the business expanded, Miller upgraded his documents and tried new methods of promotion. Receipts, originally scribbled on the stationery of the store where he rented a desk, were now elaborately printed, reciting that Miller was the manager of the "Franklin Syndicate, Stock Exchange, Bankers and Brokers, Stocks, Bonds, Wheat, Cotton." Neither Miller nor the "Syndicate" was a banker, broker, or member of the stock exchange or traded in stocks, bonds, wheat, or cotton. From the beginning and throughout Miller and his associates simply redistributed the increasing flow of receipts, with one small exception: $1,000 was deposited with a firm of brokers as a margin for speculation, all of it but $5.36 subsequently being lost. The elegant new receipt also featured a picture of Benjamin Franklin and a quotation from the great man that "The way to wealth is as plain as the road to market."

Circulars and newsletters began issuing from Floyd Street to destinations all around the country. At first Miller himself put these together but by October a literary bureau under the management of Cecil Leslie was added to deal with these matters.

Going beyond the circulars and newsletters, Miller hired an advertising agency, which inserted advertisements in 600 to 700 newspapers and was successful in placing articles in financial and other journals. One such article proclaimed:

WALL STREET ASTONISHED
William F. Miller's Franklin Syndicate a Big Winner
10 Per Cent a Week Profit.
All Former Efforts in Financial Operations Eclipsed by a New Wizard
in the Realms of Stock Manipulation.

Miller was referred to as "The Napoleon of Finance," and it was hinted that he had received pointers from the "Senatorial clique" in Washington. The byline was Cecil Leslie, the head of Miller's literary bureau.

Friday was set as the deadline for deposits that would be eligible for a dividend the following week. Early in the day, crowds, which grew week by week, would line up waiting for the office to open. Soon the police found it necessary to close the street to traffic. The presence of more and more uniformed policemen waiting in the lines to deposit their money undoubtedly encouraged others to join in.

As one entered the house, Miller was encountered at a desk signing receipts, but his handwritten signature later gave way to a rubber stamp, and his former one-man operation now required five employees.

Other, clever modifications were made. By opening the front doors and placing the receiving desks at the rear of the parlor floor, depositors were led past the window at which interest payments were made. This sight so stimulated people that many increased their deposits. Those receiving interest payments frequently decided to redeposit them at once when they saw the lines of people waiting to make deposits.

Money poured in through the mail, as letters stuffed with cash began arriving in wagonloads. At the central post office in Brooklyn, four clerks were assigned exclusively to handle the mail for the Franklin Syndicate.

It was necessary to expand the clerical force to fifty, and even they could not keep up. As money came in it was thrown on the floor in the rear. At day's end bills and coins were shoveled into barrels. There was no accounting system. Miller later said that they opened early and closed at 10 P.M., "but we never got through counting the cash until three o'clock in the morning. On Sunday mornings, we rarely concluded the task before daylight."

While this frenzy was growing, the pastor of the Congregational church to which Miller belonged raised a lonely voice in opposition. He was disturbed by the huge amounts of money Miller was receiving. The pastor expelled him from the church and asked the police to arrest him as a thief, to which a lieutenant replied, "I don't know that I'd be able to arrest the man even if I did get a complaint. Most of my patrolmen, inspectors, and detectives seem to be in it, and I'm thinking seriously of going in next week myself." It was later found that hundreds of policemen, firemen, detectives, and letter carriers were investors. For months, on certain evenings, as many as 125 letter carriers presented themselves in uniform to receive their dividends.

By October the volume of business had reached a level at which Miller found it necessary to reject deposits of less than fifty dollars because of the "congestion of detail." In that month and November the scheme reached its greatest success, totaling some 12,000 depositors and drawing crowds who formed long lines on Floyd Street. On one occasion the front stoop broke down because of the crowds. During this period the sums received daily ranged from $20,000 to $63,000. From mid October to mid November the syndicate received $648,000. After paying out $216,000, it profited in the amount of $432,000.

As in the case of Ponzi, the press was rather dormant for months while the Franklin Syndicate operation escalated in New York City and elsewhere. While some papers sensed that it was a swindle, none were able to explain just what was going on. In Boston there was a different journalistic reaction. No sooner had Miller opened a branch office there under the management of Edward Schlesinger, a stock operator of shady reputation whom Miller had taken in as a partner, than the *Boston Post* denounced the syndicate as a fraud.

At this time Miller engaged lawyer Robert Adams Ammon, a forceful personality sometimes addressed as Colonel, who had been involved in several illegal securities operations although he was never convicted. It was later claimed that the entire Franklin Syndicate operation was Ammon's and that Miller was only a front man. Ammon anticipated that the *Post* story would precipitate a run on the Boston office. To prevent that development he and Miller traveled to Boston carrying a suitcase stuffed with $70,000 in five-dollar bills, and by paying out some $28,000, the pair managed to stop the run.

In November of 1899 the more experienced and sophisticated Ammon may have realized that the days of the syndicate were numbered and decided on one final, large-scale strategy. On Ammon's advice, Miller sent the following telegram, collect, to all his depositors on Monday, November 20:

WE HAVE INSIDE INFORMATION ON BIG TRANSACTION TO BEGIN SATURDAY OR MONDAY MORNING. BIG PROFITS. REMIT AT ONCE TO RECEIVE THE PROFITS.

The next day Schlesinger arrived from Boston. He, too, sensed the end and, with a stolen $175,000, embarked on a ship for Europe where he lived handsomely in Paris and Monte Carlo before dying six years later.

On Wednesday many of the telegrams were returned when the addressees refused to pay for them. Later in the day, however, and on into Thursday mail arrived fat with cash.

By now the syndicate was being discussed more fully in the press, and on Saturday, November 25, Ammon received a telephone call notifying him that Miller had been indicted by the Kings County Grand Jury for conspiracy to defraud. Miller disappeared on Ammon's advice, hiding out in Canada after formally transferring the business to one of his employees.

On Floyd Street the crowds continued to form even though Miller had been indicted and rumors indicated the bubble was about to burst. The majority were there to invest, still lured by the promise of 10 percent weekly. Confidence in Miller continued to be strong according to a story in the *New York Times.* One of a large number of women in the crowd declared, "Mr. Miller never failed us. It is these newspapers and bankers that are causing the trouble. Nobody believes the papers.

It's envy. They'd like to make the money themselves." On November 25 a total of $30,000 was deposited in spite of the warning signs.

But the police padlocked the house and began examining the records of the syndicate. On Monday, November 27, even though the office remained closed and under police guard, people still expressed confidence in Miller.

When the Brooklyn district attorney's investigation began to focus on Ammon, the lawyer contacted Miller, advising him to return and counseling him that if convicted he would receive a light sentence and would then be free to spend his money. Naive Miller returned to New York where, in April 1900, he was quickly convicted and sentenced to ten years' hard labor in Sing Sing. In 1903, the year Ponzi arrived in the United States, Ammon was finally tried, and with Miller now testifying as a witness for the prosecution, was also convicted.

In 1905 Miller, now twenty-six years old and in ill health, was pardoned. He promptly disappeared and was not heard from again for fifteen years. Then, in 1920, a reporter for the *New York Evening World,* as part of the paper's coverage of the Ponzi development, tracked down Miller in Rockville Centre on Long Island where he operated a country grocery store and sold a little real estate on the side. Despite the reporter's retrospective view that Miller's scheme "rivalled that of John Law of 'Mississippi Bubble' fame," Miller was said by his neighbors to be one of the most trusted citizens for whom there was the greatest respect. He was, in fact, referred to as "Honest Bill."

The notion of the Ponzi scheme as a curious antique, a dust-covered phenomenon from another age, is quite inconsistent with the facts. The spirit of Ponzi is very much with us now, and the scams that bear his name are far more numerous today than they ever were. One regulatory body has warned that this con game now appears to be the biggest single fraud threat confronting average American investors.

In recent years Kenneth Oxborrow, a young farmer from the state of Washington, persuaded more than nine hundred people in the Far West to invest a total of $58.5 million in his venture. Promising to double their money, he also guaranteed earnings of 2½ percent a week ("230 Percent Oxborrow") by employing a basic, but secret, method of dealing in commodities that he discovered because of his background in farming. Less than 5 percent of the money he received was actually invested in commodities; the rest went to pay early investors and into the pockets of Kenneth Oxborrow. When he was finally jailed, many of his victims, in the finest tradition of Ponzi and Miller, expressed the opinion that he was innocent and complained about the state's interference at a time when Oxborrow might have turned the situation around and paid everyone.

In another case, a twenty-three-year-old busboy in Ohio raised $7.3 million from 2,800 investors in 1985 by promising to double their money in 60 to 90 days. The funds, which were to be used to purchase rock concert tickets that would then be scalped at premium prices, actually went to pay "interest" to early investors.

On Long Island, Robert Luongo began operating around 1971, and by the time he was closed down three years later, approximately $12 million had been invested in his plan. At first he offered 10 percent to 40 percent interest on 1-, 3-, or 12-week investments, and later it was 30 percent for 12 weeks. A network of agents talked vaguely but glowingly about investments in short-term real estate, performance bonds, aircraft, racing cars, and other real or imagined activities, but in fact, the promised interest was being paid from later receipts. New investments were collected by his agents and delivered on Thursday to Luongo, who claimed that he then drove to Philadelphia to invest the money and pick up the funds for distribution on Friday. The Philadelphia connection was probably fictional, designed to make plausible a simple shuffling of money, but Luongo and his operation were surrounded by an aura of success and prosperity sufficient to dispel any doubts.

When the law closed in, Luongo flew to Sweden, where he was arrested and later returned to stand trial. On the flight back he said that he was familiar with the life of Charles Ponzi, and that when he first started his plan he realized it would grow, but he "never dreamed it would ever catch on and grow like wildfire the way it did." When the end seemed near he had confided to one of his agents, "If this thing collapses, it will be known as a Luongo scheme and not a Ponzi scheme."

Nor should this brief roll call of some notable Ponzi schemes lead one to conclude that we are dealing with an American phenomenon. The Central African nation of Zaire was rocked in the spring of 1991 by just such an investment swindle, which seemed to capture almost everybody and even threatened to bring down the government. Michel Bindo Bolembe, a young businessman in Kinshasa, began his operation in January by opening a shop where he accepted deposits he promised would yield a 100 percent return in 4 days or 800 percent in 45 days. Even though the "profit" was generated by later deposits and such schemes were illegal in Zaire, the poverty of the country and the actual payment of the promised return combined powerfully. Soon there was a string of Bindo shops and people avid to invest slept outside in order to keep their place in line. But by May 13 Bindo stopped payment, enraging the people. Within hours the main Bindo office was burned down and rioting followed.

Common to many of the Ponzi operators is the deeply held conviction that the operation is legitimate and will not self-destruct in time. Ponzi himself exhibited this attitude to a remarkable degree, as the press of that time frequently noted. Even when he took the stand in his own defense in 1925, he testified to his belief that the business was always lawful. Consistent with this attitude was the man's serene demeanor during the hectic weeks of the summer of 1920, when new, and otherwise disturbing revelations tending to discredit him seemed to occur every few days. Years later in Italy, where he was sometimes engaged in writing his autobiography, he maintained that he was brought down by a mysterious conspiracy of officials and others whose actions were unjustified.

Transmitted to his investors, this belief undoubtedly accounted for a large part of the great faith they placed in him. A similar transference may well have occurred with 520 percent Miller and Kenneth Oxborrow, whose investors demonstrated remarkably durable loyalty. It may well be that the simplicity of the scheme belies the psychological makeup required of its operators. While there does not seem to be anything very complicated or demanding about moving cash from one drawer to another, the mind required to make the necessary subsidiary arrangements and effectively communicate the appropriate messages to the public is hardly an ordinary one.

The story of Ponzi's meteoric rise and collapse is fascinating in itself, but will also remain memorable for the lasting association between his name and the type of investment swindle we have been examining. That link is both convenient and confusing. No one would seriously question the Boston financier's right to the dubious title, and his compact name, with its opening fricative and final vowel, evocative, perhaps, of a fancy sports car or an opera singer, comes readily to one's lips. Too readily, it turns out, for there is a tendency to hang the label on other frauds and thereby blur some useful distinctions.

Some find the lineaments of Ponzi in remarkable places. The federal social security system, at least to the extent that it provides that later contributors support those who retire, has been called nothing but a gigantic Ponzi plan. Ponzi characteristics have also been detected at work in the stock market, for example, where prices are bid up and up beyond any relationship to fundamental values solely as a matter of momentum. The Greater Fool Theory, as this has sometimes come to be known, simply presupposes that the price you paid can be justified by the future appearance of a purchaser willing to pay even more. This may be a cynical way of expressing the principle, but no one doubts that the ultimate stuff of value is confidence. Securities, gems, real property all have a "market" value, which is nothing else but a consensus of their worth. Reduced to such elements, it becomes more difficult to separate the Ponzis from the pearls since the confidence exhibited in Boston in 1920 in Ponzi's notes was widespread and of a high order indeed.

More specifically, there is also a tendency to confuse Ponzi schemes with pyramid schemes. For example, in reviewing the conviction of Robert Luongo, the New York State Court of Appeals observed that he was engaged in a Ponzi scheme that was "pyramid-like." The *Wall Street Journal,* describing a Taiwan investment firm that offered annual returns ranging from 48 percent to 120 percent, reported the possibility of its being "a classic pyramid scheme that pays high interest to old investors by tapping the funds deposited by new investors instead of from investment gains." Curtis J. Lang in a long article on the savings and loan debacle in the *Village Voice* subtitled "How a Small Group of Bush-League Insiders Transformed S & Ls into Pyramid Scams—and Looted the U.S. Treasury in the Process," offered this analysis:

"At this point S & Ls became virtual Ponzi schemes. A Ponzi scheme is a financial con game named after a famous Boston swindler who tricked speculators by using the money of new investors to pay old investors huge 'profits.' There was no productive business activity at all, just an increasing pyramid of investors, not unlike a chain letter. When the pyramid-building ran out of steam, the scheme collapsed, and the last groups of investors were burned for all they'd invested."

Ponzi and pyramid schemes do have similarities. Both are fraudulent arrangements for the receipt and redistribution of money with early participants winning and those who enter later losing. In each case it is essential to continue the game with new infusions of money, for if the play ends and there is an accounting, there must be a deficit and cries of pain. But where Ponzi promised a definite return on one's investment—albeit a huge one—the possibilities in a pyramid are almost limitless as new subscribers feed those who joined before. Furthermore, the machinery of the pyramid is always explained and is, in fact, one of its alluring features, whereas Ponzi plans invariably refer obscurely to exotic investments that are really irrelevant and usually nonexistent. In some cases the pyramid seems almost acceptable socially, as in the cases of chain letters or distributorship plans, but there has never been any question about the vice of Ponzi schemes.

Some of the confusion between Ponzi schemes and pyramids can be traced, again, to nomenclature, for the pyramid is a particularly inaccurate name for a swindle that involves shuffling money, suggesting, as it does, strength, stability and endurance. In this connection, it should be noted that the pyramid, with masonic embellishments, has been chosen, along with other revered icons, to adorn our dollar bill. Beyond that, the image even conflicts with the reality of the scheme to which it refers. Because it actually involves the funneling of money back to earlier players, the better symbol might be an inverted cone.

Ponzis and pyramids can also be distinguished in historical terms. While the origin and development of Ponzi schemes is unclear, the story of the most familiar of the pyramid schemes is both recent and known in detail.

The advent of the chain letter as we now know it occurred in Denver, Colorado, in the spring of 1935, during the Great Depression. It was said to derive from a prayer letter that appeared soon after the end of World War I. Also called a "Good Luck" letter, this had an almost mythical origin, having been started by an army officer in Flanders during the war. It was based on the "magic seven": upon receiving one, you made seven copies and mailed them within seven days to seven friends. Money was not involved: Completing the chain brought you good luck; conversely, failing to forge your link meant bad luck for you.

The new development in 1935 was the addition of money. A typical "send-a-dime" letter appearing in Denver bore the heading "Prosperity Club," and the slogan "In God We Trust." Below was a list of five names with addresses and this text:

> This chain was started in hopes of bringing you prosperity. Within three days make five copies of this letter, leaving off the top name and adding yours to the bottom, and mail or give it to five friends.
>
> In omitting the top name send that person 10 cents.
>
> In turn, as your name leaves the top, you will receive 15,625 letters with donations amounting to $1,562.50.
>
> Now, is this worth 10 cents to you? Have the faith your friend had, and this chain won't be broken.

For the many who were then struggling with the bleak conditions of the Depression, the possibility of making some real money on an investment of a dime and a few postage stamps proved an irresistible temptation. By April a large part of the Denver population seemed overnight to have joined the game. On April 26, 1934, the post office in that city handled 168,695 pieces of first-class mail. On April 26, 1935, it handled 286,644 pieces. That was Friday. On Monday, April 29, 1935, the total had soared to 408,000 pieces and one hundred extra clerks and carriers had to be added to the regular staff. There was talk of a breakdown of the postal service.

From Denver the letter spread out through the West. In Hollywood the dime letter became a dollar letter and the enhanced financial possibilities brought on near mass hysteria. Whole towns were convulsed with the idea and people seemed to talk and think of nothing else. Employers were compelled to forbid mention of the topic during work hours and print shops toiled overtime turning out bales of ready-made letters requiring only the filling in of names. One local legislature considered enacting a law that would make it illegal to break a chain.

The post office was sure the letter was illegal, but who was responsible? The author could not be identified and everyone seemed to be involved. Then, again, as Postmaster James A. Farley observed, "it sells stamps." Against this background of vague illegality, specific acts occurred that were clearly reprehensible. Some people simply jumped the list, placing their names at the top, while others manipulated the list with pseudonyms or the names of friends and relatives, and others sent out more than the prescribed number of letters. These kinds of cheating were problems that would always plague chain letters, which presumed good-faith compliance with the rules by vast numbers of people. To deal with these problems, the "guaranteed" list was developed. Anyone playing the game had a notary public certify that he had mailed the fee to the top name.

Statisticians and other cooler intellects pointed out the defects of the scheme. The assumption that those below you would forward money was a doubtful one, and before some of the later participants rose to the head of the list all of the inhabitants of the community would have had to join. A mathematician explained that if it took 15,625 persons to contribute $1,562.50 to one person, a total of 244,140,625 letters would be required before each of the original 15,625 would receive the like amount. That was more than twice the population of the United States at the time. But these and other rational arguments fell on deaf ears and were usually met with one of two comments: "It's only a dime," or "My wife knows a woman who made a lot of money."

As the letter moved east it ignited some volatile fuel in Springfield, Missouri, where, according to the Associated Press, business was suspended for several days while the frenzy was at its height. For those who were unable to dispose of letters, salesmen could be hired. On top of that, a number of chain-letter "factories" or "agencies" opened for business where a staff of clerks and a notary would, for a fee, assist you in developing a letter and eliminate the necessity of selling it to your friends. After you signed it and your signature was duly notarized, the firm represented that it would sell your letter to the two customers who were behind you in line. In turn, their four letters would be sold to the customers who followed them, and so on *ad infinitum.* "It seems hardly believable that such an absurd project can draw customers into lines extending blocks," commented *The Nation,* "yet at the present writing there are more than twelve such agencies in full swing. . . . The most popular assures a return of $1,024 on an investment of a dollar and a quarter, the quarter covering the cost of mailing and notarizing and the supposed profit of the promoter."

An investigation into one such agency in Davenport, Iowa, revealed that the names of the agency's promoters and their friends were in advantageous positions and recurred frequently early in the chain. It was speculated that their profits must have been enormous.

A man who ran a garage next to one of these agencies turned it into a kind of pawnshop. He purchased watches, vacuum cleaners, and all manner of household goods for one dollar each with the agreement that he would sell them back when the customer received his chain earnings. He anticipated that only a small part of the stock would be redeemed.

Variations on the theme popped up all over, and raising the ante from a dime to a dollar—and later ten dollars—was only the beginning. The dollar chain letter evolved into the five-dollar chain telegram. One letter required the sending of a pint of liquor, another a bale of hay, while yet another called for the recipient to kiss the person at the top of the list. An abandoned wife successfully used a chain letter to locate her long-lost husband. A man with an artificial left leg circulated a letter for a right-foot shoe and received some five hundred in different sizes and conditions. The form was adapted for political purposes when a chain letter was sent to the president attacking his policies. High school students sent letters to parents in support of a teacher under fire. At *The Christian Century,* a religious journal, a planned editorial blasting chain letters was withdrawn when the publication received such a letter on the theme that war is insane and requesting each recipient to send ten cents to *The Christian Century* in order to end war.

After moving east and to Europe, the fury of the chain letter abated, and it seemed over. In fact, however, it never disappeared entirely but, under pressure from postal and other authorities, simply went underground and changed form. In the late 1970s, for example, the Circle of Gold came out of California and spread across the country. This was nothing but the 1935 Denver dime "Prosperity Club" letter updated for inflation. Now a participant paid $50 to the person who delivered the letter to him, mailed another $50 to an earlier participant, mailed copies of the letter to two other people, and added his own name to a list of twelve. Once his name rose to the top of that list he had a chance to receive $100,000.

A major problem with the Circle of Gold, like all of its predecessors, was that it used the postal system. Participants became subject to the federal mail fraud statutes, a particularly all-encompassing set of laws enforced with considerable vigor. To avoid prosecution, imaginative chain promoters took to the streets. Why, they said, we really don't need the mails at all. And that is how the airplane and the chart games were born.

These are simply chain letters without mailings, and sometimes without letters. In a typical airplane game there may be fifteen players or investors, each of whom pays a sum to enter the game. There is a pilot, two copilots, four flight attendants, and eight passengers. The crew, already "on board," attempt to sell tickets to eight passengers. As each passenger boards the "plane," he pays his fee to the copilot, who turns it over to the pilot. When all eight passenger seats are sold, the pilot, having collected the total, leaves the game, which is then split into two new airplanes. Each copilot moves up and becomes a pilot in the new game; each flight attendant becomes a copilot; each passenger becomes a flight attendant; and the game resumes. Since the postal system is not used, players need not fear prosecution for mail fraud. They should fear something else, however: Airplanes crash. These "airplanes" crash regularly.

Alternately, the promoters of such pyramid schemes use a chart, a device similar to the airplane in that it, too, dispenses with the mails. Although it lacks the charming titles of the airplane game, it has a glamour of its own. The chart game, sometimes called "The $16,000 Pyramid," appeared in early 1980 in California, where it became the rage. As many as 100,000 people attended pyramid parties and a total of almost $100 million was invested. When law enforcement agencies moved in and made arrests, there were even organized protests. The game then moved east, and by June it was the hot topic in New York City.

In this pyramid a new participant enters at the lowest level by paying $500 to the person directly above him or her and another $500 to the person in the "zero position," which is at the apex of the pyramid. Players progress upward, level by level (there are five beneath the zero position) as the lower levels fill up, until they reach the zero position and become eligible for the $16,000 prize. Progress involves bringing in new players. When 32 people join, the pyramid splits into four new charts, each having one-fourth the needed players. One's $1,000 investment can be recouped by bringing in only two more players. After a player has risen to the zero position, 128 new players will be needed to produce his $16,000 jackpot.

The chart itself and the mathematics are straightforward, but the game is embroidered with attractive details of setting, emotion, and language. Typically, the game is played at a pyramid party at which all drugs and liquor are forbidden. Prominently displayed is the large chart itself showing names, positions, and telephone numbers. An evangelical spirit prevails. In a manner reminiscent of certain charismatic church meetings, the leader and others give testimony to their belief and their winnings to the applause of the group. Every time an envelope containing a $500 buy-in is received, there are loud cheers. Pyramid players talk of "fast" and "slow" charts, "negative vibes," the need for "positive energy," and the like.

Quaint as the airplane and the chart seem, they amounted to very little when compared to the chain distribution schemes that flourished in the 1960s. Here the principles of the simple old chain letter were revived and raised to a higher level of business organization. Of many promoters who were active in this period, none made a greater impression or left more vivid memories than Glenn W. Turner.

The son of a poor South Carolina sharecropper, Turner became a ferocious salesman and showman in spite of a harelip. His line purported to be cosmetics, featuring mink oil as a special ingredient, but in reality he sold distributorships. A participant paid a fee and became a distributor, entitling him to sell the cosmetic products, but more important, entitling him to sell other distributorships. Little selling of the cosmetics actually took place, for the real money was to be made in the sale of distributorships. Those transactions were essentially the same as in the chain letter, or the airplane and chart games, in that the new participant paid one fee to the party who brought him in, another to the party at the top, and then assumed a position at the bottom of the pyramid.

In 1967 Turner had only a desk in an office in Orlando, Florida, but he possessed enormous ambition. Five years later he had parlayed $10,000 he borrowed over an uncle's signature into a conglomerate that generated a cash flow of $200 million, and in which as many as 100,000 people may have invested. He flew around in an expensive private jet, wore boots made of unborn calfskin, and was unfailingly accompanied by twin midgets. To a close assistant he confided his belief that he was Jesus Christ come again. Two main business organizations were developed to carry out his activities: Koscot ("Kosmetics Company of Tomorrow") Interplanetary, Inc., the sales arm, and Dare to Be Great, Inc., the training body.

Would-be participants were brought to staged gatherings in places like hotel ballrooms where clean-cut young men, each with a rhinestone pin of a flag and a $100 bill attached to his lapel, subjected them to the rigors of high-pressure salesmanship and intermittent sessions of "money-humming." These gatherings, called "Adventure Meetings" or "Golden Opportunity Meetings," were described by one judge as being

> like an old-time revival meeting but directed toward the joys of making easy money rather than salvation. Their purpose is to convince prospective purchasers, or "prospects," that Dare is a sure

route to great riches. At the meetings are employees, officers, and speakers from Dare, as well as purchasers (now "salesmen") and their prospects. The Dare people, not the purchaser-"salesmen," run the meetings and do the selling. They exude great enthusiasm, cheering and chanting; there is exuberant handshaking, standing on chairs, shouting and "money-humming." The Dare people dress in expensive, modern clothes; they display large sums of cash, flaunting it to those present, and even at times throwing it about; they drive new and expensive automobiles, which are conspicuously parked in large numbers outside the meeting place. Dare speakers describe, usually in a frenzied manner, the wealth that awaits the prospects if they will purchase one of the plans. Films are shown usually involving the "rags-to-riches" story of Dare founder Glenn W. Turner. The goal of all of this is to persuade the prospect to purchase a plan . . . and thus grow wealthy as part of the Dare organization.

The money-humming consisted of inducing the crowd to shout "MMMMMMONEY!" alternating with the chant "GO, GO, GO!" Uplifting songs were sung, such as this one, to the tune of the Mickey Mouse Club song:

> *M-A-K . . . I-N-G*
> *M-O-N-E-Y*
> *Making money, making money*
> *Forever let us hold our wallets high*
> *Now's the time to say good-bye*
> *To all our poverty*
> *M-A-K . . . I-N-G*
> *M-O-N-E-Y*

A special language was used to motivate participants. You were encouraged to invest by "The Program." At "The Program," people "Talked About the Money," which got everyone "Jacked Up." Sometimes you got so "Jacked Up," you became "Glazed Over," then you were in the best frame of mind to "Get that Check," all of which meant that you were "Great!" The new investor was "Great!" and "The Program" was "Great!"

Turner's critics pointed out essentially what chain scheme critics had always said: If each new participant brought in one new member a month, or twelve a year, and if each new member did likewise, after a dozen such sets, the total number of participants would be 8,916,100,448,256, or more than 2,000 times the population of the world. Turner brushed this off saying, "The Christians have been trying to saturate the world for two thousand years and they have done a lousy job with a better product than I got." The man had an undeniable style. To a woman who was staring at his harelip, he said that he put it on every morning for people like her.

By 1972 the attorneys general of thirty-nine states were pursuing Turner. When the Securities and Exchange Commission established that his distributorship contracts were securities and obtained an injunction against him, he was finished.

On this tour through the land of Ponzis and pyramids, oddities seem to be everywhere. Not the least of them, perhaps, is that such schemes are always with us and attract everyone. To this last statement every reader will silently assure himself or herself that he or she is the exception: "Not me. I am too perceptive, too experienced, or too sophisticated. I would never have been in the lines at School Street or Floyd Street or money-humming in one of those Dare to Be Great Adventure Meetings." For that reader the story of the Home-Stake Production Company may be instructive.

The Home-Stake story was first told publicly in the *Wall Street Journal* in 1974. The firm was founded by Robert Trippet, a wealthy Tulsa lawyer from a good family. In 1964 the firm began offering units of participation in its oil drilling program. Prospective investors were told their return would be 300 to 400 percent and they would also get tax deduction credits. Very little drilling was done. The operation was a simple Ponzi arrangement with later investors in effect paying large profits to those who had signed up earlier. Trippet added something new, however, in that he divided his investors into two groups. One, made up of the more powerful and astute, were paid well; the others got little. At a California site where Home-Stake falsely claimed to be drilling, agents of the company went so far as to paint farmland irrigation pipes pink and orange and put coded markings on them to suggest to investors brought out to inspect the site that they carried oil.

Because the company petitioned for bankruptcy in 1973, a list of investors became available. It was a revelation. Between 2,000 and 3,000 of the nation's wealthiest people had invested more than $100 million. The list, eventually published by the *Wall Street Journal,* included 45 people in the arts and sports, 51 businessmen, 27 lawyers, 111 charities, and 3 politicians. Some of these well-known names are listed here. Because they were among the richest, the brightest, the most powerful, and most sophisticated individuals to be found in this country with unmatched access to financial information, they deserve pondering by anyone who still believes he or she is immune to the lure of such schemes:

Alan Alda; the American Cancer Society; Jack Benny; Candice Bergen; Professor Curtis Berger of the Columbia University Law School; Jacqueline Bisset; R. Burdell Bixby, Wall Street lawyer and former head of the New York State Thruway Authority; Bill Blass; Joseph Bologna and Renee Taylor Bologna; Buffy Sainte-Marie Bugbee; Diahann Carroll; David Cassidy; Jack Cassidy; Shirley Jones Cassidy; Oleg Cassini; Philip D'Antoni, producer of *The French Connection;* Phyllis Diller; Bob Dylan; Mia Farrow; George J. W. Goodman (alias "Adam Smith"), the financial writer; Barbara Walters Guber; Thomas S. Gates of Morgan Guaranty Trust Company, a former secretary of defense; Neil McElroy of Procter and Gamble, a former secretary of defense; Senator Jacob Javits of New York; Senator Ernest Hollings of South Carolina; Claude Kirk, former governor of Florida; the American Jewish Committee; Barnard College; Baylor University; the Boy Scouts; Brandeis University; Columbia University; Cornell University; Dartmouth College; Leopold Godowsky, concert violinist and co-inventor of Kodachrome film; Andy Williams; Buddy Hackett; Elliott Gould; Michael Sovern, later dean, Columbia Law School and president of Columbia University; Walter Matthau; Walter Wriston, former board chairman of Citibank; William Morton, former head of American Express Company; a group of General Electric executives including former chairman Fred J. Borch.

JUDGE
JANUARY 16, 1926
PRICE 15 CENTS
REAL ESTATE NUMBER
SOLD!
FLORIDA
Ruth

THE FLORIDA
LAND BOOM

At its most frenzied in 1925, the rush to Florida was described as the beginning of a national shift in population scarcely less important in American history than the rush to California and the Far West in 1849. The consequences were said to be possibly as far-reaching as the descent of the Goths on Rome, the Mongols on China, the Dutch on South Africa, and the Mormon trek from Illinois to Utah.

A New York reporter estimated that ninety-nine out of one hundred of the visitors came for the sole purpose of speculating in land, buying only with the intention of reselling at a profit and thus sharing in the biggest—and oddest—boom of its sort ever known in this country. In Miami, people were real estate mad; land was the uppermost thought in everyone's mind and almost the only topic of conversation. A daily business and investment publication ran a ten-part series entitled "Making Money in Florida," cautioning that many speculators in lots would hold the bag, but admitting that "some of them have already guessed right (enormously right), and we have not the slightest doubt that in the future others will continue to guess right. It is a gamble played in the hectic atmosphere that necessarily envelops one of the most amazing real estate booms in history."

Not to be outclassed rhetorically, the *Southern Banker* offered this assessment:

> In the history of our country, as it has unfolded itself from day to day, there are words and phrases and slogans that are intertwined with the warp and woof of the periods in which they had their origin. They were words on the tip of every tongue and they showed the trend of the nation's thought. We are living now in such a time; in an era made noteworthy by a single word. It is a word to conjure with and to bring up visions of happiness in a land of plenty of ever mounting wealth. That one word is FLORIDA.

In fact, the fever that was FLORIDA had erupted before. In sixteenth-century Spain, a survivor of the ill-fated expedition of Panfilo de Narvaez fired the imagination of the country with stories of immense wealth waiting there. A syndicate was organized by Hernando De Soto who planned to sail with one ship, but so many men clamored to participate that seven ships were needed to accommodate them. Like many others before and after, De Soto failed to find riches.

Prior to 1840 there was a minor boom in the panhandle in Apalachicola and a new town named St. Joseph, but a hurricane in 1840 almost completely ruined St. Joseph. When a yellow fever epidemic occurred in 1841, the town was abandoned and the boom was over.

But none of these earlier activities could have foreshadowed the frenzy that took place in parts of the state from 1924 to 1926, and fascinated the country.

While public commentators discussed the reasons for the boom in such social and economic terms as increased prosperity and leisure time and the advent of the automobile age, the real foundation was probably laid with the construction of the Florida East Coast Railroad to Miami after 1896. In that year, the settlement that was Miami was little more than a post office with a few dwellings and one or two stores. Its population was sixty. To induce Henry Morrison Flagler to bring his railroad there, the first two settlers gave him three to four hundred acres of land. That tract was subsequently laid out as the town of Miami. By 1925, Miami had become a city of 75,000 and Miami Beach had come into existence. The expansion of the Florida East Coast Railroad to the end of the mainland, and on to Key West, was followed by other rail lines on the west coast. Connecting the two coasts of the peninsula provided access to and through the state.

In the preboom years a number of major developers added to a state that had been a winter haven for the wealthy for decades. These first sun seekers may have constituted a cadre of those who transformed Florida real estate into personal fortunes—the forerunners of those who rushed south during the boom years.

*   *   *

Carl Fisher started out as a train butcher and bicycle racer, later became a wealthy manufacturer, and in 1913, came to Miami. There he helped John S. Collins to build the first of many causeways that connect the mainland with the Keys. Fisher conceived the scheme of building a city on the long, narrow, swampy, jungle-grown tongue of land that lies between the ocean and Biscayne Bay. After ten years of work—clearing jungle, draining the swamp, building a seawall and a causeway connecting the beach with the mainland—he had created Miami Beach with 150 miles of asphalt roads and a good deal of building. By 1924, the lots in this former swamp were selling for $20,000 and more.

George Edgar Merrick, the builder of Coral Gables, an area outside of Miami billed as "America's Most Beautiful Suburb," started with land originally purchased by his father, a clergyman who came to Florida with $800 in cash. The younger Merrick added to this property and created a theme derived from the many-gabled house his father had built out of coral rock. He also developed a plan based on a uniform architectural style, which he called "modified Mediterranean." By 1926 the city of Coral Gables was well established with a business center, schools, banks, hotels, apartment houses, club houses, and canals with actual Venetian gondolas steered by Venetian gondoliers. Innovative in publicity, as well, Merrick hired William Jennings Bryan to lecture on the wonderful climate of Florida to the crowds who gathered at a Coral Gables lagoon. Bryan would sit on a raft under a sun umbrella during his oratorical labors. When he was done, there would be dancing by entertainer Gilda Gray. Bryan knew something about the magic of Florida real estate. In 1912 he bought a modest house in Miami for winter use. When he sold it eight years later, he was astonished at realizing a profit of $250,000. To the end of his days he testified to the miracles of Florida real estate, and when he died in 1925, it was said that the Great Commoner had been a millionaire.

Nor were the legends confined to the Miami area. On the west coast, D. P. Davis persuaded the city of Tampa to sell him two small islets in the bay described as "two small marshy clumps of mangrove, almost submerged at high tide." By dredging and piling sand, he created an island on which he built houses and hotels and paved streets and made a fortune.

Others were Joseph Young, the developer of Hollywood-by-the-Sea, and Addison Mizner, the architect who developed Boca Raton.

But developers such as these were following in the footsteps of Henry Morrison Flagler, whom Stewart Holbrook, in *The Age of the Moguls,* called "at least the godfather of Florida as a winter playground." From upstate New York, Flagler became one of the first business associates of John D. Rockefeller, and thus made a fortune in oil. In the 1880s, he became enamored of Florida and was shocked at the poor hotels and railroads there. In subsequent years he organized the Florida East Coast Railroad, which he eventually extended from Miami to Key West, considered one of the great engineering feats of the time. He also built a string of luxury hotels, schools, hospitals, and churches—his total investment in the state exceeding forty million dollars.

The stories of such men and their accomplishments undoubtedly contributed to the growing awareness of Florida as a place where wealth came easily, an awareness reinforced by common knowledge that parts of the state were the regular destinations of many of the wealthy class for the winter. The significance of the physical improvements that these speculators produced would soon be overlooked when news began reaching the North of a new kind of speculation in which amazing profits could be made quickly, simply by buying and reselling unimproved land.

Beginning some time late in 1924, the boom culminated in the late fall of 1925. At first it was confined to the sixty-five mile stretch between Palm Beach and Miami. Soon, however, it spread to the west coast and to the citrus fruit section in the center of the state. Jacksonville, in the north of the state, didn't experience the boom until later, however, and the "panhandle" was hardly affected at all.

In that brief period, people and money poured into the state. Bank clearings in Miami soared from $212,360,000 to $1,066,520,000, real estate transfers tripled, and the value of building permits rose from $8,391,000 to an astonishing $30,025,000. Nor was the building fever confined to Miami, for in the same period, the value of building permits in Tampa rose from $3,289,000 to $11,609,000, and in Jacksonville from $3,655,500 to $7,373,500. Banks around the state bulged with money, as deposits and loans more than doubled from 1924 to 1925. In the larger period from 1923 to 1926, bank deposits increased from $225,000,000 to $850,000,000.

The number of passengers the Florida East Coast Railroad carried in 1925 increased almost 70 percent over 1924. In the five-year period ending in 1925, the populations of Miami increased 141 percent, Orlando 140 percent, West Palm Beach 121 percent, and Lakeland 142 percent. The national population increase for that period was only 7 percent.

Nearly everywhere in Florida, it was necessary to stand in line for meals even at prices much higher than elsewhere. Lines at the best restaurants in Miami began forming at 10:30 A.M. for lunch, which was served at noon. Hotels in Miami and in Palm Beach were taxed beyond their capacities. People were sleeping in station waiting rooms and in cars. Seeking to capitalize on the housing shortage, some New York businessmen arranged to buy several car floats on which they planned to build a superstructure divided into rooms and apartments, the entire assembly to be towed to Florida to provide houseboat accommodations. An Ohio-Mississippi river steamer was brought around to Tampa for use as a hotel, and a similar expedient was followed at Jacksonville. An offer was made to charter a popular transatlantic liner for the purpose of anchoring it off Miami and operating it as a hotel.

Miami newspapers regularly published daily editions of 100 pages or more filled with real estate advertising. One day, in the summer of 1925, the *Miami Daily News* printed an issue of 504 pages, the largest in newspaper history. For the year 1925, the *Miami Herald* carried a larger volume of advertising than any paper anywhere had ever carried in a year.

Gertrude Mathews Shelby, assigned to report on the boom, joined the great migration. It was stimulated, she said, by the smell of money, which attracts men just as the smell of blood attracts a wild animal. Shelby was inclined to scoff, confident that she possessed good sense and was not likely to be fooled much, but later confessed that she became lost, gambled, remained to sell land, and made $13,000 in a month.

Her story is symptomatic. In the spring, an old friend turned loose upon her family a "colony of Florida boom bacilli" by relating how he made $100,000 in Florida in a period of months after having been down and out. His associate made more than $600,000 in six months, and together they missed an opportunity to become millionaires. He told about the big promoters—Fisher, Merrick, Young, and Davis—and, more enticing, about the successful small investors. There was a member of the Coast Guard who bought ocean frontage for 25 cents an acre and sold it for a million dollars; a returning soldier who exchanged his overcoat for a friend's deed to ten worthless acres near the beach subsequently valued at $25,000; a poor woman who bought a lot in 1896 for $25 and sold it in 1925 for $150,000; and another who took 1,200 acres on a debt in 1915 and recently received $1,200,000 for it.

Such stories were heard everywhere. A lot in the business section of Miami, sold for $800 in the early days of the development, was resold in 1924 for $150,000. A New York lawyer who owned a strip of land in Palm Beach had been offered $240,000 for it before the boom; in 1923 he accepted $800,000. In 1924 it was broken up into lots which were sold for an aggregate price of $1,500,000. In 1925 it was claimed that its value had risen to $4,000,000.

In September 1925, the *New York Times* reported in a front-page story how Mrs. Frances Cragin sold for $1,750,000 a tract of 250 acres near Palm Beach which her deceased husband had bought for a few hundred dollars. Days later the *Times* ran a story about how a single land sale in Fort Meyers attracted a line of brokers who waited all night for the sales office to open. The applications exceeded the offering by $986,000 and within an hour $1,381,000 of land was taken.

Periodicals followed suit. "So far every one seems to have made money" wrote J. Leroy Miller in *The Outlook*. Lots sold for $1,200 to $1,500, were resold, often a few months later, for $3,000 to $5,000. One owner of an orange grove near Daytona lost $75,000 because he neglected to go into town during the weekend. He did not know that prices had soared within the past forty-eight hours and sold his 43 acres for $100,000. He thought that he was receiving an immense sum, but the new purchaser immediately resold it for $175,000 and the second purchaser was about to sell it for $200,000.

Felix Isman in *The Saturday Evening Post* described how land at the Snapper Creek Canal that sold for $15 an acre in 1913 was now selling for as much as $2,000 an acre, and how at West Flagler Street and Twenty-second Avenue in Miami, land that had been sold for $30 an acre was now worth $75,000 an acre. A Miami lot, 50 feet by 135 feet, purchased in 1915 for $1,000 by the Ft. Lauderdale Methodist Church, was sold in 1924 for $30,000 and resold five months later for $80,000. Another lot was sold successively for $2,500, $7,800, $10,000, $17,500 and, finally, $35,000—the last purchaser being the man who sold it for $2,500. A property owner on the street was asked what his property was worth and said, "Well, it was worth about $30,000 at nine o'clock this morning. But at ten o'clock, the lot next to mine sold for $40,000, so I suppose it ought to bring about $50,000, as it is now ten minutes past twelve."

The sale of a nonexistent planned development in St. Augustine, according to J. W. Buzzell in the *Stone and Webster Journal,* was oversubscribed on the day of sale. The receipt of $18,405,000 far exceeded the scheduled value of $11,000,000 even though the lands were under water and required dredging and a plot plan was not even in existence at the time of the offering.

Hard-sell advertising in the North exploited the publicity. "Fellsmere Estates," a Florida subdivision planned by a New York builder, was offered in an advertisement that covered two full pages of the *New York Times* on November 15, 1925. Beginning by quoting the assessment of the *Literary Digest* that "All our gold rushes, all our oil booms, and all our free-land stampedes dwindle by comparison with the torrent of migration pouring into Florida from all parts of the country," the text skillfully played upon the feeling of excitement in the country. The reader was assured that a Fellsmere lot "should sell on paper, without being seen, because it is sold on confidence. . . ." A "reservation coupon" was to be submitted which, when received and time-stamped, would be honored in the purchase of a lot. The concluding statement that "After the offering is subscribed, prices for other lots will be increased 25 percent," which might have sounded like ordinary puffery otherwise, fit perfectly into the heated pattern of Florida land speculation.

In that pre–jet plane era, Florida was more than a few hours away from the cities of the North, and the journey could be arduous. Author Kenneth L. Roberts speculated that in 1925 two and a half million people entered the state, which at the time had a population of one million. The movement was so great, the *New York Sun* reported in October of 1925, that the railroads and steamships were taxed beyond capacity. In the summer it had become necessary to institute an embargo against building materials because of the threat of a famine. By September, the embargo was extended to include household goods, bottled drinks, and chewing gum. By the end of October, a so-called statewide embargo was declared applying to all carload commodities except food.

Gertrude Shelby chose to sail from Philadelphia and was amazed to find that she had already become a prospect for shipboard brokers. The larger proportion of migrants, however, undertook what one writer called the "Pneumatic Hegira." Another pictured it as deluxe pioneering in a modern setting with the upholstered limousine having replaced the covered wagon. Still another compared it to the rush to California in 1849, noting that "the prairie schooner had given place to the auto, the Indians to real estate agents, and the wrecks of flivvers and trucks that could not stand the pace or the impact of frequent collisions mark the Dixie Highway even plainer than did the carcasses of the oxen on the Overland Trail to the California Eldorado."

"All through the spring and summer and early autumn of 1925," wrote Roberts, "months when motor travel to Florida might have been expected to dwindle to an unnoticeable trickle—cars poured out of side streets and back roads on to the state roads in every part of the country and roared along the state roads to the main traveled highways that lead to the southeastern corner of the United States."

While the age of motor travel had begun in earnest, this was still almost a quarter of a century before the commencement of the construction of the Interstate Highway System. Undivided roads lacking such features as limited access, billboard control, and uniform signing were not the only primitive element in the adventurous jaunt south. Engine vibration combined with other noises to create an environment in the passenger compartment in which one's voice often took on a disturbing flutter. Tents and other camping equipment were usually packed, for the great growth of motels and restaurants had yet to occur. An image created in a silhouette drawing by Hendrik Willem Van Loon in *The Survey* on February 1, 1926, represented the experience of many of the boomers. It showed an open flivver piled high with suitcases and other personal belongings parked alongside a crude track. To the right, a family group is gathered around an open fire, and a seated figure—perhaps the father—holds a frying pan over the blaze. To the left, a crude sign points out the destination and gives the distance: "Florida 2,000 miles."

The overland trip was not always an isolated experience. Impromptu tent groups along the way served as convenient information exchanges. One reporter described such a group somewhere in North Carolina where rumors circulated that a cordon had been drawn around Miami to exclude strangers and that one had to wait in long lines to buy food. Out of these rumor mills came stories of shocking hotel prices, state entrance fees of three hundred dollars, thousand-dollar automobile licenses, terrible roads, yellow fever epidemics, and so on. Some members of the group told how they had sold everything, bought a car and a camping outfit, and were staking all on Florida.

Most headed for the big cities, where the atmosphere could be electric. Henry Block, a New York lawyer with extensive experience in real estate who toured the state during the boom, arrived in Biscayne Bay by boat and received a characteristic visitor's welcome: He was met at the dock by jazz music. "Airplanes circled the boat, flying dangerously close; yachts and motorboats carrying huge signs of large real estate concerns tooted horns while the band played. . . . The place seethes with excitement; there is hustle and bustle everywhere; sidewalks are so crowded one is forced into the street. Everyone seems to be in a great hurry to get—no one seems to know where. . . ."

Gertrude Shelby was similarly struck by "the whizzing pace of the people in tropical heat (for it *is* hot in Florida in summer—dripping hot)" which showed their frantic excitement. There was a sparkle in every eye, honest or dishonest. The hotel hummed night as well as day with unwanted activity. A man in the next room joyfully took advantage of the after-midnight rates to telephone New York that he had purchased ten thousand acres that day, but he was unable to tell the person he called where the land was.

"The rush is on," wrote J. Frederick Essary in *The New Republic*.

> The fever is raging. The boom cities are filled to overflowing. People crowd the sidewalks day and night and spill over into the streets. Construction gangs are working three shifts. Food and shelter are at a premium. The cupidity of rooming-house keepers and eating-house proprietors is past belief. In every town and city, real estate offices flourish like green bay trees. In downtown Miami, there are twenty to the block. They are jammed with salesmen—knickered, coatless, hatless, and sleeveless young men scouring the town for buyers.

A spirit "not unlike that of a boom on the Stock Exchange" prevailed in the state.

On Flagler Street, the main thoroughfare in Miami, almost every other store was a real estate office. The streets were filled with salesmen in golf togs selling real estate.

To another observer, "Everyone appears well dressed and prosperous and happy. . . . Nowhere does one see such an over-whelming number of big, expensive cars . . . tourists sweep through by the thousands, great schemes are hatched, millions are spent, developers found new cities every day. It is Florida of 1926: Eldorado, the Klondike, and the South Sea Bubble rolled into one."

Although the usual summer lull was expected, in 1925 the greatest crowds ever known materialized.

Boom hysteria confronted Gertrude Shelby everywhere she went on the Gold Coast, the strip between Palm Beach and Miami.

> On one of the innumerable Florida busses, bumbling overbearingly down the blisteringly hot Dixie Highway toward Miami, my neighbor

was a young woman of most refined appearance, an exceedingly pretty brunette in white crepe de chine gown and hat. Only her handkerchief-edge hinted at mourning. As usual the bus joggled loose all reserves.

"Florida? Wonderful! Came here with a special party two weeks ago. Bought the third day. Invested everything. They guarantee I'll double by February. Madly absorbing place! My husband died three weeks ago. I nursed him over a year with cancer. Yet *I've actually forgotten I ever had a husband. And I loved him too, at that!*" Values and customs are temporarily topsy-turvy in Florida.

High-pressure salesmen circulated in the streets of Miami and elsewhere, accosting strangers to whom they offered free bus trips, free boat rides, free dinners, and other gratuitous entertainment. Two real estate firms set themselves apart by offering an airplane ride and a soft drink only to those who actually purchased property.

Some of the free bus trips were afternoon affairs, but others covered hundreds of miles, lasted three to four days, and included meals and hotel accommodations—free, of course. At the end of such a journey, you would typically arrive at The Site: a stretch of barren country dotted with palmetto and pine marked with signs indicating the proposed city hall, golf course, and hotel.

It was said that there were 25,000 salespeople attached to the 2,000 real estate offices in Miami, engaged in what was almost a curb market in real estate covering the entire business district and operating throughout the whole state. Eventually, as a result of a traffic ordinance that prohibited the showing of a map or making a sale in the street or on the sidewalk, the curb activities were moved indoors. In the change that ensued, basements were cleared, lower floors redivided, porches enclosed, flat roofs built up, space between buildings boxed in, and arcades cut through buildings to provide double frontage so that there would be more spaces for selling real estate, all of which were crowded with attaché cases and customers.

New names were conceived for some of these operatives signifying their specialized functions. In addition to "high-pressure" salesmen who worked with expert "closers," there were "binder boys" who bought contracts for a quick turn, "cappers," "pointers," and "bird dogs."

The promotional tricks of the Florida land developers derived from the Southern California boom of the late 1880s, according to Homer B. Vanderblue, a Harvard professor of business economics. "The genesis of most of the tricks seen in 1924–1925 in Florida can be traced here: paper town sites sold from maps, dishonest auctions, excursions and barbecues, persons standing in line all night and paying $50 or even $100 for places in line in the morning, 'purchases' by businessmen of established wealth. . . ."

Under these pressures, as the dormant boom bacilli began to flourish, it was not long before the visitor experienced a transformation. "People in the cool, dispassionate North are quite unable to appreciate the Florida situation," one commentator wrote.

> They must be there to understand, they must talk to the people who speak of thousands and millions of dollars as though they were inconsequential and entirely within the reach of anyone willing to put himself to a little bother. Gradually they are mesmerized, as the natives are mesmerized, and begin jabbering about acreage, abstracts, and binders along with the wildest of them. When they return homeward, they seem to awaken as from a dream and are quite unable to understand their frenzy for sand, palm, and palmetto. . . .

Gertrude Shelby's reticence proved to be no match for salesmen who accosted her repeatedly in the streets and would not let her forget for an instant that she was a prospect. Refusing all the free bait, she attempted a rational inquiry, only to be told by one salesman, "Those things don't matter. All Florida is good. What you are really buying is the bottom of the climate. Or the Gulf Stream. All you've got to do is *get the rich consciousness*. There's the dotted line. You'll make a fortune." Another claimed that "The people who have made real fortunes check their brains before leaving home. Buy anywhere. You can't lose." Still, she hesitated, "clinging to such wit and caution as remained to me." After studying the area from Palm Beach to Miami, she realized that her purse was too small for the waterfront property she desired. A quest for her second choice—a "doll ranch"—led her, first, miles into the Everglades, and then to a rockpit, both of which she rejected. Then the critical event occurred which severed her remaining ties to reason and cast her into the torrent of the mania. A lot near the center of Fort Lauderdale, which she had been offered a week before at $60,000, was resold for $75,000. Two weeks later, it was sold again for $95,000. She realized that if she had risked $2,500, the deposit on the $60,000 purchase, she might have made $35,000. "Right then and there I succumbed to the boom bacillus. I would gamble outright. The illusion of investment vanished."

Gertrude Shelby may have held out longer than most of those who experienced Florida in those years. The persuasiveness of examples, as she made clear, was a powerful force operating against the bulwark of her reason and caution, but it may not have been the only force. Writer, investor, curiosity seeker, she was also a tourist exposed to all the strange conditions and unexpected influences that such travel entails, and at a time when vacation travel, especially travel to more distant places, had barely gotten under way.

A deeper understanding of how such otherwise prudent and conservative people as Gertrude Shelby were so easily conscripted by the Florida land boom may follow a few minutes' reminiscence about one's own experiences as a tourist in some foreign city.

Wandering through the Plaka in Athens or through Parisian flea markets, gazing at leather jackets in Istanbul, piñatas in Tijuana, or semiprecious stones in Rio de Janeiro, the tourist struggles silently to adjust to the value frame of reference. Of course, he has a budget, the financial plan developed before leaving for this exotic place. In his pocket, however, are those cruzeiros, drachmas, francs, pesos, or marks that he really does not yet understand. The rate of exchange is plain enough, but in a deeper, more intimate and—more important— functioning way, he has yet to incorporate these strange units of currency into the mental procedures, so thoroughly perfected back home, that allow him to know instantly whether a loaf of bread is overpriced or a shirt is a bargain.

There are additional aggravating factors. A hundred details con-
spire to pry him away from the efficient and familiar modes with which
he operates in his home environment. Signs in store windows, even the
signs which direct traffic and name streets and avenues, are in a
different, perhaps incomprehensible, language; people look and sound
strange; buildings have unfamiliar shapes and details; traffic is made up
of unusual vehicles, or made up almost entirely of the same kind of
vehicle; the smell in the air is not the smell he is accustomed to, even
the light from above, its angle and intensity, are felt to be novel.
Surrounded in this fashion by so many new sensations, it is only to be
expected that in his effort to adjust he becomes disoriented, and the
seriousness of the dislocation is in proportion to the complexity, or
novelty, of the matter at hand. So, while the newly arrived tourist may
adapt rather quickly to the idea that tipping does not exist in Australian
restaurants, it may prove more difficult to take part in the bargaining
which is almost obligatory in many places, to arrange for a guide and
organize an itinerary in a remote corner of the Soviet Union, or to make
one's peace with the multitude of beggars on the streets of Calcutta.
This is not to suggest that the dislocation is permanent or that there
will be no improvement in his ability to cope with this strange world in
time, but in the two-week period of most vacation travel it is not likely.

While it is true that Palm Beach is not Moscow and Miami unlike
Oslo, the basic principles are little changed, and if the boomers in 1925
were at least spared the difficulties of a foreign language and foreign
customs, it should be remembered that for most of the population,
travel was limited and travel outside of the country was nothing by
comparison with what it is now. For them the trip to Florida was the
equivalent of a trip to Europe or elsewhere over the seas, and while his
or her descendants would shop for artifacts in markets around the
world, the Florida tourist of the boom period was shopping for nothing
less than the land itself, the earth, the primordial substance on which
we walk and into which we ultimately pass.

Here, then, is our traveler, newly arrived in Miami and in the
middle of the boom. Having set out in his flivver what seems like
months ago from Chicago, Detroit, or New York, he is the model for,
and the antecedent of, those who, a generation and more later, would

fly all over the world in jet planes. He brings with him not only his wife and children, but the grandparents as well. In his pocket are his life savings—the accumulation of years of regular deposits in the bank or the proceeds of the sale of his haberdashery store—all of which he is prepared to invest in this marvelous state where it seems that everyone lately has been making a fortune.

Two things happen to him almost at once. A young man dressed as if he were on his way to the golf course stops him in the street and proceeds to try to sell him a piece of raw land from a blueprint. It is not an opportune time for the salesman since our traveler has just begun the subtle mental and emotional struggle to forge an understanding of what Florida is all about. He sees the flat land and compares it to the topography of the Catskills or the Smokies; compares the palms and palmettos to the deciduous trees of the North; notes the open spaces; wonders if there is an El or a bus system or whether the land is suitable for the kind of crops he has grown; asks himself whether it ever snows here in the winter and how hot it becomes in the summer. In short, he is trying to come to grips with this new place and his reactions to it, just like the traveler to a foreign city. It makes no difference that the first salesman he encounters fails to sell him, for there is virtually an endless line of salesmen who are ready to try in the future.

That night they rent a room that is too small for them, at a shocking price they would never have paid had it not become plain that the choices were few and rents uniformly high. They might also have been disturbed by the cost of dinner in a restaurant had their minds not been so distracted by the kaleidoscope of images produced by their trip and by this new, magical place and its fantasy of quick and easy wealth.

In the days that follow they are contacted by many salesmen, and find themselves chatting in public with numerous others like themselves, even though they would never have spoken to strangers in a similar fashion back home. The topic is always real estate, and gradually they begin to absorb the spirit of the time and place. They sense that the price of land here is a new concept, one that seems continuously in motion and initially difficult for them to grasp. They can only understand it as a kind of leapfrogging which requires them to note the progression of price figures and make an extrapolation.

Their resolve to be prudent weakens daily, if not hourly; and they are completely done in when they have the dubious luck to encounter someone from their hometown who came down a week before they did and has already made five thousand dollars by buying and almost immediately reselling a binder on a lot (never seen) across the state in Tampa. This news completes their conversion to speculators since it links up the whole body of their experience at home with the strange ways of the Florida land mania.

Inevitably, they find themselves in one of the myriad offices on Flagler Street, grouped around a desk studying another blueprint that tells them very little, and in the grasp of another young, knickered salesman. Only a few days before they would have been horrified at the price of twenty thousand dollars, but now they are seriously considering it. On one hand, they realize that they must either make money fast or leave soon, for the cost of living in the Sunshine State far exceeds their expectation and will soon deplete their cash resources. On the other hand, the boom bacilli are raging. They lean a little closer and ask those innocuous questions that, to the knickered salesman's practiced ear, indicate they will buy. Outside, the roar in the street is unceasing.

The only holdout is Grandpa. He has lived long enough and has experienced enough hardship that the idea of gambling all one's wealth on an unseen property does not easily fit into his understanding of the world. Standing a little apart, he rocks back and forth on his heels, fingers his suspenders, and observes to the family that the price of this lot is many times what he once paid for a working farm with improvements and livestock. But Grandpa is brushed aside; the deal closes; the binder is signed and the family is flushed back out into the street, new recruits to the army of "binder boys" who are looking for the next purchaser.

In Florida, these transactions may have been commonplace, but the full significance of their prices and the rapid movement of those prices require examination of a larger frame of reference. Florida real estate values had become national pacesetters. The sale of Miami property for more than $300 a front foot eclipsed the $212 figure for the plot at the northwest corner of Forty-fourth Street and Fifth

Avenue in New York City, and the buyer in Miami thought he had a bargain. Rents for stores on Flagler Street exceeded those at Forty-second Street and Broadway in New York City.

The people who ventured in Florida inhabited a world of prices much more modest than those to which we are accustomed. At the time a single room in the Hotel La Salle, "Chicago's Finest Hotel," ranged from $2.50 to $7.00 and a double from $4.00 to $9.00. Breakfast at the hotel was 50¢ and 70¢; lunch, 85¢; dinner, $1.25, and Sunday dinner, $1.50. A pair of men's Russian calfskin shoes with rubber heels cost $5.00. A hand-tailored, silk-lined tuxedo was $35. Toy electric train sets began at $5.75. A new gas range was $27.35 if purchased in lots of at least six. Smoked beef tongue was 29¢ a pound; flour $1.24 for a 24½ pound bag; tomatoes 14¢ for a number-two can; apples 49¢ for a box of a dozen. The fare to Bermuda from New York and back by ship was $70 including the berth and meals. A new Hudson car cost $1,250.

Residential real estate values in New York City are also worth the comparison. A house in Jamaica, Queens, was offered at $8,500; one in Douglaston, Queens, with nine rooms, three baths, and a two-car garage could be had for $19,500; in Manhattan a twelve-room Murray Hill town house was priced at $40,000; a remodeled house on East Sixtieth Street was $45,000; a ten-room duplex cooperative at Fifth Avenue and Eighty-third Street was $40,000; and an eight-room cooperative at Park Avenue and East Sixty-seventh Street featuring three baths could be purchased for $28,500.

Not only were values then a fraction of what they are now, but the opportunities for investment were considerably fewer. This was, after all, a time when the plethora of investment products that came on the scene in the 1960s and later were unknown. Mutual funds in their great numbers and variety did not exist; the large markets in options and commodities were years in the future; because the federal income tax was barely a decade old, municipal tax-exempt bonds were minuscule in comparison to what they are today. Furthermore, the income-tax-driven strategy that led many investors to seek shelters in real estate, oil, cattle, citrus groves, and phonograph records would have been alien to the 1925 investor.

Nevertheless, the country was going through a period of prosperity that would survive the Florida land boom and reach a climax years later. That prosperity was, indeed, one of the reasons often cited by those who tried to explain the boom, and as a national phenomenon, the boom demanded explanation. Among other reasons cited were the development of railroad lines and new highways, the draining of the Everglades in Florida, and the sudden realization by millions of people that the Southern California climate could be found here, at least in the winter months, little more than a few days' ride from New York, Philadelphia, Chicago, and the cities of the Midwest. In the introduction to its series of articles entitled "Making Money in Florida," the *Standard Daily Trade Service* advanced, among other reasons, the Florida soil and climate, the appearance of the idea of the winter vacation, and the growth of a leisure class of considerable numbers. The paper also observed that the boom was distinctive in that it was the first big shift in population in the motor era, was the first boom in the age of electricity, was facilitated by the use of modern machinery, and, most importantly, arrived when super-salesmanship and national advertising had developed an immeasurably great power to command people's income and savings.

The *New Republic* attributed the boom to a huge increase in the national wealth and to a change in the people of the United States. This change manifested itself in the restlessness of an enormous portion of the middle class (not to be confused with the pioneering spirit) and led to a desire to spend parts of each year in different environments and to a widespread yearning for soft living.

One writer found his answer on the globe of the world. He observed that the lines of latitude across which Florida lay, when followed, brought one to some of the most famous places for health and recreation. The mayor of Palm Beach, perhaps less seriously, reasoned that the boom was due to the superiority of Florida orange juice for cocktails. In that time of Prohibition, gin, otherwise "the vilest of liquors," was cheap and plentiful, and, when mixed with Florida orange juice, produced the more palatable, if inappropriately named, Bronx cocktail.

After its genesis was accounted for, it was inevitable that there would be a good deal of public pondering over how long the boom would last. At one extreme was the opinion of Charles Donald Fox, who said, "It will last forever, for there can be no let-up to the development of a state which offers so much to so many classes of people." More flowery, but to the same effect, was Paul O. Meredith, the secretary of the Florida Association of Real Estate Boards, who looked into his crystal ball and assured everyone that the bubble would burst "when the sun decides not to shine anymore, when the Gulf Stream ceases to flow, when the railroads lengthen their schedules and when they stop making Fords." T. S. Knowlson, writing in the *New York Times,* saw a ten-year duration because it was "topographical" (sic!), moving north from the south, and "To cover a large state in this way takes time, and I do not see how it can be accomplished in less than 10 years." Henry Block, another expert assigned by the *Times* to study the situation and write about it, was more cautious, but also wide of the mark when he offered the view that the boom would last as long as the country's prosperity.

From these curious pronouncements it would be incorrect to infer that no warning voices were heard. Joseph W. Young, the developer of Hollywood-by-the-Sea, publicly cautioned purchasers of Florida land: "Fortunes will be made in Florida. But the investor of small means must not believe that he can buy lots or acres and make money merely on the assertion of the selling agency. High prices caused by speculation will, of course, come down." After comparing Miami real estate values to those in mid-Manhattan, a *Times* reporter warned that "vir tually every dollar that has been taken out of Florida has been brought there by someone else. Ultimately the amazing profits will be paid by the unlucky final owners who find that there is no market for the parcels they purchased at prices far beyond any possible capitalization of the land's earning power." Samuel Untermyer, from his houseboat in Florida, expressed alarm at the real estate conditions, especially the number of hotels springing up all over the state. He predicted that it would take at least ten years for the winter population to reach the point at which the need for the hotel rooms being built would be met by real demand. "The orgy of unsound land speculation," he wrote in January 1926, "has about reached its apex and we may expect rapid deflation within the next six or twelve months." By then it may have been too late for many of those who had indulged in what some English visitors had called "Floridabbling."

The National Association of Credit Men in November 1925 warned of deflation and "a resulting anguish to many investors."

A more organized attempt to deal with the boom hysteria was mounted by the banking industry. In Columbus, Ohio, the banks united in an advertising campaign to keep their people at home; St. Louis banks were galvanized by the transfer of $800,000 to Tampa in one day. The outflow of hundreds of millions of dollars, and the enormous number of people who departed for Florida, elicited howls from the banking communities in Virginia, Ohio, Michigan, Alabama, Illinois, Georgia, and many other states. The Massachusetts Savings Bank League issued a statement in November 1925 cautioning their depositors not to withdraw funds to speculate in Florida after member banks reported that they were sending remittances south every day. The treasurer of one of Boston's oldest savings banks said, "The withdrawals for Florida are constant and are steadily increasing. It means that a new class of investors is affected; savings bank depositors are mostly people who cannot afford speculation." Of some three million deposits in Massachusetts savings banks, an estimated one hundred thousand were drawn on from June to October, and the withdrawals amounted to about twenty million dollars sent to Florida.

Two vacationing teachers, encountered on a bus by the peripatetic Gertrude Shelby in the summer of 1925, told her how they received a fatherly letter from their banker back home when they wrote to withdraw $500 with which they planned to speculate. Disregarding the cautionary advice, they plunged and made $1,500, which was more than a year's salary. Flushed with success, they wrote back to their banker rebuking him for interfering.

Others took to the field to stem the flow of people and money. The mayor of Indianapolis found it necessary to stage an ambitious demonstration to discourage further removal of his constituents and their money. Commercial interests in Virginia sought a special session of the legislature to appropriate money to counteract the Florida movement. In Atlanta municipal concern was expressed when more than ten thousand people left the city in a short period in the summer of 1925 and transplanted themselves to Florida. In that city and in Savannah there were acute labor problems in stores and offices since employees had gone to look for the pot of gold in Florida. In California a depression in the tourist trade and a slump in real estate sales were attributed to the diversion of interest to Florida, and in some parts of the middle west so many wealthy people transferred their interests to the Sunshine State that banks and other organizations began extensive advertising to halt the exodus.

In time the idea of "northern propaganda," as these efforts were loosely referred to, came under attack by boom spokesmen and was cited as one of the reasons for its end. In the fall of 1925 the Miami Chamber of Commerce publicly criticized northern bankers for trying to slow the remittance of funds to Florida by requiring thirty days' notice of withdrawal. After the boom collapsed, Florida papers were vocal in blaming northern propaganda and the "binder boys." Stella Crosley in *The Nation* agreed that northern propaganda hastened the collapse, but found it not vicious but truthfully descriptive. "The last thing the man with his fortunes at stake in the Florida boom really wanted was the truth. 'Truth' to him was always a flattering, exaggerated talk about Florida's climate and advantage. 'Lies' were anything the least discouraging to possible 'investors.' " As to the "binder boys" being limited to a group of "hypothetical gentlemen always of the hated Jewish extraction," she found that to be something of a joke, the truth being that "a very high percentage of all those who played in the Florida real-estate game were 'binder boys' of greater or lesser degree. Most property was bought, not for use, nor even to hold long, but to sell quickly at the biggest possible profit."

Even in Florida one of the most often told stories in that real estate–obsessed state, about how the "binder boys" were burned in Miami Beach, amounted to something of a moral fable from which anyone who was attentive could have extracted obvious wisdom. The binder boys, it was said, came down from New York City. With the Eastern European background and the accent attributed to them it was not hard to make out the anti-Semitic overtones. They churned option contracts in the peculiar way that gave rise to their name until they invaded Miami Beach. There they had the bad fortune to draw the ire of N. B. T. Roney, a respected and successful developer, when they purchased properties adjoining his. Roney and his associates cleverly set about creating a trap by systematically raising the offering prices on lots they owned. Since these advertised prices largely created the market, the binder boys soon were enraptured to find that the value of their holdings was rising daily, and they bought along with the rise. Then, a day or two before the binder-holders were required to make their heavy second payments, the Roney group suddenly announced a heavy cut in the prices of their lots. This brought the market down far below the prices the binder boys had contracted to pay for their properties. The story ends in good xenophobic fashion with the binder boys fleeing back to New York, having suffered million-dollar losses. Among those who heard the anecdote and retold it were many who were undoubtedly destined to suffer the same fate when the boom came to an end.

"Binder boys," although numerous, were not the most pernicious of those who operated in that fertile field. Fraudulent promotions generated an increasing number of complaints. One project was advertised to be "not more than three-fourths of a mile from the prosperous and fast-growing city of Nettie," but the "city" turned out to be not a city at all, but a long abandoned and burned turpentine camp.

Names were artfully—and deceptively—chosen to suggest that the project was an addition to an established city, while often this was not the case. Melbourne Gardens, for example, was about fifteen miles beyond the city limits of Melbourne, and did not even have an access road although it was advertised as "suitable for home and garden." One development was christened "Highlands" even though it was only twenty-five feet above sea level. The highest hills in topographically monotonous Florida had been known as the "Berkshires of Florida," but in keeping with the current hyperbole they were now known as the "Alps." "The Kennel Club Estates" at St. Petersburg suggested wealth and elegance, but in reality it derived its name from a nearby half-painted greyhound race track. On a larger scale the names of established California cities were simply transplanted to Florida (e.g., Pasadena, Hollywood, Santa Monica), perhaps in the hope that their prior success would be duplicated in the East.

It was a natural setting for Charles Ponzi, who declared in a signed statement in November 1925 that he was in Florida to "stage a comeback" and repay the two million dollars he estimated he still owed creditors. To accomplish this end he organized the Charpon Land Syndicate and claimed to have an option on land "near Jacksonville," which was actually sixty-five miles away. His plan involved the sale of "units of certificates of indebtedness" at $310 a unit and a guaranteed dividend of 200 percent on each certificate in three months. On April 2, 1926, Ponzi was convicted of violating Florida's trust laws.

Another promoter was the playwright, reporter, and author Ben Hecht. In his autobiography, *A Child of the Century,* he recounts how he arrived by water in Miami in the middle of the boom. He saw the furor:

> A hundred thousand people were getting rich selling building lots to each other. They raced up and down the hot sidewalks in bathing suits, bathrobes and jiggling sweaters. . . . The news of great profitable sales spread like the arrival of a Messiah. . . . Symphony orchestras played in salesrooms. Buses full of bonanza-hunters roared through the streets and down the dusty roads.

Having identified Charles Ort as one of the men behind the boom, Hecht arranged for an introduction and told him he had an idea that would help sell some of Ort's building lots on Key Largo. A short, red-faced man from Ohio, Ort was shy in conversation on any subject except Key Largo. He came to Miami with nine hundred dollars and rapidly made a fortune in a scam with a woman fortuneteller. Ort arranged with her to advise each of her clients that riches would be coming to him in the person of a man he would soon meet, who would be wearing a black derby hat and smoking a big cigar. When Ort observed a wealthy-looking man leaving the fortuneteller, he followed him to the beach where, wearing a derby on his head and smoking a big cigar, he struck up a conversation with him. Ultimately Ort sold him for $100,000 a piece of land on which Ort had placed a $500 option for a purchase price of $5,000. When Hecht met him, Ort was worth $90 million.

Hecht's idea called for a similar kind of misrepresentation, but on a much larger scale. To great fanfare he proposed to dig up "pirate treasure" on Key Largo. He buried the "treasure" himself, hoping to lure hordes of treasure seekers, thus making the sale of lots there an easy matter. Key Largo at the time was little more than jungle, but undismayed, Hecht managed to bury some authentic Spanish doubloons and two huge vases somewhere in the center of the island. The story of the treasure's discovery by a local character hired by Hecht appeared in newspapers all over the country and had the desired result.

Not only did Hecht escape retribution, he was perceptive enough to realize that the boom was certain to collapse and kept all the money he earned in a bank. Ort was not that lucky: After the decline he wound up eating beans out of a can and sleeping in a parking lot.

If the origins of the boom are somewhat difficult to sort out, its demise took on a much clearer form and even contained elements of biblical drama. The 1925 summer crowd was the greatest ever known, but gave way to a lull by late fall, and the winter crowd proved to be only a tenth of that expected. Those who waited for a rush of newcomers to buy lots in the newly planned paper cities were disappointed.

As the dates for additional payments on option contracts arrived, many of the holders defaulted either because they lacked the needed funds or because they recognized that it would be foolish to send good money after bad. In some developments 50 to 75 percent of the buyers, unable to sell and unable to meet the second payments, abandoned their "investments" to the sponsor, who could do with them as he wished. A man who had sold acreage in 1925 for $12 an acre was chagrined as it was resold successively for $17, $30, and finally $60 an acre—all in the same year. His chagrin turned to dismay when, after the deflation, he learned that every purchaser in the series of subsequent transactions had defaulted, and his only remedy was to take the land back.

It did not take long for the break in the boom mentality to demolish the whole market, demonstrating the downside risk inherent in the speculation. The possibility that leveraging one's investment, whether through borrowed money as in a stock purchase on margin or by contracting to buy land when only the deposit is available, can lead to anything but a profit seems inconceivable until it occurs, and then in retrospect seems inevitable.

Uncertainty over the Treasury Department's policy with respect to the taxability of paper profits on a land sale was mentioned as another reason contributing to the boom's end, as was a retreat in prices on the New York Stock Exchange, although some Miami real estate bond houses used the latter development as an opportunity to tout the comparative stability and attractiveness of their products.

On March 12, 1926, the *Wall Street Journal* reported that a canvass of financial men who had recently returned from Florida produced the unanimous judgment that the boom was over and that the real estate market was declining. The next month the president of the Florida State Chamber of Commerce, speaking to the "Florida Takes Inventory Congress," expressed the metaphorical view that "the gold rush was over and placer mining at an end."

By the end of the year it was reported in the North that the backwash from the boom was receding through neighboring southern states and leaving in its wake thousands of stranded tradesmen and their families. Appeals for help put charitable institutions in large cities in Georgia and the Carolinas under great pressure.

In Palm Beach, the real estate business had come to a standstill by March 1926, and the city was becoming deserted. In the business sections of Miami and West Palm Beach, where office or desk space had been scarce at any price a few weeks ago, scores of small offices closed overnight and hundreds of realtors headed north, many to Long Island, which was believed to be the site of the next boom in the summer. Most hotels were virtually empty, and northbound trains carried capacity crowds.

Stella Crosley, writing in *The Nation* in July, certified the collapse of the boom and the end of what she called "the world's greatest poker game played with building lots instead of chips . . . the players are cashing in or paying up . . . for the most part, uncountable numbers of

Americans, who believe cards and gambling sinful, have staked their all in Florida's feverish game and lost. And the roads leading northward are today black with sadder and wiser, but poorer people."

Native Floridians quipped that "The 'binder boys' are marching through Georgia," a curious phrase evocative of a historic southern destruction now inverted to imply a northern retreat.

The larger cities, like Tampa and Miami, where the streets were but lately teeming with such traffic that the authorities were forced to install new traffic and parking systems, were now "nearly as lifeless as the streets on a theater curtain."

Bank failures began to occur in the early summer of 1926. Many of the state's banks were swollen with deposits as recently as December 1925, but those that had become involved in the speculation found themselves vulnerable. When the Bankers' Trust Company of Atlanta failed as a result of a misuse of funds, the Florida members of that chain, which had committed their funds to the Atlanta bank, also failed, adding to the growing lack of confidence in Florida institutions. Bank clearings in Miami, which had topped $1 billion in 1925, declined to $632,867,000 in 1926, $260,039,000 in 1927, and $143,364,000 in 1928. By 1927, many Florida cities were having difficulty collecting their taxes. Three years later, twenty-six had gone into default on their bonded indebtedness. The Davis Islands project was bankrupt and incomplete.

Conditions had deteriorated considerably when, in September 1926 an extraordinary piece of ill fortune occurred. On the fourteenth of that month there were telegraph reports of a tropical disturbance about two hundred miles northeast of St. Kitts in the Antilles. As a result of inadequate reports, there were no indications that a storm was approaching Miami, although the barometer reading there had fallen to 27.75, the lowest ever recorded in the United States. According to the Miami weather bureau, the storm appeared suddenly and passed over the central and southern portions of the city. Then, in hurricane fashion, the winds dropped to 10 miles an hour as the center of the storm passed by. The people, unaccustomed to such a phenomenon, poured into the streets to see the damage. Thirty-five minutes later the stronger side of the storm struck with winds of 135 miles an hour. "The roar of the wind was accompanied by the crash of build-ings, flying glass, and the sounds of the sirens of ambulances and fire equipment," according to Jonathan Daniels in *The Time Between the Wars*. "Rain came in sheets as dense as fog. Torn power lines hissed and flashed. . . . Oldtimers had hardly remembered a storm like this one and newcomers had not believed such a blow possible."

Frederick Lewis Allen in *Only Yesterday* noted that the storm ironically

> concentrated upon the exact region where the boom had been noisi-est and most hysterical—the region about Miami . . . it piled the waters of Biscayne Bay into the lovely Venetian developments, deposited a five-masted steel schooner high in the street at Miami, tossed big steam yachts upon the avenues of the city, picked up trees, lumber, pipes, tiles, debris, and even small automobiles and sent them crashing into the houses, ripped the roofs off thousands of jerry-built cottages and villas, almost wiped out the town of Moore Haven on Lake Okeechobee, and left behind it some four hundred dead, sixty-three hundred injured, and fifty thousand homeless.

Every vestige of the Miami dock system was swept away. All the boats in the harbor were sunk, and Miami Beach was under three feet of water. A radio station in Miami called it the worst hurricane in the history of the country.

Although it was generally understood that the boom had already collapsed of its own weight before the hurricane, the tragedy elicited a startling spasm of mindless boosterism from Florida public officials. Governor John Wellborn Martin and others did virtually nothing to help relief operations; state aid was directed to help repair property damage while the Red Cross was left unassisted to provide for the injured and homeless. Miami Mayor Romfh said he saw no reason "why this city should not entertain her winter visitors in the coming season as com-fortably as in past seasons." The volume and persistence of such statements in the wake of the catastrophe hampered the effort of the Red Cross to raise relief funds. A lawyer for Seaboard Air Line in a *Wall Street Journal* interview acknowledged that between seventeen thousand and eighteen thousand people needed assistance, but stressed that Florida was still wonderful and would always be the "Riviera of America." He feared that in its zeal to raise funds the Red Cross would "do more damage permanently to Florida than would be offset by the funds received."

If the tragedy was not necessary to conclude the madness of a boom that had already come to an end, it is difficult to resist a sense that there had been a kind of divine intervention needed to correct human affairs that had veered too far into the abnormal. From Mount Olympus came the cleansing force sweeping away the frenzied activities, the paper profits, and even the temporary signs naming the imaginary streets and buildings of subdivisions that would not be developed.

Two years later, Oswald Garrison Villard, the editor of *The Nation,* visited the site of the boom and brought back grim news of the deflation. On the approach to Miami

> Dead subdivisions line the highway, their pompous names half-obliterated on crumbling stucco gates. Lonely white-way lights stand guard over miles of cement sidewalks, where grass and palmetto take the place of homes that were to be. . . . Whole sections of outlying subdivisions are composed of unoccupied houses, past which one speeds on broad thoroughfares as if traversing a city in the grip of death. . . .

And as to rental values:

> There is no doubt that Miami will be the cheapest place in the United States to live in during the summer of 1928. Beautifully equipped apartments rent for $15 to $20 a month. One of the most pretentious buildings on the beach, whose monthly rate two years ago was $250, now rents the same suite for $35. In 1926 one was lucky to get a double room in a private house for $50 a week. Until next November one may rent a luxurious Spanish stucco home on the bayfront, completely furnished from table-linen to radio, for $50 a month.

Having begun in the time of Coolidge prosperity, the Florida land boom had run its course before speculation in the stock market intensified culminating in the crash of 1929. As the nation entered the depression years the boom was a fading memory. Further ahead, however, lay the great development of the state—the huge growth in population, the emergence of Miami as a major commercial and financial center, the magnet of Disneyworld, and agricultural strength. Now, so many years later, there is the inclination to see almost prophetic elements in the boom. The extreme statements made then to promote the speculation have, with the assistance of a beneficent Providence, come true or perhaps even been outdistanced. The salesmen were right in a sense when they urged their prospects to buy any lot from a blueprint because they were all good, site inspection was irrelevant, and money would be made in any event. Of course, the profits they contemplated were immediate and not half a century down the road, and yet the state's determined boosters will tend to dismiss that. For them the promotional language of the boom period was true then and continues to be true. The Florida climate affords a marvelous refuge from northern winters; the population centers of the East and the Midwest are within reasonable traveling distance, and the soil is fertile. The pitchmen of 1925 would feel great satisfaction if they were to tour the state now. One can almost hear them saying "I told you so!" over and over again as the tour covers mile after mile of new apartment buildings along roads filled with traffic.

Such time travel may have a curiosity value, but smooths over the striking distortions exhibited by the boom and tends to reduce its true significance. As a large-scale migration of people and a manifestation of greed unbound, it deserves more scrutiny than it has received in recent times.

THE TULIPMANIA
REVISITED

Of all the aberrations described by Charles Mackay in his original volume, *Extraordinary Popular Delusions and the Madness of Crowds,* the Dutch intoxication with a mere flower in the seventeenth century is undoubtedly the most memorable. Many readers of that book think of the tulipmania (or "tulipomania") readily while hard pressed to recall other chapters on such diverse subjects as the slow poisoners, the hair and beard, phrases in large cities, and the Crusades. That it is, perhaps, the emblem of the book is even more remarkable because the tulipmania is covered in a scant 8 pages while the chapter on the Crusades, one of the longest in the book, takes up a full 107 pages.

Until the publication of *The Embarrassment of Riches* by Simon Schama in 1987, the Mackay book was also the only easily available source of information on the tulipmania for the general reader. The powerful and lasting memory it created in the public mind can hardly be doubted. Witness how quickly references to the mania are made in the business press when speculative activity increases or there is a collapse in prices. Two months after the October 19, 1987, stock market crash the *Wall Street Journal* looked back at the 1987 surge that capped the five-year bull market and concluded that it had "some elements of a speculative craze, echoing the Tulipmania of the 1600s, the South Sea Bubble of the 1700s and the Roaring Twenties." In 1979 when gold prices soared, the *Journal* pondered whether the market was only an "illusion of crowds, a modern repetition of the tulip-bulb craze or the South Sea Bubble." Witness, also, the link made to it by those who reported on the Florida land boom, and the nods given to it in books of investment advice. One professor of economics has described fledgling economists gathered around the campfire early in their training, listening to their elders tell the legend of the Dutch tulip speculation as the decisive example of speculative excess. Even the name has risen to a special level of acceptability, the variant words *tulipomania* and *tulipo-maniac* being defined in most larger dictionaries. The incident has clearly proved fascinating. Of what does this truly extraordinary appeal consist?

Part of the answer can be found in the contrasting elements of the story. The Dutch had already become celebrated for their serious character and their aptitude for, devotion to, and success at business. That they lost their heads over something as humble as a flower bulb suggests a delicious irony on a very large scale. But another part of the answer lies in the form of Mackay's telling of the story. Brief as it is, the emphasis is largely on the sensational; in fact, he devoted almost one quarter of that little chapter to two accounts of how invaluable bulbs were accidentally destroyed.

While rampant speculation in flower bulbs may not have occurred previously, history is not lacking in precedent. Roses were a favorite flower of the ancient Romans. As prosperity increased, people demanded roses in winter. Shiploads were brought to the city from Alexandria and Carthage, and methods were devised for making the plants bloom in December. The governor of Sicily was carried in a litter on cushions stuffed with roses, a wreath of roses on his head, another around his neck, while to his nose he held a fine linen bag filled with roses. A patrician had a bed made for himself surrounded by a rose-filled net. In imperial Rome roses were used to perfume the streets, fountains, rooms, and theaters, and in the reign of Domitian the smell of roses in public places was said to be overpowering. Horace complained that fertile land was being turned into rose gardens and that olive groves were being neglected. The economy suffered as Romans turned from food gardening to flower growing.

Curious as the Roman rose folly was, however, it lacks the essential element of the Dutch tulipmania: the financial speculation by most of the society.

As the Netherlands turned the corner into the seventeenth century, the country was poised to become the leading mercantile state of Europe. This was the great formative era in Dutch history. The war with Spain, begun in 1568 and destined to last until 1648, with an intervening truce from 1609 to 1621, would free the Netherlands from the Hapsburg empire. The people themselves had developed a national consciousness pieced together from such diverse elements as the Bible, the sea, and the Reformation. They identified themselves strongly with the chosen people of the Old Testament and were driven by Calvinist principles and a repugnance for Spanish rule. There were complex feelings toward the sea: It was the ever-present enemy, a rich source of pride since it had been made to yield up much of their land, and a biblical force connected to such stories as the Flood and Jonah and the whale.

The feeling that they were contemporary Israelites, the beneficiaries of a new covenant with God, was pervasive and powerful. Through the refraction of this vision, the Dutch saw themselves as survivors of the equivalent of the biblical Flood. They drew a parallel between their efforts to escape Spanish rule and the Jews' Egyptian captivity, flight, and the miracle of the parting of the Red Sea. Netherlanders thought of their country as the land of milk and honey and referred to scripture when separating religious and temporal authority. Extending the parallel into the future, they feared that they were destined to suffer misfortunes like those of the Israelites. In this they were concerned that their astonishing prosperity would lead to an abrogation of the covenant with God, and that after the divine protection was withdrawn they would be cast into the abyss.

The seventeenth was to be the "Golden Century" for the Netherlands. In the commercial sphere the country developed at an amazing pace into the leading power in Europe. At the core of this development was the staple market in Amsterdam and the Baltic Sea trade which carried salt, herring, wine, wood and wooden products, iron, copper, and colonial products from Poland, Russia, and the Scandinavian countries. Ships bound to these destinations carried Dutch bricks. Amsterdam grew rapidly from 50,000 people in 1600 to 200,000 in 1650, and became the financial capital of the continent. By the second decade of the century, it was also the center of the traffic in weapons and ammunition. When the Spanish closed Lisbon to the Dutch and they were no longer able to use Portuguese agents for their colonial enterprises, the Dutch East India Company was organized and the Dutch soon displaced the Portuguese entirely. The Dutch West India Company was formed in 1621 to develop New World resources, and if it proved less successful than its twin, together they seemed to cover the world. To protect this vast commerce the Dutch expanded their navy until, by 1650, it was twice the size of the English and the French naval fleets combined.

In the early seventeenth century, the population of the country was about 1½ million. The form of government was a republic, with considerable power vested in local institutions—an anomaly in Europe, where monarchical government was still the order of the day. Its society, too, was different from those in other countries. In contrast to the pyramidal shape of most of modern Europe, Schama describes that of the Netherlands as "ovoid" or "potbellied" in form, an apt description for it groups together into a great middle class all those who "sat down at more or less the same time to a breakfast consisting of more or less the same ingredients—bread, butter, cheese, fish, pastries, beer and/ or buttermilk and whey." Even the poorer citizens in this prosperous country ate well while elsewhere in Europe a majority of the population battled starvation. According to Schama, "the Republic was an island of plenty in an ocean of want. Its artisans, even its unskilled workers and its farmers (for it seems a misnomer to call them peasants) enjoyed higher real incomes, better diets and safer livelihoods than anywhere else on the continent."

Beyond the necessaries there was, for a large percentage of the population, disposable income in varying degrees. The household of a typical middle-class family was well furnished, down to the pictures that hung on the walls in profusion.

While business was the bedrock of the community, its relationship to basic religious principles was ambiguous. The success of the nation was due to mercantile genius, but the biblical injunctions against worshiping money were deeply felt and constituted a troubling—if uncertain—boundary on commercial activities. Vondel, an important contemporary poet, while a believer in the propriety of trade and the accumulation of goods, warned against the national thirst for profits:

They run, they press, they rush in greed to their affairs,
They pile up heaps of perishable goods and wares:
Great hulks are being built, vast oceans being crossed,
The vessel of the soul, though, is entirely lost.

Daily life at all levels was shaped by the useful adage "Zaken zijn zaken," or "Business is business." Sir William Temple observed while traveling through the country that it was a land "where the earth is better than the air, and profit more in request than honor; where there is more sense than wit; more good nature than good humour; and more wealth than pleasure." Perhaps the most celebrated observation of this aspect of Dutch life is that of Descartes, who wrote to a friend on May 5, 1631, from Amsterdam that "there is no one in this city, except me, who is not engaged in trade; everybody is so concerned with his profits that I could stay here all my life, without seeing anyone." The fever of business infected everyone. Even Pieter Geyl, the Dutch historian, notes that numerous witnesses were shocked to find that greed of gain seemed the prime motivation, not only of the leading class but of the entire community.

Investment was one area in which the dichotomy between the drive for gain and Bible-based disapproval revealed itself most vividly. The Amsterdam stock exchange was a problematic institution for the Dutch since it held out the promise of wealth earned without labor. Especially objectionable were those transactions involving shares either not yet in the possession of the seller or not yet paid for, a practice referred to as "trading in the wind" and one that was to become a feature of the tulipmania. It was—and is—easy to modulate these notions into that of pure gambling, an activity severely criticized in seventeenth-century Amsterdam. Disapproval not only found expression in frequent comparisons of the stock exchange to gambling dens but, more specifically, led to regulations restricting operation of the exchange to the hours between noon and two o'clock. Initially, these activities had taken place out in the open in the streets. The city fathers, while considering such trading a sink of iniquity because it seemed like gambling, also realized it was a necessary evil, and in 1608 they erected a new building for the exchange.

The atmosphere at the exchange was charged, especially as the brief two-hour period drew to a close. The ritual by which two hand-shakes signified first a sale and then confirmation of the price became a flurry of wild hand slapping. "Hands redden from the blows . . . handshakes are followed by shouting, insults, impudence, pushing and shoving." Speculation, or trading in the wind, was common. In order to move stock, a speculator would engage in bizarre acts to draw atten-tion to himself. Typically, he "chews his nails, pulls his fingers, closes his eyes, takes four paces, and four times talks to himself, raises his hand to his cheek as if he has a toothache and all this accompanied by a mysterious coughing."

Although speculation was criticized at the time on moral grounds as an invitation to prodigality and deceit, Schama takes a more un-derstanding view, observing that

> it was in fact only a more extreme form of the practices which arose naturally in an economy where delivery times were bound to be uncertain and prolonged. It was certainly no more improper than governments spending money (usually on building or campaigns) by "anticipating" (that is, realizing, through whatever source delivered the cash) revenues for coming years. In an international entrepot like Amsterdam, where a glut of capital washed around looking for places to settle, and where rumor and gossip made and ruined fortunes, it was virtually impossible to stifle impromptu speculation. If it was driven from the Bourse, the chances were that it would develop spontaneously elsewhere. For those long time lapses between the "sighting" of a commodity and its actual appearance were unbearably inviting to those in a position to manipulate rising or falling ex-pectations. And from their ingenuity, and from the impatience of the small punter to see his fortune magically transformed, there arose the great speculative manias of the seventeenth and early eighteenth centuries. More than any other phenomena, they revealed to an unnerved elite just how fragile their system of controlled supplies and buffered prices could be when faced with pressure from spontaneous market demand.

This, of course, explains considerably more than stock market speculation. In fact, it reveals the eagerness to speculate, which constituted a notable feature of the time. Warehouses were a prominent feature in the Amsterdam cityscape because of their number, but they also represented the predominant trading policies. The merchants were speculators who hoarded goods with an eye on market fluctuations. Backed by large credits, they stockpiled commodities until scarcity pushed prices up and they could sell in a favorable market. By manipulating the flow of goods with an eye to the changes in supply and demand, they could control the wine of France, the furs of Russia, and the iron of Sweden.

Fernand Braudel in *The Wheels of Commerce* relates the origins of exchanges in Europe, but makes it plain that the novelty at the beginning of the seventeenth century was the introduction in Amsterdam of a stock market where government stocks and the shares of the Dutch East India Company became the stuff of speculation. While there had been stock exchanges elsewhere, Amsterdam's was different because of its volume, the fluidity of the market, the publicity it received, and its speculative freedom of transactions. Speculation there had reached a degree of sophistication and

abstraction which made it for many years a very special trading-centre of Europe, a place where people were not content simply to buy and sell shares, speculating on their possible rise or fall, but where one could by means of various ingenious combinations speculate without having any money or shares. . . . The explanation for the volume and notoriety of speculation in Amsterdam . . . was that small shareholders had always been associated with it, not just the big capitalists. . . . "Our speculators," says Joseph de la Vega in 1688, "frequent certain houses in which a drink is sold which the Dutch call *coffy* and the Levantines *caffe.*" These *coffy huisen* "are of great usefulness in winter, with their welcoming stoves and tempting pastimes, some offer books to read, others gaming tables and all have people ready to converse with one; one man drinks chocolate, another coffee, one milk, another tea and practically all of them smoke tobacco. . . . In this way they can keep warm, be refreshed and entertained for little expense, listening to the news. . . . There then comes into one of these houses during the opening hours of the Exchange one of the bulls, or bidders-up. People ask him the price of shares, he adds on one or two percent to the price of the moment,

takes out his little notebook and pretends to write in it what he has
only done in his mind, letting everyone believe that he has really done
it, and in order to encourage in every heart the desire of buying some
shares, for fear they should go up again.

Braudel draws from this scene the conclusion that the Amsterdam
stock exchange extracted money from the pockets of small savers and
small speculators, who were formally excluded from the exchange itself
in part because there was no official quotation of prices and in part
because the brokers made small people their target.

Investment activities were not confined to stock trading at the
Bourse and its environs, however. A climate existed in which anything
could be sold for speculation. Art, in particular, was a field rich in
possibilities for bargains. John Evelyn, in 1641, was amazed to see
peasants buying paintings at the fairs:

The reason of this store of pictures and their cheapness, proceed
from their want of land to employ their stock, so that it is an ordinary
thing to find a common farmer lay out two or three thousand pounds
in this commodity. Their houses are full of them, and they vend them
at their fairs to very great gains.

Artists also speculated in paintings. Rembrandt, whose poor financial management resulted in the loss of his house and possessions, was
an inveterate auction-goer. While he may have gone to speculate, his
artist's enthusiasm regularly got the better of his business judgment
and he became known for his imprudent bidding.

Contributing to the appetite for speculation was the memory of the
capture of the Spanish silver fleet off Matanzas in 1628 by Admiral Piet
Heyn and his squadron. The value of the fleet was put at twelve million
guilders, creating a windfall for the Dutch West India Company, Heyn's
employer. The event was a public sensation and strengthened the
feeling that fortunes could be made without effort if one was lucky.

The case can be made, then, that the time was ripe for a large-
scale speculative movement focused on one kind of novel article.
Prosperity reigned; the populace enjoyed a relatively high standard of

living and many people had disposable income. Not only was investment machinery in place, but futures trading had developed and
speculation was widespread as Amsterdam, in addition to other parts of
the country, experienced a tremendous movement in goods of an
infinite variety.

If the soil for the tulipmania was fertile, what explains the selection
of this particular commodity? Why not a land boom? In a country where
land was precious, some of it won by hard effort from the sea, all of it
cloaked in a biblical aura, it would seem a more natural object of
speculative interest than a Turkish bloom. Furthermore, passing
through Amsterdam daily were such items of exotic appeal as gem-
stones, silk, Ming porcelain, and Turkish rugs, more likely candidates
for the obsession that developed. Certain exotic articles entering the
Dutch world stimulated the production of local copies, such as Delft-
ware for Ming porcelain and Flemish carpets for Turkish rugs. In
Schama's view, tulips were different because, pardoxically, they were
easily reproduced and their increasing availability fueled the mania.
This seems doubtful, for its reproducibility is precisely the characteristic that could make the flower common and unfit for speculative attention.

Mackay notes that the attractiveness of the tulip is in direct proportion to its cultivation, so it becomes progressively weaker as it becomes more beautiful. "Many persons grow insensibly attached to that
which gives them a great deal of trouble, as a mother often loves her
sick and ever-ailing child better than her more healthy offspring. Upon
the same principle we must account for the unmerited encomia lavished
upon these fragile blossoms." This may be a poetic theory, but it is not
convincing.

A more plausible analysis of the tulip's unique speculative allure is
given by Peter Coats in *Flowers in History* and Wilfrid Blunt in *Tulipomania*. The bulbs brought from Constantinople were not wild, but
cultivated. They were called "breeders," and had the unique habit of
changing or "breaking" into a variation in which only part of the original
color is maintained in streaks, feathering, or "flames." Once this break
occurs, the tulip seldom reverts to its original overall coloring, and the
children bulbs keep the new colors. It was in the unpredictability of the

break, according to Coats and Blunt, that the gambler's chance lay. Blunt quotes a seventeenth-century Dutch author's description of how this unique feature generated interest:

> If a change in a tulip is effected, one goes to a florist and tells him, and soon it gets talked about. Everyone is anxious to see it. If it is a new flower, each one gives his opinion. One compares it to this flower, another to that. If it looks like an "Admiral" you call it a "General," or any other name you fancy, and stand a bottle of wine to your friends that they may remember to talk about it.

Beyond these rather narrow considerations concerning the tulip's unique features lay the broader explanation that there had always been a special place in the Dutch sensibility for flowers and that the introduction and distribution of the novel tulip plants in the early years of the seventeenth century combined with other ingredients of a social and economic nature to fuel the intense but brief speculation Mackay describes.

In the national iconography, a verdant garden, transformed from the stockade that symbolized the great sieges of the early years of the war of independence with Spain, became a symbol of the country's prosperity. The Netherlands was a land of innumerable small gardens. "The smallest villages had their flower-growers' clubs, with their own rules, ceremonies and fetes," wrote Gabriele Tergit in *Flowers Through the Ages.* "In the spring a meeting was held to elect a tribunal to pass judgment on new flowers. Garden cultivation developed into a sort of rite. Experts walked from flower bed to flower bed, prizes were distributed, the value of novelties was discussed at length. In the evening the spring festival was celebrated with a banquet, and the talk was not about hunting or war; *on causait fleurs,* one talked about flowers," wrote the French ambassador. "Politicians, scholars, elegant ladies, all worked in the garden, planted exotic plants and sent cuttings to the botanical garden at Leiden. The most beautiful flower 'still-lifes' of the world were painted in Holland."

This was the setting for the appearance of the tulip in the Netherlands. Even before the tulipmania it occupied a special place in the world of flowers. In Persia it was a wild flower, the symbol of love and the inspiration of poets and painters, having sprung, according to legend, from drops of a disappointed lover's blood. In Turkey, it was the emblem of the ruling house and, like the fleur-de-lis in France, appeared on textiles, ceramics, and stone carvings.

The word *tulip* may have been brought to Europe along with the flower due to a misunderstanding. The correct Turkish word for the flower is *lalé*. When they were shown to Ambassador Busbecq near Constantinople they may have been described as being like "tulband," the word meaning the cloth out of which a fez is made, from which the English word *turban* is derived. Busbecq may have misunderstood an interpreter who was comparing the flower to a certain fabric.

Prized first at court and in patrician circles, the new flower reached a wider audience by the second decade of the seventeenth century. The tulip became France's favorite flower, and women pinned them to their low décolletage. The price of tulips in that country soared. A mill was exchanged for one tulip bulb; a brewery for another. The entire dowry of one bride consisted of a rare bulb, which the groom was delighted to receive. At the wedding of Louis XIII, tulips as valuable as diamonds were worn.

The tulip was first grown in the Netherlands around 1590 in Leiden, but did not become commercially important until the first decades of the seventeenth century. By 1614, poet Roemer Visscher criticized florists who wasted so much money on a plant ("this lust is surely costly") and Petrus Hondius found space in his poetic praise of the sweetness of country life to ridicule "fools who grow gardens for one flower only." The following year a character in *The Moor,* a play by Bredero, declared, "I'm not such a fool as the people who give a lot of money for a tulip."

The speculation *(windhandel)* began in 1633 in West Friesland and spread to involve the entire country, with centers of activities in Alkmaar, Rotterdam, Utrecht, Haarlem, Vianen, Hoorn, Leiden, Gouda, Enkhuizen, and Amsterdam.

According to N. W. Posthumus, the buying and selling of tulips in the Netherlands was always in bulbs, even before the mania began. Although the bulbs were sold individually in the earliest years, by 1610 it was usual to trade in beds of common-variety tulips. By 1624, however, one bulb of the Semper Augustus variety, one of the most beautiful of the flowers, was offered for 1,200 guilders. At that time there were only twelve in existence. In the following year, an offer of 3,000 guilders for two of the same bulbs was rejected, the owner claiming that he held all of them.

But what do these prices mean in present-day terms? Readers of Mackay's book know that bulb prices reached exceptional heights from the barter deals he describes, yet we remain curious as to cash values. The guilder, or florin, was the basic unit of currency and was equal to 20 stuivers. Efforts to relate the seventeenth-century guilder to to-day's dollar do not all lead to the same conclusion. Professor Peter M. Garber of Brown University, in an article on the tulipmania in the *Wall Street Journal* in January 1988, equated the guilder of 1625 to about 9 dollars. Posthumus, writing in 1929, used 40 cents as the equivalent. If that value is inflated by the total change in the consumer price index from 1929 (51.3) to the beginning of 1988 (370), the present equivalent is about $2.88 per guilder.

In 1603 one guilder was worth .9 of a gram of gold or 14.5 grams of silver. With gold and silver now at about $340 and $4 an ounce, respectively, the conversions produce present values for the 1603 guilder of $10.93 based on the gold equivalent and $2.07 based on the silver equivalent.

The failure of these different approaches to yield consistent dollar values indicated why Barbara Tuchman, after contemplating currency confusions in a note in *A Distant Mirror,* simply urged her readers to think of any given amount as so many pieces of money. While a definitive exchange ratio between seventeenth-century guilders and modern currency may escape us, it may not be important to understand the significance of the rapid movement in tulip prices and the high levels they reached because the array of values in the Netherlands at that time was quite different from those in our economic world. Schama appends typical prices in guilders and stuivers as follows:

tankard of ale	½ stuiver
twelve-pound loaf of rye bread	6–9 stuivers
weekly wage of skilled worker	2.8 guilders
small house in town	300 guilders
annual stipend of schoolmaster/predikant	200 guilders

From this it becomes evident that while the era was a prosperous one, wages and prices were considerably lower than today's and the unit of currency had much greater purchasing power, regardless of which formula is used for updating the guilders of that time. This circumstance only magnifies the significance of the prices paid for tulips during the mania. It is interesting to compare the astonishing prices paid for tulip bulbs with the 600 guilders Rembrandt accepted for each of a series of paintings of Christ's Passion commissioned by Prince Frederick Henry, and the top price of 1,600 guilders paid for a Rembrandt painting.

When the tulip trade involved actual bulbs, the buyer expected immediate delivery, although this could take place only from June to September since bulbs could not be removed from their beds before the former month and had to be replanted by the latter month. Eventually, the trade was extended to excrescences or outgrowths, which were separated from the main bulb. "Accordingly," says Posthumus, "excrescences could be bought and sold during the whole year. It is likely that soon afterward, main bulbs were also sold without being at once deliverable. In this way the speculative element was increased enormously."

An anecdote from the height of the tulipmania indicates the value of the excrescences. Although a Semper Augustus was sold for the astounding sum of 5,500 guilders, the seller claimed to have been cheated out of 2,000 guilders. When the bulb, which was in the ground at the time of the sale, was lifted out, it was found to have two lumps that would have become excrescences the following year.

Until 1633 or the beginning of 1634 the trade was still largely in the hands of professional growers and experts. But a campaign undertaken to broaden the flower's appeal was very successful and soon people with no connection to tulip culture began to buy and sell. These were the weavers, spinners, cobblers, bakers, and butchers who had absolutely no knowledge of tulips but were drawn by the prospect of easy money. By the end of 1634, speculation extended to the common varieties of bulbs.

The rising interest was spurred by new methods of selling. Sale by weight was introduced in late 1635 with the basic unit being an "ace," or one-twentieth of a gram. This meant that one would pay a premium for a heavier bulb, but the added weight increased the buyer's chances of finding viable excrescences. Ordinary bulbs were sold by the thousand aces and the very common bulbs were sold by the pound and the basket. This permitted even the poor to get in on the action. With these developments, the units of sale now ranged across a spectrum with whole beds and gardens at one end, moving to basket, pound, piece, thousand aces, and ace, depending on the season and the variety of flower.

The sale of tulip bulbs by weight also contributed to the speculation. Since the bulb's weight was registered when planted, and it was sold "on the grow," or while still in the ground, the buyer was speculating on the increase in its weight that would take place before it was lifted. This could be important. The answer of Jeuriaen Jansz, a fifty-year-old Haarlem baker to the plaintiff, dated August 1, 1636, in a lawsuit alleging breach of a contract of sale of the outgrowth of an Admiral Lieffkens bulb standing then in full bloom in a certain garden stated that the contract permitted the purchaser to cancel the deal within two days. Before that time expired, Jansz had heard conversations at the local tulip "college" in which other dealers stated that the plant in question had been taken out of the ground, the soil scraped off, and the bulb examined. Because the exact weight was not known, the plaintiff would be greatly damaged since no one would then pay even the high price that the plaintiff had paid. Knowing this, defendant Jansz had canceled the contract.

Artful marketing techniques were used. Bulbs were ranked according to rarity, with the most admired flamed and irregularly striped varieties at the top. Growers were fond of naming bulbs after themselves, adding a military title, which was more acceptable in a republic than one of nobility. So, for example, the General Bol and Admiral Pottebacher referred not to battle heroes but to growers Pieter Bol and Henrik Pottebacher.

These innovations in marketing, says Schama, were the work of a new generation of horticulturalists who broke out of the relatively genteel and circumscribed trade and changed the conditions of distribution and sale. Not only did they adjust the units of sale with their new weight units, they moved out from their nurseries and shops into the countryside by hiring salesmen to visit village fairs and other markets remote from the major bulb centers.

These intensified efforts at first caused a decline in the prices of many new kinds of tulips, but then sudden demand moved prices sharply higher. By June 1636 many varieties had tripled in price and more. A comparison of prices at that time with certain bulbs sold in December 1634 shows increases from 15 guilders to 175 guilders; 40 to 350, and 800 to 2,200. Sales volume soared. It is said that for one town in the province of Holland the total sales amounted to 10 million guilders.

The price was not always paid in cash. Indeed, as the boom progressed and prices continued to rise, it was increasingly payable in goods. The most heterogeneous lot of goods was accepted in payment, says Posthumus, such as cows, fruit, wine, yards of cloth, clothes, silver dishes, horses and carriages, land, houses, shops, and paintings. At first these goods were delivered at once, but the bulb itself would not be delivered until later when it was taken out of the ground. However, as the speculative mania developed even further toward 1636, buyers, knowing the sellers did not have the bulbs in their possession, did not pay or deliver their goods until they knew that the sellers actually had the bulbs or were certain to possess them. Then another stage was reached in which most sales took place without any basis in goods or bulbs at all. The trade in futures had degenerated into purest gamble, the seller selling bulbs he did not have against a counter value, mostly money at this period, which the buyer did not possess. Each buyer tried to sell the bulb for a successively higher price. It was possible for a speculator to make a profit of several thousand guilders, on paper, in a few days. All classes took part with the exception of the patricians, who remained aloof.

Before the pace quickened, sales had been documented by written contracts, often before a solicitor; now the volume of sales had increased so much that such formal procedures were too slow, burdensome, and costly, especially for the man in the street who was now deeply involved in the game.

Instead, informal private organizations were formed with elaborate and curious procedures where the buying and selling of tulip bulbs took place with more limited record keeping. These "colleges," as they were called, convened in inns and featured a great deal of drinking. It has been suggested that the concentration of these activities in the taverns was due to the people's desire to escape through drink the bubonic plague, from which, during August to November 1636, 15 percent of the population of Haarlem, center of the bulb trade, was wiped out. And, Braudel tells us, the plague visited Amsterdam every year from 1622 to 1628, claiming a total of 35,000 lives.

But Schama points out that this was a society of drinkers. A typical farmer's breakfast included beer and perhaps some brandywine. Drinking took place intermittently during the workday. Amsterdam alone had 518 alehouses. Deals between farmers and buyers were customarily sealed over a tankard of ale at the inn. In parts of north Holland a wool merchant was required to down at one swallow a quart flagon containing a coin. The sale was confirmed only if he emptied the flagon and caught the coin in his teeth. The Dutch had an incredible capacity for drink. At parties, toast followed toast, and when that was exhausted, they drank "at the sound of a bell, at the casting of dice, at the turning of a mill." Often wineglasses were designed without bases so that they could not stand and had to be held in the hand.

Three satirical pamphlets issued in 1637 containing fictional dialogues between two characters named Waermondt ("Truemouth") and Gaergoedt ("Greedygoods") are the source of much of the information we have on the tulipmania. Greedy had been a weaver, but like many of his fellows had become a flower dealer when the tulipmania got under way. As Posthumus observes, the weavers were passing through economic difficulties at the time and their position as independent masters was threatened. This, combined with their ability to raise some capital since they owned looms and often small houses, led to their entry into the flower trade. The big merchants, by contrast, resisted speculating in tulips, remaining more interested in the customary exchange of goods and securities.

The dialogues, which were issued after the speculation had broken, take place in Greedy's house and touch on many of the main features of the tulipmania. This was a time of primitive communication by today's standards: the world's first newspaper had begun publication in Strasbourg in 1609 and in the Netherlands the birth of the press had just taken place in 1618. In a world lacking such sources of opinion as radio, television, and a developed press, the pamphlets were an important public commentary. Not only were they read closely, in contrast to the fleeting attention given to the flood of editorial comment that pours out of the media now, it is likely that they were preserved, reread, and circulated in a manner unlike that accorded written matter in today's throwaway culture.

Judging from their satirical tone and earthy touches, they were intended to be shared by the Dutch in a fashion similar to that in which a good story now makes its way through society. It is possible to picture groups of men reading portions to each other, bent over with laughter, on streetcorners and in taverns, husbands and wives discussing them over dinner, and even the powerful perusing them in the hushed offices of the Dutch East India Company.

In the first Greedy-True dialogue, the former is full of confidence and boasts to True about the money he has made since entering the tulip trade. Even his liquor cabinet is well stocked and it's all due to the flower business, a sure thing where one's investment never fails. True notes that there had been shortages and business in general has been bad because of piracy and storms, but Greedy is unaffected: He has been making money hand over fist in the flower trade and confides to True that in the last four months he has made 60,000 guilders, although he admits most of it is on paper only.

When True expresses interest, Greedy is quick to hold out the lure: "I can let you have a small shipment, and because you're my best friend, I'll give you a special low price—say, fifty guilders less than what I'd usually get. Even better than that: if you haven't made a big profit in a month, I'll buy the whole lot back."

But how would I sell the stuff? asks True. Would people come to me or would I have to go out and sell the flowers? Greedy tells him how to do it: "First, you go to an inn. I'll give you the name of a few, but most run tulip markets. They're called 'colleges.' "

We might imagine True, some time later, hesitant but curious, entering the White Doublet Inn in Haarlem one morning in 1636. Although it is still early in the day, the large front room is filled with people drinking and talking. At the bar two small children, on tiptoe, are buying ale for the family breakfast. In a corner, a drunken couple is asleep. She has lost one shoe and leans back over a stool, her dress rising over one leg. He is facedown on a huge beer keg. True leans over to the barmaid and asks where the tulips are being bought and sold. The door she indicates opens into a rear room, and when True enters he is forced to pause while his eyes grow accustomed to the dimness and the cloud of smoke. Eventually, he makes out the candles and then the tables they rest on and the speculators. All the tables have been placed end to end in a crude circle with tulip-filled vases alternating with the candle sconces. The group is made up mainly of working men, but there are several women and children. True is not surprised at this for Greedy had told him that children took part in these trading colleges. Nor is he surprised at the volume of smoke, for most of the men wearing broad-brimmed black hats have long-stemmed clay pipes in their hands or mouths. He recalls that a well-known doctor had announced that tobacco smoke was effective against the plague and had himself kept a lit pipe in his mouth most of the day. As True stands there in the doorway getting his bearings, some of the dealers turn to look at him and from the rear of the room comes a voice quacking like a duck. Then another, very loud, roars: "There's a new whore in the house!" Since he is conducting a kind of field investigation, True tells himself, he tries to shrug off the remark.

A man who identifies himself as the company's secretary comes up to True, asks his name, and writes it at the bottom of a long list of names on a slate he carries. He then shows True to a seat and whispers that the group is now trading "by the plates." With that a stack of wooden discs or plates is distributed to the people around the table. The one True receives has written on it "one Gouda of 48 aces in N's garden." A signal is given, and two men get up and go into a corner where they are joined by two other men. True cannot hear what transpires there, but the man next to him explains it as follows: Of the four, one is the seller of the bulb, another an interested buyer, and the others were chosen by the seller and the buyer to assist in negotiating the price. The seller begins by demanding an exorbitant price, say 200 guilders for a bulb worth only 100. The buyer counters by offering 50.

The two assistants eventually decide on a price, recite it out loud, and place marks on the plates of the buyer and the seller. If the buyer and the seller both erase the marks, there's no deal. If only one of them does so, he must pay the other a consolation fee, which the college has fixed at five pence. If both of them leave the marks, it's a deal and the buyer pays the seller "wine money" of a half-penny for every guilder of the price up to a maximum of 3 guilders. The "wine money" is to be used by the seller for drinks, food, tobacco, fire, light, and girls.

Later in the day, after hours of trading "by the plates," the group reorganizes and begins selling bulbs "in the naught." Such a practice was meant to stimulate bidding because the sum in the naught would go to the highest bidder whether the sale was concluded or not. The secretary writes the amount in the circle. Bids are then shouted out at higher and higher levels until no one wants to raise the last bid. At this point the secretary calls out, "No one bids? No one once? Twice? No one a third time?" At the fourth time the bidding closes and a line is drawn through the circle. The seller then has the choice of withdrawing the offered goods and rejecting the high bid or completing the sale. If he withdraws, the winning bidder keeps the amount that has been placed in the naught. If the sale is completed, the buyer gives the seller the same amount of wine money as if the sale had been conducted "by the plates." Both procedures end up with a written agreement signed by the buyer.

Either "by the plates" or "in the naught" some sales involve bulbs actually in the possession of the seller and others do not, the sellers dealing "in the wind."

True finds it all interesting but, cautious as always, refrains from taking part in any of the buying and selling. Later he describes his experiences to Greedy and asks how much the wine money usually amounts to.

It usually covers food and drink and such things, says Greedy, and adds (hypocritically), "Of course, we must remember the poor."

Sometimes Greedy left the college early in the morning after hours of trading with more money than he brought. If the boom will only last for another few years, he says, it will be enough for him.

True, ever prudent, continues to resist Greedy's importuning. He has little money and must put it into his business. But what can you get in your business? demands Greedy. Ten percent? In the tulip business it's 100 percent, 1,000 percent, 10,000 percent, and even more.

If that's true, says True, why should anyone work? Why should merchants risk their goods overseas? Why should children learn a trade or soldiers and sailors risk their lives when they can make profits like that?

Back and forth the dialogue goes, Greedy's zeal alternating with True's caution. True is concerned that the florists will come to a bad end like their namesake and reminds his friend that Flora was a famous harlot in Rome whose beauty and charm won her many admirers. Her success made her haughty and she was known for the deceptions she practiced on her followers.

To encourage True, Greedy shows him a list of the most important bulbs he has, an inventory totaling 80,000 to 90,000 guilders, and recites some of his transactions. He started by mortgaging his house and selling some possessions to raise the cash necessary to enter the trade. When bulbs were sold whole, he bought one for 46 guilders and sold it for 515; another was bought for 20 and resold for 225; another bought for 15 was resold for 175; still another was bought for 95 and resold for 900. Even more astonishing escalations occurred when the bulbs began selling by aces and pounds. A pound of one variety, bought for 20 or 24 guilders, could be resold a month later for 1,200 guilders and more. Another variety first sold for 60 guilders a pound and later for 1,800. A third variety went from 125 to 3,600 guilders a pound. Other varieties sold by the thousand aces moved from 90 to 800 guilders, 70 to 600, and 40 to 350.

Stuff that used to be dug up as weeds and thrown away, says Greedy, has been sold for substantial prices. Everything was valuable and the demand was so great that you could get almost anything you wanted in exchange. And all of this when the bulbs were still in the earth. If it continued, flowers would become the common currency, acceptable for all payments just as conches are said to be the medium of exchange in some parts of East India.

With a certain amount of pride, Greedy gives examples of how he bought and sold bulbs for prices that were paid partly in cash and partly in goods:

- He sold a quarter of a Witte Kroonen for 525 guilders on delivery and four cows at once
- He bought two pounds of Switsers payable in 1,400 guilders in fourteen days at the bank plus a quarter of prunes delivered at once
- He sold one pound of Gheele Kroonen for 800 guilders together with enough cloth for a suit and coat, worth at least a certain sum
- He bought a pound of Witte Kroonen for 3,200 guilders payable with 200 guilders in cash, a silver dish estimated at 60 guilders, a pound of Gheele Kroonen, and the seller further transferred to Greedy his horse and coach, two silver bowls, and 150 guilders
- He bought a one-pound Genten for 1,800 guilders in exchange for "my best shot coat, one old rose-noble, and one coin with a silver chain to hang around a child's neck."
- He sold a garden with flowers and plants for 80,000 guilders payable when the flowers are in bloom, providing that the seller can retain a few flowers to the value of about 2,000 guilders.

Having gathered momentum, Greedy cannot resist recounting some big transactions to which he was not a party, including the sale of flowers in a garden for which 74,000 guilders was offered, but True alertly establishes that the sale has not been completed.

The discussion turns to the Semper Augustus, one of the super-stars of the tulip world. According to Greedy, there are only two, and one is not for sale at any price. Such a bulb might be worth 6,000 guilders, being more valuable than gold, silver, pearls, and precious stones. True admits that there is some value because of the beauty of the flower when it's in bloom, but he notes that it's perishable. He's also troubled because silver, gold, pearls, stones, and artistic works are treasured by wealthy people and it's the common people who are in the tulip business.

Greedy's desire to sell True a small shipment becomes more urgent when, after True has left for an hour, Greedy's wife returns from shopping with news that the florists are in a panic and that some goods are going for less than half what they brought last evening. Realizing he must unload some of his stock, Greedy thinks of True, who is due to return. "Of course," Greedy says, "he is a good, special old acquaintance, but everyone must look out for himself, for in business it is better to see a brother in trouble, not to speak of an acquaintance, than oneself."

But careful True is aware of the situation and tells Greedy that after having consulted with a cousin who advised him to wait, he has concluded that he will not take anything now.

Not all of the pamphlets attacked the tulipmania. A twenty-eight-page piece entitled *The Theatre of Flora,* by Cornelis van der Woude, supported the speculation. The title page depicted the reclining figure of the goddess Flora, decorated with tulips and surrounded by small garden tools. In its opening pages, the author praises himself as a peacemaker "who demonstrates with force wherein the mockers err," and describes himself as one who pitches "Reason against Ignorance." Van der Woude, who probably represented the flower traders, expressed the view that speculation should no more be condemned for the excesses of some of its participants than should wine because some greedy, insatiable bellies abuse it.

Greedy's observation that tulips were on their way to becoming the universal medium of exchange was not quite as fanciful a notion as might first appear. Not only were they exchanged in barter transactions, they were also used in wagering. In 1636, Jacob de Wet bet artist C. Coelenbier that the Dutch attempt to take a certain entrenchment from the Spanish would fail. De Wet staked a tulip bulb called the Lyons, a print by Durer, and two by Rembrandt. He lost when the Spanish gave up after a nine-month siege.

A feeling had come over the county that the tulip trade would never end, that all of Europe would participate, and that all the money from it would come to the Netherlands. And indeed it is possible to see how the phenomenon seemed to have an irresistible growth, crossing class lines and national boundaries, reaching out to include ever cheaper kinds of bulbs, and always pushing prices upward. The height of the craze took place in the autumn of 1636. Speaking of the 1636–1637 season, Greedy said, "It has been madness." It was at this time that the speculative activity concentrated on the reselling of existing sales documents. Prices were increasing so much and so fast that speculators bought up these agreements with the expectation of turning them over quickly at a profit.

To describe the phenomenon, the Dutch use the word *tulpen-woede,* which can be translated as "tulip fury," a small telltale of its scope and the intensity of energy that marked the time. Those suffering from the tulip craze were called "hooded ones" by people who kept their heads, an allusion to the hoods worn by madmen at the time. The astounding prices paid in cash, goods, and properties for certain bulbs are memorable, but not the only evidence of the psychological displacement that seems to have occurred. One story concerns a tulip maniac who heard that a Haarlem cobbler had a bulb of the same kind he had just purchased for a high price. He went to Haarlem, bought the cobbler's bulb for 1,500 guilders, and immediately ground it under his heel so that his would be unique. When he told the cobbler that he would have gone so far as to pay ten times the 1,500 guilders in order to achieve his goal, it proved to be too much for the poor cobbler, who went up to the attic and hanged himself, presumably anguished at the fortune that had slipped through his fingers.

In Haarlem, it became difficult to hire an employee; everyone was dealing in flowers. The coach builders were all booked up as the new tulip—paper—millionaires placed their orders early in preparation for the imagined grandeur of their new lives.

No painting was complete unless it included tulips. Feeling that there was a deity that dwelled in the bulbs, people refused to cut up onions for stew as a symbolic gesture in which the everyday vegetable was substituted for the precious flower bulb. Growers were understandably concerned about theft. One devised a tripwire around his garden connected to a bell, which would alert him to thieves. And since tulips were, as Greedy pointed out, more valuable than gold, silver, and pearls, the concern for such storehouses of value lying unguarded out in the open was justified.

More than a few former weavers must have spent sleepless nights listening for thieves or consumed with fears of fire or other casualties.

The dating of the collapse of the mania has been established with a strange precision. Relying in part on the dialogues, Posthumus places the stagnation on February 2 or 3, 1637. Even as late as February 1 insiders were urging people to buy and offering an eight-day guaranty against possible losses, but on February 4, there was talk of tulips becoming definitely unsalable.

Just as the record is vague in describing the exact cause-and-effect sequence by which the mania came about, so is there a lack of detail concerning its rapid collapse. The entire episode may be compared to changes in styles of a milder intensity and lesser significance, as, for example, a new mode in clothing or the introduction of a new slang expression. If it were possible to unravel the fabric of such style changes, the essentials would probably be found to consist of a few influential personalities who began wearing the new hat or the new boots or speaking the new phrase. Because these style setters were surrounded by a group ready to follow their innovations, a core of change came into existence which could, under the proper circumstances, spread across society in a significant way. There is no reason to doubt that in the genesis of the tulipmania such a group of style setters created these cores of change. And while such forces, multiplied, provide an explanation for the inflation and spread of the trade in tulips, they may also explain its deflation and demise. Negative comments, or even doubts, by influential style setters could very well have traveled through the supercharged world of the tulip dealers with terrific speed, quickly draining away the confidence and magical energy that had galvanized the Netherlands over the previous period. Added to this was the sense in some quarters that the boom could not last; even Greedy was aware of the possibility and hoped for just another few years.

After the bubble burst in the first few days of February 1637, bulb prices plummeted, the decline proceeding hour by hour. Futures contracts became completely unsalable. In Haarlem, there was panic and the matter became a national economic crisis. Those must have been days of great turmoil in parts of the Netherlands, comparable perhaps to the stock market collapses of 1929 and 1987. At the inns, there must have been bedlam in the colleges.

At stake were numerous unexecuted sales agreements, not to mention debts incurred to finance entry to the tulip trade. As the market crashed, buyers abandoned deals they had only recently been eager to consummate. A flood of litigation followed, but the courts were not inclined to enforce these contracts because they were considered gambling transactions.

Governmental intervention was slow in coming. The government had taken no part in the creation and growth of the tulipmania: the trade was almost completely unregulated, and in fact futures contracts were unenforceable by law. Had the tulipmania occurred elsewhere, the typical monarchical form of government of the time might have acted more decisively. In fact, during the next century in Turkey, events that might have led to another tulipmania were quickly suppressed. In the United Provinces of the Republic of the Netherlands, however, sovereignty was not consolidated centrally but was distributed among a number of local governmental units. Schama describes how impatient other nations became in dealing with the Dutch, who seemed to continuously refer decisions to another governmental body.

The tulipmania, then, was rather a spontaneous popular movement, unlike the major bubbles of the next century. The government played a crucial role in the Mississippi land scheme in France and the South Sea Bubble in England, so it would not be excessive to characterize them as episodes of governmental folly that engendered financial speculation. In the tulipmania, however, we have the pure model, a broad and deeply felt fascination with one kind of goods welling up in the people without any encouragement or even limiting role by the government. Its like would not be seen again for many years, but it is more nearly the archetype for many of the financial excesses of our time than any other event.

The conventional view that the duration of the mania covered the period 1636–1637 has been challenged by Professor Garber in an interesting analysis which leads him to conclude that with one exception, the movement in prices was not "obvious madness" but followed a conventional pattern. That one exception is the surge in prices of common bulbs in January 1637. To support his view, he attempts to reconstruct the price movements of rare bulbs before, during, and soon after the tulipmania and compares them with tulip and hyacinth prices in the eighteenth century. It is a curious exercise, motivated perhaps by his discomfort at the standard use of the tulipmania as one of the favored symbols of a financial bubble and apparently designed to show that it represented less crowd madness than is commonly believed.

It almost seems unnecessary to challenge the tabulations of prices Professor Garber has compiled and the graphs into which he has converted them. His thesis that the true bubble occurred only in the final month and that its significance should be reduced fails to take account of the prevailing attitudes toward speculation, the historical setting, the significance of the Amsterdam stock exchange, "trading in the wind," and the essentially crescendolike nature of the phenomenon. The notion that right up until the end the market in tulips was following an ordinary course, and one that would be repeated in the future, ignores as well the breadth of the nation's involvement in this commodity, its novelty, the shrewd and innovative selling strategies developed by the growers, and the irony involved in the juxtaposition of this most fragile and perishable of investments with the already famous business sense of the Dutch people. There is also some doubt about the relative significance of hyacinth prices in the eighteenth century since the period encompasses the abnormality of a speculation which was something of a tulipmania reprise.

One is not altogether comfortable with the professor's price study either. While his data may tend to show rapid price increases upon the introduction of a new kind of bulb or flower and then a rapid decrease as it becomes more common, that demonstration is silent with respect to the human side of the markets. The high prices paid for an unusual tulip bulb in the eighteenth century were probably paid by collectors and established dealers, an elite group which continued to attach very high premiums to such bulbs. During the mania period, however, the traffic in bulbs had extended beyond those groups even before the culmination in January 1637. It may be useful in this connection to remember our friend Greedy, a modest weaver who mortgaged his house, worth perhaps 300 guilders, in order to enter the tulip trade and soon found himself dealing in thousands of guilders.

While the government would not act at once, vitally affected bulb growers could and did move quickly as a group, meeting in Amsterdam on February 24. Even before this, when speculation was still gathering force, the bulb growers had acted collectively. Some months earlier, they had established a "kind of voluntary court of law," as Posthumus calls it, in which disputes between member dealers and customers could be arbitrated.

If the purpose of the Amsterdam conference of delegates was to find a method to prevent the ruin of the bulb growers, it was not a success. A resolution was adopted that established the date of November 30, 1636, as the dividing line. Sales entered into before that date were affirmed and should be executed. As to sales entered into later, the buyer could withdraw on condition that he notify the seller of his decision by March and pay 10 percent of the sale price to the seller. The resolution was not accepted by the Amsterdam delegate, and three of the twelve cities that voted for it conditioned their votes on the approval of their constituents. In March 1637, the burgomaster and governors of the city of Haarlem offered their opinion that all tulip sale contracts since October 1636 should be canceled. The resolution of the Amsterdam conference and the opinion of the Haarlem government, however, were only proposals and lacked the force of law. The need for direct official action was urgent.

News of the florists' resolution reach True and Greedy. The latter has been severely chastened by the recent events. Referring to a book in which he recorded sales of bulbs, he says that when he looked at it, he thought he was rich and would never have to weave again. Now, however, he wishes that he had never seen tulips.

They discuss the florists' plan for a solution to the problem and True explains how it will work. If a planter sold a bulb for 30 guilders and it was resold successively for 60, 100, and 200 guilders, anyone in the chain could pay 10 percent of the price he had agreed to pay and keep the bulb. If each declined, the next previous buyer could offer 10 percent of the price he had agreed to.

Greedy is unhappy, no doubt because he recognizes he will realize very little on his contracts. He foresees trouble on a large scale because there were so many deals, and so many of them involved insolvent people and even children who lived on charity. In the end he predicts that the moneyed people will have to absorb the losses.

True can't resist a little sermonizing. Speaking what was undoubtedly the author's mind, he says it was a stupid business and contrary to good business practice. People thought that a promise to pay was the same as payment and forgot that it was just bidding. Greedy winces.

In the last dialogue True asks Greedy whether the flowers are as valuable after the deflation as they were last winter.

Greedy doesn't think so because there's no demand for flowers. Everybody's quiet although some say they don't want to sell. There was a report that on May 1 a complete garden with valuable flowers was sold at auction for around 6 guilders. If it had been sold last year, it might have brought in 1,000 guilders. Greedy has also been with a dealer who offered to deliver seven valuable bulbs for 22 guilders and 1 stuiver. If that lot had been sold when prices were at their peak last winter, it would have gone for over 400 guilders.

The States of Holland, which was the appropriate central body to take legislative action in the emergency, refused to act until prodded by a petition from several cities including Hoorn and Haarlem. Judging by its reaction, that body was not pleased to have the problem dumped in its lap. On April 11, 1637, with the crisis entering its third month, the States of Holland appealed to the Court of Holland for counsel. Two weeks later, the court advised that it had insufficient evidence on which to act and that the gathering of the evidence should be done by the governors of the cities. Local magistrates were to use this evidence in resolving buyer-seller disputes, and if this was not possible, the information was to be sent on to the high court. In the meantime, the court proposed that all sale contracts be suspended, and that sellers be permitted to resell the bulbs. In the event the disputed contracts were later declared enforceable by the government, sellers could pursue the defaulting buyers for the difference. The States of Holland accepted these proposals and incorporated them into a resolution on April 27, 1637.

The effect of this legislation was to bar the flower dealers from enforcing their sales contracts in court and to release speculators from the obligations they had assumed. The declaration prepared by lawyer E. van Bosvelt at Haarlem on June 20, 1637, in defense of a lawsuit suggests what ensued:

> delivery and payment not being made by many and several, but a few honest people compromised by paying one, two, three, four, yes, even five, which was the utmost out of a hundred . . . such has happened in the same way at Amsterdam, der Goude, Hoorn, Enchuysen, and Alcmaer. Yes, there are also a great number of persons unwilling to pay or come to a compromise. And not only no justice was administered, but all notaries, solicitors, and ushers were forbidden by the authorities: the notaries were not to summon, the solicitors not to make plaints, and the ushers not to bring them and not to occupy themselves with these matters.

The disinclination of buyers to honor their agreements is understandable enough under the circumstances; what merits further reflection is van Bosvelt's observation that only "a few honest people" compromised by paying one to five percent of the price. Such "honesty" speaks equally of the opportunism of those who saw the reduced prices as bargains and counted on a revival of the speculative market. Greed and the gambling spirit die hard.

A return to economic stability may have taken some time. The next year the city of Haarlem found it necessary to enact a supplementary measure in January creating an arbitration panel to decide "the questions which have come forth from the flower trade." This was similar to the bulb growers' "voluntary court of law" for the resolution of such disputes except that it had official sanction. The new panel was composed of five members, met at least twice a week, and had the power of subpoena. But, like its predecessor, it could only work toward a compromise. Evidently, this soon proved to be inadequate, for in May 1638 the body's jurisdiction was changed in several important respects: not only did its decisions become binding, but the buyer could satisfy the sales contract by paying 3½ percent of the sale price, in which event the bulbs would remain with the seller. That percentage, so much less than that proposed by the Amsterdam conference of bulb growers the previous year, could not have pleased the dealers, even if it did improve their position slightly in relation to the flat suspension imposed by the States of Holland. As an official judgment of the market value of such deals at that time, however, it says a great deal about how much the speculation had inflated prices.

Among those hurt by the collapse in tulip prices was the artist Jan van Goyen. He had begun speculating in order to supplement his small artist's income. On February 4, 1637, he had entered into an agreement with the burgomaster of The Hague, Albert van Ravensteyn, to purchase two bulbs for 900 guilders and two paintings. The value of the bulbs declined so greatly that van Goyen suffered a terrible loss. Van Ravensteyn took the position that business is business and refused to compromise. As a result, the painter carried the debt for the rest of his life.

Other artists may have been involved in the speculation, but Rembrandt appears not to have been one of them. Although he painted a portrait of his wife, Saskia, as the goddess Flora in 1634, there is no evidence that he invested in tulips. Driven by a need to rise in society, he found another path to financial ruin. Having purchased a mansionlike house and busied himself accumulating works of art and antiques, he reached beyond his means, found himself borrowing more and more, and in 1658 lost his house and property.

Together with fortunes (paper or real) lost, financial hardship, and legal complications, there was an outpouring of satirical humor, both printed and pictorial, of which the three dialogues between Gaergoedt and Waermondt are but one example. Jan Breughel the Younger painted some tulips being worshiped by a pair of monkeys. One of the more memorable engravings is entitled *Floraes Mallewagen*, sometimes translated as "Flora Leading the Tulip Speculators to Destruction," dated 1637 and attributed to Crispijn van de Pas Younger (see chapter frontispiece). The picture is crowded with detail and the central theme of Flora and her speculators being carried on a land yacht—a metaphor for "trading in the wind"—has a particular pungency. Each of the four corners of the engraving contains a smaller scene depicting a tulip bed and colleges at Hoorn and Haarlem and a group of saddened flower dealers. In the wagon at Flora's feet are Good-for-Nothing, Eager Rich, Tippler, Idle Hope, and Greed all bedecked with flowers, some drinking, others holding bags heavy with gold. On the side of the vehicle are images of some of the inns that had become well known for their colleges. The sail pulls mightily, billowing out under a wind blowing flowers against it with concentrated force. The bird of Hope flutters in the air at the bow just beyond the grasp of one of the figures. Climbing up the halyard is a small figure with a belt of flowers which, on closer examination, is revealed to be a monkey, a reference to a proverb about how one's rear end may be exposed by a careless attempt to scale the heights. That the monkey is defecating on Flora and her companions does not seem to dampen their gaiety at all.

Flora, bare-breasted in the seat of honor, holds in her left hand some of the most prized tulips of the day, including the General Bol, the Semper Augustus, and the Admiral Noon, while on the ground underneath the land yacht's wheels other kinds of tulip plants are littered. Crowding behind are the otherwise sober citizens who are desperate to get aboard this marvelous contraption while they unthinkingly trample under their feet the precious articles of their livelihoods.

No one seems to be in control of the wagon and it will go wherever the flower-laden wind drives it. In the distance its fate can be made out, for a similar yacht is already foundering in the sea.

Although the mania was widespread, there was a small but violent band of tuliphobes, chief among whom was Evrard Forstius, professor of botany at Leiden. He could not see a tulip without attacking it furiously with a stick.

Mackay's brief, but memorable, description of the tulipmania comes down to us so devoid of detail and historical context that we assume such an extraordinary event could never have happened again and that the two-year period in which the Dutch became obsessed by this flower and the possibilities of wealth it presented is absolutely unique. Remarkably, there have been sequels. Not only was the same variety of plant the subject of a quite similar financial mania elsewhere, but the Dutch themselves, a century later, were carried away by another flower, the hyacinth.

It may seem particularly ironic that a tulip mania occurred in Turkey in the early part of the eighteenth century. This was, after all, the land from which the tulip was taken to Europe after it was first seen by Ambassador Busbecq in the sixteenth century. During the reign of Ahmed III (1703–1730) the same fury possessed the Turks as it had the Dutch, and the buying and selling of tulip bulbs became a favorite form of speculation. Previously neglected, flowers, and specifically the tulip, returned to favor. The grower who produced a new tulip variety was handsomely rewarded. A single order for the palace ran to 40,000 bulbs, and the palace gardens were said to contain no less than 500,000 plants. A thousand gold pieces were paid for a single bulb from Persia. This time, however, the conclusion was much different. As the speculative activity increased, threatening to get out of hand, the sultan intervened, commanding the kaimakam of Istanbul to fix the prices of the tulips and punish profiteers by banishment from the city, thereby abruptly ending the second tulipmania. Such forceful governmental action contrasts dramatically with the absence of any governmental intervention in the Netherlands. This further demonstrates that what initially appears to be simply an instance of meaningless excess may also evidence the decline in the role of a powerful central government and the concomitant rise in the personal control people exercised, for better or worse, over their own affairs. When individuals, rather than the sultan, choose their destiny, they may find to their embarrassment that they have joined Flora on her wind-wagon, but our sympathies are with them nevertheless.

In the nineteenth century, mainly in France, there was a dahlia craze. That flower was brought to Europe from Mexico around 1789, and by the middle of the next century had been developed into thousands of varieties. Sentiment for the dahlia became so strong, a philosopher cited it to disprove Rousseau's proposition that in the hands of man everything degenerates. The craze for these flowers began to take on some of the characteristics of the Dutch tulipmania. In 1838 in France, a well laid out and cared for dahlia bed was sold for 70,000 francs (perhaps $280,000 in current value, based on the relationship between gold and the franc in 1803 and a present value of $400 an ounce for gold) and a single plant was exchanged for a rare diamond.

But pride of place in any review of subsequent flower manias must go to the hyacinth mania of 1720–1736 in the Netherlands. The period encompasses the centennial of the tulipmania, a slight circumstance, perhaps, but one that emphasizes our astonishment that the Dutch would fail to remember on its hundredth anniversary a time of such abandon. This is especially noteworthy because the earlier episode appears to have been very much in the public mind. Voices were raised warning of the new mania, and some of the pamphlets that had been issued one hundred years earlier were brought out again, including those containing the three dialogues between Gaergodt and Waermondt.

The hyacinth has a long history in Europe and is mentioned by Homer. In the sixteenth century, it was reintroduced from Turkey. By about 1700 it had become so popular in the Netherlands that certain specimens commanded prices as high as 4,900 guilders.

The days of glory for the hyacinth began some time around 1684 with the marketing of the double flower. Before that time the single flower was considered the standard of beauty, the double variety being routinely destroyed, and the hyacinth had a status in the floral world beneath that of tulips and carnations. When florist Pieter Voorhelm was unable to dispose of some double blooms because he was sick, he noticed some particularly well-formed specimens and decided to cultivate them. Flower lovers liked them and would pay well for them, so Voorhelm decided to continue their cultivation. By the first two decades of the eighteenth century, hundreds of varieties had been propagated. The hyacinth had become the subject of immense interest and the flower of fashion, supplanting the tulip and other flowers and maintaining that position throughout the century.

This was a period of quiet prosperity in the Netherlands. The Golden Century had passed and the nation was no longer in the front rank of the world's powers. Well-to-do burgers were busy assembling various collections: libraries, artworks, coins, objects of nature, shells, minerals, and, of course, flowers. In one's garden it became important to display as many varieties as possible of each fashionable flower. The hyacinth was well suited for this because it exhibited endlessly varied gradations of color. As with the tulips in the previous century, the Haarlem florists showed their promotional skills, purposely cultivating a limited number of bulbs in order to push up prices.

Even the Mississippi land scheme engineered by John Law in France during the years 1719 and 1720, under the auspices of the regent, contributed to the rise in hyacinth prices. That bubble expanded across national boundaries and attracted numbers of Dutch investors. Those with less money, stimulated by the scent of money in the air, were tempted to speculate in the fashion flower. As was the case with the tulipmania, small tradespeople were drawn in.

Prices rose steadily from 1720 on and by 1733 they had reached so high a level that the hyacinth threatened to take over the role of the tulip in the previous century. Prices of 1,600 and 1,850 guilders were not uncommon. Ernst H. Krelage, whose *Bloemenspeculatie in Nederland* is the principal source on the hyacinth boom, says that the full dimension of the speculative era had already started in 1720 and covered the next fifteen years.

One view into the excesses that characterized the times is provided by a satirical fictitious "letter" that appeared in the *Holland Spectator* on August 14, 1733. The writer, a Haarlem weaver named Japik Schitspoel ("bobbin"), bemoaned the fact that his son-in-law, also a weaver, had lost his head over hyacinths. With his cousin, he had invested in a small piece of land and planted only hyacinths, to which he gave unbelievably disgusting names. He hoped to make such a big profit that he would be able to keep a carriage and horses. Consequently, he was seldom at his loom, but was always digging in the soil. He could study a flower for hours, and walked from flower bed to flower bed gently raising the leaves with a stick to inspect the growth. Visitors came daily, but Japik was afraid that they ridiculed his son-in-law. How could he talk this nonsense out of his head and avoid the unhappiness that it would cause his daughter and future grandchildren? The *Spectator* answered with a fatherly dissertation on the dangers of speculation.

The next year there was so much fear of a repetition of the tulipmania that the Gaergodt-Waermondt dialogues were reissued in a pamphlet. It included a satirical engraving from the tulipmania era, a list of current hyacinth prices, and a foreword announcing the intention of the pamphlet to be a mirror in which the present-day speculators could see themselves as money hungry as their ancestors, both victims of Flora's deception. The pamphlet ended with the following warning:

> The old whore, the wily Flora, is again exalted at the cost of many gold and silver coins. "Away mourning band! Hang up the (funeral) ribbon, here is commerce held!" calls out a flower-besotted person and many others. They feast on viewing their foolish valuables. They crawl with spy glasses near the flower bed to analyze the stamens, pistils and pollen and other niceties. Nobody can see but only a Flora's fool. Where will it go, florist? Think, think about your coins. Think of the craziest year. Think of your family. Is it for the fun? No. For the gain of the heartless ones with whom you trade? Phooey! Turn around, innocent, for it only has to do (I say it straight out) with your gold and silver coins.

This pamphlet notwithstanding, the speculation roared ahead for another two years, eliciting the publication of *Flora's Bloemwarande,* a long poem in convoluted verse satirizing some of those involved in the hyacinth in classical terms, and containing much of the information now available on the mania.

The *Bloemwarande* ("blooming park") describes a typical transaction involving one "Adelbert," a florist whose real name was Jan Bolt. Adelbert persuades a friend to buy a one-half interest in a hyacinth bulb for 1,000 guilders with only 10 percent down. Other growers and speculators hear of the sale and hasten to buy smaller interests in the same bulb, some paying cash, others mortgaging their homes or pawning property in order to share in the profit. When a newcomer expresses interest, Adelbert tells him that since a one-half interest was priced at 1,000 guilders, his offer of 600 guilders for a one-quarter interest must be refused, an indication, perhaps, of how rapidly values were rising. When the newcomer does succeed in buying a share, he joins with the other owners in talking up the price.

The speculators were mostly from outside the bulb profession and their lack of experience and knowledge often led them to commit foolish mistakes, providing inviting targets for public and private ridicule.

"Mithridates," another speculator in the *Bloemwarande* whose real name was not given, is described as being so enamored of a certain bulb he had purchased that he prepares to marry the flower nymph herself. He is pictured astride an ass on his way to the ceremony, the ass covered by a rich cloth containing gold and bells. Riding just behind Mithridates on the ass is a monkey who holds a parasol over Mithridates's head to shield him from the sun. In the middle of the crowd Mithridates must kneel before the magic fountain which spouts water only when the supplicant's love is true. In Mithridates's case, the fountain gives forth such a deluge that he is soaked and must change his clothes.

By using such names as Adelbert, Mithridates, Fabius, and Belisarius, the author of the *Bloemwarande* poked further fun at the hyacinth people, who tended to attach the most regal names to the bulbs.

Hendrik Haamblok ("Camillus") was a glazier who hoped to make a profit by speculating in hyacinths. He sold to "Livius" bulbs he represented to be the prestigious White States General. Livius, in turn, sold them to "Marcus Curtis," who planted them. To everyone's astonishment, they turned out to be Red Granaat, which were worth only a fraction of the White States General. The ensuing dispute could not be resolved even with the aid of specialists who acted as mediators, since the courts did not have jurisdiction of such matters. Ultimately a recitation of the facts and claims was recorded before a notary public. Of course, a kind of justice was meted out in the satire of the *Bloemwarande*.

Another dealer, Egbert van der Vaert, is quoted as saying that if Jupiter had known of a certain hyacinth variety, he would have preferred to take its form, rather than that of a swan, when making his amorous visit to Leda.

Lucas Nieuwenhuyzen ("Nicotiann") sold his tobacco shop in order to buy a planter of hyacinths, which he furnished in a luxurious manner. He memorized all the names of the hyacinths and believed that he knew everything about them because he possessed the most beautiful varieties. He also believed that he could change the flowers at will. To give some of them a new color he applied a yellow liquid to their petals, promising his wife a gift when he was successful. Krelage assumes she never got it.

Bartering for bulbs also occurred. In one case, linen merchants from Brabant exchanged linen for some flowers from Haarlem dealers. On discovering later that the flowers were of inferior quality, the merchants quarreled among themselves and destroyed them. Krelage interprets this incident as showing how the Haarlem dealers took advantage of people ignorant about the bulbs, many of them, like the Brabanters, from outlying provinces. These sharp dealings were practiced before and would be again.

"Astrubel," a florist named Hessen, is asked in the *Bloemwarande* whether he loves his wife or Flora more. When he protests his love for his wife, she assaults him complaining that he neglects his family, that they hardly have any bread, that the cupboards and trunks are empty, and that he is ashamed to tell her that he buys so many bulbs at public flower auctions. Later she returns alone saying that she has locked her husband up and offers to sell the case in which he displays his flowers.

The impact of the hyacinth mania on marriage seems to have been a widespread problem, for the flower dealers' wives appealed to Apollo about their situation. Flora was the cause of their problems, they wailed. Their marriages were suffering, and, since they did not even get pregnant anymore, they were denied the fruit of marriage. Unless Apollo helped them, the world would be depleted of people. The Council of Parnassus, under Apollo's presidency, found the flower dealers guilty and sentenced them to three years in the house of Lazarus (a reference to the biblical parable of Lazarus and the rich man), to which they were to be escorted immediately by thousands of Haarlem burgers. The author later visits them there and sees some of those he had earlier satirized, including Camillus, acting out their punishment by dipping water into bottomless barrels, presumably for selling Red Granaat as White States General.

Prices eventually began to fall in 1737 and a price list of 1739 shows precipitous declines from 1734 levels. The States General fell from 210 to 20 guilders, the Granaat from 66 to 16, and the Gekroont Salomon's Juweel all the way from 80 to 3.

In contrast to the tulipmania, says Krelage, the case had not made much of an impression on contemporaries. Many fewer people were involved and they could bear their losses better than the many poor and near-poor among the tulip speculators. The hyacinth speculation affected the community less deeply than the tulipmania. Evidence is also lacking as to whether the trade in hyacinths ever involved the buying and selling of futures.

The failure of the hyacinth mania to reach the empyrean heights of the tulipmania should disappoint only those perverse few who hoped for an even greater lunacy than that produced by the tulipmania. In its own right, it constitutes an episode of remarkable irrationality and is enhanced, rather than diminished, in this regard by the way it resonates with the mania of the previous century. Not the least notable feature of this encore performance is its extinction in the modern consciousness. In this, too, it is related to the tulipmania, for while the latter may be a familiar symbol in the world of economics and investment as an *in terrorem* symbol, it is a subject mostly unknown to the Dutch. That is only to be expected in view of its treatment by historians of the period. Geyl, Huizinga, Wilson, and Murray make no mention of the tulipmania. It is buried, it seems, in a potter's field reserved for national disgraces, the final resting place, no doubt, for the hyacinth mania as well.

Such flower-driven phenomena as the Turkish tulip boom, the Roman rose folly, and the French dahlia craze are all interesting, but distinguishable from the Dutch tulipmania and to a large extent, its epilogue, the hyacinth mania. Missing are the essential ingredients of broad public involvement, the complete separation of the article from its perceived market value, and the trading in futures. To Greedy and his associates at the colleges, it made no difference whether the commodity they dealt in was tulip bulbs, tea, ships, or livestock. The form of the deal had eclipsed its subject matter. The bulbs were not only never seen, they were not even in the possession of the sellers and only nominally in the minds of the parties. Therefore, it was possible—if not inevitable—that the trade became one in contracts, each buyer endeavoring to resell at a higher price the purchase contract he had negotiated. In this regard, the dahlia craze, for example, is quite unlike the seventeenth-century tulipmania. In the business of horticulture and the private collecting of flowers, high prices will always be paid for rare and unusual specimens. Therefore, it is no evidence of a mania solely that an exceptionally high price has been paid for a bulb.

To find an analogue for the tulipmania, it becomes necessary to search in more modern times and elsewhere than in the world of flowers. The Florida land boom certainly seems similar in that the investment in undeveloped land there degenerated into a mindless trade in binders. Just as in the Netherlands in 1636, those who went down to Florida in the 1920s speculated only in the contract, never viewing the property, and willingly risked a deposit in the hope that the contract could be quickly turned over at a profit.

The new issues market of the late 1960s may also bear similar comparison. The same kind of blind group obsession is suggested by the rabid interest in the shares of newly listed companies simply because of their newness without regard to earnings, assets, competitive position, or any other market factor.

Those who crowded into Boston's School Street in 1920 to give their money to Charles Ponzi were also the spiritual descendants of Greedy and his fellow tulipmaniacs. Their understanding of and interest in international postal reply coupons was equivalent to Greedy's in tulips.

Even Professor Garber, who takes up the tulipmania in order to diminish it, is impressed by its common usage as one of the ultimate symbols of financial manias. And in that select group it may stand alone for it is only that hybridized word that so evocatively packages avarice and lunacy, huge profits and fragile beauty, dread and caution.

WHEN THEY TOLD IT ON THE RADIO . . .
IT TERRIFIED THE WHOLE COUNTRY
THE WAR OF THE WORLDS
By H. G. WELLS

INVADERS
FROM MARS AND
BAT-MEN ON THE
MOON

It was Sunday night, October 30, 1938, a little after eight o'clock, and twelve-year-old Lester Charney, his sister, and brother were listening to the radio in the dining room of their grandfather's farmhouse a few miles east of Princeton, New Jersey. Like most of the listening audience they had been tuned to the Charlie McCarthy show, gathered in a tight group around the tall walnut cabinet of Grandfather Charney's radio, concentrating on the faint yellow glow of the dial as if it were a magic doorway to lands of fabulous enchantment and adventure. When Edgar Bergen, the ventriloquist, and his puppet had completed the first part of the program, Nelson Eddy was introduced to sing the "Neapolitan Love Song." Although Eddy was a popular vocalist, this was the signal for many in the audience to search the radio band for something else until Bergen and McCarthy returned. Lester turned the dial from station to station, but stopped when he heard something unusual. In the serious tones reserved for important news, an announcer was heard delivering a bulletin from Toronto, Canada. In it, a Professor Morse of "Macmillan University" reported observing three explosions that took place on the planet Mars some time before that evening. Earlier reports had been received from American observatories about the same occurrence. That seemed to be preliminary and background only, for the announcer then switched to Trenton, New Jersey, where it was reported that a huge, flaming object had fallen on a farm near Grovers Mill, New Jersey, a small town not far from Trenton. It might have been a meteor, but in any event it had been seen for several hundred miles and the impact had been heard as far north as

Elizabeth. A mobile unit was being sent to the scene and a special commentator was already on his way from Princeton. In the meantime, said the announcer, the audience would be entertained by a program of dance music coming from the Hotel Martinet in Brooklyn.

Grandfather Charney had now joined the group in the living room and everyone's attention was riveted on the radio, for the site of the impact was close by. The musical interlude was soon interrupted and reporter Carl Phillips was heard announcing that he was at the Wilmuth farm in Grovers Mill, New Jersey, having sped there from Princeton, together with a Professor Pierson. It was a strange scene that he tried to describe for the listeners, perhaps like something out of a modern Arabian Nights, he said. The object that had come hurtling out of the night sky in flames now lay partly buried in the earth. Professor Pierson speculated that there must have been a terrific impact because of the size of the hole in the earth and because there were fragments all around a tree that must have been struck as the thing came down. To Pierson it did not seem like a meteor, but more like some kind of great cylinder. Phillips then interviewed Mr. Wilmuth, the owner of the farm, who had seen the impact, and returned to a description of the scene, which was both fantastic and electric. Already a crowd had formed and hundreds of cars had been parked helter-skelter in a nearby field. The police were trying in vain to barricade the road leading to the farm, but people were forcing their way through anyway. The headlights of many of the cars were focused on the pit and the harsh illumination added to the sense of drama and expectation. The police were unable to control the crowd and prevent some bolder members from sallying up to the edge of the pit. The most daring man reached out to touch the thing, but was intercepted and led away by a policeman. Phillips drew the listeners' attention to a strange humming sound that seemed to emanate from the object in the pit. He held his microphone out toward the pit and asked the audience if they could hear it. Professor Pierson, who happened to be going by, was asked about the peculiar noise, but the only explanation he could offer was that it might be produced by the unequal cooling of its surface. At first the professor thought the thing was a meteor, but now he wasn't sure; the casing was metallic, but definitely not found on this earth. He also noted that objects that plunge to earth through the atmosphere usually are damaged by friction, but this thing remained smooth and cylindrical in shape.

Phillips then interrupted the professor's ruminations to inform the listeners in a voice charged with excitement that something extraordinary was happening. First the end of the thing began to flake off and then the top part began to rotate like a screw. Amazingly, the thing seemed to be hollow! In the background, excited voices were heard, some commenting on the action, others trying to restrain the surging crowd. But then there was a loud, distinctive noise, the ringing sound that a huge piece of metal makes when it falls to the ground and strikes a hard surface. The background voices resumed their excited babbling, but it was Phillips now who dominated the sound picture with a note of excitement in his voice that mounted moment by moment. In a terrified voice he described someone—or something—crawling out of the now opened cylinder. In the black hole he saw two luminous disks, which might have been eyes in a face. Then, with a shout from the crowd, he described something "like a gray snake" wriggling out, followed by others. There seemed to be tentacles. When the thing was in the clear it was seen as large as a bear and glistening with a horrible face that Phillips could hardly bear to look at. The eyes were black and reptilian; the V-shaped mouth quivered and dripped saliva. Slow in movement, as if unaccustomed to earth's gravity, the thing nevertheless raised itself up. The crowd shrank back in dismay.

At this dramatic juncture Phillips said he had to take up a new position with his microphone and would return momentarily. Again there was a musical interlude, this time with a piano, interrupted by another announcer declaring that this was an eyewitness account of what was happening at the Wilmuth farm, Grovers Mill, New Jersey. When Phillips returned to the air he had taken up a new position that gave him a more panoramic view of the scene. More state police had arrived and a cordon of about thirty had formed in front of the pit, although there was no longer any need to push the subdued crowd back; after what they had seen, they were keeping their distance. The police captain and Professor Pierson then had a brief conference, and the captain and two policemen formed a truce party and advanced to the pit holding a pole to which was tied a white handkerchief. Even to Phillips this seemed odd and he wondered whether the creatures would understand the meaning. As the truce party moved forward, a hissing sound was heard followed by a humming that increased in intensity. Phillips observed a strange shape rising out of the pit. There was a small beam of light against a mirror, then a jet of flame from that mirror darted right at the advancing men, striking them and setting them instantly afire. There were screams from the crowd. But the fire was not confined to the three men. Suddenly, the whole field was aflame, as well as the woods and the barns. Explosions were heard as the flames reached the gas tanks of the parked automobiles. Phillips shouted that the fire was coming his way. It was only about twenty yards to his right when there was a crash and then dead silence on the radio.

In the Charney farmhouse, Lester's little sister began to cry and Lester swallowed hard. The silence was ended by another announcer who reported that he had just been handed a telephone message from Grovers Mill. At least forty people, including six state troopers, had been killed at the Wilmuth farm, their bodies burned beyond recognition. The announcer then surrendered the airwaves to Brigadier General Montgomery Smith, commander of the State Militia at Trenton, New Jersey. General Smith declared that he had been requested by the governor of New Jersey to place the counties of Mercer and Middlesex as far west as Princeton, and east to Jamesburg, under martial law. No one could enter this sector without a special pass. At the same time a state militia force was on its way to Grovers Mill to aid in the evacuation of homes. Other military operations were planned.

A few minutes later a series of bulletins were read by one of the announcers. The charred body of reporter Carl Phillips had been identified in a Trenton hospital. The National Red Cross had assigned ten units of emergency workers to the headquarters of the state militia in New Jersey. Then the voice of a Captain Lansing of the signal corps, attached to the state militia, was heard. He was at the Wilmuth farm, and in precise, military terms he described what had become a field of battle. Eight battalions of infantry now surrounded the pit on all sides.

They did not have artillery, but their rifles and machine guns were adequate for the task in Lansing's opinion. A slightly superior tone could be heard in Lansing's voice. There was no cause for alarm. He noted that the things (whatever they might be) did not even dare to rise out of the pit. In spite of their resources, they could hardly withstand heavy machine gun fire. "Anyway," he boasted, "it's an interesting outing for the troops." It looked to him "almost like a real war." But as he was describing how a quick thrust by the seven-thousand-man force would end the matter, he interrupted himself. "Wait! There was something on top of the cylinder." At first he thought it was a shadow, but then he made out a kind of shieldlike apparatus rising higher and higher out of the cylinder. Quickly it was higher than the trees. There it remained poised with all the spotlights on it. Captain Lansing, his professional cool now lost, called out, "Hold on!" and then was silent. The radio audience next heard another announcer speaking in the gravest tones. Incredible as it may seem, he said, those strange beings who landed in the Jersey farmlands tonight were part of an invading army from the planet Mars. The battle at Grovers Mill tonight resulted in one of the greatest defeats ever suffered by an army in modern times. Of a force of 7,000 armed men there were only 120 known survivors after an encounter with but a single Martian machine. The vast number of casualties were either trampled under the machine or incinerated by its heat ray. The invader now controlled the middle part of New Jersey and had cut communication from Pennsylvania to the Atlantic Ocean. Railroad tracks had also been severed and there was no service from New York to Philadelphia. The roads in all directions were filled with a fleeing population. Law enforcement and military personnel were struggling in vain to control the panic. It was estimated that the cities of Philadelphia, Camden, and Trenton would swell to twice their normal populations by morning. Martial law was in effect in New Jersey and eastern Pennsylvania. The announcer then gave way to a special broadcast on the national emergency frequency from the secretary of the interior in Washington.

As that official somberly tried to calm the nation, Grandfather Charney went from window to window, staring out into the night. Moving with purpose, he retrieved the old double-barreled shotgun he kept hidden in the kitchen and began to barricade the door to the farmhouse with furniture.

New bulletins now issued with increasing speed. From Langham Field, Virginia, scouting planes reported three Martian machines visible above the treetops, moving north with the population fleeing ahead of them. In Basking Ridge, New Jersey, a second cylinder was discovered and army field pieces were speeding to it to blow it up before it could be opened and the fighting machine rigged. In the Watchung Mountains the Twenty-second Field Artillery zeroed in on the invaders, but a black smoke emitted by the Martians silenced the battery. A similar fate awaited eight bombers from Langham Field that were set afire by a green flash produced by the tripods. From Newark, the voice of an operator was heard warning that a poisonous black smoke, undoubtedly another Martian weapon, was moving in from the Jersey marshes. Gas masks were useless and people were urged to head for open spaces. Routes of escape were recommended.

Cal and Marie Rosenquist, who had been frozen in front of their radio in their Jersey City apartment, realized that the Martians were coming in their direction and knew what they had to do. There was no time for packing, they must leave at once. But since they might never return, they gathered up their important papers, deposited their cat, dog, and canary in the back of their car, and sped north in the belief that they could find refuge in the mountains. Since the car radio was not working, they were unable to follow the progress of the invasion. At a red light they asked the driver in a nearby car for the latest information. When he looked blank they simply raced off.

Now an announcer was heard on the radio declaring that he was speaking from the roof of "Broadcasting Building" in New York City against a background of ringing bells that he said were warning the populace to evacuate the city as the Martians approached. In terse fashion, evocative of desperate hopelessness, he estimated that in the last two hours three million people had already fled to the north. The Hutchinson River Parkway was being kept open for further evacuation. The bridges to Long Island were hopelessly tied up and were to be avoided. All U.S. military defenses—artillery, air force, everything—had been crushed. In the best tradition of heroic journalism, the announcer wondered out loud whether this would be the last broadcast, but assured the listeners that he would stay on to the end. Below him, in the cathedral, people were praying and voices could be heard singing a hymn. The harbor was filled with all kinds of boats loaded with people fleeing and still others struggled away from the docks as boat whistles were heard. It was, the announcer said, like New Year's Eve in the city with the streets jammed with noisy crowds, but this was a time of terror, not joy. From his observation post he could now see five huge Martian machines above the Palisades. The first of the giant devices entered the river and took huge strides toward the city. As he watched its progress a bulletin was given to him reporting that Martian cylinders had fallen all over the country. One machine had now crossed the Hudson and stood there ominously waiting for the others. They were huge, as tall as the skyscrapers. Now they had formed a line on the city's west side. They lifted their metal hands in unison and smoke appeared that rapidly spread over the city. The crowds in the streets saw it and, knowing what it meant, raced toward the East River, those who were engulfed by it falling like flies. The smoke was crossing Sixth Avenue now, then Fifth Avenue, and the announcer began counting its distance to him in decreasing yards until his voice faded away.

At a restaurant on East 116th Street in Manhattan the wedding reception of Rocco and Connie Cassamassina was well underway. A five-piece band dressed in maroon and gray tuxedos was playing such romantic tunes as "I Married an Angel" and "Blue Moon," and the groom, who was employed as a singing waiter at a tavern in Brooklyn, was up on the dais singing with them. A group of latecomers were visibly agitated. One of them took the microphone and said that the city was being invaded from outer space. After some moments of silent confusion and panic the guests ran for their coats and began leaving. Connie dashed up to the dais and pleaded tearfully with the remaining guests not to spoil her wedding day. Then Rocco retrieved the microphone and began singing hymns in the nearly deserted hall.

Samuel Tishman of 100 Riverside Drive in New York City heard the telephone ringing as he entered his apartment around 9:15 P.M. It was his nephew shouting in a voice he had never heard before. Frantic with fear, the nephew told Samuel that the city was about to be bombed from the air and that he must get out of the building at once. Tishman turned on the radio and heard what seemed to corroborate the information his nephew had given him. He quickly grabbed his coat and hat and a few personal belongings and ran to the elevator. When he got to the street he found hundreds of people milling about in a frightened state.

Across the country the experiences of the Charneys, Rosenquists, Cassamassinas, and Tishmans were shared by tens of thousands who were convinced that extraterrestrials had invaded and the end was near. As might be expected, the impact was greatest in the region surrounding the first Martian sighting. In a single block in Newark more than twenty families rushed out of their houses with wet handkerchiefs and towels held over their faces to protect themselves from the aliens' gas. Some of them began moving household furniture, and as a result, traffic was tied up for blocks around. In a Newark hospital fifteen men and women were treated for shock and hysteria, and calls were received from the parents of three child patients declaring that they were taking the children out and leaving the city. The New Jersey Bell Telephone Company reported that every central office in the state was flooded with calls for more than an hour. The broadcast's reference to the mobilization of New Jersey national guardsmen caused the armories in Essex and Sussex counties to be swamped with calls from men inquiring about where and when to report. Hundreds of physicians and nurses called Newark police headquarters to volunteer their services to aid the "injured," and city officials began making emergency arrangements for the population. Two grocery company executives inquired about sending food for the "victims" of the attack. The governor of Pennsylvania offered to send troops to help New Jersey. In Cranford, New Jersey, the fire chief spent a wild night chasing imaginary fires called in by citizens reporting the results of the Martian heat rays. On his travels he saw farmers armed with guns roaming the countryside looking for Martians or the militia. More than one hundred state troopers were sent in to calm the populace and disarm the volunteer defenders.

A throng of playgoers charged out of a theater in New York City when the wives of two of the men in the audience called the theater and insisted that their husbands be paged and notified of the disaster. In

Harlem more than forty people hurried to two police stations saying they had packed all their household goods and were ready to leave if the police would tell them what to do to be evacuated. The regular Sunday evening service in some small churches in this part of the city became "end of the world" prayer meetings. At the West Forty-seventh Street police station a woman walked in dragging two children, carrying extra clothing, and stated that she was prepared to leave the city. People stood on street corners in Manhattan hoping for a glimpse of the "battle." At the Dixie Bus Terminal in Midtown, officials began revising their bus schedules. In Washington Heights a man ran into the police station and, white with terror, shouted that enemy planes were crossing the Hudson River and asked what he should do. The switchboard at the Hotel Montague in Brooklyn Heights lit up around 8:30 P.M. and the elevator bell began ringing. People began coming down into the lobby agitated and shouting, "The Martians are coming" and running into the street. Callers to the Queens police headquarters wanted to know if the gas would reach as far as that borough; many said they were all packed and ready to go. Throughout the metropolitan area telephone lines were tied up as people sought to verify the "invasion" and obtain help and advice.

While the reaction was most intense in New Jersey and New York, the panic was felt across the country. In San Francisco the general impression was that the United States had been invaded from the air by an overwhelming force that was destroying New York and threatening to move west. One caller roared into a telephone, "My God, where can I volunteer my services? We've got to stop this awful thing." Chicago newspaper offices and radio stations were deluged with calls. In residential areas of St. Louis people gathered in the streets to discuss what should be done. The feeling in New Orleans was that New Jersey had been devastated by the "invaders." In Providence, Rhode Island, weeping and hysterical women swamped the switchboard of the *Providence Journal* for information and officials of the electric company received scores of calls urging them to turn off all lights so that the city would be safe from the enemy. Similar reports of disturbed people were received from Minneapolis, St. Paul, Richmond, Kansas City, Atlanta, and Birmingham. A woman ran into a church in Indianapolis screaming, "New York [has been] destroyed; it's the end of the world. You might as well go home to die. I just heard it on the radio." Services were concluded immediately. At Brevard College in North Carolina five students fainted and panic gripped the campus while many students fought for telephones to call their parents to come and get them. A man in Pittsburgh returned home in the midst of the broadcast to find his wife in the bathroom with a bottle of poison in her hand screaming, "I'd rather die this way than like that." A motorist drove through the streets of Baltimore like a latter-day Paul Revere, blowing his horn and warning of the Martian invasion. In Memphis the staff of a newspaper prepared an extra edition on landings in Chicago and St. Louis. People in Salt Lake City packed up to head into the Rocky Mountains. Out in Hollywood John Barrymore released his dogs crying, "Fend for yourselves!" At four in the morning of the following day a Washington, D.C., gas station operator was awakened by the agitated driver of a car bearing a New Jersey license plate. "Give me some gas," the driver demanded, "I'm bound for Florida and in a hurry. All hell has broken loose in New Jersey."

The panic that overwhelmed thousands on October 30, 1938 derived in part from happenstance, but especially from the uncanny verisimilitude with which Orson Welles and the Mercury Theatre on the Air dramatized H. G. Wells's *The War of the Worlds*, an 1898 novel recounting the Martian invasion of England. Welles was then twenty-three, but already a major personality in the American theater and had just appeared on the cover of *Time* magazine. CBS had offered him an hour-long weekly series of broadcasts over which he would have complete artistic control and Welles had accepted. The series, which lacked a sponsor, began on July 11, 1938, with a rendering of Bram Stoker's classic *Dracula* with Welles playing both Jonathan Harker and the vampire. The program was well received as theater and was followed by other successes including *Treasure Island, A Tale of Two Cities, The Thirty-nine Steps, The Affairs of Anatol,* and *The Count of Monte Cristo.* For the fall season the program was rescheduled for the 8–9 P.M. hour and so was in direct competition with the enormously popular "Chase and Sanborn Hour" with Edgar Bergen the ventriloquist and his dummy, Charlie McCarthy. Welles began strongly with an adaptation of *Julius Caesar,* in which a narrator was added, played with great effect by the political commentator H. V. Kaltenborn, whose voice and style were well known. Several weeks into the new season Welles decided to try the field of science fiction and came upon *The War of the Worlds.*

The first script seemed too old-fashioned and distant to Welles, so he changed the time to 1939 and the locale to New Jersey. At the conclusion of the October 23 program, Welles announced that the next offering would be *The War of the Worlds.*

A few days before the airing, Welles listened to Archibald Mac-Leish's *Air Raid* on the Columbia Workshop. Although it was in verse, it opened just before the start of the next war with an announcer on the top of a tenement roof describing the setting as his microphone picked up the sounds of women talking and children playing. Then the sound of raiding aircraft was heard, followed by explosions, running people, confusion, and screams. The added dimension of the news announcer proved realistic, as it had in *Julius Caesar,* and Welles and his associates built it into *The War of the Worlds,* but they modified it in a way that proved to be brilliantly effective.

During the preceding months the world had been listening with growing fear to the crisis in Europe and had become accustomed to news bulletins that interrupted the regular radio programming. Such an interruption had actually occurred during the Mercury Theatre's presentation of *Sherlock Holmes* on September 25, 1938. Still vivid in everyone's memory was the electrifying radio report of the explosion of the airship *Hindenburgh* the previous year. By developing the story of the Martian invasion through sudden bulletins from reporters at the scene, the Mercury group cast their broadcast in a new dramatic form of communication that automatically alarmed its listeners.

As preparations for the Sunday performance went forward, there were those in the group, including Howard Koch, the script writer, who thought the play was unbelievable. In reviewing the script, however, CBS believed it was *too* real. In addition to deleting the names of real institutions, use of which might have been deemed legally actionable, CBS cut the cries of the invading Martians ("Ulia, Ulia, Ulia") as too frightening and the passage "They're starving in heaps . . . bolting . . . trampling on each other" as too inhuman.

Cleverly put together and artfully presented as the show was, it seems unlikely that anyone, Welles included, believed it would have the effect it did. Convincing proof of this can be found in Welles's astonishment at the confused excitement that surrounded him and his associates at CBS after the program.

Still without a sponsor on October 30, the Mercury Theatre on the Air was trailing badly in the race for listeners although it had received considerable critical praise. The weekly survey of ratings by the Hooper Company had estimated that only 3.6 percent of the radio audience listened to the Mercury Theatre while 34.7 percent tuned in to Edgar Bergen and Charlie McCarthy on the "Chase and Sanborn Hour." These simple ratings failed to disclose listeners' common habit of switching from one program to another, a circumstance that would greatly enhance the credulity with which *The War of the Worlds* was received. After listening to the first section of the "Chase and Sanborn Hour" and laughing at the repartee of Bergen and McCarthy, many went dial hopping when a song came on. That was fateful, for those in the radio audience who tuned in to CBS after the beginning of the show did not hear announcer Dan Seymour state "The Columbia Broadcasting System and its affiliated Stations present Orson Welles and 'The Mercury Theatre on the Air' in *The War of the Worlds* by H. G. Wells." The *New York Times* had even featured a photograph of some of the cast of the show with a caption indicating the nature of the play. Forty minutes into the program there was another statement: "You are listening to a CBS presentation of Orson Welles and 'The Mercury Theatre on the Air' in an original dramatization of *The War of the Worlds* by H. G. Wells." But by then it was too late.

Hooper later estimated that about 12 percent of those who had originally tuned in to Edgar Bergen and Charlie McCarthy, or about four million listeners, switched over to *The War of the Worlds*.

Imaginative as the Mercury Theatre program was, there were those in the listening audience who, in their excitement, added vivid details of their own creation to the invasion from outer space. People within sight of the Hudson River claimed that they actually saw the huge Martian towers wading across the water. In Boston a woman declared that she could "see the fire." One person reported that he heard the "swish" of the Martians, another that he heard machine gun fire. A man with binoculars on top of a Manhattan building "saw the flames of battle." In Brooklyn a man called the police station: "We can hear the firing all the way here, and I want a gas mask. I'm a taxpayer." Sylvia Holmes of Newark ran out into the middle of the street saying over and over, "Don't you know New Jersey is destroyed by the Germans—it's on the radio." A rumor circulated that President Roosevelt had been on the radio telling everyone to pack up and go north. An NBC executive who tuned in to the show was appalled at the thought that his network had been scooped by a story so colossal that no one would survive long enough to report it.

The first half of the program ended with New York City invaded by the Martians and enveloped by their deadly gas. The last "announcer" was choking to death on the roof of the "Broadcasting Building," and the final refugees were meeting their doom in New York harbor. In the second half a lone survivor was revealed. The destruction of the Martians by bacteria was recounted and a new world was to be built. Across the country, however, there were thousands in terror and flight who had not stayed to listen to the second half. Nor did they hear the announcer identify the fiction, or the hurriedly prepared closing re- marks of Orson Welles in which he explained that it was all a joke, that the Mercury Theatre group had wanted to perform a Halloween stunt, but "we couldn't soap all your windows and steal all your garden gates by tomorrow night . . . so we did the next best thing. We annihilated the world before your very eyes and utterly destroyed the CBS. You will be relieved, I hope, to learn that we didn't mean it, and that both institutions are still open for business."

The happenstance by which as many as four million listeners failed to hear the opening announcement of the Welles's show because they had been laughing at a puppet on another station was not the only improbability. A careful listener could have picked up signals of the fiction from the alteration of certain names. Much more glaring was the considerable action, encompassing long periods of time, which the play would have the audience believe was compressed into some forty minutes. During that broadcasting time people traveled long distances, police and military forces were assembled, battles were fought, and governmental bodies deliberated. More than that, the story encompassed the departure of the invaders from Mars, so the brief time interval of the broadcast also included the Martians' journey through space to Earth. Of course, it could not all have happened in forty minutes, but that thought did not enter the minds of the panic-stricken. Nor were many astonished when Carl Phillips, the first reporter, who was "killed" by the Martians' rays early in the program, reappeared in the second half. Somewhat less conspicuous but nonetheless still available as clues to the fiction for those with keener perceptions were such made-up names as "Langham Field" and "Macmillan University."

Feedback from the national panic created a different kind of turmoil in the studios at CBS. Before the first part of the program had ended, the main switchboard had lit up and was unable to handle all the incoming calls. In the control room a member of the staff was heard telling a caller, "Of course it isn't real," and then hanging up abruptly to continue with the play. Police began arriving at the studio and stood around peering through a glass at Welles and the other members of the cast. When one officer tried to enter the studio to find out what was going on, he was brusquely pushed out. The mayor of a midwest city called demanding to speak to Welles and shouted, "There are mobs in my streets! Women and children crowding my churches! Violence, looting, rioting! If this is just some crummy joke, then I'm coming to New York to punch you in the nose!"

As the show ended there was a crowd outside the studio composed of policemen, newspaper reporters, and photographers. The phones continued to ring incessantly. Welles and most of the cast slipped out by a back door to continue an all-night rehearsal of a Broadway play.

The following day the event was front-page news. "Not since the Spanish 'fleet' sailed to bombard the New England coast in 1898," declared the *New York Herald Tribune*, "has so much hysteria, panic and sudden conversion to religion been reported to the press of the United States as when radio listeners heard about an invasion from Mars." (The reference was to a period in the Spanish-American War when uncertainty about the whereabouts of the Spanish admiral created such fear on the Atlantic seaboard that the government finally found it necessary to rig old—and useless—Civil War monitors and anchor them along the coast with naval reservists aboard.)

At a press conference at CBS, Welles gave four reasons why the audience should have recognized the fiction: (1) the action was clearly set in the future, in 1939; (2) the broadcast took place at the regular weekly Mercury Theatre time period and most of the earlier shows had been fictitious; (3) at the beginning and twice during the broadcast listeners were told that it was a play; and (4) the "Man from Mars" had become such a familiar fable that the audience should have understood that the program was not true.

Scriptwriter Howard Koch experienced the sensation of the broadcast in an unusual way. Exhausted, he had gone home to sleep early, unaware of the play's effect. The next morning he went out to get a haircut. "There was an air of excitement among the passersby. Catching ominous snatches of conversation with words like 'invasion' and 'panic,' I jumped to the conclusion that Hitler had invaded some new territory and that the war we all dreaded had finally broken out." When Koch asked his barber what had happened, he was shown a newspaper with a headline that read, "Nation in Panic from Martian Broadcast."

CBS issued an apology to the public and promised not to "use the technique of a simulated news broadcast within a dramatization when the circumstances of the broadcast could cause immediate alarm to numbers of listeners." The Federal Communications Commission, which had received twelve protests, studied the matter for a while but took no action, although its chairman characterized the program as "regrettable."

A wave of litigation broke over the network involving claims for personal injuries allegedly caused by the broadcast. Typical was a $50,000 suit by Sara E. Collins, a stage actress who attributed severe nervous shock to the program. John Houseman, Welles's co-producer in the Mercury Theatre, recalled that none of the claims was substantiated, but that a request for a pair of black shoes, size 9B, from a man in Massachusetts who had been saving for them, but used the money to escape the Martian invasion, was honored in spite of the lawyers' protests.

Indignation was a main element of the public response. The *New York Times* warned, sternly, that "Radio ought to act promptly to prevent a repetition of the wave of panic in which it inundated the nation." Iowa Senator Clyde Herring called for legislation to curb such "Hallowe'en bogeymen."

But some pondered the deeper significance of the event. *The Nation* discussed the main causes of the panic: "the psychological carryover from the European crisis which had the listening audience in a constant state of excitement; the compulsive force of the human voice issuing from the upper air; the mass attitude toward the wonder workings of science, which has become as credulous as that of the Dark Ages towards religious miracles," but went on to identify the more immediate causes as stemming from a deeper source, "the sea of insecurity and actual ignorance over which a superficial literacy and sophistication are spread like a thin crust."

Dr. Alice V. Keliher, chairman of the Commission on Human Relations of the Progressive Education Association, admitted that "American education has a few embarrassing questions to answer."

In *The Christian Century* James McBride Dibbs decided that "Either we shall have to be protected from radio by censorship of programs or by the licensing of receiving sets to a select group or we shall have to grow up."

Heywood Broun wrote that although he did not hear the broadcast, he was still terrified, but for a different reason: "We have much more reason to fear censors than octopi from the distant skies." He also doubted that "anything of the sort would have happened four or five months ago. The course of world history has affected national psychology. Jitters have come to roost. We have just gone through a laboratory demonstration of the fact that the peace of Munich hangs heavy over our heads, like a thundercloud."

Perhaps the most pungent piece of analysis was that of Dorothy Thompson in her influential column, "On the Record," in the *New York Herald Tribune*. Calling it "the story of the century," and "one of the most fascinating demonstrations of all time," she offered a macabre list of what the Mercury Theatre group had accomplished:

> They have demonstrated more potently than any argument, demonstrated beyond question of a doubt, the appalling dangers and enormous effectiveness of popular and theatrical demagoguery.
>
> They have cast a brilliant and cruel light upon the failure of popular education.
>
> They have shown up the incredible stupidity, lack of nerve and ignorance of thousands.
>
> They have proved how easy it is to start a mass delusion.
>
> They have uncovered the primeval fears lying under the thinnest surface of the so-called civilized man.
>
> They have shown that man, when the victim of his own gullibility, turns to the government to protect him against his own errors of judgment.

Far from blaming Welles, Thompson would have given him a congressional medal and a national prize. She saw in the program a contribution toward the understanding of such contemporary terrorisms as Hitlerism, Stalinism, and anti-Semitism. Hitler managed to terrify all of Europe, but he had an army and air force; Welles demoralized a nation with a single microphone.

Four morals were drawn by Thompson: no political body must ever control radio; popular education had failed to train even the educated in reason and logic; popularization of science had led to gullibility and new superstitions rather than a truly scientific attitude; and the power of mass suggestion was the most powerful force in the world.

The aftershocks of the broadcast were still being felt throughout the nation's sensibility when Hadley Cantril, a Princeton University psychologist, undertook a study of reactions to the incident and an explanation of the mass panic. The results of that study, published in 1940 as *The Invasion from Mars, A Study in the Psychology of Panic*, are a curious blend of expeditious field work, speculation, and reflected astonishment at individual reactions to the event. Now, a half century later, at a time when our exposure to television has made the average person more skeptical, if hardly more cultured, than his predecessor in 1938, many of the case discussions in the Cantril study seem bizarre and his methods of analysis quaint and old-fashioned.

But Cantril correctly saw in the event a unique opportunity to study a panic with modern tools. He rejected as superficial and misleading the statement of one prominent social scientist that "as good an explanation as any for the panic is that all the intelligent people were listening to Charlie McCarthy," and sought both deeper psychological meanings in the panic and lessons for the individual that might enable him to deal more capably with such incidents in the future.

Beginning one week after the broadcast, Cantril and his staff gathered information mainly from interviews with 135 persons, most of whom had been upset by the program, and all of whom were located in the New Jersey area, a sampling which might be criticized as too small and too localized, especially in view of Cantril's own statement that "Probably never before have so many people in all walks of life and in all parts of the country become so suddenly and so intensely disturbed as they did on this night."

Sifting through this data, Cantril attempted to assess how panic behavior was affected by the individual's critical ability and personality and by the listening situation and the cultural context in which the broadcast occurred. "Critical ability" proved to be somewhat elusive, comprising elements of innate intelligence and education, but modified also by such personality traits as insecurity, lack of self-confidence, fatalism and religiosity, and the situation in which the listener found himself. By the latter Cantril referred to the manner in which an individual learned of the event. His conclusion—not startling—was that critical ability could protect one against panic but it could be "over-powered either by an individual's own susceptible personality or by emotions generated in him by an unusual listening situation."

Finally, Cantril attempted to evaluate the cultural setting of the broadcast. Here he reflected on such unsettled conditions as the long economic depression, the complexities of modern life that seemed to many people beyond their understanding, the war scare in Europe, and the "thrill of disaster." Such cultural dislocations, he concluded, "probably account in large measure for the emotional insecurity we have found so important and for the lack of critical ability discovered especially in the lower education and income brackets of the population."

Conscious, perhaps, of the deficiencies in his analyses and the shakiness of his conclusions, Cantril deprecatingly added a nicely ironic flourish by quoting H. G. Wells's observation that "the forceps of our minds are clumsy forceps and crush the truth a little in taking hold of it."

If the Cantril study can be faulted as self-evident, it is also entertaining for its individual case histories, adding further color to a dramatic event, almost like an epilogue. Important, too, is Cantril's appreciation of the significance of radio in the panic:

> By its very nature radio is the medium par excellence for informing all segments of a population of current happenings, for arousing in them a common sense of fear or joy and for enciting them to similar reactions directed toward a single objective. It is estimated that of the 32,000,000 families in the United Sates 27,500,000 have radios—a greater proportion than have telephones, automobiles, plumbing, electricity, newspapers, or magazines. Radio has inherently the characteristics of contemporaneousness, availability, personal appeal, and ubiquity. Hence, when we analyze this panic, we are able to deal with the most modern type of social group—the radio audience—which differs from the congregate group of the motion picture theatre and the consociate group reading the daily paper. The radio audience consists essentially of thousands of small, congregate groups united in time and experiencing a common stimulus—altogether making possible the largest grouping of people ever known.

It may not have fit neatly into his discipline, but a further consideration of radio as a method of sounding the alarm would have been appropriate. A thousand years ago on the coast of England, the sudden appearance of a breathless sentry running toward the village shouting about Norsemen was sufficient to spur everyone to action and result in the rapid evacuation of the village. But the village over the hill would remain ignorant of the approaching threat. In 1938, however, with radios in more than 85 percent of houses in the United States, the

alarm could be raised everywhere almost at once. It was no longer
necessary to dash back to the village or send a mounted messenger, for
the news was broadcast everywhere instantly. Even radio's companion
modern device, the telephone, did not have the potential for sounding
the alarm so quickly since that method of communication is essentially
person to person. This is not to suggest that the power and meaning of
radio were unrecognized at the time. Such phenomena as Franklin D.
Roosevelt's Fireside Chats and the perverse propaganda strategies of
Joseph Goebbels and the Nazis had given ample evidence of that. What
made *The War of the Worlds* broadcast different, however, was that
it demonstrated, if not for the first time certainly in the most startling fashion, how radio could galvanize the populace into immediate
action.

Another lesson of the broadcast, only hinted at at the time, was the
awesome power of radio to manipulate its audience. There had already
been some criticism of radio's inclination to distort, especially in
advertising messages. Now, however, the medium's true potential in
this regard was revealed. If it was one thing to steer a few consumers
to a certain toothpaste through subtly misleading commercials, it was
quite another to send thousands screaming in terror into the night to
seek refuge in the mountains. This aspect of the broadcast may have
been obscured by the many stories of irrational reactions, but now it is
clear that the program was a watershed event in the history of
electronic communications, foreshadowing the more pervasive influence television would later wield in shaping public attitudes and
events.

Twenty-six years after its first publication, in a preface to a new
edition of the book, Cantril told how he had often been asked whether
such a thing could happen again. "The questioners usually imply that
we are now somehow too sophisticated to be taken in by anything so
fanciful. Unfortunately, I have always had to reply that of course it
could happen again today and even on a much more extensive scale."
Now, many years later, we might be inclined to boast of even greater
sophistication and doubt that it could happen in our time. But before we
commit ourselves to that answer, we might do well to consider some of
the history of *The War of the Worlds* subsequent to the 1938 broadcast.

On November 12, 1944, a radio station in Santiago, Chile, broadcast the play with local details. Although it was claimed that advance notice had been given, many people were terrified. In some quarters of the city residents ran through the streets to escape while others at home were reported to have suffered nervous upsets and heart seizures, and an even greater panic occurred in the city of Valparaiso. The governor of one province dispatched a telegram to the minister of war declaring that the provincial troops had been placed on alert and he had mobilized the artillery to oppose the Martian invaders. The use of an actor impersonating the minister of interior and references to such institutions as the Red Cross helped convince listeners of the truth of the account and gave rise to numerous complaints later. In January of the previous year the government, mindful no doubt of wartime conditions, had issued an order severely prohibiting sensational radio broadcasts that could cause public alarm, but the fines imposed were generally felt to be inadequate to compensate for the harm suffered by many in their homes as a result of the scare.

The Chilean episode, however, paled by comparison with what happened in Ecuador five years later. In February 1949 the radio station in Quito broadcast a version of the Martian invasion in which local place names and other details were again substituted for the original English setting. In bulletinlike fashion, the invaders were reported to be approaching Quito in the shape of a cloud after destroying the town of Latacunga, miles to the south. The air base at Mariscal Sucre had been captured and there were many dead and wounded. An actor identifying himself as the minister of interior was heard appealing to the people to be calm "in order to be able to organize the defense and evacuation of the city." Then the "mayor" arrived and declared, "People of Quito, let us defend our city. Our women and children must go out into the surrounding heights to leave the men free for action and combat." The voice of a priest begging for mercy in the catastrophe was heard. The city's church bells sounded and the announcer, who said he was reporting from the tallest building in Quito, said he could see a monster approaching from the north engulfed in fire and smoke.

At this point hysteria had driven most of the city's population out of their homes. Men dressed only in pajamas and nightshirts and women

in nightgowns and slippers raced up and down Quito's hilly streets in
confusion. Many believed the country was being attacked by Peru
while others said it was a Russian invasion.

The show's producers, who may have lacked authority to broadcast the play, belatedly became aware of the panic they had caused and
frantically appealed to the people to be calm, assuring them that it was
all a fiction. But when they finally succeeded in convincing them, the
situation became a crisis of another kind. What had been terror only
moments before now became wrath. Infuriated by the deception, a
mob of Quitenos formed in front of the three-story building of the
newspaper, *El Comercio,* which also housed the offending radio station, and began breaking its windows with stones. Groups in the mob
then set the building on fire at various places, and, as if that was not
enough, they removed the fire hydrants and blocked the firefighters
from extinguishing the fire. About one hundred people were in the
building when the mob attacked and some managed to escape through a
rear exit. Many were forced to the third floor where some leaped from
the windows as the flames approached. Others formed a human chain
from balconies and windows, but the chain broke and some people fell
to the ground. Of the four policemen initially on the scene, one was
beaten by the crowd and the others, helpless, could only call for
reinforcements. Police assistance was slow in coming, ironically because police units had been sent out of the city to investigate the scene
of the "invasion" reported on the radio.

Eventually, army troops were called out and tanks and tear gas
were used to clear a way for fire apparatus to reach the burning building
and restore order. When it was over, six people had been killed and
fifteen others injured. Of the *Comercio* building only the front was left
standing.

In the investigation that followed, Alfredo Vergara Morales, one of
the actors who used the name "Eduardo Alcaraz" on stage, was
arrested on criminal charges and jailed. He placed the blame rather
squarely on the shoulders of the station's artistic director, Leonardo
Paez, who may have gone too far in pursuit of verisimilitude. Paez had
planted stories in the local newspapers about flying saucers in the area

before the show aired, purposely did not announce that the program was fictional, and was pleased by the sensation it produced. It was Paez, too, who had ordered the doors locked so that the actors would not be disturbed during the performance, a circumstance that Alcaraz believed contributed to the riot. The police were searching for Paez but it was believed that he had fled the country.

Not all of the rebroadcasts of *The War* produced similar results. A 1968 broadcast in New York City was uneventful and in San Antonio the caution of the show's producers who had alerted police in advance appeared unnecessary as the three hundred calls to the station elicited by the program were from listeners who wanted to obtain a record of the broadcast. On the fiftieth anniversary of the Welles's broadcast fifty stations across the United States presented an updated version of the original without creating any reported panic.

But as recently as 1974 a program on station WPRO in Providence, Rhode Island, based on the original *War* but with some details changed, seriously frightened listeners. Broadcast at 11 P.M. on Halloween, the play began with "a meteorite falling in Jamestown, Rhode Island," and developed the Martian invasion from there. Providence, it will be recalled, was a city where the 1938 broadcast created a major disturbance, but there seemed to be no memory of that. After receiving complaints from the public, the Federal Communications Commission admonished the station for failing adequately to inform listeners that the program was not real.

Across the Atlantic, the Martians were permitted to invade Portugal in 1988 courtesy of Radio Braga, producing panic among residents of the northern part of that country. There, as in Ecuador in 1949, the reaction evolved from terror into anger, and a crowd of two hundred people stormed the radio station in protest after learning that the program was a play.

The facts that we have placed men on the moon, established satellites in space, and photographed distant planets at relatively close range may not have insulated us from such fantasies. If anything, technological progress, coupled with futuristic films and television plays, may have made us even more vulnerable than the victims of

Grovers Mill. In the words of Ken Howard, director of Northwestern University's clinical psychology program: "It could easily happen again. If something like that came on the air today, it would seem even more believable. I think we still have a mindset to be afraid of some unknown enemy and we've been socialized by a whole variety of movies and television shows to be open to the notion of extraterrestrial life— probably more than ever before."

No doubt the passage of more than fifty years has created in us that condescension with which we tend to view the human reactions of bygone time. It's easy for us to feel that those who were frightened by Orson Welles were vulnerable to such a deception because they were more innocent, less aware, perhaps less educated, and altogether less in control of their world and less capable than we are. In itself that is a misleading notion, and it might be useful to cast one final look around the landscape of *The War of the Worlds* to see how well the story holds up.

The original book by H. G. Wells, as Isaac Asimov has pointed out, has a considerable political dimension. Published in 1898 at a time when the British empire was at its zenith, it postulated a fine irony. For centuries Europeans had been the invaders, "discovering" and then subjugating other parts of the world. The fictional appearance of the Martians turned that state of affairs upside down: Now the historical invader experienced the sudden appearance of the aliens, the terrible weapons and strange ways, and ultimately its own destruction.

That meaning should not have been lost when Howard Koch substituted Grovers Mill, New Jersey, for Woking, England, for the United States had given ample evidence over the years of its predilection for colonialism by its actions in Central and South America, the Philippines, and elsewhere. This country, like the England of 1898, had a national experience of expansion—of *invading others*—and was completely unprepared for the singular experience of *being invaded.* Now, half a century after Orson Welles's play and nearly a century after H. G. Wells's imaginative fiction, the American international experience continues to be more nearly like a nineteenth-century colonial power than not. And we are, then, no better prepared for an invasion than were Victorian England and the America of 1938. Even Montezuma and the Aztecs, in spite of a long series of victories and locally unmatched power, were better prepared for the appearance of the bearded white men from the sea than the British were, or we are, for the extraterrestrial invader.

The unlikelihood of life on Mars has been determined only as recently as 1976 by sensing devices landed on that planet's surface. But even that may be irrelevant, for the search for life in the galaxy is now accelerating, and many people believe that contact with another intelligent life force is inevitable. We may be speaking here simply of communication, something considerably less than the sight of the tentacled monster rising out of the pit in Grovers Mill, but the event is difficult to imagine nonetheless.

Arthur Clarke, in *Childhood's End,* tells of the appearance on earth of space ships with otherworldly beings who, although they promptly take control of earthly affairs, remain both silent and hidden from human view for years. This is partly because they are devil-like in appearance, but also because they understand the trauma humans would suffer in the first contact with beings from another world. No doubt such a vast traumatic wave will sweep over the world when the Search for Extraterrestrial Intelligence (SETI) project one day in the future makes contact with beings elsewhere in our galaxy. It remains to be seen whether we, or our descendants, will behave with appreciably more poise than those who listened to the Mercury Theatre on the Air that night in 1938.

By placing the first contact with extraterrestrials here on earth and giving it a hostile character, H. G. Wells's clever fantasy contained an intensely dramatic potential, which was stunningly realized by Orson Welles and his associates. The Wells-Welles assumption that the first contact between humans and extraterrestrials would take place on earth—so plausible on Halloween 1938—seems less likely now. It would appear more likely that it will occur elsewhere in the universe, especially since science has ben armed with powerful new devices enabling it to probe space, and that it will be benign, or at least not confrontational. Such an event may lack the elements of terror and panic that characterized the Mercury Theatre broadcast, but will be sensational nevertheless.

*   *   *

In fact, the event *was* a sensation when it occurred in the summer of 1835, and if it proved to be a journalistic hoax, the public's reaction to it is well worth considering nevertheless.

It began with a small notice in the New York *Sun* on Friday, August 21, 1835, under the headline "CELESTIAL DISCOVERY."

"The Edinburgh Courant says—'We have just learnt from an eminent publisher in this city that Sir John Herschel, at the Cape of Good Hope, has made some astronomical discoveries by means of an immense telescope of an entirely new principle.' " Nothing further appeared for four days. It was the subtlest baiting of the hook by a man who was to demonstrate considerable gifts of imagination and showmanship. That man was Richard Adams Locke, a young Englishman employed as a reporter for the *Sun,* who had arrived in New York in 1832. Educated at Cambridge, and claiming descent from John Locke, the famous philosopher, Richard Locke was interested in astronomy and was mindful of the public's appetite for news in the field. At the time there were reputable scientists who believed that there was life on the moon. Some of them claimed they had discovered roads, fortifications, and other artificial works upon the moon's surface. Only weeks before in the summer of 1835, *The Unparalleled Adventures of One Hans Pfall* by Edgar Allen Poe had appeared in the *Southern Literary Messenger.* That story contained the detailed account of how a citizen of Rotterdam traveled to the moon by balloon. It is the voyage rather than the lunar discoveries that make up most of that tale, although the narrator teasingly promises at the end to relate some of the wondrous things he learned of the denizens of the moon during his five-year sojourn there. The possibility of extraordinary lunar discoveries, then, was alive in the public consciousness, ready to be exploited by some opportunistic journalism.

The substance of the moon discoveries began to appear in the *Sun* on Tuesday, August 25. After the brief, but intriguing notice of August 21, the readers were led into what seemed like a technical explanation of telescopes and how Sir John Herschel, a famous British astronomer of the day, had made a great breakthrough in the field, devising an instrument of such enormous power that the most minute observation of the moon's surface was now possible. In itself, this was inspired on Locke's part, for Sir John Herschel was widely known to the public, as was his father, the astronomer William Herschel, who had discovered the planet Uranus. More recently, Sir John had been in the news as a result of his activities in Cape Town, South Africa, where he was to establish an important new observatory. (Sir John, it should be noted, knew nothing of the ensuing hoax until months later, but he found it quite amusing.)

The August 25 account, captioned "GREAT ASTRONOMICAL DISCOVERIES LATELY MADE BY SIR JOHN HERSCHEL, L.L.D., F.R.S.&C. AT THE CAPE OF GOOD HOPE," contained a byline indicating that it had been first published in a supplement to the *Edinburgh Journal of Science.* By presenting the news under the auspices of an established and respected scientific journal, Locke again showed his cleverness, but also made an error which surprisingly went unnoticed. The correct name of the journal said to have published the supplement was *The Edinburgh Philosophical Journal.*

The new telescope, according to the first account, utilized a lens weighing 14,826 pounds and could magnify objects forty-two thousand times. The problem that an object grows fainter as it is magnified was said to have been solved by Herschel by focusing the image from the telescope on a polished glass plate and illuminating it with the intense light from lime heated by a hydrogen-oxygen flame. The illuminated image was then magnified by a powerful microscope and the greatly enhanced image was projected upon a wall in the fashion of a camera obscura. With this arrangement Herschel was able to survey the lunar surface in the closest fashion. The remarkable apparatus had been manufactured in England and shipped to Cape Town.

The first *Sun* account opened with a grand rhetorical flourish trumpeting "recent discoveries in astronomy which will build an imperishable monument to the age in which we live, and confer upon the present generation of the human race a proud distinction through all future time." Before embarking on the technology of the new telescope, however, it left no doubt as to the nature of the discoveries by claiming that Herschel "has affirmatively settled the question whether this satellite be inhabited, and by what order of beings."

With the second installment began one of the great travelogues of all time. The first viewings revealed a fairy-tale landscape, greenish-brown basaltic rock columns and a shelf of the same material profusely covered with dark red flowers, the first evidence of lunar organic life. Excitement was high in the observatory at the Cape for this meant that the moon had an atmosphere capable of supporting terrestrial life, and there was no reason to doubt that animal forms would eventually be discovered. The surveillance continued showing more of the features of Earth's satellite: a forest of trees similar to "the largest class of yews in the English church-yards," a level green plain and a forest of firs, and then an inland lake or sea, blue, with huge waves, featuring white sand beaches bounded by "wild, castellated rocks, apparently of green marble." Elsewhere the delighted astronomers saw groups of obelisks apparently made of amethyst, other astonishing geological features, and then, on a wooded hillside, "herds of brown quadrupeds, having all the external characteristics of the bison . . . but more diminutive." The animal had "one wildly distinctive feature, which we afterwards found common to nearly every lunar quadruped we have discovered; namely, a remarkable fleshy appendage over the eyes, crossing the whole breadth of the forehead and united to the ears. We could most distinctly perceive this hairy veil, which was shaped like the upper front outline of the cap known to the ladies as Mary Queen of Scots' cap, lifted and lowered by means of the ears." Herschel speculated that the veil was a natural design intended to protect the eyes of the animal from the great extremes of light and darkness to which they were periodically sub-jected.

The next animal was even more remarkable. Blue-gray in color, about the size of a goat with the head and beard of that animal, it had a single horn like the legendary unicorn. The strange beasts were grace-ful and sociable and Herschel and his associates took pleasure in watching them playing in woody glades. When viewers in the Cape Town observatory sought to touch the image of the animal's beard, it would bound off as if it was aware of the threatened contact, suggesting that it might possess some kind of extrasensory faculty. Further on, a large, branching river was found with birds like the pelican and the crane. While they seemed to be feeding, Herschel was unable to observe any lunar fish, but there was a glimpse of "a strange amphibious creature of a spherical form, which rolled with great velocity across the pebbly beach, and was lost sight of in the strong current."

On later nights they saw volcanoes erupting as well as dormant volcanoes all so numerous that it was conjectured that they were connected in subterranean fashion. Other animals came into view: quadrupeds similar to the bisonlike creatures seen before, but larger; dazzling flocks of white and red birds; a small kind of reindeer; a kind of elk; a kind of moose; a horned bear; and the biped beaver. The last was truly remarkable, resembling the earthly beaver in most respects, but lacking a tail and walking on two feet. "It carries its young in its arms like a human being, and moves with an easy gliding motion. Its huts are constructed better and higher than those of many tribes of human savages, and from the appearance of smoke in nearly all of them, there is no doubt of its being acquainted with the use of fire."

Pressing on, the searchers found a huge island which featured hills "pinnacled with tall quartz crystals, of so rich a yellow and orange hue that we at first supposed them to be pointed flames of fire"; a lunar palm tree with distinctive large, crimson flowers, a tree bearing melons; herds of miniature zebra; several kinds of blue and golden long-tailed birds like pheasants; multitudes of univalve and other shell-fish along the shores. In another region observers were again staggered by the grandeur of the scenery and speculated that the long lines of yellow metal seen hanging from crevices were pure gold. Here, too, were unusual fauna: a quadruped with an amazingly long neck, a head like a sheep with two long, spiral horns, disproportionately long front legs, and a very bushy white tail that curled high over its rump and hung two or three feet by its side; as well as sheep identical to those in England in very large herds. It was here, however, that the greatest of marvels was to be seen: "flocks of large winged creatures, wholly unlike any kind of birds" descended in a slow, even motion from the cliffs and lit on the plain. A more powerful lens was employed and the observers could make out three parties of these creatures walking erect, in a dignified manner, their wings now disappeared. The most powerful lens was then substituted and the beings came into sharp focus:

> They averaged four feet in height, were covered, except on the face, with short and glossy copper-colored hair, and had wings composed of a thin membrane, without hair, lying snugly upon their backs, from the top of the shoulders to the calves of the legs. The face, which was of a yellowish flesh color, was a light improvement upon that of the large orang outang, being more open and intelligent in its expression, and having a much greater expansion of forehead. The mouth, however, was very prominent, though somewhat relieved by a thick beard upon the lower jaw, and by lips far more human than those of any species of the simia genus. In general symmetry of body and limbs they were infinitely superior to the orang outang; so much so, that, but for their long wings . . . they would look as well on a parade ground as some of the old cockney militia! The hair on the head was a darker color than that of the body, closely curled, but apparently not woolly, and arranged in two curious semi-circles over the temples of the forehead. Their feet could only be seen as they were alternately lifted in walking; but from what we could see of them in so transient a view, they appeared thin, and very protuberant at the heel.

The creatures seemed to be engaged in conversation with impassioned gestures of hands and arms. Herschel concluded that they were rational beings capable of producing works of art and contrivance. Later they were seen lying on the ground with their remarkable wings fully extended and disporting themselves in the water. In tantalizing fashion, the account also noted certain "habits of these creatures, who were of both sexes which led to results so very remarkable that they should be laid before the public by Sir John himself in view of the incredulousness with which they would be received." The scientists named them "Vespertilio-homo" or bat-man, and concluded that "they are doubtless innocent and happy creatures, notwithstanding some of their amusements would but ill comport with our terrestrial notions of decorum." With these veiled remarks Locke added the allure of sex to a story already overflowing in reader appeal.

The astronomers were sometimes impeded in their survey of the moon by fog and clouds, all products of a remarkable earthlike, humid atmosphere. On a clear night, however, while scanning yet another lunar area, they first observed a mountain ridge 340 miles long consisting of a single crystal and then came upon an obvious work of art in a valley, a kind of beautiful temple made of sapphire or other blue stone with square, tapering columns and a yellow metal roof. Although no devotees could be seen around this temple or several other temples that were later found, it was not long before Herschel discovered groups of beings similar to the bat-men seen earlier. These were larger than Vespertilio-homo, lighter in color, and in every respect superior. They were busy eating fruit and seemed very happy and even polite, sharing choice pieces with each other. In scenes evocative of paradise, these happy, angellike creatures engaged in such innocent activities as eating, flying, bathing, and lolling about, while other animals wandered among them without fear. The peacefulness of these creatures and the apparent absence of any carnivorous or ferocious species inspired Herschel with the greatest joy. Later the astronomer was to find other groups of these angelic beings that were immeasurably more beautiful and produced numerous works of art of incredible quality.

Except for some discussion of how the new telescope was used to investigate the rings of Saturn, this brought to an end the six installments of the report. It covered but a brief period of days, but caused a sensation in New York where the city became wild with excitement and little else was talked about. By the afternoon of August 21 no copy of the *Sun* could be bought at any price. The paper's readership increased day by day thereafter with the presses unable to print enough copies to satisfy the demand. When the fourth installment appeared on August 28, the brash, little, relatively new *Sun* had become the world's largest newspaper, with a circulation of 19,360 as compared with the 17,000 of the great London *Times,* which had been founded at the end of the eighteenth century.

Although the story, pumped up with Locke's vivid imagination, seemed like something out of Scheherazade, it was widely accepted by the public. Poe, who was drawn in to the matter, among other reasons, by his recent *Hans Pfall* story, said, "Not one person in ten discredited it, and (strangest point of all!) the doubters were chiefly those who doubted without being able to say why—the ignorant—those uninformed in astronomy—people who *would not* believe, because the thing was so novel, so entirely out of the usual way. A grave professor of mathematics in a Virginia college told me seriously that he had no doubt of the truth of the whole affair."

During the excitement, crowds in the thousands formed daily at the offices of the *Sun* seeking more information, or perhaps hoping, by gathering at the place where the sensational news was being disseminated, to experience the discoveries more intensely and for a longer period of time. One observer said that "the almost universal impression and expression of the multitude was that of confident wonder and insatiable credence." Public opinion seems to have fed upon itself in order to credit the news. In the crowd besieging the offices of the *Sun* one morning, a highly respectable elderly gentleman in a fine broadcloth Quaker suit completely persuaded the few doubters around him by asserting, in the calmest, coolest, and most unquestionable manner, that he was fortunately engaged in business at the East India Docks in London when Herschel's vast, seven-ton lens and the whole gigantic apparatus of the telescope was loaded on board ship for transportation to the Cape of Good Hope and that he, himself, had seen it lifted by crane. The estimable gentleman, as a final guaranty of trustworthiness, added that the story's reference to a loading at St. Catherine's Docks was an error on the part of the Edinburgh writer. In the crowd listening to this testimonial was Richard Adams Locke himself, who was flabbergasted at what he heard but remained silent. On another occasion a respectable person in the crowd was heard to affirm that he had in his possession a copy of the *Edinburgh Journal* "Supplement" from which the *Sun* was taking its daily stories and that the paper's reporting was faithfully done and without any additions or alterations.

With rare exceptions, the press was taken in. The *New York Times* declared that the writer of the supplement "displays the most extensive and accurate knowledge of astronomy, and the description of Sir John's recently improved instruments, the principle on which the inestimable improvements were founded, the account of the wonderful discoveries in the moon, &c., are all probable and plausible and have an air of intense verisimilitude."

"No article," said the *Daily Advertiser*, "has appeared for years, that will command so general a perusal and publication. Sir John has added a stock of knowledge to the present age that would immortalize his name and place it high on the page of science."

The *Mercantile Advertiser* ran the story with a veiled attribution to "a cotemporary [sic] journal of this city" with the note that "It appears to carry intrinsic evidence of being an authentic document."

Under the headline "STUPENDOUS DISCOVERY IN ASTRONOMY," the editors of the *Albany Daily Advertiser* gushed that "We have read with unspeakable emotions of pleasure and astonishment, an article from the last *Edinburgh Scientific Journal,* containing an account of the recent discoveries of Sir John Herschel at the Cape of Good Hope."

A similar ecstasy was forthcoming from *The New Yorker:* "GREAT ASTRONOMICAL DISCOVERIES!—By the late arrivals from England there has been received in this country a supplement to the *Edinburgh Journal of Science* containing intelligence of the most astounding interest from Prof. Herschel's observatory at the Cape of Good Hope. . . . The promulgation of these discoveries creates a new era in astronomy and science generally."

The *U.S. Gazette* affirmed that the account had been published before—that is, in the *Edinburgh Journal of Science.*

On September 1, 1835, the *Sun* published these and other extracts, calling them "but a handful of the innumerable certificates of credence and complimentary testimonials issued by the country's press."

The sluggishness of editors around the country was not the least remarkable circumstance of the affair, in view of the intense competition that marked journalism of the day. (So bitter was the rivalry that editors of competing papers were sometimes known to assault each other when they met on the street.)

Locke had the articles reprinted into a pamphlet and sold sixty thousand copies in a month. The *Sun* also reprinted the story in pamphlet form and sent copies to London, Edinburgh, and Paris. From those cities the news spread through Germany, Italy, Switzerland, Spain, and Portugal. English and French journals were full of the subject, but there was no attribution to an American source. Some Paris papers reported elaborate and energetic debate in the prestigious French Academy of Sciences on the authenticity and credibility of the Cape of Good Hope discoveries.

In spite of the eventual disclosure that the matter was a hoax, pockets of belief continued to exist for many years in out-of-the-way areas in Europe where people insisted that the discoveries were true. New editions of the *Moon Hoax* pamphlet appeared for more than twenty years.

William N. Griggs, writing of the event in 1852, described it as a balloon, "and no serial vehicle ever performed a more illustrious or extensive voyage, for it maintained its wondrous flight until it had accomplished the entire circle of the globe, and had filled every civilized nation, in succession, with enthusiastic astonishment and delight."

The New York *Herald* correctly guessed that the story was a fiction and even the identity of its author, but it fell to another New York paper, the *Journal of Commerce,* to blow the whistle, and it did so in a somewhat ignominious manner. The *Journal* had decided to reprint the *Sun* story about the moon discoveries, but before it started, it had a lucky break. Locke happened to have a friend among that paper's reporters whom he warned not to go ahead confiding that he had written the story himself. The *Journal* did an abrupt about-face, denouncing the story as a hoax and revealing Locke as the real author.

There is some question about the true purpose behind the moon story. While the *Sun* undoubtedly aimed at a commercial reward, which it richly received, Locke seems to have had something more in mind than an elaborate practical joke, for he claimed to have intended the work to be a satire. One source quotes him as saying, "If the story be either received as a verifiable account, or rejected as a hoax, it is quite evident that it is an abortive satire; and, in either case, I am the best self-hoaxed man in the whole community." Some intrinsic evidence is available to support this interpretation. Once the reader penetrates the technical discussion of the new telescope, he finds himself voyaging in a fabulous land, which sometimes seems to be paradise, studded with precious stones and occupied by humanoid beavers, telepathic unicorns, speedy spherical frogs, and libidinous bat-men. The profusion and exotic character of the invention alone suggest that its creator strove for something other than mere plausibility and sought to make fun of something or someone.

Poe apparently agreed, noting that while the story was "made the subject of (quizzical) discussions in astronomical societies," it also "drew down upon it the grave denunciation of Dick (whose school was the real object of it, as a satire)." Thomas Dick was a Scots astronomer who proposed constructing huge geometric forms in the wasteland of Siberia in order to communicate with the moon. He also believed that calamities like earthquakes and hurricanes were produced by humanity's sins. Whatever Locke intended, however, Poe, as a professional spinner of similar tales, could not resist expressing his admiration for what was "the greatest hit, in the way of sensation—of merely popular sensation—ever made by any similar fiction, either in America or Europe."

At the same time, Poe felt constrained to point out why the story should not have been believed in the first place. The notion that the power of a telescope could be enhanced by adding bright light from an artificial source to the faint image it produces he dismissed as "rigma role," not even bothering to point out, as others did, that the artificial light would simply wash out the image, not brighten it. The lunar topography described, he argued, was at variance with accepted facts, as was the atmosphere and bodies of water claimed to have been found on the satellite. The discoveries were also to be faulted for failing to show the lunar animals "walking, with heels up and head down, in the manner of flies on a ceiling. . . . The *real* observer," according to Poe, "would have uttered an instant ejaculation of surprise . . . at the singularity of their position; the *fictitious* observer has not even mentioned the subject, but speaks of seeing the entire bodies of such creatures, when it is demonstrable that he could have seen only the diameter of their heads!"

Separated by more than one hundred years, the Moon Hoax and *The War of the Worlds* are similar enough to warrant comparison. Both gave evidence of an appalling public credibility, a tendency hardly diminished by the progress in science and technology that occurred after 1835 and the spread of learning through education. The comments of *The Nation* and Dorothy Thompson in the fall of 1938 pointing out the public's gullibility, the apparent failure of education to train people to think reasonably and with logic, and the tendency to worship science blindly in a manner reminiscent of the religious faith in miracles exhibited in the Dark Ages could all have been applied to the country's reaction to the astounding astronomical discoveries of 1835. No social scientist or professional ancestor of Hadley Cantril studied the Moon Hoax, but if such an analysis had been made, its conclusions might not have been very different from Cantril's.

The Moon Hoax comes down to us surrounded by a layer of good-natured feeling. It did not occur at a time when world war was on the horizon, and there was no Federal Communications Commission to look into its more serious implications. The most distinguishing element between the hoax and *The War of the Worlds,* however, seems to be the aesthetic distance between the public and the events described. The Martian invasion took place on our soil and affected us immediately; there could be no leisurely reflection about the incomprehensible war machines from Mars wading the Hudson River and attacking the populace of New York City with poison gas. Two hundred and forty thousand miles away, however, the strangest beings presented no threat at all. It will be pointed out that Locke's lunar world was peaceful, but even if its denizens exhibited the most ferocious conduct, the avid readers of the *Sun* would not have experienced the terror felt by radio listeners in 1938, but rather would have viewed the experience like visitors to some wonderful zoo.

Just as the listeners in 1938 were fooled by artful packaging that adopted the special news bulletin technique with which the public had become familiar, so too did the Moon Hoax use clever packaging, if of a somewhat different form. The brief advance notice, the attribution to the respected Edinburgh journal, the use of Sir John Herschel, and the long technical discussion about the new telescope all shaped the story in a credible way. And if it seems to us now, at an even greater remove in time, that the 1835 world should have shown some skepticism about the magical scenes and creatures that paraded across Sir John's viewing screen, what shall we say about the gullibility of those in 1938 who failed to notice that correspondents made long trips, armies were mobilized, airplanes were dispatched, battles were fought on land and air, New Jersey was traversed, and other implausible events were completed all in a period of minutes?

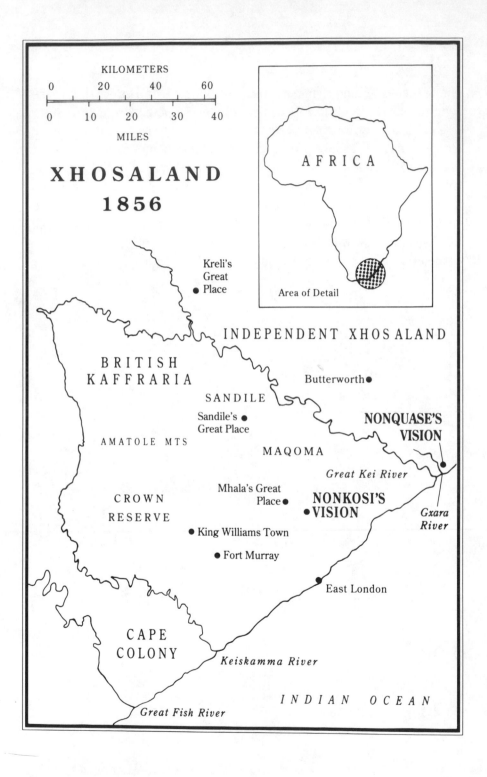

KILOMETERS

0   20   40   60

0   10   20   30   40

MILES

XHOSALAND
1856

AFRICA

Area of Detail

Kreli's
Great
Place

INDEPENDENT XHOSALAND

BRITISH
KAFFRARIA

Butterworth

SANDILE

Sandile's
Great Place

NONQUASE'S
VISION

AMATOLE MTS

MAQOMA

Great Kei River

CROWN
RESERVE

Mhala's Great
Place

NONKOSI'S
VISION

Gxara
River

King Williams Town

Fort Murray

East London

CAPE
COLONY

Keiskamma River

INDIAN OCEAN

Great Fish River

THE DESTRUCTION
OF THE XHOSAS

There is a thing which
speaks in my country . . .
—Kreli, king of the Xhosas, 1856

News of the defeat of the English by Russian forces in the Crimean War in 1854 reached some of the native people of South Africa in a strangely refracted way. It was encouraging to learn that the hated English were not invincible, but the reports were especially significant because it was believed that the Russians, like the Africans, were black. In the larger eastern Cape region it was frequently remarked that "the Russians are black people like ourselves, and they are coming to assist us to drive the English into the sea." While such remarks could only be whispered in that part of the region under British domination, beyond the frontier they were openly proclaimed by members of the Galekas, one of the Xhosa tribes under Kreli, the paramount Xhosa chief or king.

The Xhosas had good reason to hate the English. Members of the larger Nguni group of native people, the Xhosas may have numbered about 140,000 in 1848 and were largely engaged in herding and hunting. Even before the British took possession of the Cape from the Dutch, initially in 1795, there had been friction between the whites and the Xhosas. Skirmishing had begun in 1778 as Dutch settlers, searching for better land to the east, came into contact with tribes moving westward under the pressure of an increasing population. At first the whites formed a commando to deal with the Xhosas, but that eventually proved ineffective and the colonial government was required to provide military forces. In 1781 the whites succeeded in driving the Xhosas over the Fish River. The British policy at first sought to prevent interaction between the whites and the Xhosas, and a neutral zone was created toward that end. This neutral zone, in which occupation by both white settlers and natives was prohibited, was created by annexing Xhosa land and expelling the tribespeople from it. Over the years the zone was moved farther and farther east until in 1835 the government had taken land as far east as the Kei River and proposed to remove all Xhosas who lived west of that boundary. In that year a new, more enlightened policy was adopted. The latest annexation was canceled and treaties were entered into with chiefs between the Kei and Keiskamma rivers. But that policy also failed to establish order, and alternating raids by the Xhosas and retaliatory expeditions by the whites followed. A third policy phase was then commenced in which annexation of native land resumed, but the white government attempted to exert rule over the tribes through their own chiefs. The strategy of a neutral, unoccupied frontier zone was accompanied by a policy of relatively dense settlement on the British side. This may have contributed to border problems in that it presented to the Xhosas raiding prospects that they could not resist.

Over a hundred-year period to the middle of the nineteenth century there were in this region between six and nine wars, the exact number depending on the precise point at which raid and retaliation became formal war. The Xhosas had vastly superior numbers, but because they consisted of a number of small independent chiefdoms, were poorly armed, and fought on foot, they were no match for the well-armed, mounted, and organized whites. Although they fought desperately to retain their land and freedom, they were regularly defeated.

The latest of these conflicts, as well as the longest and most damaging to the Xhosas, extended from 1850 to 1853 and ended in yet another British victory. Known as Mlanjeni's War, it was named for a young Xhosa witch doctor and prophet who had rapidly become a national figure by purifying the natives of evil witchcraft and instilling in them a fighting spirit based on supernatural matters. Mlanjeni was only eighteen when the war began, a member of the Ndlambe tribe of the Xhosas, whose chief was Mhala and which occupied an area west of the Kei River. The Ndlambes were one of a number of Xhosa tribes that were under British control living in an area that had been designated as

British Kaffraria and made subject to the rule of the Cape Colony government after the previous war, which ended in 1847. Mlanjeni's call, which extended into independent Xhosaland to the east and beyond and to Xhosas working in the Cape Colony to the west, prophesied a British defeat in which the guns of the British would shoot hot water and tribesmen who carried a certain root or rubbed it on their bodies would be invulnerable. Among the preparations required was the selective killing of cattle. In addition to a few animals that were to be sacrificed to Mlanjeni, dun and yellow cattle were to be slaughtered, perhaps because they suggested the color of the English, or perhaps because they were considered unnatural.

When it became immediately apparent that the Xhosas were not immune to bullets on the battlefield, Kreli, the Xhosa king, sued for peace, an appeal which then Governor Sir Harry Smith ignored, leading to three years of ugly and destructive warfare. By the time the fighting ended in 1853, some 16,000 Xhosas were dead, together with some 1,400 on the colonial side; Sir George Cathcart had replaced Smith as governor of the Cape Colony; and Xhosa territories that had been captured by the British were reallocated to the detriment of the tribes living there. Specifically, the area of the Amathole Mountains where some of the most difficult fighting had occurred was established as a Crown reserve and forbidden to any Xhosas. Mlanjeni, the architect of the war, died of tuberculosis six months after its end, and Sir George Cathcart soon left for the Crimean War, to be replaced as governor by Sir George Grey.

The governors of the Cape Colony had done little to endear themselves to the Xhosas. Imperious Smith had forced the proud Xhosa chiefs to choose publicly between the "staff of peace" and the "staff of war" which he held, and had, among other indignities, compelled some of them to kiss his boot. Cathcart, a similar dandy, pursued many of Smith's brutal strategies, but at least agreed to permit the chiefs to continue to administer tribal affairs. It fell to the brilliant, enigmatic Grey to deliver the most crushing blows to the Xhosas.

Grey arrived at the Cape in December 1854 and wasted little time in establishing new policies. He reversed Cathcart's decision to continue the powers of the Xhosa chiefs in tribal affairs and sought actively to break their power. Identifying the legal fees and fines that the chiefs traditionally collected in their judicial capacity as the source of their power, he ended that arrangement, replacing it with a system in which the chiefs received salaries from the colony and thereby became its employees.

For the Xhosas, who had known only defeat at the hands of the British, and to some of whom it must have seemed that the white men could never be vanquished, the information about their losses to a mysterious people known as the Russians in a distant land across the sea must have been wonderfully encouraging. Together with the general good tidings came the specific piece of information—itself no doubt greatly satisfying to the Xhosas—that Sir George Cathcart had charged in the wrong direction in one of the battles in the Crimean War, surrounded himself by Russians, and was killed on the spot.

Such was the state of affairs for the Xhosa people when, on an evening in April 1856, a young girl of the Galeka tribe went to a pool in the Gxara River to bathe. This was no ordinary girl, for Nongquase was the niece of the witch doctor and prophet Mhlakaza, the most renowned seer of the Xhosas, and a prophesying medium herself. She returned to the village on the run calling out excitedly for her uncle. At their garden near the river she had seen ten black strangers who wanted to talk to her, but she became frightened and ran home. After hearing her account, Mhlakaza went to the garden and remained there until it was dark. The village sensed that something important had happened and a crowd gathered the next morning in front of Mhlakaza's kraal. The prophet confirmed what his niece had told him. There were strange men at the pool who were black like the tribespeople, and there were very beautiful cattle, too. Mhlakaza had been amazed to see among them his own brother who had died a few years ago. The strange men identified themselves as messengers from the abode of the ancestors in the bowels of the earth below the river. They had risen, together with the cattle, in order to help their descendants, the living Xhosas, in a wonderful way. If their commands were obeyed, the tribal ancestors would all arise in the flesh in pools and kraals throughout the country. Chiefs, warriors, prophets of old, and all departed loved ones would be restored to a youthful life. Aged members of the tribe would experience renewed youth. Furthermore, the pastures would be filled with countless beautiful cattle, corn pits would overflow, and lost fertile lands would be recovered. As if all of these blessings were not enough, there would be even more: A great wind would arise and the English oppressors would be driven into the sea.

But there was a condition, and it was an awful one: In order to bring about the resurrection and blessings the people must put aside all witchcraft, they must kill all their cattle and destroy all their grain, and they must abandon all work in the fields.

There was consternation among the villagers. One excited woman asked how they could do such things without starving to death. Mhlaka-za endeavored to quell these doubts. He agreed with the strangers and accepted the condition. If the people obeyed, they would be rescued; if not, they would be forever doomed and remain under the control of the white people.

The enormity of the condition cannot be understood without considering the special relationship that existed between the Xhosas and their cattle. The animals were loved, as one commentator observed, in the way the Arabian loved his horses. When, toward the end of the eighteenth century, the San, a hostile tribe, killed the favorite ox of the Xhosa chief, the chief ordered the extermination of the whole San tribe. The Xhosas loved the animals individually and loved to herd them, training the herd to answer whistle signals. The horns of oxen were bent into shapes regarded as beautiful. Cattle were displayed at dances and made the subject of poems. In some areas oxen were trained for riding, packing, or racing. A man would even identify himself with a favorite ox.

Cattle were also at the heart of Xhosa rituals. They were the appropriate sacrificial animal in ceremonies relating to puberty, marriage, sickness, and death, and were exchanged for nubile women. The gate to the cattle byre was one of two shrines in the village. Milk would only be drunk in the homes of fellow clansmen.

There were other circumstances that might have tended to make the prophecy questionable in the minds of the villagers. Some forty years earlier, Makanda, another powerful prophet, had predicted a similar resurrection of the ancestors if the people gave him their cattle, and more recently, there was the failure of Mlanjeni's prophecy, which involved a limited slaughter of cattle. The memories of those events were still vivid in the minds of many. Even though Makanda had been imprisoned by the British on Robben Island thirty-seven years earlier and had actually drowned in an escape attempt, his return was still expected.

Mhlakaza was now the most renowned Xhosa prophet and had great influence, but not all of the tribe's members were persuaded. Nobanzi, the blind wife of Kwaza, one of the councilors of Kreli, the Xhosa king, openly confronted the prophet. Accusing him of talking nonsense, she predicted starvation and death. It took great courage to challenge Mhlakaza in this fashion, for he was a powerful personality with high standing in the society. Nobanzi was a convert to Christianity, but her religion and good sense may not have been the only reasons for her attitude. A previous sufferer of cataracts, she had come under the care of Mhlakaza, who plastered her eyes with cow dung. When the plasters were removed, the witch doctor found a beetle and a spider and declared that the blindness was caused by two of Nobanzi's friends who had bewitched her. As the blindness progressed, however, Nobanzi lost all faith in the healer.

In the commotion that followed her challenge, Nobanzi was reviled as a witch, weapons were drawn, and the blind woman was struck on the head and knocked down. But Mhlakaza sprang to her defense and saved her life, saying that she was harmless and, as an Unbeliever, would never experience the blessings of the day of liberation. Later that day, as she recuperated in her hut, she heard the bellowing of cattle as her son and husband set about killing the animals that had sustained the family.

During the following weeks Nongquase visited the enchanted pool often at the urging of Mhlakaza. Sometimes she stood waist deep in the water while talking to the strange messengers. They had come from the Place of Refuge, they said, and brought orders from a great chief, known only to the oldest living tribesmen, and from the tribe's ancestors. Everything in the country was to be made new.

The important news from Mhlakaza's kraal spread swiftly throughout the land occupied by the Galekas and beyond. Frequent visits were made to the magic pool by chiefs of other tribes under the guidance of the prophet and Nongquase. Together they peered into the water, and some, seeing moving shadows and the reflections of the leaves of wild banana plants growing along the bank, imagined that they were witnessing the first movements of the rising of their ancestors and cattle. When a heavy rain caused the river to overflow, the bodies of drowned oxen floating in the water were pointed to as the vanguard of cattle that would soon rise. Later, Mhlakaza brought back from the seashore a European-style black cap trimmed with gold braid and boasted to the villagers that it was evidence that their ancestors were destroying the white men over the seas.

Not all of the visitors to the Gxara were convinced, however, and while the prophecy was spreading, its ultimate course remained tentative until about June 10, 1856, when King Kreli himself came down from his Great Place at Hohita to investigate. Kreli was now forty-seven, immensely wealthy and powerful and, at the same time, beloved by his people for his accessibility, courtesy, and fairness. But Kreli may also have been undergoing an emotional crisis at the time caused by his inability to produce a son who would survive him and the circumstances surrounding the death of a close advisor. What Kreli saw in the company of Mhlakaza and Nongquase is not known, but the experience turned him into the prophecy's most powerful proponent. The king thereupon ordered the Xhosa nation to obey Mhlakaza's directions, and, as a gesture, commenced a renewed cattle killing by slaughtering his favorite ox, an animal celebrated throughout the country.

Fabulous stories were now circulating. It was said that Kreli had seen a famous horse once owned by Mhlakaza, long since dead, now restored to life. The dead child of the prophet himself had been brought back from the grave. A heavy ear of the finest corn had been examined and identified as a sample of that which the earth would produce after the resurrection. Some people even claimed to have seen the risen heroes appear out of the Indian Ocean on foot and on horseback, march before them, and then sink beneath the waves.

The power of the prophecy, growing in intensity and extending, was such that even other tribes, outside the Xhosa group, came to believe in it. A deputation from the Fingoes was sent to Mhlakaza concerning their role, but the prophet told them there was no message for them and, like the white men, they too would be swept away on the great day.

But while the ranks of the Believers swelled, there were many, like Nobanzi, who did not believe, including a number of influential leaders, although among the Unbelievers more than a few slaughtered their livestock and burned their food supplies as a matter of simple obedience to tribal command. Notable in this group were Kreli's chief councilor, Gxabagxaba, and Buru, Kreli's uncle, who was second only to Kreli in the tribe. Both opposed the prophecy, but complied nevertheless. Buru and his favorite wife were later found starved to death in his kraal. Gxabagxaba became unbalanced mentally as a result of starvation, and although he was treated at a mission station, he, too, died.

Even among the pilgrims to the Gxara there were those who came away unpersuaded. Notable in this group were Nxito, the elderly chief who ruled over the immediate area in which Nongquase lived, and chief Ngubo, Kreli's first cousin, who visited the prophetess specifically to confront her. When the girl refused to see Ngubo because he had not killed his cattle or destroyed his corn, warning him that he would die if he saw her, he beat her and called her an impostor.

With opinion divided, it became necessary to mount a campaign if the prophecy was to succeed. For this purpose Mhlakaza set out on foot one day to consult with Kreli at his Great House near the Quora River. As he moved through the countryside, he made a striking picture. A powerfully built man, he was fully dressed in the attire of a priest-diviner. His headdress consisted of the skins of monkeys and baboons; from it hung a distended ox bladder which signified that he was an important person in whose honor cattle had been killed. The tails of wild cats and jackals were laid across his shoulders. He carried bags of skins and plaited grass that contained medicines and such bewitching items as wild bird feathers, dried blood, snake skins, dead lizards and insects, and powdered colors, roots, herbs, and tree bark. Around his neck were horns used to suck blood from sick people and withdraw bewitching matter as well as the canine teeth of carnivorous animals. His face was painted with red clay and around his body he wore a wrap of leopard skins, a mark of distinction.

Striking as the figure of Mhlakaza might appear to the modern reader, it would have been even more startling to his contemporary, Nathaniel James Merriman, archdeacon of Grahamstown, for Merriman would have recognized him as his former servant, Wilhelm Goliath. By a strange series of events, Mhlakaza/Goliath spent several years in the colony where he became fluent in Dutch, was baptized as a member of the Methodist Church in Grahamstown, and was married in a Christian ritual to a Mfengu woman. In 1849 he became the personal servant of Merriman, then newly arrived and charged with supervising the Anglican church throughout the eastern portion of the Cape Colony. Merriman's method was somewhat peculiar in that he would walk from settlement to settlement, often covering great distances. In these travels he was accompanied by Goliath, and during an eighteen-month period they tramped many miles together sharing adventures and discussing religion. Out of these experiences, perhaps, arose Goliath's desire to become a member of the Anglican church and a "gospel man." Acceding to Goliath's wish, in 1850 Merriman confirmed him as the first Xhosa to become an Anglican. It is no small irony that the man who was later to become one of the central figures of the Cattle Killing was avid during this time to preach Christianity to the Xhosas and was, himself, intolerant of Xhosa religious practices.

But Merriman's duties eventually confined him to Grahamstown and the happy days on the road came to an end. Goliath, who may not have been a completely satisfactory servant, no matter how enthusiastic his religious feelings were, was dismissed. In time he went to live in Kreli's country near the Gxara River.

Arriving at Kreli's Great Place, now, Mhlakaza reported that cattle were being slaughtered and grain destroyed by many but that others were hesitant and awaited word from Kreli. Wholly committed to the prophecy, Kreli had already killed more than two hundred cattle in the royal kraals, but he was disturbed because Sandile, the chief of the Gaika tribe, had refused to join in the killing, and Mhala, the Ndlambe chief, was proceeding too slowly. It seemed clear that the ultimate fate of the prophecy depended on Sandile, but he reported that he was in a difficult position. While he professed a desire to join the Cattle Killing, he was under the jurisdiction of the British, who opposed the sacrifice, and in his brother, Maqoma, he saw a claimant for his throne who would use the killing to further that end. Kreli sent messengers to Sandile, reminding him that all the Xhosas derived from a common lineage and that while the British recognized a split between their ancestors the resulting change in tribal allegiance was contrary to Xhosa law, which clearly established Kreli as the paramount chief. Accordingly, Kreli demanded compliance with the Cattle Killing.

By the time Kreli's message had been delivered, Sandile's situation had become even worse. His aged mother threatened to disown him, saying: "It is all very well for you, Sandile; you have your wives and children, but I am solitary; I am longing to see my husband, and you are keeping him from rising and me from being restored to all the freshness and the vigor of a blooming maiden." Maqoma had visited the Gxara with Mhlakaza and had seen his father's spirit struggling to rise and return home and had relayed this to their mother.

In the case of Mhala, chief of the Ndlambes, resistance to the prophecy took a different form. Mhala himself was a devoted believer in Mhlakaza and had killed all but one of his cattle, but he had been unable to persuade the members of his tribe to do so in the face of strong opposition to the prophecy by the British. Although renowned for his personal bravery, he had suffered several military defeats, which had eroded his leadership. Resistance to the prophecy seemed to be connected to territorial pride: members of the tribe believed— perhaps incorrectly—that the rising of the ancestors was to take place at the Gxara River, and they wondered why their ancestors could not rise in their own country. Can't we meet our loved ones here? Mhlakaza and Nongquase were not well known here and they had no right to interfere in the sacred affairs of their tribe, which had its own prophet, Kulwana.

Through either contrivance or fortuitous development this problem was resolved in January 1857 when Nonkosi, Kulwana's eleven-year-old daughter, entered the picture. Like Nongquase, she was a medium, and, at a large pool in the Mbonco River she began to experience startling visits from otherworldly beings much like those experienced by Nongquase.

First, a man suddenly appeared waist deep in the pool and said he was Mlanjeni, the famous prophet. He had come from the abode of the ancestors in the bowels of the earth beneath the deep water of the pool to raise the dead and directed Nonkosi to tell the people about his visit. On the next day the little girl heard cattle bellowing and saw their horns sticking out between the reeds and rushes. The sharp horns were very long and bent and six cows were seen rising out of the water. Mlanjeni appeared and milked two of the cows on the riverbank for Nonkosi. The cows were the most beautiful she had ever seen and their milk the sweetest she had ever tasted.

Other important developments followed. Once Nonkosi saw the heads of five men in the pool struggling and shouting, "We are rising! We are rising!" Mlanjeni named them as deceased chiefs. Another day fire shot out of the pool and set Nonkosi's little reed shelter aflame, terrifying her. Mlanjeni explained that the ancestral chiefs were about to rise and shelters should not be built around the pool as the fire accompanying their rise would destroy them.

Then came the day that Nonkosi told her father how she had accompanied Mlanjeni to the wonderful place where the spirits of the tribe's dead people lived. Without knowing she had moved she suddenly found herself in a beautiful land where she saw hundreds of kraals filled with cattle, sheep, goats, and pigs. The huts were round and smoothly plastered. Mlanjeni explained that he could not give her anything to eat as the food there would kill anyone who came from the living world above the pool until such time as all cattle and grain had been destroyed. In departing the wonderful land she was carried up a long hole by Mlanjeni and, when they reached the top, she found the water of the pool spread over it. Mlanjeni explained that the water was held up there by a sort of cloth. As he left her, Mlanjeni directed the girl to tell all the people to join with Mhala in slaying cattle and destroying grain; they must obey the commands of the ancestral spirits. When she reached the bank of the pool Nonkosi found that her legs were wet.

Her father expressed great surprise at this and declared that the news must be spread among the people. Soon, Kwitshi, Nonkoshi's uncle and one of Mhala's councilors, approached her and informed her that the rise of the chiefs and the cattle was imminent and urged her to attend at the pool every day.

It was not long after that Nonkosi heard the loud bellowing of oxen across the pool. She looked at the reeds that lined the bank and saw them move as the long, curved horns of oxen appeared. Nonkosi had never seen better horns. Rich corn covered the rocks and floated on the water. Mlanjeni's head broke the surface, followed by others, and they shouted, "We are rising! We are the people who died!" Mlanjeni announced the names of each of the others, famous chiefs who had long since died. Before he disappeared, Mlanjeni told Nonkosi that Makanda was not among the chiefs because he was still alive and might yet return home. This was an important detail, for Makanda, as has been noted, had been captured by the British and imprisoned on Robben Island. Although he had actually died while trying to escape, many believed he was still alive.

These revelations from the Mbonco pool, reported by Nonkosi to Kulwana, immediately spread throughout the tribe creating a sensation and greatly accelerating the slaughtering of cattle in its final stages. But months earlier the prophecy had already produced great changes in the people and the land. Throughout the country, preparations were being made that involved more than the slaughter of cattle, and slaughter itself proceeded at the rate of hundreds a day. Houses were strengthened and cattle kraals enlarged for the great day. The tools of cultivation were discarded as were personal ornaments; farming came to a halt. Xhosas laboring on public works in the colony left the job believing that the sounds of their picks and shovels might prevent the coming of the new cattle. Corn that had been stored for future use was dug up and destroyed, and the meat of the slaughtered cattle putrefied across the landscape because the Believers were ordered not to eat it. Some Xhosas, initially believing that the prophecy permitted the disposal of the animals by sale as well as slaughter, drove their cattle to the markets at King William's Town and East London, where they sold them at severely reduced prices because of the glut. "The movement seems particularly to have been one of the common people," wrote Charles Brownlee, the commissioner assigned to the Gaika tribe, for many of the chiefs opposed it, although Kreli's official endorsement must have had considerable effect.

A displaced sense of reality seemed to prevail, astonishingly untempered by a string of fateful days on which the prophecy failed to occur. Brownlee recorded how "The people are led by a strange infatuation. In the midst of their ruin they are happy and contented and in the confidence of the fulfillment of their expectations they now no longer make a secret of what was at first so carefully concealed." His superior, Commissioner J. Maclean, during a depressing ride through part of the territory, everywhere "found the people cheerful, although the neglected fields spoke plainly of the woeful and calamitous hereafter—starvation and death—I spoke to several, but they merely smiled."

In October the prophets were heard from, directing the people to adorn themselves anew in celebration of the great day. Anticipation quickened and old women who had given up decorating themselves years ago now appeared made up, ornamented, and waiting for the restoration of their youth. But by that time so many cattle had been slaughtered and so much corn destroyed by Kreli's people that hunger had become a condition of life. The first death by starvation had occurred in late September.

During the months in which the movement grew and preparations were made, the exact day for the great event remained unspecified. In its earliest form, as expressed by Mhlakaza and Nongquase, the prophecy may have contemplated an event to occur only when all the conditions had been fulfilled. By its very nature, however, there must have been an increasing clamor for a specific date. Some believed that the resurrection was to take place as early as the first full moon of June

1856. When that date passed uneventfully there was considerable disappointment, the first of what was to become a series of increasingly bitter disappointments.

At Kreli's Great Place a meeting was convened at which Mhlakaza was severly criticized, and under great pressure, the prophet named the full moon to occur in mid-August as the "moon of wonders and dangers." It would be an awesome spectacle, he predicted. Two suns would rise red over a certain mountain, and then collide. In the darkness that followed there would be a great storm that would level all but the houses of the Believers. The righteous dead and the new cattle would then appear at the mouths of the local rivers, and the English and their allies would retreat into the sea which would rise up in two walls and engulf them.

Many of the Believers waited expectantly on the night before the magical day unwilling to sleep. There was dancing and revelry and frequent inspections of the new cattle enclosures. But when the "moon of wonders and dangers" failed to bring forth the prophecy's promise, anticipation and joy turned into disillusion and anguish. Kreli issued orders to suspend the Cattle Killing and sent urgent messages to Mhlakaza.

If the delusion had ended at this point, it would not have been the tragedy it became, for the slaughter was not yet wholesale and large numbers of animals remained. It was a curiosity of the phenomenon that this disappointment actually fueled the prophecy and led to its much greater impact in the months to come.

Mhlakaza and Nongquase had an explanation for what came to be known as the First Disappointment of August 16, 1856. The prophecy failed to materialize, they said, because some of the people had sold their cattle rather than slaughtering them. The distinction seemed plausible because the bellow of the dying animal was believed to signify its spirit, which should have been preserved according to the prophets. In any event, Kreli accepted the explanation at once, took steps to prevent the further sale of cattle, and in September visited the Gxara for the second time, receiving from Mhlakaza proofs of the prophecy sufficient to renew the king's enthusiasm.

As the movement grew and subsided and grew again, surviving a series of failures, marked always by a deep and increasingly bitter rift between Believers and Unbelievers, certain acts and decisions by Governor Grey may have had the effect—unintentional, no doubt— of encouraging belief in the prophecy. Early in September Grey arrived at the frontier, where he spent the better part of a month instituting a new system of administration for the Xhosas. Henceforth, each chief would be assigned a magistrate appointed by the colony who would establish a local police force and maintain law and order. The effect was to transfer control from the chief to the magistrate, who was a government employee, and it caused deep resentment among the Xhosas, inclining them further to look for help in some supernatural fashion.

Later in the same month Grey sent Kreli a threatening letter warning him of the consequences of the Cattle Killing and demanding that he stop it:

"I shall consider you as the guilty party and will punish you as such. You have seen that I have been a good friend to you and to your people, and I desire to continue so—but if you force me to take a contrary course you shall find me a better enemy than I have been a friend, for your conduct has been most unprovoked."

Kreli replied that he was astonished the governor should send him such a letter before consulting with him, but that "there is a thing which speaks in my country, and orders me and my people to kill all our cattle, eat all our corn, and throw away all our witchcraft wood, and not to plant, and to report it to all the chiefs in the country—in reporting this to the other chiefs to kill their cattle. I was ordered to do so by the thing which speaks in my country."

By late October Grey decided on a water-borne show of force. Without giving adequate thought to its implications, he arranged for H. M. S. *Geyser* to enter the Kei River. The appearance of the ship in the Xhosa heartland was immediately interpreted by the local tribes as an act of war although it was ordered only to make a survey. Because the captain had been drunk and failed to pick up a pilot, the ship entered the river by the wrong channel. Proceeding a short distance, it sent out a boat, which capsized. Of the five men in it, one refused to return to the *Geyser,* walking all the way home to East London up the coast. The event was seen by the Xhosas as a great victory and proof of the validity of the prophecy. As the story passed along it took on different shapes: Kreli's dead father was said to have destroyed the ship with a wave of his hand; Mhlakaza had driven the crew mad; the new people had sunk the ship, leaving one survivor to report the event. As a result some Unbelievers were converted and the killing of cattle increased.

The command to cease cultivation was an important branch of the prophecy, which tends to be slighted by the conventional reference to the phenomenon as the Cattle Killing. In the prophetic view, renewal required not only the disposal of livestock and food supplies but complete abstinence from producing new food supplies by farming. The normal agricultural timetable called for sowing during a period beginning with the rains in late August, but not later than mid December. In the division between Believers and Unbelievers there were a certain number of Xhosas who hedged their bets, perhaps by cultivating while slaughtering their cattle or by slaughtering only some of their animals. Believers who sought to convert others saw a special opportunity in the farming cycle. If cultivation could be prevented until December, there would be no harvest and Unbelievers would be further pressured to subscribe to the prophecy. Women played an important role here for they performed most of the cultivation, and many refused to proceed even though their husbands demanded it. Tiyo Soga, the Xhosa missionary, wrote that "The women, the cultivators of the soil in Africa, were the warmest supporters of the prophet, as they rejoiced in the anticipation of getting crops without labour."

In September, after Grey had established his new system of magistrates and police, Sandile, who was long undecided about participating in the prophecy and had previously denounced the Cattle Killing, declared that he would no longer cultivate. That was a significant decision, for not only was the chief the nominal owner of all the land and thus controlled the farming cycle, Sandile was the senior chief in British Kaffraria and a bellwether for Believers and Unbelievers.

By December there was awful hunger. Many people had reduced themselves to a state of destitution months before, surviving only by going to those who continued to kill their cattle and sharing the meat. Old people and children were seen to faint from hunger. People wore special "hunger belts" which they tightened around their middle to ease the pangs and women and children searched for roots and mimosa bark to eat. The accumulated effects of the prophecy were terribly visible in others ways. Carcasses dotted the landscape and the land stank with carrion. Even the vultures were unequal to the task. At one station hundreds of tribespeople passed daily on the way to sell the horns and skins of their slaughtered cattle. Usually talkative, they were now silent. When missionaries pointed out their folly, their eyes flashed and they gnashed their teeth in anger.

December 11 was widely expected to be the new date for the rising. When that day, too, came and passed, the prophecy faltered once again, but Kreli, perhaps fortified by positive messages from the Gxara, persevered with his policy. New explanations for the failure were given: The new people had been insulted and refused to appear, or the ancestors of the Unbelievers had interceded. It was said that the ancestors were unhappy with those who had failed to kill their cattle; the great day was still ahead; wonderful things, auguries of the event, were being seen at Mhlakaza's kraal. The prophet told everyone that before the fabulous occurrence the sun would rise in the west and then unite with the moon. The earth would be shrouded in darkness and the heavens would rain powder. The houses of the Unbelievers would be destroyed by fire.

The nation had become divided between Believers and Unbelievers in an increasingly disturbing fashion. Driven by their belief in the promised paradise and encouraged by the prophets to think that the prophecy's repeated failures were due to the nonparticipation of their fellow tribespeople, the Believers ("Amathamba") turned their frustration and anger on the Unbelievers ("Amagogotya").

For the latter, too, it must have seemed to be a matter of life and death, but for more ordinary reasons. Their vision of the future contained no rising of new people, abundant new food supplies, and the end of the English; rather, they foresaw famine, hardship, and death. But in prudently preserving their cattle and cultivating their land they aroused the enmity of their neighbors. This schism in faith led to armed encounters between the two groups and cut across the most stable tribal and family ties. Families were often split on the issue with fathers and sons or husbands and wives in fierce opposition. As the struggle between Believers and Unbelievers went on, the lives and property of the Unbelievers were increasingly threatened. After an attack in which some were killed, Brownlee permitted many to move onto a reserve and come under government protection. Sandile's councilors, Soga and Tyala, were obliged to flee for their lives and take refuge at a mission.

The tension between Believers and Unbelievers and the ready explanations for the prophecy's repeated failures both reflect its curious dynamic. As a prediction of future events, it seems to have been artfully contrived to attract adherents, or at least to escape criticism. Since the central idea was that the people could bring on the millennium by their pure and complete obedience to the prophet's instructions, it was easy to say that nonoccurrence was due to a failure to comply, thereby placing responsibility on those who doubted. This was more than a convenient excuse, however, for it could and did lead to angry explosions between those who desperately sought the promised paradise and those who, with equal desperation, sought to avoid starvation, just as it explained the powerful drive to convert the Unbelievers. It is this curious, self-propelling feature of the prophecy that explains how it took hold across the nation and survived a series of developments that should have defeated it.

With the turn of the year 1857, events seemed to quicken. Sandile, who had wavered for many months while weathering severe pressures from Believers, Unbelievers, and the government, made his final decision and it turned out to be a tragic one. Early in February a large crowd assembled at his Great Place, including Commissioner Maclean, Brownlee, and two of Sandile's councilors, Tyala and Soga. Maclean began by expressing his government's hope that Sandile would not acquiesce in Kreli's plan. Brownlee then spoke of his long relationship with the tribe. He characterized Kreli's movement as calculated to bring disaster and suffering to the people and denounced Mhlakaza as wicked and an impostor to be shunned and despised. In a loud voice, audible even to those outside the royal hut, Brownlee exclaimed, "Never! Never! Never!" thereby gaining as a nickname the Xhosa equivalent ("Napakade"), which he was to carry ever after. Brownlee also argued that Kreli had no right to interfere with tribes west of the Kei who were subjects of the British government.

Baba, an old councilor, railed at Brownlee: "Why cannot you leave us alone? You say we will starve; when we are hungry, as you say we will be, hunger will testify against us!" Brownlee replied that he would write down those words and remind Baba of them when hunger testified against him.

Tyala and Soga had long urged Sandile to remain loyal to the government, and before Sandile rose to speak, they restated their view that there had been enough of strife and false prophets, that the most important goal was peace, and that they should side with the government.

But Sandile had finally made up his mind. While he had initially followed Brownlee's urging and opposed the Cattle Killing, he now reversed his decision. Sandile, too, was a much-beloved chief, sensitive to the will of his people, but was often criticized as indecisive and lacking in leadership. Now, after alluding to the conflicting forces brought to bear upon him, Sandile announced his decision to support Kreli as the paramount chief of the Xhosa nation and directed all his subjects to kill all cattle and destroy all grain. There were tears on Tyala's face as he left the hut.

Communications between Kreli and the prophets at the Gxara River also became more numerous and urgent at this time. When Kreli learned that the government was massing troops along the frontier, he asked Mhlakaza to consult the oracle, but the prophet replied that the spirits were mute. Further efforts proved futile and when the chief and thousands of his warriors visited Mhlakaza's kraal for advice, Mhlakaza was not to be seen. As belief in the prophecy began to fade, however, word was received from the divine that the spirits of the ancestors had been on their way to the living world, but had turned back when they learned that several chiefs and councilors had failed to obey their commands. Kreli was advised that if the next full moon rose blood red, he should come to Mhlakaza, for that would be a sign that he had found favor with the spirits.

When the next full moon did rise blood red, Kreli traveled to Mhlakaza accompanied by eighteen councilors and five thousand warriors. Many were afraid to approach because they had not fully complied with the prophesy, so Kreli met with the prophet alone. On his return the chief reported many strange sights and, most importantly, definite instructions. All remaining livestock must now be killed except for one cow and one goat for each family. If that was done, the day of resurrection would occur eight days after Kreli returned home. On the fateful day the sun would rise late; when it reached its zenith, it would become blood red and suddenly set where it had risen. A great storm would follow with thunder, lightning, and darkness. The stage had been readied for the final climax. These last, specific directions stimulated the people to make one frantic, final effort to bring on the promised paradise. The remaining animals were killed, immense new corn pits were dug, the huts were prepared for the storm, their doorways reduced in size to discourage the entry of animals associated with witchcraft and the space about the hut cleared and swept so that reptiles, which signified ill fortune, could not approach.

As early as the seventh day the weary, famished families entered their huts to await the great event. They passed the long hours in a silence unbroken by the sounds of livestock, for the cattle kraals were empty. The first gleamings of sunrise were met with the greatest expectation. But the sunrise was unexceptional and there was nothing unusual about the sun's passage across the sky. It did not stop, neither did it change color nor reverse its course. No storm developed and the reborn ancestors and the bountiful cattle and grain were nowhere to be seen. Throughout the day the Believers hid in their houses behind securely fastened doors peeping out occasionally through little holes until the sun disappeared.

The thought occurred to many that a mistake had been made and the supernatural events were to occur on the ninth day. Repressing their disappointment, they resumed their vigil, only to be disappointed even more keenly on the following day. This became known as the Great Disappointment of February 16–17, 1857. Years later one Believer recalled:

"I sat outside my hut and saw the sun rise, so did all the people. We watched until midday, yet the sun continued its course. We still watched until the afternoon and yet it did not return, and the people began to despair because they saw this thing was not true."

Even now Mhlakaza managed to preserve both his reputation and belief in the prophecy. His latest explanation for the failure was that the resurrection had been delayed because two of the chiefs in the netherworld had quarreled as to which of them had the right to rise first. Under these harrowing conditions, the people now suffering famine and having experienced a series of events that would normally have disillusioned them completely, it is evidence of their remarkable faith that they would again prepare for the great resurrection. On May 28, 1857, Brownlee reported that the tribe was once more getting ready to receive the new cattle and the plentiful grain. Needless to say, they failed to materialize.

Conditions across the land had already become seriously unsettled. Starving, angry tribesmen began roving about in bands, stealing from and killing people who had not slaughtered their cattle. It became too dangerous to travel. As early as March 15 Brownlee reported that "The utmost confusion reigns throughout the country, parties large and small invest the land and are stealing cattle and committing murders on the owners of cattle wherever they are able. Last week I heard of 31 Kafirs being killed, either in defending or in taking cattle."

The government moved to establish order in the area under its jurisdiction. All Xhosas found with weapons in hand were banished and thieves attempting to escape were shot. The arrival of a legion composed of Germans had a stabilizing effect, although they proved difficult to control.

The worst of the calamity was now about to take place. Many in the tribes who had waited patiently for months began to leave their kraals in June looking for help once deaths by starvation occurred. But there were still those awaiting the miracle. One poor old man was found dead with his head hanging over his corn pit. He had gone with his last breath to see if the marvelous corn had come. And there were still those who studied the sun during the day and the moon at night, who daily inspected empty cattle kraals and corn pits. Women and children wandered the fields searching for roots. In Kreli's tribe, especially, the suffering was great. Many were so emaciated that they died on the way to get help. "Want among those who have destroyed their cattle has reached the highest pitch," Brownlee wrote on July 28, 1857.

Twenty years after the experience Mrs. Brownlee was still sickened when she recollected scenes of starvation and death. The first sound in the morning and the last at night was the endless, pitiful cry for food. It seemed to her, watching the crowds of breathing skeletons with hollow eyes and parched lips come in crowds and crawl along, that the prophecy had come true in some perverse way and that the dead had indeed risen from their graves.

Brownlee had laid in a supply of a thousand bags of grain in anticipation of the famine, but his efforts and those of others in the colony had limited effect. Corn and meat were given daily to all who came and lighter fare to the sick and children. For hundreds it was too late: they got one meal and died. Others were too far gone to eat anything. Still others were so voracious that they scoured the area stuffing any food they could find into their mouths and thus became sick. Mothers took food from their children, the strong wrested it from the weak.

Among those struggling toward the colony for help was the family of Nobanzi, the blind woman who had challenged Mhlakaza when he first revealed the prophecy. Mhlakaza himself, suffering from starvation, had left the village on the Gxara River for the seashore where he hoped to find food, but instead found death. The departure of the prophet was the signal for all the villagers to leave. Most set out in the direction of King William's Town in the colony.

King William's Town was about seventy miles from Kreli's country. In the streets of that town the inhabitants were distressed to see living skeletons going from house to house seeking food. Soup kitchens were set up by the civilians and the worst cases were sent to the Native Hospital. Daily truckloads of the dead were taken to the cemetery for burial. Police patrols and rescue wagons like the one that discovered Nobanzi searched the far hills and valleys, but many tribespeople were never found. There were those in the tribes who avoided King William's Town for one reason or another and pressed on toward the Fish River.

Instances of cannibalism began to occur. Near Fort Beaufort the police came upon three women emerging from a thicket over which smoke had appeared. Entering over the protests of the women, they found the heads of three children whose bodies had been devoured. Near the Fish River a man carrying an exhausted child lagged behind his wife. When she returned, she found that he had killed their little daughter and was roasting one of her limbs over a fire. In a fury she struck him with an ax and killed him.

To their credit, some of the leading citizens in King William's Town organized the Kaffir Relief Committee in July 1857 upon the initiative of Henry Cotterill, the bishop of Grahamstown, to provide food and other assistance to the starving Xhosas. To his great shame, however, Governor Grey discouraged the committee and manipulated its early demise. In Grey's view the suffering of the Xhosas could be readily ameliorated by putting them to work. In this he displayed one of the uglier Victorian social attitudes, believing that honest labor was the answer to poverty and hardship no matter the degree or how occasioned.

Brownlee estimated that more than 20,000 died in the calamity, 30,000 entered the colony and obtained work, and at least 150,000 cattle were killed. Other estimates put the human mortality at 40,000 and the cattle slaughter as high as 300,000. The population of certain chiefdoms between the Kei and Fish rivers dropped from 104,721 to 37,697 in 1857.

The Xhosa nation was irremediably wrecked. The people who had survived were scattered and many were absorbed into the colony and forever separated from their old world. The event became known, with some justification, as a national suicide.

Of the principal actors, Nongquase, the young prophetess, was protected and taken beyond the Bashee River to the tribe of Kreli's uncle. Kreli escaped capture and also fled to this land. Nonkosi was orphaned by the deaths of her parents and although all her relatives died in the famine, she was cared for by people living near the Mbonco River. Sandile signed a bond of loyalty with the government before the movement was over. Mhala, whose tribe had practically ceased to exist, led a band of robbers until his arrest. Because feelings were running so high, the government decided that the lives of those who took a leading part in the catastrophe were in danger and transferred them, including the two girls, to Robben Island by sailing ship, to be released when the intense hatred abated.

Nongquase, sometimes referred to as the most powerful woman and the most tragic figure in the history of South Africa, lived on, marrying, producing two daughters, and dying in 1898. Little was heard of the subsequent life of Nonkosi. Sandile was wounded in a war with another tribe in 1877 and died a few days later. Kreli, one of the architects of the killing, ironically lived the longest, dying in 1902 in seclusion, exiled from the old tribal lands.

It was inevitable that an event of such magnitude would give rise to rumors that it had been brought about for political reasons. Prevalent soon after the disaster was the idea that the Cattle Killing had been an elaborate native strategy intended to unite the loosely organized Xhosa tribes for one concentrated offensive against the English. Evidence of a variety of kinds seemed to support this theory. The fact that horses, so useful in war, were not among the animals killed seemed to point in this direction, although guns and spears were sold by the natives in their distress. Brownlee was convinced of the military intention at the time, although his belief later faded. He had come to that conclusion initially because of the absence of prior public discussion in Kreli's council, unusual for such an important issue, and also because Kreli was alleged to have said, "Everyone will fight now."

More concrete and so more persuasive were the results of the investigation into the affair that Commissioner Maclean began in October 1857. Kreli was beyond his jurisdiction, but Nongquase and Nonko-

si were summoned for questioning at Fort Murray. Nonkosi was the
first to arrive. After a period in which Maclean and his wife became
acquainted with the little girl and succeeded in winning her confidence,
she was formally interrogated and a record made of her answers.

At first, she told about the magic pool on the Mbonco River,
Mlanjeni, and the appearance of the departed chiefs. But when Maclean
looked closely into her face, reminded her that some chiefs had admitted the deception, and assured her she had nothing to fear if she told
the truth, a different story began to emerge. While she continued to
profess belief in the supernatural events, she admitted that she had not
seen them herself, but was told them by her uncle, Kwitshi, who filled
in for her all the descriptive details including the names and appearances of each of the dead chiefs. At one time Kwitshi warned her that if
she told anyone that he had instructed her in what to say, they both
would be strangled.

Maclean decided to bring in Kwitshi for questioning, and sent out a
mounted patrol to scour the country for him. After some pursuit,
Kwitshi was apprehended just as he was attempting to cross the
border. Brought back and examined in November 1857, Kwitshi admitted directing Nonkosi. He blamed Mhala, who forced him to do it in
order to drive the English from Xhosa country and take their property.
Neither Kwitshi nor Mhala believed in the prophecy. Some of the
events at the pool were staged by Kwitshi who hid behind the rushes
and reeds bellowing like an ox and holding horns aloft for Nonkosi to
see. He also called out loudly, "We are rising! We are rising! We are
the people who died!" Mhala, Kulwana, and Kwitshi also arranged for a
man to impersonate Mlanjeni at the pool.

Mhlakaza was determined to drive the English out, and Kwitshi
described taking part in many meetings attended by the prophet and
various chiefs in which he heard plans being formed for the killing of all
cattle so that the people would be forced to steal from the English and
bring on a war. According to Kwitshi,

> It was believed that, if the people killed all their cattle, they would be
> free from encumbrances and all would be able to attack—no one

would have to stay at home to care for cattle, and the English would have nothing to take from the people.

It was said that the Government had deprived them of their country and they were determined to have it back. . . .

These plans were upset because all the people did not kill all the cattle at the same time. In this way, some were starving when others still had cattle, and, in the end, the tribes were unexpectedly broken up and the people scattered. . . .

In April 1858 Nongquase was escorted to Fort Murray for questioning. In general she affirmed the visions she had seen at the Gxara River and gave no indication that the strange happenings might have been staged, as seems to have been the case with Nonkosi at the Mbonco River. But Nongquase did report hearing Kreli say he wanted to drive the English out of the country and welcomed the assistance of the spirits. She also recounted how Mhlakaza once stated he "wished to be a non-killer." Later, when the prophet was starving, Nongquase often heard him say he regretted killing his cattle and destroying his corn and blamed Kreli as the sole cause of the killing, which was done for the purpose of leading the Xhosas to war with the English.

In the reminiscences of Charles Brownlee and his wife we can make out the prevailing imperial English attitude to the self-destruction of the Xhosas. Beyond their direct experience of the horrors observed and their personal feelings for some of the natives, one senses their exasperation and inability to comprehend the native mind. Unspoken but nonetheless powerfully felt by the Brownlees and the other colonial administrators was the conviction that these events took place beyond the frontiers of civilization in the dark heart of a savage world they could not hope to understand. That reaction was probably magnified at the center of the English empire when reports of the Xhosa disaster were received back home in England. Those reading such reports were undoubtedly astonished at the barbaric nature of the Xhosas and their capacity for self-delusion and may well have silently complimented themselves as more advanced and sophisticated people, certainly less credulous when presented with such fantastic prophecies.

In fact, however, many of those who were astonished at the reports coming out of South Africa had exhibited their own capacity for self-delusion not many years before when London was severely disturbed by an old prophecy of cataclysm that resembled, in some ways, the Xhosa episode.

In the early months of 1842, the year after Charles Mackay's *Extraordinary Popular Delusions* was first published, London was alive with rumors that the city would be destroyed by an earthquake on March 17. The rumor was said to derive from two prophecies, one more than six hundred years old. That source was an alleged manuscript from the year 1203 which predicted a widespread calamity:

> *In eighteen hundred and forty-two*
> *Four things the sun shall view*
> *London's rich and famous town*
> *Hungry earth shall swallow down.*
> *Storm and rain in France shall be,*
> *Till every river runs a sea.*
> *Spain shall be rent in twain,*
> *And famine waste the land again.*

The other was attributed to John Dee, the astrologer, in 1598:

> *The Lord have mercy on you all—*
> *Prepare yourselves for dreadful fall*
> *Of house and land and human soul—*
> *The measure of your sins is full.*
> *In the year one, eight and forty-two,*
> *Of the year that is so new;*
> *In the third month of that sixteen,*
> *It may be a day or two between—*

Perhaps you'll soon be stiff and cold.
Dear Christian, be not stout and bold—
The mighty, kingly-proud will see
This comes to pass as my name's Dee.

Mackay refers to the matter briefly in a footnote in which he says the alarm was limited to "the wide circle of the uneducated classes" and also questions the existence of the 1203 prophecy. Whether or not the prediction could be traced back more than six hundred years, it was very old, indeed, and seems to have been broadly known throughout the city by word of mouth passing from one to another, down the generations, until it became part of unwritten London lore comparable, perhaps, to the common belief that the sewer lines in New York City are inhabited by huge albino alligators.

As the fateful day approached, it was originally reported that the lower classes of Irish were the only people affected. This later proved to be inaccurate and may have been prompted by the kind of cultural condescension that inhibited English thinking about South African natives and other colonial people, the Irish being treated as something like members of a South African tribe who happened to come from a neighboring land across the Irish Sea. The excitement among the Irish in the eastern part of the city was very great, reported the *Times* of London on March 4. Many had already left for distant parts of the country and for Ireland, and others were preparing to leave. From concerned relatives and friends in Ireland came letters begging loved ones to leave and so avoid destruction.

The prophecy had a kind of territorial precision. In one form it was believed that the anticipated earthquake would destroy the "big churches," including St. Paul's Cathedral and Westminster Abbey, but would not extend eastward of Stepney Old Church, so those in flight knew where safety began. In another version, however, fifteen miles of countryside beyond the city were destined to be swallowed up. A week before the fateful day some saw early evidence of the event, insisting that St. Paul's had already sunk five feet, other churches two feet, and the Custom House, in the words of the *Times*, "reported to be fast disappearing in the bowels of the earth." The newspaper claimed that many of "the poorer classes of the Irish people" visited these buildings to see for themselves how far they had already disappeared and one man near St. Paul's was heard to say, "Faith, now, the great big church don't look so high as it did some time ago."

As the clock ticked down, however, it became evident that the delusion was not confined to any one ethnic group, economic class, or section of the city. By March 10 the *Times* admitted that belief in the prophecy was not confined "to the lower and more ignorant classes of Roman Catholics, but is participated in by many belonging to the Wesleyan and other sects," and was not only very popular in the East End of London but was influential in the West End as well. In Marleybone a former police constable sold a good business to finance his escape and a clerk resigned a well-paying position for the same reason.

Some observers were reminded of a similar event in 1750 when a prediction that London would be destroyed by an earthquake on April 2 created alarm among the nobility and gentry as well as the lower classes, prompting a noticeable exodus into the countryside. Several women were said to be making "earthquake gowns" in which they intended to sit outdoors all night. On the evening preceding the expected disaster the green fields surrounding the city were filled with a great number of people assembled on foot, and in chairs, chaises, and coaches waiting fearfully for the earthquake to begin.

On March 17, 1842, an outside observer might have witnessed extraordinary scenes in some London neighbourhoods. Although many residents had left, the larger number of inhabitants remained. "The frantic cries, the incessant appeals to Heaven for deliverance, the invocations to the Virgin and the Saints for mediation, the heartrending applications for assistance, heard on every side during the day," impressed the *Times* reporter with the power with which the prophecy had gripped the minds of the people. "Many persons from whom better things might have been expected were amongst the number who fled London to avoid the threatened catastrophe." The panic proved a blessing to the railways and the Gravesend steamboat companies.

Long before the boats' departure times shore points were thronged by crowds of well-dressed people carrying enough provisions for a six-week trip. As one boat came along the London Bridge wharf to take on passengers a stampede ensued, and within minutes there was hardly standing room aboard. Trains were filled for several days in advance of the event and people who could not afford boat or rail trudged out of the city in several directions seeking refuge and a view of the demolition of the great metropolis.

It is easy to distinguish the London prophecy of 1842 from the Xhosa Cattle Killing. Credulous and agitated as the Londoners may have been, they did not destroy their livelihoods, there was no expectation of the millennium, and the prophecy had no political dimension. There were no reports of deaths in London and the existence of the English people was never threatened. Significant as those differences may be, they fade before a larger meaning that encompasses both people, black and white, civilized Londoners and South African "kaffirs." The credulity of the Xhosas, scoffed at by the English, was matched by that of those Londoners who believed in the prophecy. It is not too much to say that the English capacity for delusion matched that of their South African contemporaries in light of the considerable advantages of education, knowledge, and life in a great city then at the center of the Industrial Revolution, all available to residents of London but not to those beyond the Fish River. If delusion, as a psychologically altered state, can be thought of as a voyage to a distant land during which one progressively casts off the wisdom accumulated at home to cope with life, the distance traveled by the terrified Londoners may have been comparable to that traveled by the desperate Xhosas.

Similar thoughts may have been in the mind of Charles Brownlee when he wrote to his superior, Commissioner Maclean in British Kaffraria as the Cattle Killing was proceeding on its calamitous course:

> It seems absurd that a shrewd and reasoning people like the Kaffirs should be led astray by such reports as have for the past few months been in circulation, and that they should be giving up a certainty for an

uncertainty. But if we should reflect on the wonderful delusions in our own land, in the last and present centuries, and even in our own day, some measure of astonishment may be removed that a superstitious people who have always regarded their chief doctors as inspired should be led astray, when the delusion is pleasing and its realisation desirable.

SOCCER

The Central American countries of Honduras and El Salvador share a border of some 180 miles and the kind of passion for *futbol,* as soccer is known in Spanish, that regularly flares up into violence around the world. In 1969 that violence led to an actual, but undeclared, war replete with machine gun duels, air bombings, tank deployment, and the invasion of Honduras by Salvadoran army forces. Before a tentative truce was arranged, an estimated 2,400 people died within the first weeks of fighting, and the conflict continued intermittently for years. Ryszard Kapuscinski, the highly regarded correspondent for the Polish Press Agency, has reported much grimmer figures: 6,000 dead, more than 12,000 wounded, some 50,000 deprived of their homes and fields, and many villages destroyed.

Ill feeling between the two countries had been growing for some time because of economic and social problems. El Salvador is much smaller than Honduras, but the 3.25 milion people who lived there in 1969 were crowded while its larger neighbor to the north was sparsely populated. Prior to 1969 more than 300,000 Salvadorans had moved into Honduras, causing border incidents for years. Aggravating this situation was the relative industrial prosperity of El Salvador, the envy of Hondurans and the source of frequently cited distinctions between the more affluent and sophisticated Salvadorans and the poorer Hondurans.

A law enacted in Honduras in 1962 restricted the ownership of designated lands to native-born Hondurans. In April 1969, as a result of increased animosity toward Salvadorans, the government began to enforce the law. On June 4, 1969, Honduran army units forcibly removed 54 Salvadoran families from their homesteads along the border in an action referred to by the Honduras press as "cleaning the area of *guanacos,*" using a pejorative term for the Salvadoran settlers, which is commonly translated as "bumpkins."

Against this background the three-game series of a regional World Cup match between the soccer teams of the two countries took on a special added meaning. The match already had its own importance of a very high order—at least for soccer fans—since the winner would advance to the final if it defeated Haiti, and, in vying for the celebrated World Cup itself, would have a rare opportunity to bring fame and glory to itself and its nation. The observation of one commentator that the playoff games were "less trivial than one might imagine" hardly conveys, with its double minimals, both the emotional intensity generated by the sport in this region and the opportunity for international prestige afforded by the match.

The first game was to be played in Tegucigalpa, the capital of Honduras. The night before, the visiting El Salvador team was subjected to the kind of extra-playing-field offensive that is not unknown in Latin America. Honduran fans gathered about the hotel where the El Salvador team was staying and maintained a din throughout the night. By leaning on their car horns, exploding firecrackers, stoning the hotel windows, beating on tin cans, and so on, these enthusiasts did their best to deprive the players of any sleep. The next day the groggy El Salvador team lost by a score of 1–0.

In El Salvador, eighteen-year-old Amelia Bolanios became so distraught while watching her country's team go down to defeat on television that she rushed to the drawer in which her father kept a revolver and put a bullet into her heart. This was neither the first nor the last fan suicide in the volcanic world of soccer, but the public reaction to Amelia's death was unique.

El Nacional, the El Salvador newspaper, began with the astonishing proclamation that "The young girl could not bear to see her fatherland brought to its knees." The population and the government went considerably further and decided to treat her as a national heroine. Her funeral became a televised event with trappings that might have been expected for a fallen head of state. In the procession there was an army honor guard, and the president of El Salvador together with his ministers marched behind Amelia's flag-draped coffin, followed by the nation's soccer team.

Now came the second game in the series, to be played in San Salvador, El Salvador. It was only eleven days after the first evictions of Salvadoran families by Honduran forces, and the funeral of Amelia Bolanios had brought feelings to an intolerable level. Pictures of the dead girl were displayed along the route of the visiting Honduran team. At the hotel in San Salvador the night before the game the Honduran players were treated to the same kind of "shivaree" that their opponents had received in Tegucigalpa, but with more violence. During the night-long racket the windows of the hotel were broken. The following day it was deemed necessary to escort the Honduran team to the stadium in armored vehicles.

When the El Salvador team now triumphed on the field in the second game, many Hondurans in the stadium were attacked and mauled by the local crowd. Hondurans elsewhere in the city were subjected to vigilante beatings and internment, and their homes and shops were looted and burned. The Honduras government reacted to this incident by severing diplomatic relations with El Salvador and stepping up the expulsion of Salvadoran campesinos. At first, El Salvador closed its borders hoping to force Honduras to relocate the expelled Salvadorans, but this action proved ineffective.

Concern over the strong feelings surrounding the third, and final, game of the match led the authorities to remove the game to the neutral territory of Mexico City. There, on June 27, with 1,700 policemen assigned by nervous officials expecting violence that never developed, El Salvador prevailed. On the soccer field there was ample good sportsmanship: players embraced and shook hands. Back home, however, both countries called up military reinforcements and deployed their troops.

In the first few days of July there were isolated incidents of air attacks and border clashes, and by July 9, Salvadoran troops had invaded Honduras. At one point troops reached to within seventy-five miles of Tegucigalpa, the capital and major city of Honduras. The announced purpose of the invasion, according to El Salvador, was to defend the human rights of their countrymen and put an end to Honduran genocide. We are not at war, said the El Salvador foreign minister, but there is a "state of aggression" by Honduras. By July 19 the organization of American States (OAS) estimated 2,000 had been killed in the fighting; Reuters, however, put the count at 2,400.

The conflict continued in spite of mediation efforts by neighboring nations and the OAS, until August 3 when El Salvador finally agreed to withdraw about ten thousand of its troops under heavy threat of condemnation and possible sanctions by the OAS. It was not the end, however, for even though both sides had agreed to a truce, the fighting was to erupt again and again for years.

Uncomfortable, perhaps, with the "Soccer War" label, historians correctly point out that the deeper causes of the event antedated the soccer rivalry, an observation that neither diminishes the game's potential for violence nor does much to illuminate the way wars begin. While it seems probable that these Central American countries would have gone to war anyway, it was the regional playoff games that in fact brought the heated situation to its flashpoint. And if it is true that Honduran-Salvadoran problems reached beyond the soccer stadium, it is also true that the attack on Pearl Harbor, for example, was only the precipitating—and by no means the only—cause of the American-Japanese conflict in World War II.

Currently, soccer is the world's most popular sport. One hundred and forty-seven countries are members of the international body that regulates the game, a total that exceeds by thirteen the nations that participate in the Olympics. The World Cup, contested every four years, plays to the largest television audience in the world. In 1978 it was estimated that the final game was watched by more than two billion people, or almost half of the world's population. In countries where it is a passion, soccer is played everywhere, from dusty yards in which barefooted boys kick around a crude "ball" made of socks, to Rio de Janeiro's huge Maracana Stadium which seats 210,000.

Together with its vast popularity, the game engenders intense feelings among its fans. Victories can be celebrated with the most protracted jubilations. When Brazil won the World Cup for the third time in 1970 and retired the trophy, the entire country cavorted in excitement for two days, leaving 44 dead and 1,800 injured. Conversely, when the Brazilian team was eliminated in the 1982 World Cup, despair was such that one fan committed suicide and another attempted it. The wildness and sustained enthusiasm that went on in Rome in 1983, when the city won the Italian national championship for the first time in forty-one years, was said by older Roman witnesses to have surpassed even that experienced when the city was liberated from Nazi rule in 1944. Exuberance in stadium grandstands seems boundless, expressing itself in cheering one's team or vilifying the opposing team, their fans, or the referee. In some countries, the extent and depth of interest in the game raise it to the level of a pervasive cultural force. There is a popular adage in Brazil that every town in the country has at least one church and one soccer field— "Well, not always a church, but certainly a soccer field." Fans of the Flamengo Club in Rio de Janeiro recall as children cheering the team even before they could talk and recognizing the Flamengo flag before the national flag of Brazil. In Liverpool, England, where it is said that "you get football before you get the baby bottle," a former club manager observed, "Some people think football is as important as life and death. I can assure them it is much more serious than that."

As exemplified by the Honduras–El Salvador history, soccer also has a potential for group violence, a potential unmatched by any other sport. The history of the game is so filled with incidents of attacks— upon fans, referees, players, and bystanders—riots, stampedes, and other casualties, it makes one wonder whether such violence has not become a permanent feature.

The modern game is not much more than a century old but comes to us with a colorful and ambiguous provenance. A kind of football was played in China as early as the time of Christ, and involved a single goal with a small, high opening through which the players tried to kick the ball in alternating fashion. In ancient Greece and Rome three different kinds of games were played, each with a hair-filled ball of a different size, but while modern soccer is said to derive from them, all permitted the use of hands and it is unclear whether kicking was permitted, much less emphasized.

According to English folklore, the game can be traced back to
sometime around 1050 when two workmen found a Danish skull on an
old battlefield and began kicking it around, partly to retaliate for the
recent Danish occupation. Apocryphal as this story may be, it sounds
the right chord of anger and symbolic revenge for the beginning of a
sport that was destined to record so many instances of violence.

By the twelfth century a team ball game was being played throughout England that featured both kicking and the use of hands. Often
played with roads, trees, and buildings marking the playing field and
goals at each end of the town in which the game took place, these were
mob affairs. Games lasted for hours in which town contested against
town, parish against parish, married against unmarried. Little was
forbidden on the field: A player might be attacked in almost any fashion
in order to keep him or her from the ball. If the rules failed to suggest
modern soccer, the bloody reality of the play and the usual property
damage do. The game grew so popular that in 1314 the king forbade it
be played in London, as he felt it led to a breach of the peace. In 1349 it
was further prohibited because the casualties it produced reduced the
number of trained and able archers needed to defend the kingdom.
Similiar laws were enacted throughout the fourteenth, fifteenth, and
sixteenth centuries, but their very repetition evidences the growing
popularity of football.

Eventually, the game was moved to a proper playing field and rules
were adopted, so that by the end of the fifteenth century it was known
as a game in which the ball was propelled exclusively by kicking. In
spite of continued opposition, football began to be played at colleges in
the sixteenth century. Despite these refinements and its spread
throughout society, it was still the disorganized and bloody sport of
mob football. Philip Stubbes offers this description in his 1583 publication *The Anatomie of Abuses:*

> Rather a bloody and murderous practise than a felowly sporte or
> pastime. . . . For dooth not everyone lye in weight for his Adversary,
> seeking to overthrow him . . . though it be upon hard stones? . . . So
> that by this meanes, sometimes their necks are broken, sometimes

there backs, sometimes their legs, sometimes their armes; sometime one part thrust out of joynt; sometime another; sometime their noses gush out with blood, sometime their eyes start out; and sometimes hurt in one place, sometimes in another. . . . And hereof groweth envie, malice, rancour, choler, displeasure, enmities, and what not els; and sometimes fighting, brawling, contention, quarrel picking, murther, homicide, and great effusion of blood, as experience dayly teacheth.

A milestone was reached in 1845 when new rules were written for a game played at Rugby School that made further refinements in order to minimize violence. Mob football disappeared; at the elite private schools two kinds of football were played, one permitting the use of hands and the other prohibiting it. The formation of a "Football Association" (the word *soccer* derives from "as*soc*iation") at Eton in 1863 marks the commencement of the modern era of the game. The Rugby Football Union was established in 1871.

Soccer was a patrician activity until the late 1870s when an effort was begun to teach it to the working classes, partly to deal with urban crime but also to instill in workers the Victorian virtues of hard work and civic pride.

The reformulation of the sport and its spread from the aristocratic public schools through the middle and working classes coincide with the zenith of Great Britain's colonial empire. That coincidence explains how soccer came to be exported around the world, took root in Africa and Asia, and became the most popular of team sports. Along with their English language, their Anglicanism, their Victorian values, and such technological advances as steam power and modern weaponry, the British colonizers brought with them that curious kicking game in which one group is pitted against another. That they also brought the team game of cricket, which took root far less tenaciously, should not be ignored, for it may suggest something of the primordial appeal of soccer.

By the time of World War I the game occupied such a special place in the culture of Great Britain that it even played a part in the conflict.

Among other military conventions that became obsolete in the Great War was the idea of sportsmanlike conduct on the battlefield. Perhaps to demonstrate such conduct, British troops began an attack on the western front in 1915 by kicking a football toward the enemy lines. The practice was adopted everywhere and soon became a customary act of bravado. In October 1917, for example, it was used in the British attack on Turkish positions at Beersheba. Perhaps the most famous instance, however, was when Captain W. P. Nevill provided a football to each of his four platoons in the Somme attack. The attack was begun when a lead soldier got off a good kick that rose high and traveled well toward the German lines. We can only imagine that in some inexplicable way the good kick cheered the soldiers who followed the ball into the enemy's fire. Captain Nevill was killed instantly.

If the British empire explains how the sport came to be played so widely, the dismantling of the same empire contains a clue to the politicization of the game and reveals some of the sources of the violence with which it has been played since the end of World War II. With declining economic and military power, Great Britain was unable to resist the rise of nationalism that swept the modern world. The same force that produced feelings of political unity and a clamor for independence by otherwise diverse peoples could also be spent in the mock war that takes place on the soccer field. That would be especially likely in the case of new nations, uncertain of their roles in the world, lacking economic and military might and eager for glory. As former colonies evolved into new nations, it is not surprising that some of the worst instances of soccer violence can be attributed to misplaced nationalism. If the Soccer War of 1969 between Honduras and El Salvador is the most egregious example, it is not alone, and in fact, follows by only seven years incidents in west Africa that almost seemed to be a tryout or dress rehearsal for the later conflict.

Here the participants were the countries of Gabon and the Republic of the Congo, and the ignition was provided by the Tropical Cup, the local version of the World Cup. To Africans, the Tropical Cup is the equivalent of baseball's World Series in the United States, and the match between Gabon and the Congo in September 1962 would determine which of the two teams would challenge for the Cup. The first game, played in Libreville, Gabon's capital, resulted in the Gabonese winning 3–1. At the second game, in Brazzaville, capital of the Congo, there was tension in the stands from the opening whistle. When Gabon scored first, the Congolese band refused to play the fanfare, traditional when either side scored. At the end of the game the scoreboard showed that the Congolese team had won by the same 3–1 score that had determined the first game in favor of the Gabonese. Most of the 20,000 fans, however, thought the score should have been 5–1, and blamed the referee who had nullified two of the Congolese goals. This was important because if the goals had been allowed, the Congo would have won the series on points. Congolese fans were so infuriated that a phalanx of policemen was required to see the referee safely off the playing field. Irate Congolese stoned cars, attacked Gabonese residents, and burned their homes. More than one thousand frightened Gabonese sought refuge at a Congolese army base on the outskirts of the city. The president of the Congo appealed for calm and declared a day of mourning for those who had been killed.

When news of Gabon's defeat reached Libreville, a rumor spread that the Congolese had mobbed the Gabonese team and beaten two players to death. Although the return of the Gabonese team scotched this rumor, old feelings of animosity toward Congolese living in Libreville were so inflamed that for two days Gabonese mobs roamed the city attacking Congolese residents. The police took no steps to quell the rioting until the night of the second day, but by then the Congolese quarters of the city had been burned to the ground.

The Gabon government complained that the Congo had displayed exceptionally bad sportsmanship and announced it was breaking off all athletic relations. On September 22 Gabon expelled three thousand Congolese residents because of the bitterness growing out of the soccer match. The Congolese were herded into concentration camps and packed aboard ships for the journey of several hundred miles down the coast to Pointe-Noire.

The president of the Congo appealed to President de Gaulle of France for help.

While some observers were thunderstruck at the extent of the violence, others noted that winning had become a matter of national honor throughout Africa. When a good European team came to play, it tried to win the first game by a close score and allow its opponents to tie all the others. A larger truth about soccer may have been expressed by a British diplomat who noted, "There are two things every diplomat, no matter what his nationality, dreads more than anything else short of war. One is for your country to dispatch a goodwill naval visit and give three thousand of your sailors shore leave. The other is to try to build international friendship through football."

The Soccer War of 1969 and the 1962 conflict between Gabon and the People's Republic of the Congo may stand alone in that soccer-induced violence led to such governmental actions as the taking of lands from alien residents, deportations, and war. But such extreme measures are less astonishing when considered in light of the political significance attached by some governments to the outcome on the playing field. President Mobuto Sese Seko dispatched the Zaire team to World Cup competition with the exhortation "Win or die!" Even that chilling disjunctive may not have been a first, however, for at the 1930 World Cup final Argentinians shouted, "Victory or death!"

On the occasion of the Brazilian team winning the World Cup for the third time in 1970, President Emilio Medici's address to the nation virtually made the team a political instrumentality. "I feel profound happiness at seeing the joy of our people in this highest form of patriotism. I identify this victory won in the brotherhood of good sportsmanship with the rise of faith in our fight for national development. I identify the success of [our national team] with . . . intelligence and bravery, perseverence and serenity in our technical ability, in physical preparation and moral being. Above all, our players won because they knew how to . . . play for the collective good."

Soccer victory has enormous political significance in the lands where the sport is a near religion, but the game's relationship to the political process goes beyond that. Public understanding of and interest in the game have been made to serve both the ends of domestic and international governmental programs and even the electoral process. In 1973 when the Brazilian government disappointed the people by the size of the increase in the minimum wage, some sugarcoating was added in the form of fifteen thousand free tickets to a big holiday game. This was consistent with a policy of maintaining low prices for many stadium seats, a policy reminiscent of that pursued by Imperial Rome designed to placate the citizenry and which moved Juvenal to say of the typical Roman, "He longs for only two things—bread and the big match."

In the realm of international relations it was the considered opinion of some knowledgeable observers that the Falklands war between Great Britain and Argentina could have been averted by threatening to exclude Argentina from the 1982 World Cup, and sportswriter Michael Roberts was convinced that barring sport-crazy South Africans from soccer and other matches "probably carries more weight than all the arms embargoes, economic sanctions, and liberal handwringing put together." Similarly, the refusal of Arab teams to meet Israeli teams and Indian teams to meet Pakistani teams are extensions of foreign policies to the playing field.

But the influence of the game, or, more precisely, the public's intoxication with it, has been felt at the earliest steps of the political process as well as in the formulation of governmental policies. To communicate its election campaign message effectively to the El Salvador electorate in 1984, the right-wing National Republican Alliance staged a soccer game in San Salvador in which its team played a team representing the opposing Christian Democratic Party. The organizers no doubt felt they had discovered a wonderful medium for communicating their political message. The National Republican Alliance accused the Christian Democrats of being Communists, an accusation dramatized on the playing field when that team stripped off the green shirts with which they began play to reveal red shirts. During the game figures representing President Reagan and the United States Ambassador to El Salvador made appearances on the playing field. It is almost superfluous to mention that the National Republican Alliance team won.

Nationalism and the tendency to politicize the game account for much of soccer violence. In Europe, with good transportation and cities relatively close together, the spate of recent riots has been attributed, at least in part, to historic national rivalries. For the 1966 World Cup final between England and West Germany one London newspaper considered the headline "Remember Dunkirk!" In 1980 Jewish and Arab teams were playing in the Galilee when a referee's decision led to an attack upon him by the Arab shooter. A mob of five thousand Arab spectators stormed the field shouting, "Khomeini!" and "Down with Zionism!" The Jewish players barricaded themselves in the locker room for two hours while the Arab mob tried to batter down the doors. The riot was eventually broken up by police using tear gas, warning shots, and an armored vehicle.

Even more frequently, a soccer match will provide an arena for the acting out of local allegiances, ethnic loyalties, or religious convictions together with xenophobia and other prejudices which are the ugly reverse sides of those emotions. When La Barça of Barcelona plays Real Madrid the issue is the dominance of Castilian culture and the Catalan struggle for independence. In Glasgow, Scotland, the meetings of the Celtics (Catholic) and Rangers (Protestant) are treated as semi-annual religious struggles. In Lima, Peru, there is racial rivalry among soccer clubs, and in Buenos Aires and Rio de Janeiro the rivalry is based on ethnic background and class.

Bringing teams together from different provinces, cities, towns, or villages can generate the most intense feelings of allegiance comparable to those produced by international matches. When in 1967 a referee made a disputed call in the first half of a game in Kayseri, central Turkey, between the home team and one from the city of Sivas in the neighboring province, the crowd of ten thousand watching the game erupted in a riot in which rival fans fought each other with pistols, knives, and broken bottles in the stadium and the streets of the city. Troops and police used rifles with bayonets to control the fighting in which forty-two died and some six hundred were injured. When news of the event reached Sivas and it was learned that most of those who had died were from Sivas, rioting began there with buildings believed to be owned by people from Kayseri set afire. Before police and the army regained control, eleven shops, a hotel, and a score of cars with Kayseri license plates were destroyed. Troops were ordered to the border between the provinces, roads between the cities were closed, and intercity bus service was suspended.

It is the thesis of Janet Lever in *Soccer Madness* that sport helps complex modern societies cohere, that soccer promotes societal integration for its fans, and that the game has had an important role in creating modern society. Even she, however, admits that soccer can be a divisive force. By magnifying old distinctions, reviving old hatreds, and encouraging irrational behavior, soccer tends to tear at the fabric of society.

This potential for divisiveness has even crossed national boundaries and served to focus hatreds against the Western world. After the Republic of China team was defeated by Hong Kong in Peking on May 19, 1985, and was eliminated from the World Cup, thousands of Chinese fans rampaged outside the stadium, menacing and attacking all foreigners while screaming, "Foreigner! Foreigner!" The event seemed to bury the "friendship first, competition second" precept of former premier Mao Tse-tung, especially since at the end of the game the Chinese team refused to shake hands and bottles were thrown at the departing Hong Kong players. It certainly embarrassed the current government, which was energetically trying to attract foreign investment and technology.

Feelings of national pride, ethnic and religious identification, and even local allegiance all call into play powerful emotions which can be magnified enormously by the setting in which they are played out. With many thousands of excited people compressed into small areas, often with opposing fans having access to each other, the tinder for an explosion can be provided by what would otherwise be an ordinary occurrence. Such was the case in the calamity that occurred on May 24, 1964, in Lima.

The eagerly awaited game scheduled to take place that afternoon pitted Peru against Argentina. It was an important match because its outcome would determine which national teams would represent South America at the Tokyo Olympics, and it had long been sold out. By game time the gates to the new 53,000-seat National Stadium were locked because its capacity had been reached but a large crowd still milled around outside. Inside, feelings were high. Because of soccer's reputation for trouble, police wearing steel helmets, armed with pistols, truncheons, and tear gas, and accompanied by police dogs, had been stationed in front of the grandstands. To prevent fans from getting to the players and the referee, a nine-foot-high chain-link steel fence surrounded the field.

The first half saw both teams play aggressively but without scoring, adding to the tension in the crowd. Halfway through the second half, Argentina scored. The Peruvian team responded vigorously and minutes later scored what seemed to be the tying goal. But the Uruguayan referee disallowed the goal, declaring that he had stopped play by whistling in order to call a foul against Peru before the scoring play.

The decision enraged the Peruvian spectators. Hundreds of bottles and seat cushions were thrown on the field. Bottles were even thrown through the windows of the scoreboard keeper's booth.

Over the nine-foot steel fence climbed a man called Bomba ("Bomb"), a nickname he had earned by his crazed exploits at soccer games, but his efforts to get at the referee were frustrated by the police. Another man then gained the field only to be taken into custody by the police. By this time the referee decided it would be imprudent to continue and called off the game. If his decision sought to avert further trouble, it had the opposite result. Groups of fans poured from the north stands and tried to climb the fence; the police on the other side clubbed their hands through the mesh. Other groups tore open the fence by kicking it in concert. The police first tried to deal with the frenzied people racing onto the field by using truncheons and police dogs. Fires were started in the stands and a retaining wall was demolished, its bricks hurled at the police. The referee and the players ran from the field and escaped with their lives only because a police detail rushed them into a secure locker room and took them by bus to a remote part of the country.

When the police commander saw the escalating violence, he determined to separate the mob from the police and directed his men to lob tear gas grenades at the fence in order to repel the enraged fans. But a breeze blew the gas into the stands. Perhaps because they saw this, the police began throwing the tear gas grenades directly into the stands.

Among the packed spectators there was coughing and blindness. Because of the size of the crowd and the closeness of quarters, it was impossible for anyone to reach fresh air. In one electric moment individual efforts suddenly gave way to an irresistible panic-stricken mass movement to the exits. The tunnels that led under the stands were only fourteen feet wide and narrowed to ten feet as they neared the exits. In the stampede men, women, and children were trampled to death. Three policemen were murdered: one strangled with his necktie, another thrown from the upper stands, the third stomped to death.

At the north end of the stadium the steel doors at the end of the tunnel had been locked because the attendants wanted to see the last part of the game. Those at the head of the mob begged and screamed but the thousands of maddened people desperately pressing forward behind them could not be stopped. Bodies piled up in increasing numbers against the doors, most of the victims suffocating or being trampled to death.

One young man who survived described the scene:

> The crowd carried me halfway down the tunnel without my feet touching the floor. I felt as if I were being squeezed to death. People were screaming for their children, calling for God's help. I thought I was gone. But I was lucky. I was squeezed upward and my head, chest, and one arm were free and in the air. Then the steel gate swelled out like a balloon and burst. Some people on top scrambled out. I couldn't move out of the vise I was in. I must have passed out. When I awoke, I was in a hospital. The doctors had put tubes in my nose. One leg had to be stitched up, and the other was broken in three places.

Outside the stadium hoodlums hurled stones at the police, turned cars over, smashed and burned buildings, and looted stores. The dead and injured were laid out in appallingly long rows and then transported to hospitals and temporary morgues where crowds later formed chanting, "Revenge!" and "Down with the police!" Another crowd marched on the National Palace demanding to see President Fernando Belaunde Terry to protest police brutality and—incredibly—to seek his intervention in having the soccer match officially declared a tie.

The government proclaimed a state of national emergency throughout Peru and suspended constitutional guarantees for thirty days in order to investigate the tragedy. First reports indicated that three hundred died and five hundred were injured, but an exact count of the fatalities proved impossible.

Responsibility for the catastrophe was not easily fixed. The referee insisted that he had acted in good faith and with impartiality. The police commander, citing his duty to protect the players and the referee, defended his use of tear gas claiming that there was no other way to control the mobs. Even this brief account makes it plain that the causes were many, including poor crowd control, bad judgment, the locked exit gates, and even the design of the stadium. But rising up above all these causes was the attitude of the soccer fans themselves, a collective state of mind so charged that it could produce the mobbing of the field and the later panic. When, some days later, Pope Paul VI called on fans to curb their enthusiasm and avoid such tragedies, saying that sports "must be without passion in athletes and the public," he exhibited both an understanding of how the Lima riot came about and ignorance of the realities of soccer mentality.

The 1964 Lima disaster may have accounted for the greatest death toll ever at a sporting event, but it was neither the first nor the last in a long series of such incidents. As a result of overcrowding, riots, and panic reactions, 33 died at Bolton, England, in 1942; 42 in Turkey in 1967 in the Kayseri-Sivas incident described; 72 in Buenos Aires in 1968; 66 in Glasgow in 1971; 48 in Cairo in 1974; 16 in Calcutta and 19 in Greece in 1981; and 24 in Colombia and 100 in Moscow in 1982—and this is by no means a complete list.

Several disasters were added in 1985, one of which seemed to alert the world to an awful increase in soccer violence. A fire in an old wooden grandstand at the stadium in Bradford, England, prior to a game on May 11 claimed the lives of 56 people, many of whom were elderly and unable to escape onto the playing field. The full horror of the fire that swept the stands in minutes, including the picture of a man aflame on the field, was witnessed by television audiences around the world. Ironically, the stadium lacked the tall fences installed on many fields to protect the players and the referee from the fans and thus many were able to save themselves from the fire by fleeing onto the field. Since the rear exits had been padlocked to prevent people who had not paid from entering, and there were no fire extinguishers, rushing onto the field was the only way the flames could be avoided.

In the investigation that followed there were reports of smoke bombs being thrown before the fire broke out and how members of "Ointment," a gang known for soccer violence, had purchased greenhouse fumigation devices before the game.

Almost eclipsed by the Bradford fire was a soccer riot in Birmingham on the same day in which hundreds of fans fought with police on the field leaving 1 dead, 17 injured, and 125 arrested.

But it was the riot at Heysel Stadium in Brussels on May 29 that was especially shocking. The game, in which teams from Liverpool and Turin played for the Cup of Champions, had not begun when the British fans left their section in the stands, pushed over a steel barrier surmounted by barbed wire that separated them from the Turin section, and attacked the Italian fans. In trying to escape, the Italians pressed against a retaining wall, which collapsed. Most of the Belgian police had been stationed outside the stadium and many of those inside were on the playing field, leaving too few to deal with the riot in the stands. Thirty-eight people died and more than two hundred were injured, most of them Italian fans.

Live television coverage showed scores of Italian fans crushed under a fallen barrier and lying in bloody heaps in the stands. In spite of the carnage, the authorities decided to go ahead with the game, perhaps fearing another eruption if the game was canceled, a fear possibly based on the memory of the referee's decision in Lima in 1964. Prime Minister Craxi of Italy protested the decision, but was told by his Belgian counterpart that the decision was made purely for reasons of security. One observer said watching the game was like dining in a restaurant where someone had just died. The Heysel Stadium incident was a considerable embarrassment to Great Britain, the once imperial country that had casually exported soccer and now seemed to be exporting soccer hooliganism. Prime Minister Thatcher expressed her disgust at the affair and announced that Britain would contribute $317,500 to a special fund for victims of the riot and families of the dead. Belgium barred British teams "until further notice," and the English Football Association prohibited English clubs from playing on the continent for one year.

The attention of the world now became focused on the violence of soccer. Of course, none of this was new, but it was one thing to read about it in the back pages of the newspaper and quite another to sit in your living room and actually see the blood, to see fans crushed under a pile of bodies, to see hands held out as silent pleas for help, to hear the injured and dying crying out. More particularly, the phenomenon of

British hooliganism and soccer violence became a subject of public debate. A West German television station, which had shown an hour and a half of the melee but refused to broadcast the game, exclaimed, "Such horror at a soccer match has never been seen in European history. We find this violence unbelievable. What kind of people are these?"

What kind of people, indeed, and why do they behave the way they do? The answers tend to cluster around four points: (1) the nature of the game evokes violence; (2) the social conditioning of the fans and crowd psychology lead in the same direction; (3) the media encourage such behavior; and (4) the very design of the stadium is a contributing factor.

Is there something about the game itself that stimulates violence in its observers? On the surface it would appear to be a harmless athletic contest. David Cort in *The Nation* compared it to some other kinds of team sports. Baseball, in his view, lacks passion because of its restrictive rules; in football the passion is open but melodramatic; basketball is "made somewhat comic by bare skin and the preternaturally tall boys slapping one another." In soccer, however, he sees

> a faceless rabble rushing up and down the field. Long-distance runners caught in a squirrel cage, the players pant out the long scramble to nowhere. These are the disinherited of the earth. A soccer game can be compared only to forms of frantic insect activity. It takes a scientist to tell which ants are eating which . . . the game remains a confused hurly-burly. Perhaps that is why it leads to patriotic riots. Since one's own side is ignominious, one cannot possibly afford to give the ignominious opponents any magnanimous admiration. The fans hate the enemy without qualification. Life is symbolized as a mean, desperate, endless, exhausting, futile shambles, as in fact life is in many of the 131 countries where soccer is played.

Partly on target, partly off, Cort seems to have missed the essentially interruptive, if not static, nature of baseball and football. Action occurs intermittently, and if it is explosive, it is both preceded and followed by relatively long spells in which nothing happens. This view was colorfully expressed by Soviet Premier Khrushchev when, asked what he thought of the first American football game he saw, he said, "All fall down, all get up. All fall down, all get up." Even basketball, a game in which play is more continuous, is interrupted every few seconds by a score or a foul.

Clive Toye, an authority on soccer, sees something in the game uniquely inflammatory. In his opinion, "Soccer simply lends itself as the perfect nucleus around which violence and tragedy can be built, offering, as it does, passion, proximity, and primitive conditions as fuel for the savagery. Its passion stems from the nature of the game in which inches and seconds turn fans from despair to joy to despair again. Missing is the more measured attack on the emotions of most other team sports in which there are set plays and times out to give tempers a rest." Yet the rhythm of a game or the continuous movement of its play hardly seem related to its potential for eliciting violence among its spectators, and inches and seconds that take fans from despair to joy to despair can be found in other team games.

Even further afield was the analysis of Michael Novak of the American Enterprise Institute who suggested that soccer breeds violence because it is played with the feet, a frustrating procedure in a manually oriented manufacturing world.

A more plausible explanation was offered by George Orwell: Soccer is "war minus the shooting." Orwell, reflecting on a 1945 tour of Britain by a Moscow soccer team, which even then was marked by fighting and animosity, wrote

> I am always amazed when I hear people saying that sport creates goodwill between the nations, and that if only the common peoples of the world could meet one another at football or cricket, they would have no inclination to meet on the battlefield. . . . At the international level, sport is frankly mimic warfare. But the significant thing is not the behavior of the players but the attitude of the spectator; and, behind the spectators, of the nations who work themselves into furies over these absurd contests, and seriously believe—at any rate for short periods—that running, jumping, and kicking a ball are tests of national virtue. . . . As soon as strong feelings of rivalry are aroused,

the notion of playing the game according to the rules always vanishes. People want to see one side on top and the other side humiliated and they forget that victory gained through cheating or through the intervention of the crowd is meaningless. Even when the spectators don't intervene physically they try to influence the game by cheering their own side and "rattling" opposing players with boos and insults. Serious sport has nothing to do with fair play. It is bound up with hatred, jealousy, boastfulness, disregard of all rules, and sadistic pleasure in witnessing violence. . . . If you wanted to add to the vast fund of ill will existing in the world at this moment, you could hardly do it better than by a series of football matches between Jews and Arabs, Germans and Czechs, Indians and British, Russians and Poles, and Italians and Yugoslavs, each match to be watched by a mixed audience of 10,000 spectators.

Orwell is right, and his truth encompasses not only soccer but other organized sports as well. Most notably, it applies to the quadrennial Olympics, which have long been a testing ground for national pride and a place for settling old grievances. One of the more indelible images from these games is of the water polo match between Hungary and the Soviet Union in the 1956 Olympics. Played just after the Russians had brutally crushed the Hungarian revolt, it was simply an extension of that conflict and turned the water red with blood. Anyone persuaded of the correctness of Orwell's analysis can hardly avoid the conclusion that the wonderfully entertaining Olympic games also add to that vast fund of ill will in the world. And since preparations for the momentous World Cup and the Olympics both begin so far in advance of the final contests, which are separated from each other by two years, these two huge tournaments are always in the public eye. Orwell's truth is undiminished by its application to other sporting events, however, and goes far toward answering our first inquiry simply because the war without shooting that is soccer is played so widely and has such a great and dedicated following.

A different view was expressed by Sir Norman Chester, the deputy chairman of the Football Trust. The violence of English football, in his opinion, was due not to the play of the game but to such external circumstances as its ability to draw crowds from the lower classes; the practice of large groups of fans traveling to games in other cities, leading to confrontation between home and visiting fans; and the league organization, which emphasizes winning. While undoubtedly valid, these considerations seem rather secondary and may be more effect than cause.

An investigation into the social background of the spectators and the psychology of the crowd yields an abundance of theories. Especially since the events of 1985, the subject of soccer violence has given rise to a variety of explanations from these perspectives, almost all of which seem plausible, if not compelling.

A French psychiatrist attributed the violence of English soccer fans to the English cultural characteristic of keeping a stiff upper lip and denying violence. The country's soccer fans were especially violent, according to him, because they were reacting to the national denial of violence.

Unemployment was often cited as an underlying cause giving rise to frustrations that were released at the football stadium. In 1985, it was pointed out, the British unemployment rate was 13.5 percent, rising to 25 percent in Liverpool, a city in which half of the twelve thousand members of the largest soccer fan club were then unemployed. It has been noted that support for local soccer teams is strongest in those cities with the highest levels of crime and unemployment, the game apparently providing a source of group pride for people who have been relegated to the sidelines of society. Among them fighting is one of the few sources of excitement, meaning, and status available. A 1980 study of British soccer hooliganism found that 80 percent of those charged with soccer-related crimes were either unemployed or manual workers.

The fact that most of the soccer rowdies are young men has received considerable attention. The inadequacy of outlets for youthful energies was one explanation. Others saw a similarity with the youth gangs in some American cities, the soccer fan clubs providing both a sense of belonging and, when fighting began, anonymity. Like the street gangs of Chicago and New York, too, the soccer fan clubs featured dress codes, proprietary phrases, and other elements indicative of a strong organization. One Chelsea club calls itself "The

Anti-Personnel Firm." After they attack rival fans they leave gold-embossed calling cards that read, "Nothing personal—you have been serviced by the Anti-Personnel Firm." Manchester United fans chant, "We hate humans!" Millwall supporters have a different chant: "Nobody likes us! We don't care! 'Cause we are Millwall! Mill-WALL!" The Birmingham City Zulu Warriors emit a Zulu cry while on the attack and leave business cards with their victims reading, "Zapped by a Zulu." The cards of the Chelsea Headhunters state, "You have been nominated and dealt with by the Chelsea Headhunters." The members of another club wear surgical masks while on the attack.

The prominence of British fans in these annals of violence is deserved (on the continent it is called "the English disease"), but should not be understood as an exclusive franchise. Among Dutch and German youth there is a similar pride in fighting at soccer matches and riots have occurred in Spain, France, and Italy.

Eric Dunning studied English violence at European soccer games for years and linked up the predilection for fighting with "a close identification with the local community. They fight on behalf of their community against other comparable communities. . . . There is a sense of ownership of territory even though it is temporary." An expert on political violence stressed the human need to belong to a group: In the past young men went to war, an activity that provided purpose and excitement. Soccer now fills this void.

Class friction was advanced as another explanation. Auberon Waugh, in *The Spectator,* spoke for many: "We have always known there were two Britains, one extraordinarily mild and pleasant, inhabited by mild, tolerant, kindly people, the other utterly disgusting, inhabited by brutal, malevolent louts." Also cited was the restlessness of the lower middle classes, a condition that had earlier produced such youth problems as Teddy boys, skinheads, mods, and rockers.

Drinking before and after the game was frequently deplored. In Brussels the Liverpool fans had been drinking throughout the day before the evening match. Alcohol is known to inhibit one's judgment and to provide a ready excuse for behavior that the same person would normally suppress while sober. In support of this explanation it was pointed out that the banning of alcohol at games in Scotland considerably reduced incidents of violence.

The tone and circumstances of the game itself may induce violence. Cheering and shouting can be seen as a kind of aggression that can escalate into more overt, physical action. Dr. Jeffrey H. Goldstein, a Temple University psychology professor, saw in the violence at a soccer match the end result of a chain of aggression that had started much earlier. The spectators, seeing an aggressive sport, tend to become more aggressive themselves. Although he also cited high unemployment as a contributing factor, the main cause was "nationalism pure and simple. . . . In an era of instant communication, people increasingly are making nationalist issues of international sporting events . . . [which] have become tests of the rightness or wrongness of ideology." The same theme was echoed by Dr. Thomas A. Tutko, a professor of psychology at San Jose State University: In the relative absence of wars "it has been the athletes who have taken the identities of warriors, especially so at international sports events . . . the riots go beyond soccer in that many fans sense that coming under challenge— and perhaps defeat—is their whole concept of what they stand for and agree with." If these thoughts seem familiar, they should, because they partake of the same larger idea that George Orwell expressed four decades earlier: Soccer is war without the shooting.

In short it was a field day for academics, politicians, journalists, and almost anyone who had access to a public pulpit. Not everyone was convinced that soccer violence was a serious issue, much less a national or even an international problem, however. Anthropologist Desmond Morris, author of *The Naked Ape*, pooh-poohed it as "ritual rowdiness" with little or no bloodletting, merely threat displays as in the animal world. He saw in soccer fanaticism "quasi-religious elements and trappings of churchgoing as it used to be: the chanting, special costumes, rhythmic clapping and the rest." The singing of the Liverpool end-zone crowd reminded him of a cathedral choir.

The *Times* of London took a similarly tranquil view: "In the array of issues confronting the British government in 1985, soccer violence should not bulk large. A more relaxed administration might indeed— without in any way condoning gross offense against public order outside sports grounds—see some function in the rituals and crowd activity of the big urban soccer clubs. For government to take unto itself the capacity to prevent sporadic local outbursts smacks of the nanny state at its most cloying." This editorial appeared in April 1985. After the events of the following month the *Times* changed position; declaring the game of soccer as good as dead, it abandoned its lofty petulance about nanny intervention.

Conspicuous by its absence in the debate was the name of Gustave Le Bon (1841–1931), the acknowledged founder of social psychology, whose *The Psychology of the Crowd* was a pioneering work and one that helps to understand soccer violence. First published in 1895, *The Psychology of the Crowd* even then declared, "The substitution of the unconscious action of crowds for the conscious action of individuals is one of the principal characteristics of the present age," and "The age we are about to enter will in truth be the *era of crowds*." Le Bon saw that in a crowd the individual's personality tends to disappear and a collective mind forms, "a single being . . . subject to the law of the mental unity of crowds." Three factors give rise to this phenomenon of the crowd as a separate psychological entity: (1) the individual's feelings of invincible power, allowing him to yield to instincts that he would otherwise have restrained, due to the anonymity of the crowd and immunity from responsibility; (2) the contagion of acts and feelings characteristic of a crowd; and (3) suggestibility, of which contagion is a result. "By the mere fact that he forms part of an organized crowd," Le Bon points out, "a man descends several rungs in the ladder of civilization. Isolated, he may be a cultivated individual; in a crowd, he is a barbarian—that is, a creature acting by instinct." Almost a century old, these thoughts are still compelling, and we might imagine Le Bon at Heysel Stadium in 1985, Lima in 1964, or many other soccer games for that matter, looking on with a sad but knowing expression.

The media's responsibility for soccer violence gives rise to much narrower issues. Newspaper accounts of damage done to railroad trains by fans traveling to and from soccer matches in the 1950s gave the phenomenon an unfortunate prominence against a background of disorderly youths, which seemed one of society's more serious problems. Television followed and soon it seemed as if fights and other disturbances were part of the sport. James Walvin, who has written several books on the social aspects of soccer, is especially critical of television. He notes the increasing frequency of rowdy incidents at soccer in England since 1960 and connects it to the growth in ownership of television sets. With television covering more and more of the events both on and off the field, the home audience began to see behavior that was inspired by the presence of the cameras. Not only had the stadium terraces become a stage on which fans could act out their team loyalties and demonstrate their pugnacity, it was even possible to see themselves on the screen at home later on. Television had this effect on other public events, Walvin admits, but soccer was especially vulnerable because of its regularity, its ubiquity, and its international nature.

Finally, stadium design comes in for its share of blame. Terraces where rabidly partisan fans are forced to stand for up to three hours packed tightly together can hardly contribute to anything but frayed tempers and belligerent possibilities. Sir Philip Goodhart, a Conservative Member of Parliament, was of the opinion that there is relatively less violence at sporting events in the United States because its stadiums accommodate far fewer standees; seated crowds are less likely to riot. Such features as the locked exit doors at the stadium in Lima, the old wooden stands at the Bradford stadium, the inadequate fence separating rival fans, and the too easily demolished brick wall at Brussels all contributed to those disasters. Even those design modifications intended to avert or curtail it led subtly, but powerfully, to violence. Segregating opposing fans may seem to protect them from each other, but it also establishes dangerous borders and creates feelings of territoriality that too easily encourage warlike thoughts. The high fences or moats that surround many fields do insulate players and referees from irate fans, but are also omnipresent reminders of what has happened in the past as well as the likelihood of recurrence.

Lesley Hazleton, a British professor transplanted to the United States for ten years, attended a match between Arsenal and Manchester United in North London on her return, and was appalled at both the conduct of the fans and the manner in which they were processed. Police surrounded the field. The lowest price admission was to the terraces—huge, open structures where fans were required to stand throughout the game. Those who entered the terrace turnstiles were frisked by the police for weapons. Because of the crowds there and the reluctance to surrender a good location, urinating in place was common. Manchester United fans were confined to one end of the field, Arsenal fans to the other. In each of the two terraces the fans were penned in between high steel fences, and the terrace was bordered by empty concrete strips that served as buffer zones. At game's end the visiting fans from Manchester were not permitted to exit at first. Hundreds of police, some mounted, others with dogs, controlled the railroad station and cleared the street leading to it from the stadium. With a low-flying helicopter overhead directing a powerful searchlight on the evening scene, Arsenal fans were led out of the stadium and placed aboard a train. Only when that train had departed and the station platform was again empty did the police bring out groups of Manchester fans for the next train. In that way, alternating trains between the two rival groups of fans, the police hoped to maintain complete separation and avoid any rowdyism.

The events of 1985, culminating in the incidents at Bradford and Brussels, may have shocked the world, but they were actually part of a trend that had long been in operation. For years, too, stadium and club managements and government officials had been struggling to deal with the problem of soccer violence. In South America it was common to create a moat around the playing field to protect the players and the referee from the fans. As late as the 1960s this seemed preposterous to the English, an attitude that has since disappeared. By 1974, Sports Minister Denis Howell recommended that the same kind of dry moat be constructed in English stadiums to protect those on the pitch. Many stadiums also rely on high fences. The eight stadiums in Buenos Aires, for example, enclose their playing fields with twelve-foot-high wire fences topped by barbed wire.

In England in 1989 five hundred police were assigned to certain soccer matches where violence was anticipated and as many as one thousand were deployed for the worst games. For the oldest spectators among the soccer-loving part of the population this was a far cry indeed from the old days. In 1923, a single policeman on a white horse was sufficient to clear thousands of fans from the field at London's Wembley Stadium. Now tear gas and trained dogs are routinely provided, and closed circuit television monitors and metal detectors are standard installations. In Africa, when Zaire and the Congo play, military forces are required to patrol the field. One referee assigned in 1984 to the European Cup final in Rome, between Rome and Liverpool, decided that three thousand police were not enough and engaged a group of karate experts to provide more protection.

But force and walls were not the only techniques tried. In Birmingham City the local club arranged for a parade of attractive girls in miniskirts during intermission in the hope that truculent males would be diverted. After the national embarrassment of the antiforeigner riot in Peking when Hong Kong defeated China, the Chinese government announced that in the future prizes would be given to the most decorous crowds.

In Argentina, after a number of small-scale soccer riots in a period of several weeks in 1955 that could be quelled only by firemen with hoses and police with tear gas, the Football Association announced that games would henceforth begin at 7:45 in the morning, in order to avoid the "incendiary qualities of the afternoon heat" and the spectators' temperament. The sale of soda pop was also prohibited in order to deprive fans of the bottles, which were one of their favorite forms of ammunition, although the large chunks of cheese that spectators brought to the game and also used as missiles were not banned. How effective these changes were is not clear, but twelve years later the newspaper *Cronica*, after listing the incidents of violence of the previous Saturday, was still struck by the "climate of exasperation, irascibility, and lack of attention" at soccer games. When a really partisan crowd was aroused it was noted that none of the aforementioned methods moat, high wire fence, or mounted police could hold it back. Then the fire brigade was called in.

In England other remedial steps were taken. Special football trains to away games were eliminated and some clubs with particularly aggressive fans were required to play certain games away from their home fields. Mindful of the territorial basis of fan hostility, the authorities have also removed some games to a completely neutral site, as was done in the third game of the elimination match between Honduras and El Salvador in 1969. A related tactic was unveiled in connection with the 1990 World Cup. While the final was scheduled for Rome, and most preliminary matches were held at other major Italian cities, the English team, with its feared hooligans, was required to play its first three matches at Cagliari on the island of Sardinia. Because the city could be reached only by ship or plane, it was hoped that better control could be maintained over the eight thousand genuine fans and five hundred hooligans expected from England. Unfortunately, the schedule called for England to play the Netherlands in the third round, a team also noted for the rowdyism of some of its fans.

By the spring of 1987 the ninety-two professional English soccer clubs announced the latest proposal for controlling hooliganism: One-half of the stadium would be set aside for hometown fans, and visiting fans, as Ms. Hazleton observed, were to be kept separate from the local group. In addition, a membership identity card system was to be instituted in the hope that it would better enable the police to identify and control the rowdy fans.

But an evil spirit sometimes seems to be monitoring the game of soccer, ever ready to turn events to its malign purposes. It is possible to see in the history of the game how that spirit made the playing field the venue for conflicting nationalistic passions, ethnic loyalties, and other allegiances. Later it was the breeding ground for soccer hooligans who may have begun their belligerent activities at the stadiums and based them on club loyalties, but eventually embarked on random violence hardly connected to the game at all. And all along, that evil spirit was active in stirring up mad stampedes and blind mob activities. It must have been that same evil spirit that caused the disaster at the Hillsborough stadium in Sheffield, England, on April 15, 1989.

Scheduled for 3 P.M., the game involved the Liverpool and Nottingham Forest teams and was to be played at the neutral Sheffield site. Although Liverpool was known to have many more fans than Nottingham Forest, both groups received the same number of tickets. With the stadium sold out, a large crowd appeared at the end that led to the terraces reserved for the Liverpool fans. Many Liverpool fans apparently had shown up without tickets in the hope that somehow they could gain admission at the last minute. Police trying to control that outside crowd grew fearful of what one called a "life-threatening" crush. The crowd was so forceful that a police horse was lifted off the ground. When it appeared to the police commander that the enormous pressure of this crowd of screaming fans might cause a wall to collapse and crush many people, he decided to open the gate to the terrace just as the whistle blew to signal the start of the game.

The excited crowd rushed forward into the stadium, creating an irresistible human tidal wave that drove into those fans already on the jammed terrace, forcing them forward. Separating the terrace from the playing field was a strong ten-foot-high steel fence that had been erected to keep fans from entering the field. To ensure that it could not be climbed, the top of the fence was bent back in the direction of the terrace. Those nearest to the fence were now driven helplessly into it, many being crushed to death. Others were trampled. Television and newspaper pictures showed horrible scenes of fans being pressed into the metal squares of the fence in agony. While at the entrance fans continued to push in, unmindful of what effect they were having, at the front of the terrace people were screaming for help and others were seen on the ground, their faces turning blue. Because of the fence's design it was impossible to escape by climbing over it. Ninety-three died and some two hundred were injured in the disaster, the worst in British sporting history.

It was a terrible irony that the fence, specifically designed to curb fan violence, had been so obviously responsible for the casualties. There was the additional irony that the victims were Liverpool fans, the same group that four years earlier had a part in the Brussels calamity.

If it sometimes seems that all who attend soccer stadiums are either wild-eyed barbarians bent on violence or mindless candidates for a stampede, one American traveler in Italy has given testimony to some exceptions. While at a game in Trieste, he found himself next to a man who was accompanied by two monkeys. They were rather large, about three feet tall, with long tails and intelligent faces. Their attention seemed to be focused on the playing field and they were well behaved. At halftime the man gave them each a banana, which they ate slowly. Before the end of the game they left, perhaps in order to avoid the crowd.

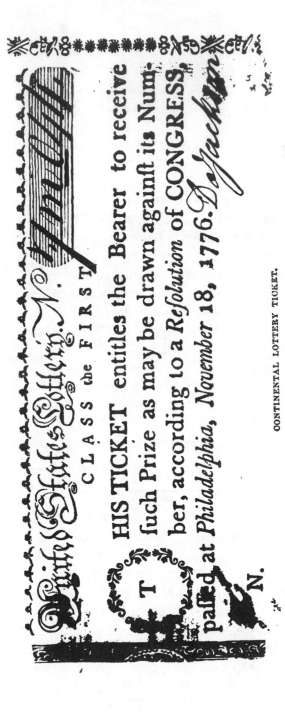

United States Lottery. N.º *Wm Cliff*

CLASS the FIRST

T

HIS TICKET entitles the Bearer to receive fuch Prize as may be drawn againft its Number, according to a *Refolution* of CONGRESS, paffed at *Philadelphia, November 18, 1776. Do Juckfon*

N.

CONTINENTAL LOTTERY TICKET.

LOTTERIES 7

> The Lottery, with its weekly
> pay-out of enormous prizes,
> was the one public event to which the
> Proles paid serious attention. It
> was probable that there were some
> millions of Proles for whom the
> Lottery was the principal if not
> the only reason for remaining alive.
> It was their delight, their folly,
> their anodyne, their intellectual
> stimulant. Where the Lottery was
> concerned, even people who could
> barely read and write seemed
> capable of intricate calculations
> and staggering feats of memory.
> There was a whole tribe of men
> who made a living simply by
> selling systems, forecasts
> and lucky amulets.
> —George Orwell, *1984*

The United States' third love affair with lotteries began in 1964 when New Hampshire launched the first state-run lottery of the modern era. New York followed in 1967 and by 1990 twenty-eight states, the District of Columbia, and two United States territories were in the business. With aggregate annual sales of lottery tickets running about $17 billion and advertising expenditures approaching $200 million, this unique, state-operated monopoly had quickly become one of the largest industries in the nation. When the New York lottery offered a jackpot of

$45 million in December 1988, 37.4 million tickets were sold in three days. The number of people participating was equally impressive. The word *lottomania* began to appear in the press, and columnist George F. Will, aghast at the size of the states' bookie operations and the energy and imagination with which they were promoted, declared sententiously, "Once upon a time, mass irrationality was considered a menace to democratic government. In this age of lotteries, manufacturing mobs is a government goal and mass hysteria is an important ingredient of public finance."

The lottery concept is old and rich in dramatic potential. It figures frequently and significantly in the Bible and its imaginative possibilities are still being mined by modern storytellers. The longer history of the lottery is relevant principally as background since the form we are discussing is of relatively recent vintage. The Bible contains twenty-one references to the use of lots as a selection method, eighteen of which are in the Old Testament. Moses, for example, was instructed by the Lord to take a census of the people of Israel and divide the land among them by lot. (Numbers 26:55–56) The replacement of the apostle Judas, who had hung himself, by Matthias was effected by lots, the other apostles appealing to the Lord to show them which of the two candidates He had chosen. In Periclean Athens the members of the Council were chosen by lot, and the same procedure was used to select the presiding officer who would serve for one day only. Such an unpredictable election gave assurance that the officeholder's exercise of his great powers would be free of bribery and corruption. Among the reforms instituted by Solon in Athens in the sixth century B.C., the jury system involved the selection of citizens by lots to sit and decide cases.

Far from indicating the Divine Mind or selecting the head of the council or a jury, the lottery was exploited for purposes of amusement in Imperial Rome, where Augustus and Nero used it as a device for giving away property and slaves during Saturnalian feasts and other entertainments.

Organized commercial lotteries first appeared in Europe in the fifteenth century in towns in Burgundy and Brussels for the purpose of raising money for the poor and to fortify defenses. Between 1520 and

1539 Francis I of France authorized both public and private lotteries in several cities. But the prizes in these early ventures consisted of property, and it was not until the lottery in Florence in 1530 that money was offered. This innovation was such a success that it spread to other Italian cities. With the unification of Italy, the first national lottery was created in 1863 to provide income for the state. Lotteries remained popular in France until the reign of Louis XIV when the king himself and several members of his court won the top prizes in a drawing. Whether this was coincidence or contrivance, the event created such suspicion among the public that the king returned the money for redistribution and lotteries fell out of favor.

In England the course of the development of the institution influenced the American experience. Queen Elizabeth I chartered a general lottery in 1566, to raise funds for harbor repairs and other public purposes, which had some unusual features. The grand prize of 5,000 pounds was followed by lesser prizes, partly in cash, partly in goods, and the lottery was advertised as being "without any blanckes," which meant that each of the 40,000 tickets would return at least a quarter of their value (10 shillings) in cash or goods. Furthermore, ticket buyers were to be free from arrest for seven days for any except major crimes, a guaranty which probably led to many a footrace between criminals and the sheriff's men to the lottery ticket office.

In spite of these attractions, the tickets, which were first offered on August 23, 1567, did not sell. To stimulate buying, the lord mayor of London posted a notice in September guaranteeing the honesty of the lottery, but that, too, was ineffective. By January 3, 1568, the queen postponed the drawing because of lack of interest. Other efforts followed, but it was not until January 11, 1569, that the drawing was finally held.

The seventeenth and eighteenth centuries witnessed a lottery boom in England in which the government came to rely more and more heavily on the device for purposes of revenue. New techniques were developed for their promotion, and their influence spread throughout society. The Virginia Company held a lottery in 1612 to provide supplies for the colony in the New World. With a first prize of 4,000 crowns' worth of silver plate, this lottery offered special extra chances for those who bought quantities of tickets. Churches were among the larger investors. Other lotteries were held for such public projects as waterworks, church buildings, charities, roads, and fisheries, and to pay the English soldiers.

Cromwell and the Puritans suppressed lotteries, but they reappeared when Charles II was restored to the throne, and continued to grow in popularity. By 1693 the government had turned to the lottery to raise money for a war against France. Attendant upon the growth of lotteries was the growth of abuses. The preamble to an act of Parliament in 1699 that banned such draws for ten years referred to "evil-disposed persons" who "set up many mischievous and unlawful games called *lotteries* . . . and have thereby most unjustly and fraudulently got to themselves great sums of money from the children and servants of several gentlemen, traders and merchants, and from other unwary persons, to the utter ruin and impoverishment of many families . . . by cover of several patents or grants under the great seal of England for the said lotteries." After the ban expired, private lotteries were held until 1739 when they were finally prohibited by Parliament, but public lotteries continued to be used, notably for the building of Westminster Bridge in 1739 and the British Museum in 1753.

Because of abuses, a rising chorus of complaints that, among other things, lotteries encouraged mass gambling, and the view that the national glory was ill served by a system of public finance that relied on such schemes, all lotteries were finally banned by Parliament in 1826. By that time the income tax had been developed as a more dependable method of producing revenue and the lottery had long since established itself across the ocean in America.

The institution was well known in this country even before the Revolution. Private lotteries seem to have appeared first as a means of selling larger properties at a time when currency was in short supply. With the exception of the Quakers, who vigorously and continuously opposed them on moral grounds, religious groups not only acquiesced in the use of lotteries but commonly availed themselves of the device to raise money. While such activities were increasingly used to pay for public works, more and more local legislators were persuaded of the social evils of unregulated lotteries, and laws prohibiting unlicensed drawings were adopted in many of the colonies.

America's experience with this form of gambling was quite extensive up to the Revolution. And while there were critics, there was a consensus that the technique was morally acceptable and politically necessary. In the development of that consensus a key part was played by the silence of the clergy, a silence that undoubtedly was induced by the fact that the church was frequently the beneficiary of the games. Lest this seem too much like bribery, it should be noted that there was an ongoing debate which continued after the Revolution over whether lotteries were acknowledged and approved by the Bible or whether they were inimical to the broader principles of faith expressed there.

Since recourse to the institution to meet war expenses characterized the colonial period, it was to be expected that the lottery would be put to similar uses during the Revolution. Two months after the British defeated Washington at New York City, the Continental Congress authorized a lottery to raise funds for the military. All but the smallest prizes were payable in treasury bank notes redeemable in five years, a feature designed to maximize the amount of cash produced by the lottery and an early model for the present practice by which states provide annuities rather than immediate cash payments to winners. Tickets for this lottery initially sold well, but interest in it then faltered and the government did not make much on it.

The states also authorized lotteries to help the fight for independence, and private lotteries for other purposes continued to be held. British forces in this country also put the game to use.

With the surrender at Yorktown in 1781 and the emergence of the new nation, a flood of new drawings took place, produced in part by unsettled financial conditions and the inability to raise money by taxation. Over the next thirteen years about one hundred lotteries were initiated for such purposes as bridges, hospitals, schools, Harvard and Dartmouth colleges, the improvement of river navigation, roads and streets, mills and factories. That inveterate lottery player, George Washington, the first president of the United States, purchased twenty tickets at six shillings each in the 1789 Virginia lottery, which raised money to pave the streets of Alexandria.

In spite of an economic depression, the War of 1812, and the panics of 1819 and 1837, the lottery continued to grow. Moral objections were muted, perhaps out of necessity: In the words of one clergyman, describing the purchase of a ticket by a church, the "devil's water was used to turn the Lord's mill." Two significant developments were the appearance of ticket brokers and ticket contractors. The brokers bought tickets in large quantities at a discount and resold them through shops and branch offices. By 1815 it was said that every town with a thousand people had such a middleman. The contractors took over the entire operation of a lottery for a fee, and used the network of brokers to distribute the tickets. Some writers have seen in these developments the primitive origins of the modern private banking and stock brokerage houses. Perhaps as a result of these brokers and managers, lotteries were promoted and their tickets sold across state lines so that what had been small localized drawings now became regional and national affairs. More energy and imagination were applied to the sale of tickets. Open accounts could be established at ticket agencies where prizes were credited and purchases debited monthly. Handbills were broadcast and street placards used. Newspaper advertising offering wealth to the greedy gullible proliferated. Some of the texts have an uncanny resemblance to present-day pitches: "Nothing venture, nothing have" (echoing New York's recent "You have to be in it to win it"); "Delays are dangerous"; "Now is the time to fill your bags." A broadside advertising the Harvard College Lottery in 1812 warned, in verse,

> That none can "reap who never sow,"
> Requires no argument to show;
> Alike 'tis clear—none Prizes gain
> Who never Plough the Lottery main.

One agent boasted of the winning tickets he had sold and referred to "that *tickling, pleasing,* painful sensation which always arises from having undrawn tickets in one's pockets." Another firm in Rhode Island noted that " 'The demand receives its lustre from the labor bestowed on it'; and the many capital prizes sold by G & D [the selling agent] are like so many lottery stars, which will be considered by the knowing ones of primary magnitude and brightness." One seller recounted recent experiments in which a blind person could be made to see flashes of light by bringing him in contact with a voltaic pile. "In like manner, a person in the gloom of poverty may be made to perceive very lively and numerous flashes (say 20,000) of good fortune by bringing one extremity of a ragged bank bill into communication with the Book-Store and the other with the Lottery-Office, one door west of Central Building." Agents often advised the public to buy now since ticket prices would be increased later.

Sales of ticket fractions and sales on the installment plan were possible and one could even lease a ticket for a day. If it was drawn, then the lessee became the winner; if not, it was returned to the office. As the game grew more complicated, opportunities for sharp dealing proved irresistible to the unscrupulous. Many vendors sold more fractions than were contained in a ticket, including one in New York who sold nineteen eighths of a ticket that turned out to be a winner. Others sold numbers which could not win.

"Insurance," or "Policy," was common by the nineteenth century. Since the drawing of tickets could extend over weeks and even months, bets were made on whether a certain number would be drawn the following day. This practice, seen already in the English lotteries, became a common adjunct and evolved into the illegal "Numbers" and "Policy"* games of the modern era. Insurance was lucrative for the ticket agents and the source of many complaints. Neither the managers who operated the lottery nor the game's beneficiary received any of the money bet in this fashion. To end the practice new procedures were adopted in the 1820s to shorten the drawings, but they were not effective and some of the states took legislative action to outlaw it.

---

*Policy should be distinguished from Numbers, which first appeared in the 1920s and went on to become the main illegal lottery in New York and other Northeast cities. In Policy a three-digit number, often taken from the handle, or total amount wagered, at local race tracks, or the payoffs at certain races, was drawn daily. Small bets were possible, a system of runners was used, and payoffs were immediate. Like Policy, Numbers led to a proliferation of techniques for picking a winner, usually based on dreams or arcane associations. While these superstitions may have been irrational, they nevertheless suggested to players formulas for winning, encouraging them to believe they had a measure of control over the outcome. Numbers has not only survived the advent of state lotteries but has served as the model for one of the successful games offered by the state lottery agencies.

*   *   *

In the new era of prosperity that followed independence the federal government decided to enter the lottery business. When, in 1792, ordinary revenues proved inadequate, Congress authorized the corporation governing the proposed capital city of Washington, D.C., to institute lotteries for important civic purposes. The two games that were organized proved failures, however, and the promoter lost everything as a result of litigation.

Nevertheless, the subsequent period from 1790 to 1860 saw approximately 130 separate lotteries by the states for public purposes excluding those for schools and transportation improvements. In a variation of this theme, permission was sometimes sought to use the lottery procedure in order to sell property, the seller receiving a portion of the revenue and the property offered as the prize. Notable among the instances of this use is the petition of Thomas Jefferson. Although he had been a lottery opponent, he found himself heavily in debt in his eighties, and, unable to sell his real property, he appealed to the Virginia Legislature for a lottery license to facilitate the sale. His petition is eloquent in defense of the lottery as both a substitute for taxation and a means of selling unique property, but when read together with his listing of the offices he had held and the services he had rendered, and considered in relation to his previous long hostility to the idea, it verges on the pathetic. Approved after considerable resistance in the legislature, the Jefferson lottery was not successful. Even though the governor presided at public meetings of the lottery, it was a time of economic depression and sales were disappointing. Eventually, public subscription to support Jefferson seemed to make the lottery irrelevant, and it was abandoned.

Louisiana went even further with respect to such property raffles, permitting anyone to dispose of his property in this manner from 1826 to 1841 if the state treasurer appraised it and two percent of the appraised value was paid into the state treasury.

The flood tide of lottery activity occurred in the last decade of the eighteenth and the first decades of the nineteenth centuries when, according to one historian, there was a wheel in "every city and town large enough to boast a court-house and a jail. . . . The State of the Wheel became as regular an item in the papers as the ship-news or prices current." A Pennsylvania newspaper commented on August 24, 1790, that "The lottery mania appears to rage with uncommon violence." A year later a Boston paper said, "Every part of the United States abounds in lotteries." Massachusetts especially was a hotbed. A clergyman in Salem reported how five lotteries were in progress at one time in 1790, ticket sales proceeding "amazing rapid, hundreds sell at a time for speculation, and there is hardly a person who is not an adventurer, and sometimes large parties buy conjointly so as to pay themselves their money again." A special edition of a newspaper was issued just to announce the winners of one game.

In New York City revelations of fraud in the conduct of lotteries had only a temporary effect, and in spite of tighter state regulations and a constitutional prohibition of all but existing games, by 1825 a contemporary wrote, "If the city did not appear like a huge lottery office, with innumerable departments, it was because the citizens were too excited by the rage for moneymaking to see it as it really was." There were reported to be more than 160 lottery offices in the city, and in 1827 one newspaper described the impression formed by visitors that "one half of the citizens get their living by affording the opportunity to gamble to the rest." A British traveler in 1833 was astonished at the hordes and style of lottery agents: "They are numberless in Broadway. Their puffing exceeds all belief. Each collector called heaven and earth to witness that he was the luckiest among his worthy colleagues. One of them went so far as to affirm that he had paid prizes to a larger amount than would liquidate all the debts of bankrupts in the United States."

As the idea of America as the land of opportunity became popular, so did the corollary notion that the likely path to superiority and distinction was by wealth. And if getting-rich-quick was a major theme, the lottery was the obvious instrument. "The desire to grow rich, and to grow rich rapidly, are the besetting sins of our country," wrote one government official after the War of 1812. A similar view was expressed in 1840 by Professor W. G. Goddard of Brown University:

> Lotteries . . . are rendered especially mischievous in this country by the nature of our institutions, and by the spirit of the times. Here, the path of eminence being open to everyone—but too many are morbidly anxious to improve their condition; and by means, too, which in the wisdom of Providence were never intended to command success. A mad desire for wealth pervades all classes. . . . It generates a spirit of reckless speculation; it corrupts the simplicity of our tastes; and . . . it impairs not infrequently . . . the obligations of common honesty. Upon these elements of our social condition and character, the Lottery system operates with malignant efficacy. . . .

Opposition at this time was intermittent and ineffective to curb the public's enthusiasm, even though some raffles failed either through poor management or a disenchantment caused by surfeit. A division of opinion characterized ecclesiastic institutions: On the one hand they were among the more numerous of the beneficiaries; on the other hand the means of producing those benefits were morally questionable. While the religious authorities waffled, there were isolated incidents that indicated their quandary. The records of the James Street Methodist Church of New York show the disbursement of funds for the purchase of a ticket in 1790. In 1813 the Missionary Society of New York was forced to search its conscience when a ticket turned up in the contribution box. After a long discussion, a final decision was deferred until after the drawing.

Slowly, however, criticism began to appear in newspapers and periodicals. The Philadelphia *Eye* ran a series in 1808 assailing lotteries, bemoaning, in the first of the pieces, that "even the clergy . . . have forsaken us" and "have permitted the ends to justify the means, and flourishing churches have been raised by iniquitous lotteries." In 1818 the *New York Post* took a strong anti-lottery stand, and in 1827 not only reaffirmed its position but refused to carry lottery advertising. *Niles Weekly Register* in 1826 assailed the games as "always objectionable" and a "fraud upon the oppression of the poor and unreflecting." In 1818 the Society for the Prevention of Pauperism in the City of New York placed lotteries second in a list of the principal causes of poverty, just after drink, a ranking endorsed by the Baltimore branch of the organization three years later. In a popular book satirizing lotteries written from a broker's point of view Thomas Mann said, "The Broker's wealth is the Heart and Soul of the Beggar's Wallet; the amount spent around the country on every other kind of gambling was nothing compared to the lottery, which flourished because of that 'Little Flippant Thing' called *Fashion,* at whose Shrine are offered daily sacrifices, from the Crowned Monarch, down to the Hatless Vagrant."

The investigation of the lottery system by a New York legislative committee concluded by damning it, particularly the high commissions paid to salesmen to attract women, children, apprentices, servants, and the poorest and most ignorant, and found that the only aspect of such a system for raising money it could approve was "the cheerfulness with which it is paid." In Massachusetts in 1821 the disclosure that the managers of several lotteries had continued to draw eight more classes after the approved amount had been raised while the city, which was to be the beneficiary of the games, had still not received any money, went far toward organizing public opinion against the system. A grand jury investigating lotteries in New York City described them as "an evil of the most alarming nature, both in a moral and pecuniary point of view."

Such negative publicity had its effect in eroding public enthusiasm for lotteries. By April 1829 the managers of the Literature Lottery in New York were distressed when only 37½ percent of the tickets had been sold.

A spirit of reform that extended to all institutions in the decades beginning around 1830 helped consolidate the formerly sporadic criticism of lotteries and led eventually to their abolition. The fraud that seemed to attend all levels of the games and their negative social effects became the targets of the opposition, replacing the desultory debate over whether or not the Bible condoned lotteries.

In Pennsylvania, an anti-lottery drive spearheaded by the Quakers led to the first abolition law in 1833, followed quickly by similar legislation in Massachusetts. Other states moved to outlaw or restrict the games either by statute or constitution and by 1860 all but three states, Delaware, Kentucky, and Missouri, had done so. The battle to suppress lotteries was hard fought over some three decades, in part because the majority of the press was long sympathetic to them, a position attributable to the considerable advertising revenues brought in by lotteries.

But with the Civil War and the unsettled conditions that followed, there was a revival of lotteries. In some states the prohibitions were repealed, in others illegal activity increased and was overlooked. The Kentucky State Lottery became national in scope. A common strategy used by illegal operators in this period was to identify themselves as "gift companies," which purported to deal in straight merchandise sales. In such an offering there would be "gifts" of cash and merchandise and the purchaser of a chance would receive a sealed ticket describing his "purchase."

The mobilization of anti-lottery forces against this revival led to new victories on the state level, and new involvement by the federal government. In 1876 Congress made it unlawful to use the mails to carry any letters concerning any sort of lottery. Two years later the United States Supreme Court upheld the law in a case brought on when the Louisville, Kentucky, postmaster refused to deliver mail to a lottery company.

This should have been the end of the lottery system in the nation, but it was not. Instead, the demise of other lotteries by state action and the new postal ban, which eventually proved to be unworkable, combined to clear the way for the largest and most spectacular lottery of all. For decades the Louisiana lottery enjoyed a virtual national monopoly, which it exploited to the fullest and protected with such political skill that it often seemed indestructible.

By constitutional amendment Louisiana changed its policy and again authorized lotteries in 1864. Two years later the legislature granted the first license. The birth of the lottery destined to become an infamous giant among such schemes occurred in 1868. Its parent organization was a New York syndicate which had appeared in New Orleans in 1865 with Charles T. Howard and John A. Morris its principal operators. By bribing the carpetbagger Louisiana legislators, the group succeeded in obtaining a twenty-five-year charter, which gave them a monopoly on lotteries and tax exemption. While most lotteries were required to pay out in prizes three-quarters of the take, the Louisiana scheme gave the syndicate the right to retain a whopping half, and extracted an annual payment to the state of a mere $40,000.

Daily public drawings began on January 2, 1869, with two wheels initially under the supervision of a former state treasurer. From the start the operation was a phenomenal success. The first year's take of more than $1 million grew, before long, to an estimated $30 million to $60 million annually, of which—still—only $40,000 went to the state until 1890 when that payment was increased to $1,250,000. A year after its start, the Lottery Company had a branch in every major city in the country and there were agents almost everywhere in smaller cities, towns, and villages. It was estimated that 93 percent of its enormous revenues were generated outside of the state of Louisiana. In New Orleans by 1891 there were 108 places selling tickets. Lottery fever raged through the city. According to Peggy Robbins in *Smithsonian,* "The passion to 'play lottery' led to small thefts by servants and clerks, and big embezzlements by businessmen; bank depositors withdrew their savings to join the gamble; housewives boasted that they bought a ticket every single day; people chose numbers according to voodoo charts, dream predictions, their children's ages, the fish count in a catch, and the Pope's birthday; and priests were kept so busy blessing tickets brought to them by Catholics that the archbishop was compelled to forbid such practice."

Under Howard and Morris's direction the enterprise expanded enormously and consolidated its political influence. Bribes to legislators resulted in the increase of penalties for selling illegal tickets and the defeat of efforts to charter a rival company. The police, and most local newspapers as well, were said to be under Howard's control, and the company was active and effective in securing the election to office of people sympathetic to its aims.

Such power eventually led to public criticism, and by 1878 the *People's Vindicator* of Natchitoches described it as a "nuisance stinking in the nostrils of all good men." Elsewhere in the country sentiment was turning hostile to the lottery. Anthony Comstock was particularly energetic, raiding the company's New York offices repeatedly. In Philadelphia, Alexander K. McClure, editor of the *Times,* was a vociferous foe.

While the drawings were, in fact, honest, they became the subjects of rumors of fraud, and in order to dispel those rumors, the company hired two southern heroes to add their luster and reputation for integrity to the drawings. Generals Pierre Gustave Toutant Beauregard and Jubal Anderson Early were glorious figures from the Civil War, but they were also in financial trouble. For a sum estimated at between $10,000 and $30,000 annually each, the two war horses agreed to preside over the public drawings. Just before the annual Extraordinary Drawing of June 5, 1877, they issued a public statement that the procedure was fair. On the stage they made an imposing sight, Beauregard with snow white hair and moustache and Early badly stooped. They were not the only icons of honesty employed, for the actual drawings were performed by two boys from an orphanage who were escorted to the stage by a group of nuns.

The company generated extraordinary wealth for its principals. Stockholders received annual dividends of from 110 percent to 170 percent in the period from 1887 to 1890. Morris became a millionaire many times over, the owner of an estate in New York and numerous homes in this country and in Europe, a thoroughbred horse breeder, and the owner of the Westchester Race Track.

With the end of carpetbagger rule after federal forces left in 1877, the legislature managed to cancel the company's charter in 1879, but within months its managers succeeded in including a charter in the new state constitution.

By 1890 anti-lottery forces were better organized and were publishing their own newspaper, *The New Delta*. But a bill to recharter the company presented to a legislature that was initially hostile to the lottery eventually passed after intense lobbying and bribes by Morris. Money flowed freely, and intimidation was used as well. In the words of one contemporary observer, as soon as a legislator was converted to the lottery "they set . . . a 'death watch' over him, that is, they had him accompanied night and day by two or three of their henchmen, who effectively prevented all communication with him." *The New Delta,* perhaps carried away by its advocacy, reported a series of incidents accompanying the bill's progress that taxed credibility: In the House on two separate occasions a vote in favor of renewing the charter was blocked when a legislator preparing to vote for it became ill and was forced to withdraw. Final passage was accompanied by "the most violent storm which ever raged in Baton Rouge. The rain poured in torrents, the winds lashed the walls of the State House in fury, the thunder rolled in deep toned disapprobation of the outrage which was being perpetrated, the lightning played almost constantly around the building, and just as the Representative who had it in charge cast his vote the capitol was struck by lightning." The Senate followed suit and although Governor Francis Nicholls, who had lost an arm in the battle of Chancellorsville, vetoed the bill with the statement that "I will never permit one of my hands to assist in destroying what the other was sacrificed in endeavoring to uphold—the honor of my native State," the veto was overridden.

The antilottery forces persevered, however, and eventually obtained legislation in other states prohibiting the sale of Louisiana lottery tickets. But it was the federal law making it a crime to send lottery materials through the postal system that finally ended the lottery since it changed it from a national operation to one restricted to Louisiana, where it could no longer survive. So great was the lottery's reliance on mail that it amounted to an estimated 45 percent of the entire business of the New Orleans post office.

The demise of the giant Louisiana lottery was both the end and not the end of lotteries in this country. State-authorized games would not be seen for seventy years until New Hampshire decided to reenter the field. But "Insurance," which had been spawned in England in the late eighteenth century, flourished in this country, and boomed in New Orleans under the auspices of the Louisiana Lottery, was to survive the death of its parent, transform itself, and continue to grow.

No account of lotteries in the United States can be considered complete without attending to the history of this vigorous, illegitimate offspring of the legalized games. Insurance was doubly illegitimate. In the first place, it existed outside of the licenses granted by the states and therefore its proceeds never reached the states or the designated beneficiaries. In the second place, many states specifically outlawed the practice.

Originally a sideline in the lottery shops of London, Insurance became the diversion of the nobility. Robert Walpole wrote in 1789 that it was the reigning fashion then "to go, after the opera, to the lottery offices, where their Ladyships bet with the keepers. You choose any numbers you please; if it does not come up next day, you pay five guineas; if it does, receive forty. . . . The Duchess of Devonshire, in one day, won nine hundred pounds." The clerks who handled these bets and the outside salesmen who drummed up trade were called "Insurance solicitors." The receipts given bettors were called "Insurance policies" or "lottery policies" from which the name "Policy" evolved.

In this country, Insurance was a part of every lottery by 1800 and seemed to generate most of the fraudulent practices associated with the drawings. Although it continued to grow in popularity, it remained a minor part of the lottery business until the movement to abolish lotteries. "The death agonies of the Lottery proved to be the growing pains of Policy," according to Herbert Asbury, author of *Sucker's Progress, An Informal History of Gambling in America from the Colonies to Canfield,* "and as the former was gradually legislated out of existence in America the latter took its place as the one system of gambling in which everyone could participate. While the lottery was trembling on the brink of legal extinction, Policy was being established on a firm foundation throughout the United States, and it continued to expand as new areas were settled and the country increased in population."

The Policy shops in New York and other cities originally quoted bets on the drawing of the New Jersey lottery, but when that lottery was abolished around 1840, lotteries drawn in Covington, Kentucky, were used. Occasionally drawings of illegal lotteries in Georgia and Missouri were also used, as well as the Louisiana Lottery after 1868.

Games like lottery and its bastard offspring Policy admit of no systematic approach favoring logical analysis, but depend solely on random events. Because of that, their players are often inclined to superstition, their selections based on hunches, dreams, and other portents. In the South, particularly, fortunetellers, dream books, and other magical procedures were consulted. Asbury describes such a time-tried bit of necromancy still popular today. "Before going to bed the player moistens the index finger of his right hand with spittle and outlines an X on his forehead, and when he is sound asleep 'they' will appear and give him a number which is bound to win if played immediately." In New Orleans in the late nineteenth century parakeets were hired to select the numbers to be played.

The social evils of Policy were recognized early: Not only did it lead to fraud and divert betting proceeds into private hands, away from government and public projects, its lure proved irresistible to the poorest in society, thereby encouraging theft and leading to hunger, homelessness, and other social problems.

Legislation banning Policy began appearing in 1805 in Pennsylvania and by 1848 ten states had such prohibitions. After the Civil War many other statutes were enacted in the continuing, but unsuccessful, war against the game. Policy is unique in that, with one exception, it was never legal anywhere in the United States, a circumstance that hardly mattered, for its history is one of uninterrupted growth. The exception was the state of Louisiana, which in 1880 granted a Policy monopoly to the Louisiana Lottery Company when it renewed that company's charter. That event almost immediately turned the state's cities into vast Policy shops. "Before long," wrote a New Orleans historian,

> the city was Policy mad. Visitors to New Orleans in the 80's remember well the open Policy booths in the main business streets of the city, and the lines and crowds of negroes and whites that thronged the "book," seeking to bet their nickels and dimes on the innumerable combinations of figures which superstition or fancy dictated. There were Policy booths in front of laundries, bar-rooms, groceries and markets. There were instances where as much as $5,000 was paid for a stand if the location were favorable enough, which might not be more than four feet square of space, with a small table and a chair. More than a hundred Policy shops existed in New Orleans. The profits from the Policy game, in which there were two drawings daily, were large enough to pay all the expenses of the Lottery proper in which the drawing was monthly, leaving the profits from the national business, over the payment of prizes, clear gain.

The tide of legislation against Policy hardly slowed the game. New York City, which had from 300 to 350 Policy shops in Manhattan alone in the 1840s and 1850s, became the center of a nationwide system with the advent of Zachariah Simmons, the first Policy king. When Simmons first came to New York after the Civil War, the Policy fever raged there as violently as it did in New Orleans after 1880. It was estimated that one-fourth of the city's population of 900,000 played regularly, and the number of Policy shops had risen to between 600 and 700. Simmons and his brothers initially set up a few lottery offices and Policy shops, but had grander plans. With Tammany Hall he agreed upon a division of the spoils and police protection. The independent Policy dealers were not receptive to his plan until one day in the summer of 1870 when every Policy shop in the city was raided by the police and closed for the day. That powerful gesture was enough, and most of the dealers joined Simmons's Central Organization, which then proceeded to rule most of the Policy operations in New York, dividing the city into districts and assigning rights. By the following year Simmons's control not only included three-fourths of the shops in New York but extended to Policy as far west as Milwaukee and as far south as Richmond.

In addition to his organization of the game, Simmons modified it to reach even poorer players. The smallest Policy bet had always been a nickel; Simmons unveiled what he called "the envelope game" in which bets of from one to five cents could be made and "drawings" held every ten to fifteen minutes. Offices for the new game were opened in the poorer sections of the cities and it was popular for many years among Blacks and schoolboys.

The envelope game "drawings" were not really drawings at all, but simply a group of numbers arbitrarily selected and posted by the shop's managers. That was not the only such manipulation of winning numbers attributed to the Simmons group. Allegations were made that the drawings in Kentucky were tampered with and even that numbers drawn there were changed after arriving in New York. Anthony Comstock, the implacable enemy of lotteries and Policy, claimed to have found two notes initialed by Simmons requesting certain numbers. In one amazing coincidence that befuddled players and angered critics, the commissioners of the Kentucky State Lottery and the commissioners of the Frankfort Lottery of Kentucky on August 25, 1879, separately certified identical thirteen-digit winning numbers in their lotteries. Simmons was a manager of both lotteries.

By 1900 the Policy king was Al Adams, a former railroad brakeman from Rhode Island, and there were some 800 shops in New York. Winning numbers were said to be drawn twice every weekday in Kentucky by a blindfolded child, but in fact they were selected in New York City by the Policy kings, and in such a fashion that winnings would be minimized and the public's losses—or the Policy profits— maximized. Like Simmons, Adams established a power base in Tammany Hall, but with the enormous fortune he acquired through Policy he became a megalomaniac, employing a publicity man to distribute to the world news of his eminence. One such release boasted that "Al Adams is like unto Andrew Carnegie in that, being a marvelously successful businessman himself, he has drawn around him a corps of men almost equally brilliant as himself, not the least of whom are his four sons."

But the Society for the Prevention of Crime, also known as the Parkhurst Society, had Adams in its sights. A raid of his offices yielded evidence connecting him to the Policy business, which led to his conviction and a jail sentence. Soon after his release he killed himself.

The imprisonment and death of Adams marked the decline of Policy. The new reform administration in New York continued to attack the game, and other cities drifted away from the Central Organization. By 1915 Policy was no longer a significant part of American gambling and disappeared after World War I.

Even this brief history makes evident a certain ambiguity in the meaning of the term *lottery*. The procedures used by Moses to distribute land to the Israelites and by the ancient Athenians to fill public offices, on the one hand, and on the other the financing arrangements found in seventeenth- and eighteenth-century England are both similar and in need of distinction. If the common denominator is the selection by lots, the objectives or emphases are quite different.

Resorting to a lottery to accomplish a fair result is one thing; exploiting the gambling appeal in the lottery form is quite another. And if those who abdicate responsibility for awful or complicated decisions involving life and death and other heavy matter by deferring to a Higher Judge suffer no loss in dignity, those who abdicate in order to encourage a big public gambling casino are not entitled to plaudits.

These conditions have powerfully shaped the history of government-sponsored lotteries in this country and are the source from which spring not only the current lottomania, which has engulfed both the public and the states, but also the growing criticism that has accompanied it.

The reappearance of the public lottery in New Hampshire in 1964 seems astonishing at first: The game had been banned so uniformly and for so long, and the New England puritan heritage seemed inimical to a return to this form of gambling. In fact, however, public sentiment about gambling had been undergoing a change for many years. The states had increasingly permitted horse racing and bingo, Nevada had legalized gambling casinos, and commercial sweepstakes had become a popular marketing technique. The idea of state-run lotteries had been in the legislative air for years and New Hampshire first considered such a bill in 1937. Because it had no sales or income taxes, New Hampshire depended heavily on property taxes, which had reached oppressive levels, and in aid to education it ranked last in the nation. On top of all this, the state's population contained a large number of foreign-born and an above-average number of Catholics, groups known to be more receptive to lotteries. The 1963 bill, which provided for two sweepstakes a year, limited the number of retail outlets, and earmarked revenues for school districts, was approved by the governor, who bowed to the will of the people and cited "constantly increasing demands for school facilities, at a time when our people are already carrying a cross of taxation unequaled in American history."

By its terms subject to a popular referendum, the scheme was approved by the people in 1964 and began operation with the other states watching closely. The first New Hampshire games priced each ticket at three dollars and required the player to write his name and address on it. Since the drawings were made from the tickets sold and collected by agents, it was some time before winners were announced. Initially, prizes amounted to a low 31 percent of revenues. Sales proved to be disappointing, however, and revenues declined for five years. The future of the modern state lottery seemed uncertain. New York was the second state to take the plunge, approving a constitutional amendment in successive legislatures in 1965 and 1966. Notwithstanding opposition by both candidates for governor, one of whom was the incumbent, and the Board of Regents, the proposal passed easily. The New York lottery began as a monthly drawing with tickets priced at one dollar, but it, too, languished. In these early years it began to look as if the golden promise of the lottery was a chimera.

The corner was turned in 1970 when New Jersey entered the field with a new and faster game featuring a fifty-cent ticket that did not require the bettor's name and address, weekly drawings, and the payout of 45 percent of revenues in prizes. The new game was immediately successful and produced $30 million for New Jersey in the first six months. New Hampshire and New York adopted the new game and other states enacted lottery legislation modeled on New Jersey's.

Other improvements followed. Computer networks permitted immediate participation; new, more exciting games were introduced; and, perhaps most importantly, modern marketing techniques were used. Among the new games was the instant winner involving a "scratch-off" ticket with which the player learned at once whether he had won or lost. Not only was this more exciting than the traditional passive drawing which involved a long waiting period, it was a technique well known to the consuming public since it had been used extensively by product marketers.

Another new game was a computerized version of the illegal Numbers game. Like its illegal model, the new game permitted a player to choose a three- or four-digit number, as well as variations on their sequence, and offered daily prizes.

Perhaps most popular of the new games, and certainly the most publicized, is lotto. In lotto, players pick a small group of numbers from a larger field of numbers and have them registered by computer. The drama in lotto and the reason for its explosive growth derives from its rollover feature. If no one wins, the total amount is added to new bets. Snowballing week after week, the top prize can reach huge proportions as illustrated by jackpots of $45 million in New York in 1988, $69.9 million in Illinois in 1989, and—biggest of all—$115 million in Pennsyl-

vania in 1989. As the amount grows and news of the giant treasure is
adroitly spread, the lines of ticket buyers begin to lengthen.

Since the avowed objective of state lottery agencies is the
maximization of revenues, it was natural that they would turn to
Madison Avenue and employ the most modern techniques available to
persuade people to play. Surveys revealing who the heavy bettors
were and identifying those most likely to bet were followed by marketing programs that targeted those groups. Advertising was timed to
coincide with traditional paydays and the receipt of such governmental
benefits as Social Security payments. These advertisements stressed
the fun of the game, the size of the grand prize, and the possibilities of
wealth. In New York one series on the theme "All you need is a dollar
and a dream" showed ordinary people telling of the fantasies they
would realize when they won. "I'd buy a place in the country," dreamed
one player, "the country of Spain." Others mused that "I'd buy a
baseball team for Brooklyn," or "I'd buy out my company and have my
boss work for me." An Oregon ad declared, "PLAY MEGABUCKS NOW
AND YOU COULD BE A WINNER THIS SATURDAY NIGHT," going on to
embellish the dream:

> Imagine this.
> You pick up a Megabucks play slip now.
> Choose 6 of the 42 numbers available.
> (Or ask for "Quick Pick" and let the machine pick 'em for you.)
> Then, on Saturday night, you sit down to watch the Megabucks
> show.
> Your ticket is clutched tightly in your hand.
> The numbers are picked.
> Your numbers!
> And suddenly, your life has changed.
> Suddenly, you're rich.
> Could it happen?
> Absolutely!
> But, you have to do more than just imagine.
> You have to play.

The theme was reduced to its most compressed form in a Michigan ad
that said, tersely, "The rich. Join them."

Closely related to this theme was the promise of escape from economic constraints. Playing—and winning—the lottery meant one would no longer need to work. In a New Jersey ad a harried ballpark vendor of soda and popcorn is pictured saying, "If I win Pick 6, I won't have to do this anymore." A controversial Chicago ad that appeared on billboards in ghetto neighborhoods said, simply, "This could be your ticket out."

Implicit in these public messages was the notion that winning was not only possible, it was somehow *very* possible. A 1987 advertisement for the Washington state lottery made it seem easy: "It was Saturday night. I took my change down to the store for the lotto game. I got two chances at a buck a pair and by 7:05 I was a millionaire."

With the appearance of criticism that the odds against winning were extraordinarily high, the lottery agencies developed rebuttal ads cleverly fashioned to emphasize the possibility. In a Michigan television spot a man says he has a better chance of being struck by lightning than winning the lottery. He is immediately hit by a bolt, after which, scorched and smoking, he says, "One ticket, please." A similar ad in Oregon shows an elderly man in front of a general store complaining that nobody ever wins the lottery. When three winners emerge, he goes in to buy a ticket.

Some ads purported to show how to pick winning numbers by picturing a random assortment of objects together with their numbers, a message that would appeal to those familiar with the Numbers game and the many superstitions that surrounded it.

Lottery advertising has been extensive as well as whimsical and sophisticated. The total advertising expenditures for state lotteries has been estimated at $200 million a year in 1988, representing 2 percent of their total operating expenses, a figure almost double that for all United States corporations in 1984.

These promotional efforts had their effect. Viewed as a single enterprise, the state lotteries would rank thirty-eighth according to gross sales in the *Forbes* magazine 500, and, in terms of profits, those of the lotteries exceed the combined profits of IBM and Exxon, the two national profit leaders in 1987, each of which requires a multibillion-dollar asset base and vast numbers of employees to generate their profits.

These bare business data translate into some astonishing human figures. By 1988 annual lottery sales had reached an average of almost $100 per capita in states where the games had been legalized, or about $240 for each family, and in Massachusetts $234 was spent on lotteries *per capita*. The number of tickets sold reached bewildering levels. In one morning Pennsylvania sold 11 million lotto tickets. Late in 1988 New York was selling 28,000 tickets a minute for a $45 million lotto game, producing a three-day total of 37.4 million.

Riding the tide of a nationwide interest in gambling, state lotteries became a phenomenon themselves and the word *lottomania* was heard more and more often. When the 1985 New York lotto prize climbed to $41 million, then the largest jackpot ever in North America, people in New York City waited in rain in lines that stretched down the block and around the corner. In upstate New York there were similar queues on rural roads and in Amenia a Connecticut septuagenarian who had waited in line for five hours fainted when he finally reached the counter. Revived, his first words were "Can I have my tickets, please?" Stories began to appear of lottery plungers like the young couple who quit their jobs, sold everything they owned, and purchased $15,000 worth of tickets over a three-month period, all of which presumably lost.

Unusual behavior did not stop at state boundaries. When the 1989 Pennsylvania lotto jackpot climbed to a record-breaking $115 million, people from all around the country and beyond were drawn by the siren call. So many people from New York took the Metroliner to Philadelphia on the final day that it was called the Lottery Fever Express. A New York office worker drove down just to buy $8,000 worth of tickets. Four people from Chicago flew in, bought 800 tickets, and immediately returned. A woman from Oakland, California, flew in to play, impelled by her horoscope's prediction that it was a good day for money. Others made special trips from Texas, the Far West, and even Europe. So many wanted to buy tickets in large numbers that some vendors imposed arbitrary limits in order to keep the lines moving. At a busy outlet near the train station in Philadelphia the limit was set at 200 for each person, and even then buyers had to wait for as long as six hours. A strange euphoria developed in the city, fed by fantasies of wealth and the shared experience of buying tickets. Employees left their jobs for hours to play and were greeted on their return by smiling bosses who inquired pleasantly of the numbers they had chosen. In the streets people waved their tickets in the air and cheered each other.

Four years earlier the *New York Times* had commented on a similar mood that descended on that city on the eve of the $41-million drawing: "They stood in long lines chatting to one another while blocking in the numbers. Birthdays, ages, addresses, fractions of Social Security and telephone numbers. When asked their systems, they answered with old chestnuts like 'Does Macy's tell Gimbels?' When blessed with a 'good luck,' they promptly good-lucked back. Once they'd put the ticket someplace safe, the fantasies took over."

Elsewhere in Pennsylvania the 1989 lotto fever raged as well. A photograph of the area outside a ticket vendor's office in Shrewsbury showed a road filled with cars and people and a line stretching out to the horizon. The offer of a Westchester, New York, radio station to give away Pennsylvania lotto tickets created such congestion on telephone lines that the promotion was canceled at the request of the telephone company.

While lottomania may have reached a crescendo with the 1989 Pennsylvania game, it had become a familiar phenomenon before then. The already mentioned statistics of the lotteries' rapid success tell the story dispassionately; a more dramatic point of view was that shared by the many thousands of vendors who sold the tickets. The restricted outlets in the first modern lottery in New Hampshire had evolved into large networks of such agents, typically newsstands, drugstores, convenience stores, supermarkets, and liquor stores, numbering thousands in every state. Selling tickets and operating their computer terminals, they manned the barricades against the assaults of determined lottery players. What this experience behind the counter was like may be indicated by one Maryland vendor who exclaimed, "It's gone beyond a cycle. It's gone beyond a habit. It's become a mania. These people are obsessed."

In the states' rush into the lottery business the rich national history of the game seems to have played no part, with one exception. The Louisiana lottery, last of its kind, national in scope and unequaled in its corruption, was probably the reason why the new lottery legislation made the state itself the proprietor of the game and gave it monopoly power. There was very little historical precedent for this, but the memorable lesson of the Louisiana Lottery seemed to be that the granting of a lottery franchise to private interests led inevitably to corruption, and the way to avoid those risks was by state ownership of the business. This feature, common to all the current lottery schemes, has raised some of the most troubling issues about these games and elicited some of the most pungent criticism.

The enormous success of lotteries in the 1980s was responsible, in the view of some, for the national resurgence of interest in gambling in general, but even if that was not true, the incessant publicity that accompanied lotteries would have led to criticism. By the end of the decade, that criticism had coalesced into three points: lotteries were a sucker bet; they were a poor way to raise funds; and their success required of the states some very un-government-like—if not downright immoral—behavior.

So far the state lotteries have been, with a few minor exceptions, free of the frauds that haunted their predecessors especially in the nineteenth century, but there has been a rising chorus of complaints nonetheless that the games are not fair. The main targets of these complaints are the payout rates and the odds against winning. The payout, or the percentage of total bets returned to winners as prizes, barely averages 50 percent, a feature usually set forth in the enabling legislation. It is perhaps ironic that the Louisiana lottery, which inspired the states to assume the proprietorship of modern lotteries, itself paid out only 50 percent, a figure that contributed both to its great wealth and its infamous reputation. In some cases the payout in today's games is considerably less than 50 percent: In 1988 New York paid out only 39 percent of lottery receipts and Kansas paid 44 percent. From the balance, the expense of operating the lottery are met and the residue is paid to the state. But a comparison with other forms of gambling reveals that the lottery payout is the lowest of all. In casino gambling, horse racing, and jai alai the rates range from 75 percent to 98 percent. Bets with a bookie on the outcome of a sporting event return more than 95 percent, and when a group of friends bet among themselves it is 100 percent. Most galling of all, perhaps, the illegal Numbers game pays back more than its state lottery imitator, somewhere between 60 percent and 70 percent.

And if the payout rate is a little too abstract to be appreciated by the fevered mind of the lottery player, the same cannot be said of the odds against winning. Here we are close to the heart of the game: What chance does a ticket buyer really have of winning the big prize? Once understood, the answer is astonishing both for the remoteness of the possibility and the artful way in which the state lottery agencies subordinate that possibility to dreams of wealth. In a lotto game in which 6 numbers out of 48 must match those drawn, the odds are 1 in 12.3 million. The odds improve when it is a 6/42 lotto game; there they are only 1 in 5.2 million.

What do those numbers mean? When the game's odds are 1 in 5 million, the average person is eight times likelier to be struck by lightning than he or she is to win the jackpot. Jean Lemaire, a professor of actuarial science at the Wharton School of the University of Pennsylvania, compiled a list of events more likely to occur than winning the $115 million jackpot in the 1989 Pennsylvania lotto. These included the suicide of your neighbor that afternoon and your own death in a car accident the next time you drove, assuming you use your car five times a day. He also postulated an imaginary player who purchased one ticket a week and determined that he would have to live at least 553,058 years to be 99 percent sure of winning. Finally, if all of the 102 settlers on the *Mayflower* and all of their descendants each purchased one ticket a week until today, there would be 80 chances out of 100 that no one would have won.

It should be said in defense of the lotteries that games other than lotto offer more favorable odds. In a three-digit game in which the digits must be selected in the right order the odds are 1,000 to 1, improving with variations relaxing the order, and in the "instant" or "scratch-off" games, with prizes of $50 to $100, 1 out of every 4 players is a winner. But this is almost irrelevant since the theme of most lottery advertising is the winning of million-dollar jackpots.

In further defense of the lotteries it should be noted that the chances of winning are sometimes printed on the betting slip itself, as in the case of New York's "Cash 40" game. This information, however, is presented in small type and can hardly be expected to mitigate the effects of insistent advertising campaigns that leave bettors so obsessed with dreams of millions of dollars that their minds have been effectively sealed against winning possibilities of millions to one.

The results of a study by the Delaware State Gambling Commission revealed that few players knew the real odds against winning the various games. Charles Clotfelter and Philip Cook, authors of *Selling Hope: State Lotteries in America,* a scholarly analysis of the phenomenon, examined lottery advertisements in this light and found that only 20 percent provided any information on odds and that information was usually about winning any prize as opposed to the grand prize. "In contrast," they point out, "over half the advertisements in the sample mentioned the dollar amount of prizes—almost always the grand prize. Bolstering this emphasis on prizes over probabilities, the ads give a distorted impression of the probability of winning with their frequent portrayal of players who have won large prizes."

Superstitious practices in the selection of numbers are also encouraged by advertising. In some ads would-be players are advised on how to pick numbers by observing such ordinary details of daily life as the number of cherries in a bowl or cuff links on a dresser. In the now-familiar interview with the jackpot winner the press carefully reports how the number was crafted out of a combination of such random matters as birth dates, license numbers, or the date of the death of Billy Martin.

Prominent among the superstitions long associated with such forms of gambling is the notion that a number is "due" because it has not been drawn in a long time. In fact, in the cottage industry of lottery advisers this belief is responsible for a great deal of painstaking accounting, purportedly showing which numbers are ready to come up and which will not because they have already appeared. This conviction must spring from some deep level in human nature since it is unaffected by probability experts' explanations that the frequency with which a number has appeared in earlier games means nothing with respect to its possible appearance in the next game.

The "perceived probability," to use the nice phrase of Clotfelter and Cook to describe the ticket buyer's feeling about his chance of winning, is much greater than the real probability. The responsibility for that discrepancy, which may be huge, must be traced back to the state lottery agencies which, with their aggressive and misleading advertising emphasizing the winning of prizes and the fulfillment of dreams, lead the bettors away from any contemplation of the real odds that would very well discourage playing.

While the low payout rate and the enormous odds have been the main targets for those assailing the unfairness of the lotteries, the method of payment of prizes has also been criticized. Million-dollar prizes turn out not to be million-dollar payments, but annuities by which the winner is paid annually over a period of many years sums of money totaling the prize. No great financial sophistication is needed to perceive the difference. Not only is the disbursement by the state less, the recipient is deprived of the value of most of the advertised prize for years, and, in a time when inflation has been acknowledged as a fact of life, each payment is destined to contain cheaper dollars.

Two powerful forces combine to make the state lotteries irresistible. "The people want it," said the governor of New Hampshire in 1963 when the idea was being revived. Indeed, the public sentiment throughout the nation has been heavily in favor, with the exception of many of the southern states and North Dakota, where lottery referenda suffered their only defeats in 1986 and 1988. If that was not enough, the reluctance of legislators to vote for new or higher taxes would provide any additional needed motivation. Alan J. Karcher, formerly majority leader and speaker of the New Jersey Assembly who went on to write a book critical of state lotteries, has described how otherwise responsible and dignified legislators would go into hiding in the cavernous State House during a vote on a tax bill.

If a legislator's duty only requires him to carry out the will of his constituents, this combination of circumstances would seem to present a clear choice for him. But is that his duty? Across the country legislators and governors have spoken out initially against proposed state lotteries and then approved them because the people wanted them. These abdications are of a piece with the larger pattern of abdication that characterizes the use of lotteries in decision making, but the consequences in this case may be immeasurably more serious.

Since the state lotteries have come upon the national scene as a tax substitute, it is only fair to consider them in those terms. Karcher has called them "repressive and rapacious," and a system "that uses promotions that target the poor, and that markets tickets in a manner that is often abusive and exploitative. These indeed," he says, "are the three 'sins' of the states: avarice, conscious oppression of the poor, and hypocrisy."

A basic principle in taxation calls for the imposition of burden in direct proportion to the payer's ability to bear it. In a word, taxes should be progressive. The opposite, a tax that falls more heavily on those least able to pay, is called regressive, and while there may be some continuing debate, it seems reasonably clear that the state lotteries constitute such a regressive tax.

In general, the income tax is progressive in that its rates rise as does the taxable income. Even simpler impositions like the sales tax are still seen as fair to the extent that the amounts paid are directly related to the size of the purchase, although its impact on poorer people has been criticized as disproportionately large and it has been labeled regressive. Contrasted with these approaches is the lottery, a tax substitute that distributes the burden only in accordance with the intensity of one's impulse to gamble. Since that impulse may be strongest among the disadvantaged, a group targeted by a great deal of state lottery advertising, it is not surprising that they bear a large part of that burden. Even by comparison with the regressive sales tax, the lottery is seen as inordinately unfair in its impact.

"Rapacious," as well as "regressive," said Karcher. The reference here is to the policy of the state lotteries to maximize lottery revenues or at least make certain that they do not decline, a policy that derives from the treatment of the lottery as a tax substitute. If, in its search for revenue, government took the traditional route of imposing or increasing taxes, it would be assured of a stream of receipts that would be reasonably predictable and would rise and fall with economic changes. But lottery receipts are hardly predictable and are tied to economic conditions only in the loosest fashion. Because of this the state lottery agencies have been forced to act like private entrepreneurs, marketing their product as aggressively as soap, toothpaste, candy bars, or beer are marketed. This policy decision has cast the states into an unprecedented role: Constantly developing new games, filling the airwaves and the press with their insistent appeals to play, they have left far behind their traditional governmental functions and in this heady environment are every bit as combative and concerned for the bottom line as the typical, profit-driven businessman.

Perhaps even more. The typical businessman is kept in check by a network of legal restraints imposed by state, federal, and local laws, but the state's lottery monopoly insulates it from such controls. No regulatory body supervises lottery advertisements to ensure that they are not misleading or requires a warning that betting may be imprudent. Clotfelter and Cook point out that the Federal Trade Commission requires that the advertising of certain sweepstakes disclose a number of facts including the odds of winning all prizes. There is no reason to distinguish these games from the lotteries except that the latter are state-owned.

One of the colorful figures from this nation's past is the snake-oil salesman, a dynamic operator traveling from town to town offering from the rear of his wagon nostrums capable of curing any ailment from ingrown toenails to heart disease, dropped womb to spinal curvature. With the recognition that consumers needed protection in the marketplace and the development of a more regulated economy, these itinerant salesmen disappeared from the land. How remarkable it is that many decades later their spiritual descendants have reappeared at state capitals around the country offering, in the form of lottery prizes, a cure-all that holds out even more promise than did the old snake oil. Not only will the jackpot provide the means for healing any physical problem, it will also dispel any unhappiness, such is the ameliorating effect of a large sum of money. The only reason these hard-sell promotions, last heard from the rear of a horse-drawn wagon, are not restrained is because they emanate from state agents and employees.

There are other inconsistencies. We acknowledge and accept—often grumblingly—the activities of the state as imposer and collector of taxes, but until now we have not seen its promotional activities in this field. Since the lottery is a tax substitute, it is only fair to test the propriety of its promotional programs here by turning it around and applying it to other taxes. How appropriate would it be, for example, for the state to encourage by advertising those transactions that yield greater tax revenues?

Casino gambling, legal in Nevada and New Jersey, may not be advertised in most states, including those that have a lottery. Valid economic distinctions may be made based on whether the monies gambled wind up in the home state or not, but since the opposition to the casino gambling advertising is based on moral considerations, the difference between them and home-grown lottery advertising seems hardly to be a difference at all.

Even before the appearance of the New Hampshire lottery in 1964 there existed a tradition of sanctifying the lotteries by earmarking their proceeds for some worthy purpose. In this way the proposal seemed more attractive to those who were considering it, whether legislators voting on a bill, a governor pondering approval, or the people in a referendum. But this cleansing tactic—using "the devil's water to turn the Lord's mill"—has proved to be deceptive. While providing, for example, that lottery proceeds shall be applied only to education, the realities of the states' budget-making processes usually defeat that objective. As the budget is being prepared, the availability of lottery monies usually means that other state funds will not be appropriated for that purpose, even though those who approved the legislation may have expected that they would supplement and be in addition to those appropriations.

In their headlong rush into the lottery business the states have taken a radical step into the world of private enterprise. With the steady expansion of government in this century, public functions that take on some attributes of the private sector of the economy have become increasingly common. One example is the proliferation of public authorities, entities that function in some ways like private enterprises, to finance, build, and operate roads, bridges, transit facilities, and other needed projects without the necessity of a referendum on state borrowings. Another is the system of industrial revenue bonds, which extend the benefits of municipal bond tax exemption to deserving businesses. Other, more specific, examples include state-owned liquor stores and off-track betting parlors.

But in this area the state lotteries remain unique. Although the states' assumption of the role of proprietor of these games may not be remarkable, the policies they pursue in operating them certainly are. Driven, as we have seen, by the need to maximize lottery revenues, the states have pursued the betting public with a vigor and lack of conscience that is astonishing. In advertising directed at people most vulnerable to the impulse to gamble and least able to afford it, cleverly designed to obscure the tremendous odds against winning with fantasies of wealth and personal dreams, the lottery agencies have been unrelenting in their efforts to recruit new players and encourage repeated play.

Long ago in the history of lotteries the doubtfully moral means was justified by a socially desirable end. Always open to question, that logic is now being pressed into even more extreme service. If lottery gambling can be said to be justified by the funds it generates for education, for example, that justification, according to proponents, embraces even the kinds of advertising that the states now use. But there exists a range of behavior in the moral spectrum so extreme that even a goal as desirable as school aid cannot be used to justify it, and it seems clear that some time in the early 1970s the states crossed an invisible—but important—moral frontier when they set out to push people to play their lotteries no matter what the consequences.

Several examples, hypothetical and real, one from the sixteenth century, two from our time, may help locate that frontier. The offer to ticket holders of freedom from arrest for seven days in order to spur interest in an English lottery in 1566 could not be duplicated today, although the volume of crime and the ease with which arrestees pass through our criminal justice system and return to the streets might argue for its adoption. The reason is that the means chosen to accomplish the end in this case simply goes too far.

The sovereign has also entered into the business of selling packaged liquor and operating off-track betting parlors, activities where the product is morally questionable and its excessive use is recognized as socially destructive. It is interesting to compare the subdued nature of the state's marketing efforts in behalf of its off-track betting parlors with those pursued for lotteries. In New York, off-track betting ads feature a warning to "Bet with your head, not over it," a well-intentioned, if ultimately unintelligible piece of advice that might well be inserted in lottery ads. Conversely, if the state marketed its off-track betting operation in the way it markets its lotteries, the encouragement to participate in this form of gambling might prove unacceptable, although this is by no means certain. A much clearer contrast is afforded by a consideration of state-owned liquor stores. If the states pursued with this business a program aimed at converting individuals to use its products similar to that used with their lotteries, the uproar that would follow would be understandable. We still await the outcry over the combined efforts of the lottery agencies to turn us into habitual gamblers. The distinction in the latter case may be found in the dramatic potential of each vice. The connection between heavy drinking and the death of a child in a highway accident through drunken driving is direct, plain, and compelling; if the results of excessive gambling are more diffused, that does not necessarily mean they are less injurious in the long run.

In his indictment of lottery advertising, Karcher discusses what he calls the "denigration of the work ethic." The message of many of these ads seems to be that success and happiness result from the lottery, or, in other words, from gambling and luck. This road map to a better life should be compared with our traditional guide that stressed education, ability, and hard work. At a time when American productivity has become a national—and perhaps international—issue, it ill becomes our states to counsel us to depend on luck. Perhaps it is too much to expect our state governments to act as moral exemplars; at the least we should not be subjected to state campaigns that erode national goals.

The social contract theory of government may be vulnerable to many criticisms, but it still expresses some deeply held convictions about the nature and role of government. Even with the expanded sphere of government operations, no one would venture the thought that in the bargain we made with government, in which we gave up our wild freedom in exchange for the safety and limitations of a civilized society, we ever expected to find the sovereign urging us daily to take to gambling.

The invisible history of our country is being compiled even now. Some time in the future a researcher may be astonished to learn how in the last third of the twentieth century it was the governments of our states that led us down into the moral swamplands.

DOWSING

If the procedure appears simple, its meaning and validity remain unclear after more than four hundred years of testimonials and denials, debate and experiment. A person walks slowly but purposefully across a field, holding in front a small, Y-shaped tree branch. Suddenly, the point of the branch twitches and turns down. The branch holder announces that there is water flowing beneath the ground. In some cases he or she may even specify the depth of the subterranean water course, the volume of the flow, and whether the water is potable.

In his chapter on "Fortune-telling," Mackay accords "divination by the rod" a brief three sentences. It was practiced by the Egyptians, he tells us, and "In comparatively recent times, it was pretended that by this means hidden treasures could be discovered. It now appears to be altogether exploded in Europe." Mackay's decision to treat the subject, no matter how fleetingly, as a kind of fortunetelling is puzzling, for dowsing is a technique generally employed for identifying existing—albeit subterranean—conditions, and not for predicting the future. In any event, his perfunctory remarks hardly scratch the surface of a field that has produced a literature so voluminous one can tire simply from studying its bibliographies. It is a peculiarity of the craft that it inspires its adherents with the kind of intense belief and urge to convert one might expect from religious missionaries. This need to convert unbelievers undoubtedly contributes to the surprisingly large amount of writing on the subject.

The first definite appearance of dowsing seems to have occurred in the fifteenth century in Europe although claims for a greater antiquity are quite common. One authority places it at no less than 7,000 years old, and others speak as well in millennia. Passages in the Old Testament are often cited to show its existence in Biblical times. So, for example, Moses, following the Lord's instructions, struck the rock at Horeb and water came out of it from which the thirsty people drank

(Exodus 17). "Rhabdomancy," a dowsing synonym, is derived from ancient Greek words, an etymology that suggests to some that the Greeks knew of the practice. Similarly slight indications exist that the Chinese and other peoples were familiar with the practice although it is never clear whether the claim contemplates divination by rod of water or other underground materials, or the use of rods to predict future events. Reference is sometimes made to the Aquilegus in Roman times, an official responsible for finding water, but dowsing seems not to have been one of his methods; instead, he proceeded by carefully observing certain herbs, briars, reeds and trees, insects, and vapors, and by the use of tests to detect other natural signs. Never completely convincing, the effort to secure a considerably longer history for dowsing than that commonly attributed to it is no doubt polemical in nature. Just as a business might boast of its reliability by advertising the year it was established, so the greater history of water divination might add to its validity. By similar logic some of the subject's apostles are at pains to find dowsing-like activities in the cultures of primitive peoples, as if the wider realm in which it is practiced, like its older vintage, gives proof of its reliability.

Perhaps the first specific reference to dowsing occurred in a 1430 writing by a mining surveyor in which a rod was described that responded to "metallic exhalations." It is significant that dowsing was initially developed as a technique for locating underground mineral veins and it would be many years before the craft was put to use to determine the presence of subterranean water.

By 1518 the use of the rod was sufficiently established to be included by Martin Luther in his list of acts that violated the First Commandment. It would not be the last time that the craft would draw the opprobrium of the church.

The written record really begins, however, with the publication of *De Re Metallica* by Georgius Agricola, a doctor in a mining camp in Bohemia. Agricola, born Georg Bauer, had steeped himself in mining lore and had labored for years on his great work, which was richly illustrated with woodcuts. His publication contained the first detailed description of the use of the rod to detect minerals underground and a woodcut showing the different stages of the procedure. Even here in this first work on dowsing there is disagreement as to its validity. Agricola wrote:

> There are many great contentions between miners concerning the forked twig, for some say that it is of the greatest use in discovering veins, and others deny it. Some of those who manipulate and use the twig, first cut a fork from a hazel bush with a knife, for this bush they consider more efficacious than any other for revealing the veins, especially if the hazel bush grows above a vein. . . . All alike grasp the forks of the twig with their hands, clenching their fists, it being necessary that the clenched fingers should be held toward the sky in order that the twig should be raised at that end where the two branches meet. They then wander hither and thither at random through mountainous regions. It is said that the moment they place their feet on a vein the twig immediately turns and twists, and so by its action discloses the vein; when they move their feet again and go away from that spot the twig becomes once more immobile. The truth is, they assert, the movement of the twig is caused by the power of the veins, and sometimes this is so great that the branches of trees growing near a vein are deflected toward it. On the other hand, those who say the twig is of no use to good and serious men, also deny that the motion is due to the power of the veins, because the twigs will not move for everybody, but only for those who employ incantations and craft.

Paracelsus, a contemporary, also dealt with the subject in a post-humously published work. He was also a skeptic, observing that these divinations "are vain and misleading and . . . have deceived many miners. If they once point rightly, they deceive ten or twenty times."

Sir William Barrett, who devoted a lifetime to dowsing and with Theodore Besterman wrote a major work on the subject; concluded that the divining rod probably originated in the Harz Mountains of Germany, and speculated that it was an outgrowth of the notion that metallic ores attracted certain trees which consequently drooped, in telling fashion, over the veins of ore beneath them. A branch of the tree was therefore cut and moved around to see exactly where it would be attracted down.

By the end of the sixteenth century dowsing for minerals was common in Germany and had spread westward in Europe, arriving in Cornwall, England, with German miners who were imported to work the mines there.

Explanations for the phenomenon during this period took a number of forms. The most common, and that advanced by learned men, was that it was based on "sympathy," or "attraction and repulsion." Another view was that the rod functioned as a result of demoniac influence, a dangerous thought at the time. Still others believed that the operator, as well as the rod, had a divinely given faculty. Perhaps as a result, the rod was sometimes surrounded by Christian ritual, laid in the bed of a newly baptized child, given that child's name, and adjured with prayer before use in the field. In Cornwall, miners believed that the rod was led to ore deposits by fairies, the custodians of the earth's mineral treasures. Against these theories, quaint and varied, were opposed the conviction of authorities like Agricola and Paracelsus that the use of the rod was simply a superstitious practice affording no guarantee of success.

The development of the rod as a tool for water divination is usually credited to the baroness de Beausoleil in the seventeenth century. However, in their book *The Diving Rod: An Experimental and Psychological Investigation,* Barrett and Besterman write of an earlier use which they found in a biography of Saint Teresa of Spain. "Teresa in 1568 was offered the site for a convent to which there was only one objection—there was no water supply; happily, a Friar Antonio came up with a twig in his hand, stopped at a certain spot and appeared to be making the sign of the cross; but Teresa says, 'Really I can not be sure if it were the sign he made, at any rate he made some movement with the twig and then he said "Dig just here"; they dug, and lo! a plentiful fount of water gushed forth, excellent for drinking, copious for washing, and it never ran dry.' "

The baroness de Beausoleil and her husband were active in developing mines for the French government and were well-known diviners. The baron was one of the foremost mining authorities of the time, and with his wife had traveled extensively through the mining regions of Europe where he had worked for dukes, emperors, and even the

Pope and had conducted similar activities in the New World. Because their efforts at locating mines in France had gone largely unrewarded, the baroness in 1640 submitted to the duke de Richelieu, the real ruler of France, a long report describing their activities, listing the mines they had located all over France, and setting forth a program which, if followed, would make the king of France the richest of all Christian princes and the French the most fortunate of all peoples. This report, entitled *The Restitution of Pluto,* described five methods for locating mineral treasures and undergound water: opening the ground, observing plants that grow on the surface, tasting surface water, smelling the vapors that ascend from the soil, and using sixteen instruments the most important of which was the divining rod. "The ancients," she wrote, "that is to say our ancestors, used any available forked stick from hazel or other nut trees which, by a virtue, inclines and dips over those places where sources of water or metals are located, whether beneath earth or water. Not everyone can use the rod."

Richelieu's reaction to this promising report was astonishing in its nature and severity. Both the baroness and her husband were arrested and placed in separate prisons where they both died. The abrupt end of the Beausoleils' career may have been brought about by charges of sorcery, a problem they had encountered over the years.

Adding considerably to the reputation of the Beausoleils as the first water diviners is the story of the discovery by the baroness of the mineral waters at Chateau Thierry. On a visit to the village in 1629 she had surveyed the area with mysterious instruments, including seven different dowsing rods, and was able to convince the inhabitants that waters with curative powers ran beneath the courtyard of the inn at which she was lodging. Even here there was some disagreement. A doctor who had participated in verifying the baroness's find and recorded the events in a book rejected the notion that she had divined the hidden springs, offering his opinion that her success was due, instead, to acute observations of such telling clues as the discoloration of cobblestones over the mineral-rich waters.

By 1658 dowsing was sufficiently important to warrant examination in an academic thesis at the University of Wittenberg. After lengthy consideration, the author concluded that the rod did move, but in most of the cases it was due to fraud and deception. In the other cases the movement was purportedly due to a pact with the devil. It is some indication of the lively interest in the subject that this dissertation was reprinted twice and was followed by many similar scholarly works in succeeding years.

While instances of individual dowsers multiplied elsewhere in Europe, in Spain there developed an entire class or race of such diviners. Called "Zahouris," a word that has been linked to the Zohar, the principal book of mystical Judaism, these were people who could look into the bowels of the earth and see water or minerals. Unlike traditional dowsers, they did not require a forked twig or any other instrument. Some of them were said to be able to see into the human body and make out the various organs. A fine magical aura surrounds this shadowy group. The power was said to be possessed only by those who were born on Good Friday, or, in another version, by those born at the precise moment when the Passion was being chanted, and it could be exercised only on certain days such as Tuesdays and Fridays. Zahouris were reportedly capable of seeing under ground to a depth of twenty pike handles and were characterized by a peculiar inflammation around the eyes. It is almost needless to say that there were many people who questioned their power and still more who saw in them the work of the devil.

Toward the end of the seventeenth century what seemed to be a new application of the rod developed with the sensational appearance of Jacques Aymar, a figure of near-mythical proportions in the literature of dowsing. The story involves a grisly and apparently insoluble crime, an extraordinary detective, a long and arduous pursuit, and the eventual capture of a culprit. In 1692 the bodies of a husband and wife were discovered in their wine cellar in the city of Lyon. They had been brutally hacked to death with a butcher's cleaver. Although the police found that the contents of the couple's strongbox had been taken, they were unable to find any clues as to the identity of the killers. In the neighboring province of Dauphiné, Aymar had become well known as a *sourcier,* able to locate underground waters, and also capable of tracking criminals. In desperation the authorities brought him to the scene of the crime. As the police looked on, he is said to have walked back and forth, holding a forked stick, sweating and trembling. When he stood over the spots where the bodies had been found, the stick twisted in his hands. It was almost as if Aymar were a dog that had gotten the scent, for he then took off at a fast pace through the city with curious people following him. The path led out of the city to a gardener's house beside the Rhone River. Inside, the rod plunged violently over an empty wine bottle, and a table and three chairs. Aymar declared that the fugitives were three in number and had stopped here in their flight to drink some wine. The gardener's children confirmed these matters. The chase went on. Farther south, in the town of Beaucaire, Aymar's rod led him to the local prison. When the warden arranged for a lineup of prisoners who had recently been arrested, the magic wand dipped in front of a nineteen-year-old hunchback who had been jailed only an hour earlier for petty larceny. Aymar reported that the rod indicated that the man had participated in the double murder, but was not the main villain.

Returned to Lyon, the hunchback at first denied everything, but when taken back over the route Aymar had taken, and identified by people who had seen him, he eventually broke down and confessed. He had acted with two others, he said, but they had done the actual killing.

Aymar's apparent success encouraged the authorities to send him out again in pursuit of the others, this time accompanied by a troop of archers. Now the rod led the group to the Mediterranean port of Toulon, where Aymar determined that the fugitives had departed the previous evening for Genoa beyond the jurisdiction of the French authorities.

In Lyon the hunchback was tried, convicted, and broken alive on the wheel, purportedly the last person in Europe to suffer that awful punishment. When witnesses at the trial corroborated all of the details discovered by Aymar's rod, he became a celebrated figure throughout Europe.

There was speculation that Aymar possessed a unique ability to detect a special *matière meurtrière*, or "murderous matter," emitted by a murderer, but he claimed to be able to track a specific person, rather than a murderous trail. When in pursuit of a murderer, he said his temperature rose until he felt faint, his pulse raced, and he even spat blood. He tested an article by placing his foot on it while holding the rod. Although he could locate water as well as murderers, evidence of the latter agitated him so violently that he said he could not be confused as to the nature of the cause.

Moral dowsers like Aymar were well known in the area around Grenoble and Dauphiné. In addition to using the forked twigs traditionally to locate minerals and water sources, dowsers were able to track criminals and establish property boundaries even when they had been secretly changed by former owners. Particularly astonishing was the claim by this special breed of diviners that their rods would dip only over that which they wished to find. If they sought a felon's trail, for example, the rod would not move over underground water.

Such a skill was a great novelty and Aymar was brought to Paris where he was subjected to a number of experiments by the prince of Condé in which his repeated failures began to erode his celebrity. That decline accelerated when he became involved in a series of morally questionable activities. In one case he was hired—presumably by her lover—to determine whether a young lady had been faithful. He secretly approached the lady and asked for money if she wanted him to give the desired report. Because of such incidents he was forced to leave Paris. Back in the countryside, he was engaged by a Catholic group to trace Protestants alleged to have murdered a number of Catholics, and based on his report twelve Protestants were executed. Aymar seems to have been a pliant individual lacking in conscience. It was reported that he had been persuaded to roam the streets of country villages with his dowsing branch and indicate whether any of the women in the houses he passed had "soiled their honor." That adventure stirred up a considerable clamor.

Dowsing had long been on the frontier of black magic and had been debated for years in ecclesiastical councils. To cleanse it of any association with witchcraft, a potentially dangerous matter in the seventeenth century, a dowser would pronounce a special incantation before proceeding, such as the following: "In the name of the Father and of the Son and of the Holy Ghost, I adjure thee, Augusta Carolina [the baptized name of the rod] that thou tell me, so pure and true as Mary the Virgin was, who bore our Lord Jesus Christ, how many fathoms is it from here to the ore?"

In 1659 the dowsing rod was denounced by an important Jesuit leader as an instrument controlled by the devil. Considering the preoccupation with demons and the perceived prevalence of witches, it is remarkable that this mysterious tool for finding minerals and water not only survived but flourished. The implications of dowsing's new field, as brought home by the Aymar episode, were not lost on the church. The important functions of determining guilt by using the elaborate procedures so carefully developed and long followed by the church could not be preempted by something as simple, lacking in control, and affording so many opportunities for manipulation as a wayward tree branch. In 1701 the Inquisition issued a decree prohibiting the use of the divining rod in the "moral world" for tracing criminals, determining boundaries, or settling lawsuits and the like.

The interdiction seems proper to us now, but may have lacked consistency and certainly was ironic. Procedures not too dissimilar had long been approved for determining guilt or innocence. A girl accused of witchcraft would be cast into a body of water bound hand and foot, her innocence established only if she floated. Equally brutal trials by fire or ordeal were just as alien to any real search for truth and provide a background against which moral dowsing may even seem a relatively responsible and innocuous, if unusual, method of proceeding.

Those who use Aymar to bolster dowsing's credibility point out that the story is not hearsay, but has been set forth in court records and other documents that afford guarantees of trustworthiness. But questions about the man's initial exploit remain. Aymar's subsequent chicaneries raise doubts about it, as did his repeated failures to pass the prince of Condé's tests. Some authorities point out that the hunchback's confession may not have been voluntary, not an unlikely possibility in an age when torture was regularly used as part of a suspect's interrogation. It has also been suggested that Aymar had received important information even before he took out his dowsing stick at the crime scene.

If Aymar and his moral dowsing had a brief, but brilliant, career in Europe, the apostles of dowsing point to similar uses elsewhere. Barrett and Besterman describe like procedures in use in a number of locations, including Calcutta and Central Africa.

The next large figure on the dowsing stage was also a Frenchman. Barthélmy Bleton was born around 1750 in Dauphiné, the same province from which Aymar came, and became well known as a *sourcier* or water diviner, credited by some with transforming Dauphiné from an arid land into one of the richest provinces in France. His talent was discovered at the age of seven when he experienced a fainting spell on a rock. When he was removed and later brought back to the stone, the spell recurred. Upon excavating the ground beneath the stone, an abundant spring was found.

Unlike Aymar, Bleton did not practice moral dowsing, but he enjoyed a solid reputation in Dauphiné, where there had always been some who thought Aymar was a charlatan. Bleton's technique was somewhat different as well. He used a nearly straight rod which he perched on his outstretched index fingers. When he was over an underground spring the rod would rotate on its axis eighty or more times per minute, and he would be subjected to a convulsive spasm that affected his diaphragm and elevated his pulse. The rod was merely a prop, for Bleton would experience the physical reaction even without it. Only subterranean flowing water created these effects; neither stagnant water nor the water in rivers or lakes made any impression on him. Bleton's power was subject to fluctuations. It was said to be greater in dry weather and before meals, and disappeared entirely when he was ill.

Pierre Thouvenel, a highly successful physician, became interested in Bleton and brought him to Paris, where his success in a series of tests created great public interest. It was Thouvenel's theory that dowsing worked through electromagnetic forces, a departure from the old views that the rod moved by sympathetic attraction, but in the mainstream of the fascination at the time with the effect on living things of electricity and magnetism.

Among the public tests that Bleton passed successfully was one in which he traced an undergound pipe to a fountain in the Faubourg St. Denis while he was blindfolded; another in which he traced an underground aqueduct, starting in the Luxembourg Gardens, for 15,000 yards with such precision that the official in charge of the system declared his tracing could serve as a dependable plan if the official charts were lost; and yet another in which an assembly of five hundred people, including many notables, were all persuaded of his ability.

But these public tests represented only a small part of the experimentation. Thouvenel, assisted by Professor Jadelot of Nancy, a respected medical authority, subjected Bleton to more than six hundred trials over a period of two months, and Thouvenel reported that they never once were able to deceive him.

As a result of the publicity that resulted from his feats in the public tests in Paris, Bleton was employed by the queen of France for whom he is said to have found a number of springs. Together with the scientific investigations, there exists a considerable number of field reports and testimonials that constitute a kind of catalog of Bleton's success.

But the record, as is so often the case in the history of dowsing, is not lacking in dissent. One writer speculated that Bleton's successful public displays in Paris may have been, in part, a newspaper concoction and that, in any event, the locating of buried water pipes was due more to keen observation than anything else. It was also noted that Bleton was frequently unable to locate subterranean water courses and failed completely in the new church of Saint Genevieve, a completely dry site, where he declared there were many streams large and small. Some authorities relate that as the queen's *sourcier* he had failures at Trianon.

Lalande, a celebrated astronomer, claimed to have exposed Bleton by demonstrating that the rod, as held by the dowser, could be made to rotate by sleight of hand. The attack was taken up by Henry Decremps, who included Lalande's instructions on simulating the rotation of the rod in a book on magic that was popular in France and England. Dowsing partisans are quick to point out that the rod and its movement were superfluous to Bleton's power, but the prestige and influence enjoyed by Lalande, no doubt augmented by Decremps's book, crushed Bleton and Thouvenel. The dowser was regarded henceforth as a fake and Thouvenel, whose career at one time seemed to offer limitless prospects, also suffered in his reputation. With the coming of the French Revolution, Thouvenel emigrated to Italy. In that country he associated himself with Pennet, another accomplished dowser, continuing both his experiments and his battle with the scientific community to adopt his theory that electromagnetism was the key to the divining of water.

Yet another Frenchman now appears on the scene, affording an interesting comparison with his predecessors. The Abbé Paramelle was born in 1790 and in 1818 took up his religious duties in the department of Lot in southwestern France. The eastern half of that department was well watered, but the western half was arid and poor, a situation that puzzled Paramelle since both areas received the same rainfall. In the hope of locating water sources in the dry parts of the department he spent two fruitless years tramping about, earning a reputation as an eccentric hunting for lost treasure. But the abbé was persistent as well as perceptive and analytical. After nine years he believed he had developed a system for locating underground water and, with the financial assistance of the impoverished localities, set about demonstrating it.

His success was remarkable. By 1843, 338 wells had been dug in Lot at sites he had chosen and 90 percent yielded abundant potable water at the depth he had indicated. He himself estimated that in a twenty-five-year career he located more than 10,000 underground water sources at which between 8,000 and 9,000 wells had been dug. His failure rate was approximately 5 percent. Soon after his initial successes in Lot he relinquished his ecclesiastic duties and thereafter spent every day, except Sunday, from sunrise to sunset for nine months of the year searching for water.

As his fame grew, there were critics, as well. One writer in 1842 attributed his success to impressions, sensations, and convulsions, and, doubtless, diabolic visions: "The only difference between Paramelle and other sorcerers is that he conceals the diabolic signs he receives, glossing over his magical proceedings with a lot of scientific jargon." To rebut such allegations, Paramelle wrote a work on his craft in 1856 that was published in four editions in France and translated into German and Spanish.

The techniques he described are unlike those of the ordinary dowser. He never used a divining rod and stated that it would never turn in his hands. Instead, he theorized that underground water courses behaved much like flowing water on the earth's surface. The location of the channels in which these subterranean streams ran could be determined by careful observation of the surface. In general, the impermeable stratum that was the bed of the underground body of water corresponded to the surface formation. A valley or long depression indicated the presence of a stream below. Even in level country he claimed to be able to detect the slight clues that indicated water. These outward signs were caused by the natural tendency of the surface to conform to that of the buried bed in which the hidden water flowed, and also by the subsiding of the surface due to subterranean erosion. He furthermore estimated the volume of the water in relation to the area drained and judged its quality from the character of the surrounding soil. From these principles it is clear that his *modus operandi* was more like that of a geologist, albeit a self-trained one, than a sourcier.

Paramelle insisted that he had no special faculty and that anyone, after a few months of study and practice in the field, could match his proficiency as a water finder. With this conclusion Barrett and Besterman disagree, pointing out that in spite of the wide readership of his book, no second Paramelle appeared. The reaction of Barrett and Besterman to this Frenchman is rather complicated but worth pondering. Their *The Divining Rod: An Experimental and Psychological Investigation,* published in 1926, is at once a valuable source in the field and a partisan work that seeks to validate dowsing. To them Paramelle's phenomenal success could not be explained simply as a matter of shrewd observation in the field and correct speculation. "We believe," they said, "that the experience he had gained by long observation in the field, and the instinct he had thus acquired, accounted for a good deal more than he could rationally explain. Hence, like the successful dowser of past and present times, it was his subconscious far more than his conscious faculties that were concerned in the process of water-finding." In other words, they would place Paramelle in the great tradition of dowsers even though he did not act or talk like them, and they would enshrine him in the pantheon of water diviners along with such notables as Aymar and Bleton.

Two British dowsers of the late nineteenth century are also to be found in that pantheon. W. S. Lawrence, a native of Bristol, discovered that he had the gift when he was twenty. A stonemason by trade and the father of twenty-six children, Lawrence was a practicing dowser for nearly seventy years, achieving a long series of successes that produced many testimonials from the nobility and businesses. His technique was different from other diviners in that he used a flat steel wire formed into a kind of horseshoe first. Its motion indicated minerals as well as water, and required Lawrence then to use a forked hazel twig, which would respond only to water. He was convinced that without the steel wire and hazel rod he lacked any power to locate water. An eyewitness described what happened when Lawrence detected a source:

> I can only describe the antics of that twig as a pitched battle between itself and him! It twisted, it knocked about; it contracted and contorted the muscles of his hands and arms, it wriggled and fought, and kicked, until it snapped in two—and then—what made it painful to watch until you got used to it, the old man reeled and clutched hold of any one nearest to him for a few moments. It evidently exhausts him very much, though afterwards I asked him what effect it had on him, and he said it only made his heart beat *most* violently for a short time.

Lawrence seems never to have been subjected to rigorous scientific testing, but all who knew him considered him to be scrupulously honest and a rare man of principle.

John Mullins was also a mason, but in 1882, at the age of forty-four, he formed a company with his two sons and devoted himself exclusively to dowsing and well digging. He was said to have located more than 5,000 water sources and to have brought in some 700 wells. When he contracted to dig a well at a site he had dowsed, he would waive payment if a good supply of water was not obtained. In view of the considerable cost of making a well, this policy powerfully evidenced his faith in his ability and no doubt enhanced his reputation considerably.

Mullins used a twig from almost any tree, but found the lancewood and boxwood too stiff for the purpose. The rod would turn for him only over running water and gave a positive indication over a buried pipe only when the valve was open. His practice was to search for water during the dry season, for at other times he believed he might be misled by transient draining of surface water. From the violence of the rod's motion he claimed to be able to estimate the depth and volume of the water's flow. According to Mullins he could detect gold as well as water and the testimonials include a description of how he located a coin buried for the purpose. There is nothing in the record, however, to indicate whether he ever employed his unique ability to search for real treasure.

Barrett and Besterman lavish attention on Mullins, reciting perhaps too many testimonials to his successes, both in England and in Ireland, and claim to have been unable to find one instance in which he failed. One scientific test was aborted, however, when Mullins, irritated by a blindfold roughly applied, tore it off and declared he would not have his honesty, unquestioned in thirty years as a dowser, called in question now. In another episode in Ireland the local people made Mullins drunk and "turned his performances into a laugh."

The reputation of a dowser is created slowly by word of mouth and its incremental construction is such that reported failures may be fatal. That reputation therefore is typically both local and fragile. A dowser may be celebrated in a valley or a few counties, but rarely does his fame extend far and wide. Another factor inhibiting the greater publicity of its practitioners is the uncertain classification of water divining: Among most people it would be placed somewhere on the vague frontiers separating magic, art, and science. It is because all these factors limit the notoriety of dowsers that the case of Henry Gross is so exceptional. Unlike any other dowser, his ability and successes were trumpeted across the country in determined and protracted fashion by a formidable publicist, Kenneth Roberts, a journalist and novelist.

Roberts had deep roots in New England: He traced his family back to the seventeenth century; sought, in some of his novels, to correct what he perceived as inaccuracies in the standard histories of Maine; and made his home on a farm in Kennebunkport, Maine. On his farm he had located a number of springs by using local dowsers, but he had always entertained doubts about the craft until he met Gross. A game warden from Biddeford, Maine, Gross not only dispelled Roberts's skepticism, he turned him into a passionate and tireless champion of dowsing.

Henry Gross and His Dowsing Rod, the first of three books written by Roberts on dowsing, appeared in 1951. In it he describes how, when he first met Gross, the dowser had a limited ability to detect water. He could not, for example, determine the depth of the water vein or the volume of its flow. In time, however, according to Roberts, Gross's power increased to an astonishing degree. Not only did he become able to determine depth and volume, but he could also make these determinations from a map or a picture, thereby dispensing with the need for a visit to the site. And even that was not all. "The sudden widening of dowsing power," to use a phrase coined by Roberts in *Henry Gross,* enabled Gross to query his divining rod and elicit answers from the rod's movement that were invariably accurate. In the winter of 1949 Gross dowsed his brother's property for water by holding the stick over a photograph of the property and asking it questions.

> [I] . . . asked whether there was a vein of water on the land shown in the picture. The stick went down, meaning that there was. I then had my son-in-law take a pencil and move it slowly across the picture. The first time he traced a line parallel with the road, and about 30 feet from it. The rod didn't move. The next line was traced parallel with the first, but through his door yard. Right in front of his greenhouse door the stick went down. I asked how many feet it was from the door to the vein—one, three, five and so on—and the stick said 16 feet. I asked whether the water was good to drink; the stick said Yes. I asked what direction the water was coming from: the stick said from the west and in line with Mrs. Johnson's (his neighbor's) house. The stick said the vein was flowing 7½ quarts a minute.

Later he found that he could dowse a property for water without going to the site and without a map or a picture, needing only the name of the locality or the name of the owner of the property.

Nor was the power of Gross's miraculous rod confined to the search for water. It could tell him whether a certain person was at home; it could locate a lost outboard motor at the bottom of a lake; at a camp for girls it correctly picked out individuals merely by being told their first names. As time went on Gross came to believe that he could divine ore veins as easily and accurately as veins of water.

These years were marked not only by the surge in Gross's dowsing power but also by the wholehearted commitment of Roberts to the field and the enormous energy he expended in proselytizing among unbelievers and contending with critics. Roberts was a prickly individual with a well-known reputation for truculence. A long list of his aversions included Franklin D. Roosevelt ("I think . . . [he] has broken every promise he ever made"), most historians ("like most professional men . . . [they] should have stuck to farming"), and Henry Ford and the makers of cheap automobiles who in his view "have done more to promote unrest and unhappiness in the United States than has any other agency." It was inevitable, of course, that this energetic and opinionated missionary for dowsing would strike sparks. The Brattleboro, Vermont, *Reformer* was particularly hostile, accusing Roberts, "a supposedly reputable author . . . [of] upholding the ancient hoax of water witchcraft," and speculating that he had "become a partner in buncombe that was hatched in the Dark Ages and continues to victimize thousands of credulous folk every year." For his part, Roberts struggled to throw off the name "water witching" by which dowsing was known in the United States. He had several reasons, one of which was genealogical. In 1692 an ancestor had been convicted of witchcraft, excommunicated, and hanged in Salem Village. The phrase was derived in corrupt fashion from the French word *sourcier*, meaning "one who locates water." When transformed into *sorcier*, which means "witch" or "magician," it brought to dowsing the negative connotations of the black arts.

On one battlefield Roberts contended with scientists who insisted on subjecting Gross to tests which Roberts felt were inappropriate. When Professor J. B. Rhine, a well-known researcher into the paranormal, visited Kennebunkport, Roberts was chagrined that he insisted on an experiment in which Gross was asked to tell whether water was running in an underground pipe or had been shut off. To Roberts such experiments were irrelevant. The important thing was the results in the field. It is not known whether, as a careful student of the history of dowsing, Roberts was aware that Barthélmy Bleton had undergone similar tests in Paris toward the end of the eighteenth century and, according to some reports, passed them splendidly.

And yet the greatest triumph of Henry Gross and Kenneth Roberts was about to happen. Roberts owned property in Bermuda and spent considerable time there. The island had always lacked wells for drinking water, a deficiency that had been met by collecting rainwater from roofs and leading it into storage tanks. When this was explained to Gross one evening in Kennebunkport, the dowser was puzzled; it seemed unlikely to him that such a large island could lack underground spring water. Thereupon Gross consulted his rod, which informed him that there were three sources of good drinking water on Bermuda, some eight hundred miles away. A map was produced, and in further consultation with the rod the exact locations were marked.

Much of the balance of *Henry Gross and His Divining Rod* is devoted to how Roberts struggled in Bermuda with a variety of problems including widespread disbelief, bureaucratic inertia, and his own limited fund of patience. But he reports eventual success, and to memorialize it he placed a brass plaque in the room in his Maine farmhouse where Gross had first performed his telepathic dowsing.

The book was not a success, however, and Roberts's publisher was increasingly unhappy when he insisted on writing two more books on the same subject, each of which fared rather poorly. In *Water Unlimited* and *The Seventh Sense* he related further experiences of Henry Gross, including his success in finding water at a leprosy settlement in eastern Nigeria and his failure to find it at Tikal, the long-lost Mayan city being excavated in eastern Guatemala. But the main purpose again was polemical and Roberts continued to debate scientists and others who disagreed with him about dowsing. The power of the rod, he predicted, would rank with electricity and atomic power when its potentialities were more clearly understood and utilized. As for Henry Gross, Roberts called him the equal of da Vinci, Copernicus, and Galileo.

Roberts's continuing effort to throw off the term "water witching" as a pejorative name for dowsing is a reminder of the many names by which the practice has been known. To dowsing and water divining must be added the European names radiesthesia, cryptesthesia, and rhabdomancy. In the United States it is known not only as water witching but also water smelling, channel surveying, wishing for water, doodlebugging (a common term also for oil divining), water prophesying, peachtwig toting, and switching. In Germany the diviner is called *Wassersucher* ("water seeker") or *Rutengänger* ("rod walker"); in France, *sourcier* ("spring finder"); and in Switzerland, *Brunneschmoker* ("water taster"). The divining rod itself is called a *Wünschelrute* or *Schlagrute* ("wishing rod" or "striking rod") in Germany; *Wichelroede* in Dutch; *baguette divinatoire* in France; *bacchetta divintoria* in Italy, and *varilla adivinadoria* in Spain.

The tools of the trade are similarly varied. While hazel and willow twigs seem preferred, even Agricola referred to a number of different kinds of trees and mentioned iron and steel rods as well. Divining rods have also been made of such diverse materials and articles as a stalk of grass, scissors, a steel spring, a walking stick, candle snuffers, and even a German-style sausage.

There are variations in form as well as material. While the Y-shaped branch may have been the standard, Bleton's implement was a straight twig with a slight curve. Some operators have used tapering sticks or a portion of a fishing rod. Others employ large, circle-shaped lengths of aluminum or a wire bent into the shape of a *P*. An old Spanish device consists of four small metal needles, each of a modified *Y* form, to be operated by two people. A dowsing rod sought to be patented in England in 1889 by a Texan as a means of detecting gold and silver underground consisted of a flask containing some of the valuable metal. When suspended over the underground mineral the flask was supposed to vibrate. Sometime in the early part of the nineteenth century a pendulum began to be used. It is not uncommon for a dowser to use a twig first to make a rough, preliminary determination and then the pendulum for a kind of fine-tuning.

Once the implement acts, however, the dowser must still determine the depth of the water. In some cases his estimate is based on the violence of the rod's action, although it is unclear whether this indicator is not also responsive to the volume of the flow. Other dowsers measure the surface distance between the points at which the

rod's movement commences and where it exhibits the greatest violence and proclaim that as the vertical distance that must be excavated
to reach the vein. A rare few, like Henry Gross, need only enter into a
conversation with the instrument.

The view of many in the field that the divining rod itself is not
indispensable to the procedure has not discouraged the invention and
promotion of many elaborate devices that are advertised as guaranteed
water and mineral finders. Barrett and Besterman, in 1926, referred to
an "Electro-Terreohmeter," an "Electro-Geodetic Mineral Finder," a
"Patent Automatic Water Finder," and a "Vibrator," as well as a large
number of mechanical oil finders in the United States and even a ring
invented by a Somerset man that would prevent the dowser from
"feeling any untoward sensations." Christopher Bird, in *The Divining
Hand: The 500-Year-Old Mystery of Dowsing,* reports on a Czech
invention consisting of a tube mounted on a tripod hooked up to a
stethoscope through which the operator is said to hear acoustical
waves sent out by subterranean water veins.

Varied in its nomenclature and the tools of its trade, elusive in its
principles, dowsing has also tended to a kind of expansiveness in
function only some of which we have touched on above. Starting as a
miner's technique for locating underground minerals, it evolved into its
now best-known form as a procedure for finding water. It was not long,
however, before the divining rod was operating in the moral world
determining criminal guilt, land boundaries, and even chastity. But
even that is far from the sum total of its applications.

It was natural that in the modern world, with its heavy dependence
on oil, divining would become an accepted method for finding such a
subterranean treasure that uniquely combines the precious character of
rare minerals with water's fluid properties. Paul Clement Brown,
reputed to be a successful doodlebugger in recent years, is the subject
of an admiring chapter in Bird's *The Divining Hand.* In the field, Brown
used a pendulum consisting of a small container filled with oil. When the
device signaled that he was over a body of petroleum, he employed an
additional procedure for determining the depth of the oil, or the amount
of oil the body will produce. Holding the pendulum steady with one

hand, he would start a stopwatch which, according to Brown, read off ninety feet of depth for every minute. When the pendulum started to move in a counterclockwise movement, he marked the time (depth), an indicator of the upper surface of the oil. He continued timing the pendulum until its motion ceased at the point determining the bottom of the body of oil. According to Bird, Brown had a long list of successes as an oil dowser and eventually turned to dowsing for minerals with similar results. Brown seems one of the stars in the field, for he had the very rare capability of dowsing from a map. Using his characteristic pendulum he liked to start on a mountain peak, and, by using the motion of the pendulum, claims to have been able to locate the approximate boundaries of the deposit. Unlike Henry Gross, however, Brown then had to make a field investigation to perfect his divination.

Although he is unable to explain how it works, Brown believes that he functioned as a kind of transmitter sending down a "mental wave," which was reflected back by the deposit he was looking for. It was not instantaneous, but proceeded at ninety feet a minute. And Brown's "mental wave" apparently could be tuned in or calibrated for any kind of deposit. Not only did he claim to be able to locate bodies of oil and minerals underground, but he applied his special talent to the search for a sixteenth-century Spanish ship that was believed to have gone down at the mouth of the San Luis Rey River near Oceanside, California, carrying more than $50 million in gold. According to Bird, Brown was successful in locating the wreck, using a mysterious device called an "attractometer," but ocean currents have ever since made raising the wreck impossible.

The discovery of this long-lost ship by dowsing should seem unremarkable to those who recall, for example, that Mullins had no trouble finding buried gold coins in a test of his prowess. To the growing inventory of divining's applications we add that of finding lost things.

Nor is the dowser's sphere limited to the subterranean world. In Canaan, New York, a transplanted Frenchman who owned a gas station diagnosed automobile engine problems by using a dowsing pendulum. On the coast of Maine a man used a plastic dowsing rod to determine where on the horizon the next ship would appear, its speed, and its distance. A Benedictine scholar used dowsing in World War II to help Swiss art experts detect forgeries.

Bird reports the case of Vo Sum, a South Vietnamese naval officer who was able to apply the technique in connection with the thousands of people who had been lost during the war in Vietnam. First he determined whether the individual was living or dead by suspending his pendulum over a photograph of the person. If the person was alive, Vo Sum would then move the pendulum over a map to find him or her. He also was successful in locating missing ships and intercepting a junk carrying opium, putting questions to the pendulum in a manner similar to that of Henry Gross.

Even the U.S. Marine Corps experimented with divining rods. During the Vietnam war it tried them out as a means of locating booby traps, pongi pits, and underground tunnels, but ultimately declined to adopt them officially. This was not the only wartime use to which dowsing had been put, however. In World War II, according to Ben G. Hester in *Dowsing: An Exposé of Hidden Occult Forces,* the British Admiralty employed two dowsers to map-dowse enemy harbors for ships worth bombing, and German sea captains used the method to locate allied shipping. Heinrich Himmler, head of Hitler's SS, is said to have arranged for a school for dowsers during the war.

Evolving even further, the craft became a procedure for making medical diagnoses. Bird credits Father Jurion, a Parisian, with promoting this use sometime after the end of World War II. He had been a traditional dowser since 1930 and was inspired to move into the medical field by three other clerics who were also dowsers. The first was the Abbé Bouly, who had already earned a solid reputation as a *sourcier* and after World War I had applied his skill so successfully to locating unexploded artillery shells that he was said to be able to indicate before excavation whether they were of German, Austrian, or French manufacture. Looking for new fields in which dowsing could be employed, he selected what he called "the world of microbial variations." The second source of inspiration for Jurion was Father Bourdoux, a missionary in the jungles of Brazil who used the new discipline of "radiesthesia" to identify which plants in a given region could be used as remedies for ailments. The Abbé Mermet, a Savoy dowser, extended the procedure to human illnesses as early as 1906.

Father Jurion's long career as a medical dowser was marked by conflict with the French medical association, which charged him with the unauthorized practice of medicine and brought him to court on six separate occasions. In time he became the spearhead of a new group of such practitioners now numbering more than one hundred in France.

Jurion's technique involved putting a series of questions to his favorite pendulum, a shiny crystal. In "yes-no" fashion the pendulum would answer such questions as "Is there something wrong with the patient's brain?" or "Should any value be attributed to the blood tests?"

In the more common form of medical dowsing, however, a pendulum would be suspended over the patient's body, sometimes using the free hand as an "antenna" or "screen," interposing it between the pendulum and the patient. The gyration that the pendulum produced over a healthy part of the body was supposed to change to oscillation over the unhealthy part. It is also claimed that the number of oscillations would indicate the seriousness of the disease. The technique could also be applied to a patient's blood, urine, or saliva specimen, and many believe that the sex of an unborn child could be determined infallibly by the pendulum.

As veterinary medicine is related to human medicine, it should come as no surprise that dowsing has also been practiced on animals. Bird includes photographs of French dowsers ministering to a huge draft horse and a sickly lamb during the years 1932 to 1933.

Le Vicomte Henry de France was a dedicated dowser who brought the discipline into the dining room. In his 1948 work *The Elements of Dowsing*, he wrote that as long ago as World War I it was known that the clockwise gyration of a pendulum, suspended over a piece of food and adjusted over the operator's free hand, signified that it was good for him. If the gyration was counterclockwise, the food was not suitable. De France takes credit for perfecting this "primitive method," as he calls it. Some of the further principles of "alimentary radiesthesia," the name he gave this procedure, are these: If the pendulum's gyration turns into oscillation, this might mean only that the portion is too large—therefore reduce it and try again; if the food is bad for you, the oscillating movement produced by the pendulum without the screening hand will be parallel with the front of your body; if it is good for you, the oscillation will be toward you and away from you. He even developed what he called a "system of coefficients." Pendulum oscillations over the food usually do not exceed 20 in number. If less than 10, the food is either mediocre or too large in quantity; if 15 to 20, it is very good. Alternately, he proposed a ruler of at least 40–50 centimeters to measure the length of each oscillation which, presumably, bears a relation to food suitability similar to the number of oscillations. This "radiesthesia of food" led de France to conclude that, at least for himself, cereals, fruits, and vegetables rated most highly, followed by milk, butter, and eggs, and lastly meat, and that water is the preferred drink.

Even in a dowsing application as rarefied as "alimentary radiesthesia" there is some relationship between the divining implement and the subject being examined, although that relationship may be only one of proximity. All but the most thoroughgoing of skeptics may admit of some marginal possibility that emanations from the subject are being sensed by the dowsing instrument, or that the dowser's subconscious has been mysteriously brought into play by the presence of the materials. It is when we come to telepathic dowsing, with such variations as divination from a map or picture, and the disappearance of the relationship of proximity that we seem to enter into a radically different and even more incredible world. What are we to make of Henry Gross who converses with his rod in Maine and locates underground water in Bermuda, or of Vo Sum who uses similar methods to find lost ships and people, or even of those medical radiesthesiasts who arrive at a diagnosis simply by questioning their pendulums? Of this extrasensory aspect of divining, de France, who called it "teleradiesthesia," ponders "whether we are not dealing with one of the most extraordinary discoveries of all time—on a par with the atomic bomb!" Even among those who believe in the more conventional kinds of dowsing there are considerable numbers whose faith falls short of that needed for these ultimate leaps.

One powerful reason for this disbelief may be traced to the similarity between these advanced forms of dowsing and parlor activities such as the Ouija board which suggest mind reading and communication with the Beyond. The Ouija board, too, will answer questions, although most of us do not take it seriously. While Ouija boards and talking and turning tables are all of comparatively recent vintage, they are really modifications of a similar, centuries-old device, the magic pendulum. Ancient Romans employed an antecedent of the Ouija board by suspending a pendulum in a glass and reciting the alphabet while it gyrated or oscillated, noting when the pendulum rang against the glass.

Evon Vogt and Ray Hyman, who set out to examine dowsing in a more rigorous manner in *Water Witching U.S.A.*, take up this and related phenomena in a chapter entitled "From Talking Horses to Talking Twigs." They begin with Clever Hans, a horse that astonished Berlin in 1904 with his ability to answer any question put to him by his owner. Among other things, he could count, do simple arithmetic, spell, identify people and things by name, and even express a preference for some kinds of music. He did these things in response to questions put to him, answering by tapping a hoof, shaking his head, or indicating letters on a board or objects on a shelf. It even developed that Hans could do these things when his master was absent. He was sensational.

A commission of outstanding scientists and animal experts examined him and were unable to find evidence of signals being given or prior training. A more incisive investigation ultimately revealed that the horse was actually responding to subtle cues given by the questioner; when the questioner himself did not know the answer, the animal was unable to answer. The same technique has been employed by human mind readers who have developed acute abilities to pick up muscular cues given by those whose minds are being "read," and Vogt and Hyman show how it is also at the bottom of such apparent mysteries as table turnings, talking tables, and Ouija boards. The common denominator is "ideomotor action," involuntary motor behavior caused by mental activity.

Table turning had become so popular in mid-nineteenth-century England as a sure way of communicating with the next world that

Michael Faraday, the great physicist, felt obligated to look into it. He was able to demonstrate that those at the table actually initiated the movement although they were unaware of it. Ironically, he concluded his report with an apology for having written it: "I am a little ashamed of it, for I think, in the present age, and in this part of the world, it ought not to have been required."

It is this same ideomotor action that Vogt and Hyman advance as the explanation for the movement of the divining rod. Here, just as with the tables and the Ouija board, those involved are unaware that they are causing the motion. Kenneth Roberts, who saw in dowsing evidence of a "seventh sense," rejected this analysis. So, too, would most dowsers. The literature, so largely anecdotal and testimonial, is filled with accounts of the rod acting violently in the dowser's hands. The description of how the rod turned so strongly in spite of the operator's grip that the bark was torn off appears often enough to constitute a familiar theme. For those who have felt the rod move, the ideomotor action explanation is no more convincing than it is for those at the tables or the Ouija board. But Vogt and Hyman show how ideas create imperceptible muscular movement and that implanted ideas (suggestions) can grow incrementally in this way into a sudden, large, muscular contraction. Well reasoned as it may be, the Vogt and Hyman analysis has not been applauded by the dowsing community. Not only does their work highlight the "water witching" name for dowsing that was particularly odious to Kenneth Roberts, it refuses to give credence to any of the better-known diviners, and ultimately seems to reduce the magic in the field to little more than some chemical reactions in the human nervous system.

Not quite. Vogt and Hyman pull up short of calling dowsing superstitious nonsense that must be eradicated at all costs, deciding, finally, that it is a form of "magical divination." As such, it may have some redeeming social value such as encouraging farmers and others to search for water, although it is clear they have no faith in its reliability. Even that qualification can hardly be expected to please dowsers, for it amounts to little more than relegating them to the same category as shamans and witch doctors, purveyors of useless mumbo jumbo tolerated by condescending intellectuals mainly because of their traditional roles in a benighted society.

In their opposition, Vogt and Hyman stand in a long line of naysayers that extends back to the origins of dowsing, and even their scientific explanation for the phenomenon, built up as it is with more recent advances in psychology and embroidered with modern psychological phrases, is not completely original. Agricola had noted that since the rod would not work for everyone, its motion must have been due to human manipulation. In 1645 Father Kircher demonstrated that a divining rod never reacted unless it was held by a human hand, and in 1692 Pierre Lebrun suggested that the movement was due to "prior intention." Michel Chevreul reported to the French Academy of Science in 1852 that the cause of the divining rod "does not belong to the physical world, but to the moral world; I think that, in most of the cases in hand, in which the wand is held by an honest man who has faith in it, the movement is the consequence of an act of the mind of that man." Years earlier Chevreul had investigated the magic pendulum and reached a similar conclusion that the pheonmenon was the result of involuntary muscular movement in the hand, induced by mental processes.

From the beginning, dowsing had been condemned as a superstitious and vain practice even without regard to the possibility of demoniac influences. Such was the view of Agricola and Paracelsus in the sixteenth century, and when Sabine Baring-Gould published *Curious Myths of the Middle Ages* in the mid nineteenth century, dowsing was featured. In 1917 the U.S. Geological Survey found it necessary to review the history of the practice and state a similar conclusion in an official paper on the divining rod. In an introductory note, O. E. Meinzer observed that dowsing still had a strong hold on the popular mind. Calling water witching "practically useless," he wondered "whether so much investigation and discussion have been bestowed on any other subject with such lack of positive results. It is difficult to see how for practical purposes the entire matter could be more thoroughly discredited, and it should be obvious to anyone that further tests by the United States Geologic Survey of this so called 'witching' for water, oil, or other minerals would be a misuse of public funds." The paper itself, written by Arthur J. Ellis, sketches the history of dowsing, relates how the delusion spread, and quotes, with approval, the following rhetorical, but unequivocal, verdict of R. W. Raymond in 1883:

> To this, then, the rod of Moses, of Jacob, of Mercury, of Circe, of Valentin, of Beausoleil, of Vallemont, of Aymar, of Bleton, of Pennet, of Campetti—even of Mr. Latimer—has come at last. In itself it is nothing. Its claims to virtues derived from Deity, from Satan, from affinities and sympathies, from corpuscular effluvia, from electrical currents, from passive perturbatory qualities of organo-electro force are hopelessly collapsed and discarded. A whole library of learned rubbish about it which remains to us furnishes jargon for charlatans, marvelous tales for fools, and amusement for antiquarians; otherwise it is only fit to constitute part of Mr. Caxton's "History of human error." . . . It belongs with "the magic pendulum" and "planchette," among the toys of children. Or, if it be worthy the attention of scientific students, it is the students of psychology and biology, not of geology and hydroscopy and the science of ore deposits, who can profitably consider it.

Ellis's paper was followed by other publications from the Geological Survey generally maintaining the same critical position, notwithstanding persistent pressure from dowsers to modify it.

Traditionally, those who tried to explain dowsing fell into one of two camps: the psychological or the physical. Either the rod moved because it was attracted by some force, or the mind of the operator somehow caused it. That simple division masks an astonishing variety of ideas. The first theory to appear postulated a natural law of "sympathy" similar to the law of gravitation. Speculation that there was a natural affinity between certain things led to the belief that there was a special sympathy between a tree bough and subterranean metals and that such a force moved the divining rod. A refinement of this theory appeared in France in the eighteenth century based on the notion of corpuscular action. "The corpuscles," wrote William Price in 1778, that rise from the Minerals, entering the rod, determine it to bow down, in order to render it parallel to the vertical lines which the effluvia describe in their rise. In effect the Mineral particles seem to be emitted from the earth; now the Virgula, being of a light porous wood, gives an easy passage to these particles, which are also very fine and subtle; the effluvia then driven forwards by those that follow them, and pressed at the same time by the atmosphere incumbent on them, are forced to enter the little interstices between the fibres of the wood, and by that effort they oblige it to incline, or dip down perpendicularly, to become parallel with the little columns which those vapours form in their rise.

It was an extension of this theory to the *matière meurtriere* said to emanate from a murderer that was offered as an explanation for Jacques Aymar's feat.

With discoveries in electricity and magnetic fields, these new, invisible forces seemed to provide the most plausible explanation and one that remains popular. It was Thouvenel, working with Bleton, the famous dowser, who, around 1780, first expounded the idea that there was an electrical explanation. The movement of the divining rod, in this view, was due to a combination of weak electrical currents that existed in the earth and a magnetic field that surrounded the dowser. To demonstrate the theory, Thouvenel and others attempted to show that a dowser's ability to detect water was affected by interposing insulating materials between him and the earth. Charles Latimer attempted to prove the same theory in the United States in 1875, a century after Thouvenel, and there are still those who profess to have assembled evidence demonstrating it.

Other physical theories deserve mention. Sir W. H. Preece, in 1905, rejected the idea that dowsing is explained by electrical or magnetic phenomena, concluding instead that "it is mechanical vibration, set up by the friction of moving water, acting upon the sensitive vertical diaphragm of certain exceptionally delicately framed persons." A Count von Klinckowstroem attributed the movement of the divining rod to the energy it received from the rays of the sun and the moon, and the leader of the German dowsers' association saw dowsing as the "rudiment of an atavistic sense of smell."

But if dowsing has traditionally been explained either in physical or psychological terms, a special word must be said for the paranormal. While this is, in one sense, a psychological explanation, it is also more than that, involving mysterious forces which may exist and operate independently of the human psyche. It is evidenced not only by Kenneth Roberts's "seventh sense," but by the other telepathic dowsers we have discussed. Bird is especially receptive to such ideas, sounding, at the end of his book, a kind of exalted coda in which he groups dowsing with such mysteries as clairvoyance, precognition, unidentified flying objects, and extraterrestrial intelligence, all indicative of a multidimensional universe.

The tendency to see the paranormal in dowsing may be due in part to recent changes in the field. In the first edition of their book, in 1959, Vogt and Hyman commented that European diviners were better organized than their American counterparts. Twenty years later, in the second edition, they noted not only the appearance of the American Society of Dowsers based in Vermont but a membership largely made up of "urban dowsers," people living in or near cities with higher income and more education than their rural cousins. Where the rural dowser was primarily concerned with the search for water, the urban dowser found "new 'uses' for his divining: the location of underground objects placed there by man (water and gas pipes, telephone cables, sewers, and graves); the location of lost objects (gold balls, mislaid rings, watches, coats, runaway pets, and missing persons); medical dowsing (detection of diseases, determining which organ is infected, and predicting the sex of fetuses); the prediction of future events (the date a new car will be delivered, whether or not a business deal is wise, and the winners of the Kentucky Derby); the analysis of personal character (determination of honesty and dishonesty)."

Many urban dowsers, according to Vogt and Hyman, have been recruited by the American Society of Dowsers through their interest in occult matters and the supernatural. This side of the society is reflected in the books it offers for sale to its members, which include a healthy sprinkling of works on Edgar Cayce, human auras, pyramid power, crystals, soul travel, and ESP.

In another sense, however, the paranormal is not a new dimension in dowsing. As long ago as 1926 Barrett and Besterman concluded that dowsing is purely psychological and has no physical basis, but they also were convinced that the diviner has supernatural powers.

The debate, now in its fifth century, continues. A major issue generating considerable emotion is the significance of the field experience. Roberts, for example, was especially irritated at the experiments selected by scientists and their refusal to look at field results. "It works" is the insistent cry of the dowsers, "and that's all we need to know." Believers, therefore, point to successes in the field, trot out innumerable testimonials, and rest their case.

To Vogt and Hyman this is unsatisfactory because it is not scientific. Testimonial evidence produced under casual conditions has been proven to be unreliable. Furthermore, these case histories fail to indicate whether the successful location of water was due in part to the reading of surface indications, and in any event, a useful statistical analysis of dowsing activities in which successes and failures are tabulated has never been made. Most disturbing to them is the view that although dowsing cannot be demonstrated by currently accepted scientific standards, it remains valid and therefore science should make an exception of it. That view, redolent of the paranormal which has recently become more prominent in the world of dowsing, is often expressed in terms of analogies taken from the history of science. Since the most astute scientists of the past were frequently in error, goes this argument, so may their descendants now be mistaken in rejecting the validity of the divining rod.

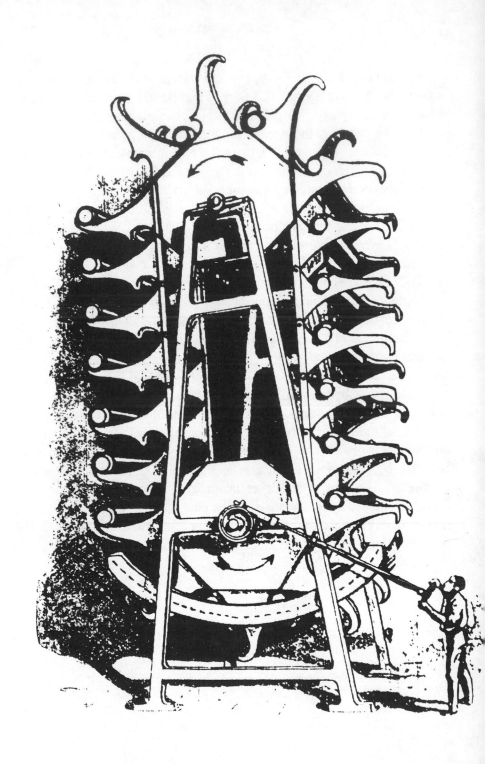

PERPETUAL
MOTION

The idea of a machine that could create the energy needed for its operation has long seemed within man's grasp. Arthur W. J. G. Ord-Hume, an engineer and writer on the subject, has explained graphically in his *Perpetual Motion: The History of an Obsession* why it seemed so plausible to the early artisans:

> Perpetual motion surrounded him on a grand scale—the sun rose and set, the moon waxed and waned, the seasons changed, the tides ebbed and flowed. Water and wind cost nothing and their natural abundance could not be overlooked. The forces of Nature existed everywhere and their harnessing was itself seen as a form of perpetual motion. What was needed to grind corn automatically or pump water continually was considered nothing extraordinary, and the ways of having your work done for you were believed many and varied.

In the third century B.C. Archimedes of Syracuse was said to have invented a sphere and an artificial heaven which showed the movement of the planets; it was a machine which moved itself—an automaton, a self-moving device. But the oldest drawing of a perpetual motion machine is that by Villard de Honnecourt, a thirteenth-century architect (figure 1). Accompanying the crude sketch is this comment: "Many a time have skillful workmen tried to contrive a wheel that shall turn of itself: Here is a way to make such a one, by means of an uneven number of mallets or by quicksilver." Because the drawing lacks perspective, in the style of the time, it fails to show clearly that the wheel is at right angles to the axle and the frame. Each of the mallets is loaded with a weight and hinged on the rim of the wheel. When the wheel is put in motion the mallets on the ascending side are brought close to the

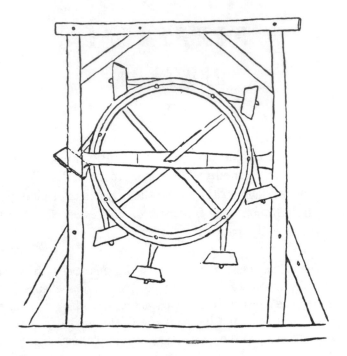

Figure 1

rim, flip over at the apogee, and then are extended, by gravitational force, as they descend. In theory, the wheel, once started, would produce its own energy and continue to rotate. In actuality, friction slowed and then ended the motion.

That de Honnecourt's wheel could not work did not discourage countless inventors over the next seven centuries from basing their claims to a perpetual motion machine on the same general design. Among them were men who went on to establish reputations for legitimate achievements. Even the great mind and interest of Leonardo da Vinci were captured by the idea, if only briefly. One page of his sketchbooks contains six drawings of overbalanced wheels, essentially like de Honnecourt's, shown in figure 2. The sketches lack any commentary but there can be no doubt of their purpose. Three of these wheels are designed to operate partly submerged in water. This modification, intended to take advantage of the buoyance of some substances in water, is almost an admission of the failure of the basic design, and itself has been repeated over and over again by later

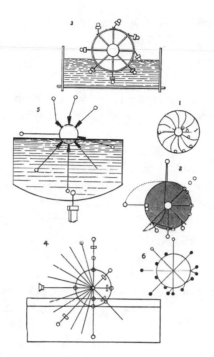

Figure 2

inventors. Number 5 may involve a magnet positioned to attract the wheel's spokes at the nadir of the wheel's revolution, further evidence, perhaps, that the simple machine was not working.

Dr. John Dee, in a preface to a translation of Euclid in the sixteenth century, reports seeing a perpetually turning wheel: "A wonderful example of farther possibilitie, and present commoditie," and "a thing almost incredible."

Cornelis Drebbel, a Dutchman known as an alchemist, magician, and professor of the black arts, but also engineer to King James I in England, developed such a machine, which was exhibited and presented to the king on May 1, 1610. It was said to demonstrate "that the Heavens move, and not the earth," and that it was "perpetually in motion, without the means of steele, springs, and waights."

King Charles I was given a demonstration of such a device some time during the period 1638–1641. The proponent was no less an individual than Edward Somerset II, marquis of Worcester, who otherwise had a considerable reputation as a scientist and inventor. No plan of the wheel survives, but it was described in Worcester's *Century of Inventions* published in 1655 under the title "An Advantageous Change of Centres" as follows:

> To provide and make that all the weights of the descending side of a wheel shall be perpetually further from the centre, than those of the mounting side, and yet equal in number and heft to the one side as the other. A most incredible thing if not seen, but tried before the late king (of blessed memory) in the Tower, by my directions, two extraordinary ambassadors accompanying his majesty, and the duke of Richmond and duke Hamilton, with most of his court, attending him.
>
> The wheel was fourteen feet over, and forty weights of fifty pounds apiece. Sir William Balfour, then lieutenant of the Tower, can justify it with several others. They all saw that, no sooner these great weights passed the diameter-line of the lower side, but they hung a foot further from the centre, nor no sooner passed the diameter-line of the upper side, but they hung a foot nearer. Be pleased to judge the consequence.

There is little doubt that Worcester had built a wheel like those described by de Honnecourt, da Vinci, and many others.

Worcester's interest in these devices was not limited to the over-balanced wheel. In the *Century of Inventions* he also describes

> How to raise water constantly, with two buckets only, day and night, without any force other than its own motion, using not so much as any force, wheel, or sucker, nor more pulleys than one on which the cord or chain rolleth with a bucket fastened at each end. This, I confess, I have seen and learned of the great mathematician Claudius his studies, at Rome, he having made a present thereof unto a cardinal; and I desire not to own any other men's inventions, but if I set down any, to nominate likewise the inventor.

When Charles I was defeated in 1645, Worcester fled to France. On his return he was first imprisoned in the Tower of London, was later freed by Charles II, and then went on to develop a "water commanding engine," which is generally considered to be the forerunner of the modern steam engine, a device that was largely responsible for Britain's subsequent prosperity.

Henry Dircks's history of the search for perpetual motion, written in the middle of the relatively enlightened and technically sophisticated nineteenth century, is peppered with the author's impatience with and disdain for those who sought the chimera. He was puzzled how such a great man as Worcester fell "into the common, vulgar error of believing in the possibility of perpetual motion; and not only so, but publicly exhibiting a machine pretending to that character." Dircks notes that eminent scientists of the seventeenth century declared perpetual motion possible, but Worcester went beyond that, claiming to have obtained practical results. "Hence he leaves us no alternative but to declare that he propounds either a truth or a falsehood; and if false, that he was either himself mistaken, or deceived by others." The obvious possibility that his lordship might have been a fraud seems never to have entered the author's mind.

By the end of the seventeenth century, quicksilver, which de Honnecourt mentioned in his thirteenth-century sketch, was being added to models of the wheel. In models with the quicksilver modification, the spokes of the wheel were hollow and ended in pouches on the rim, thus permitting the magical substance to move back and forth to assist the wheel's motion.

Three patents for perpetual motion machines were recorded by the British Patent Office in the seventeenth century, and that number doubled in the next century. In the period between 1760 and 1780 London was said to abound with perpetual motion seekers and their public exhibitions. With characteristic asperity, Dircks observes:

> When we consider that in addition to these hopelessly imbecile efforts, numerous ingenious plans have, in addition, been made public in various scientific journals and early philosophical treatises, it becomes only the more remarkable that men's minds should not have long since lost all faith in such fruitless mechanical speculations. The present history affords abundant evidence of reproductions, rather than of progress; of taking a circular path ever leading to the same starting-point, instead of going beyond the fallacies of bygone ages.

In Germany, an engineer who had adopted the name Orffyreus (Johan Ernst Elias Bessler) devoted considerable effort to the problem and achieved a certain renown at the beginning of the eighteenth century. After experimenting with some three hundred different models, he claimed to have succeeded, but destroyed the device when the Hesse Castle government taxed it heavily. But Orffyreus persisted, and his second "successful" wheel was exhibited to the landgrave of Hesse, who permitted it to be placed in operation in a room that was then locked and sealed. After two months the room was unlocked and the wheel was found to be spinning at the same speed. The wheel became famous and the nobility and learned men came to observe it. A certain Baron Fischer described its operation in this fashion:

> The wheel turns with astonishing rapidity. Having tied a cord to the axle, to run an Archimedean screw to raise water, the wheel then made twenty turns a minute. This I noted several times by my watch, and I always found the same regularity. An attempt to stop it suddenly would raise a man from the ground. Having stopped it in this manner [and seeing that] it remained stationary (and here is the greatest proof of a perpetual motion), I commenced the movements very gently to see if it would of itself regain its former rapidity, which I doubted; but to my great astonishment I observed that the rapidity of the wheel augmented little by little until it made two turns, and then it regained its former speed. This experiment, showing the rapidity of the wheel augmented from the very slow movement that I gave it to an extraordinary rapid one, convinces me more than if I had only seen the wheel moving a whole year, which would not have persuaded me that it was perpetual motion, because it might have diminished little by little until it ceased altogether; but to gain speed instead of losing it, and to increase that speed to a certain degree in spite of the resistance of the air and the friction of the axles, I do not see how any one can doubt the truth of this action.

Not everyone was persuaded of the triumph. One critic wondered why one of Orffyreus's servants, who fled in fear for her life, had in her possession the written oath her master made her swear to preserve the device's secrecy. Orffyreus was a suspicious type as well as an

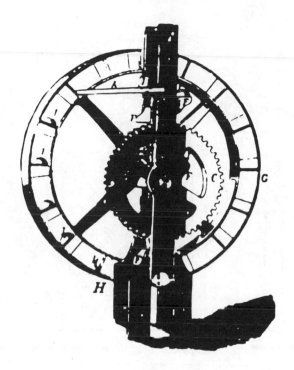

Figure 3

the device's secrecy. Orffyreus was a suspicious type as well as an irascible personality. The wheel was kept in a locked room to which visitors did not have access; they observed, instead, a rope connected to it by means of which the machine did work. It was also noted that certain parts of the wheel were carefully covered with canvas so that the inside could not be seen. When the landgrave engaged a Dutch philosopher and engineer to examine the wheel, Orffyreus was so outraged that he smashed the wheel to pieces.

The reinvention of the wheel continued. In 1790 we find the scheme of Dr. Conradus Schiviers (figure 3). Here a wheel with compartments is connected to an endless belt that carries balls to the top of the wheel and deposits them in the topmost compartment, where their weight turns the wheel. At the bottom of the revolution the balls fall out of their compartment onto the endless belt, which again lifts them to the top of the wheel. The wheel turns the belt, which operates the wheel. But these reciprocal motions could not be sustained.

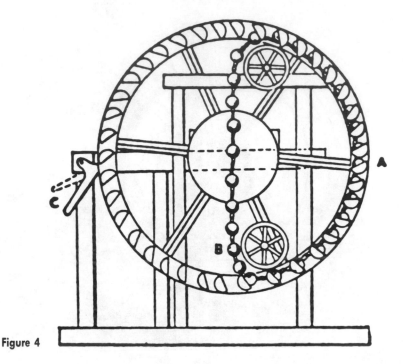

Figure 4

A century later we find a modification of Schiviers's wheel (figure 4): Here the balls are connected to each other and so there is no need for the belt, but the result is the same. At the left the lever C may be a brake to prevent the wheel from spinning too fast, more evidence of the boundless confidence and optimism of this special breed of inventors.

A British patent issued in 1866 to Henry Prince of Manchester described a wheel immersed in water with air bags and weights on the rim opposite each spoke. Air entering the bags on one side of the wheel displaced the weights and caused the wheel to rotate, or they floated in the water. At the same time the bags on the other side of the wheel were deflated by their weights. Dircks's acid comment: "This singular specimen of modern mechanical stupidity was duly honoured with a final and complete specification."

The principle of the overbalanced wheel evolved over time into increasingly complicated applications, but there were exceptions. Figure 5 shows the plan of F. G. Woodward, a graceful construction which

Figure 5

at first glance might suggest a piece of modern sculpture or the kind of gewgaw found on an executive's desk. Closer examination, however, reveals it to be the same unbalanced wheel.

Capillary action was enlisted by Sir William Congreve, a Member of Parliament and inventor of a rocket, around 1827 (figure 6). Both sponges and weights are positioned on the endless chain, which is placed in water. As the sponges on the vertical side absorb water, the increase in weight moves the chain down. On the upper leg the weights squeeze the water out of the sponges. Different in form as it may be, this is really the overbalanced apparatus again.

In the March 1925 issue of *Science and Invention* we come upon the huge device shown in figure 7. Scaled up it may be, but of course it is nothing but the omnipresent wheel. Here, again, an attendant (the inventor?) stands ready to apply the brake if the machine begins to run away with itself.

The quest for an ever-spinning wheel, started at least as long as seven centuries ago, continuous even now. Although the U.S. Patent

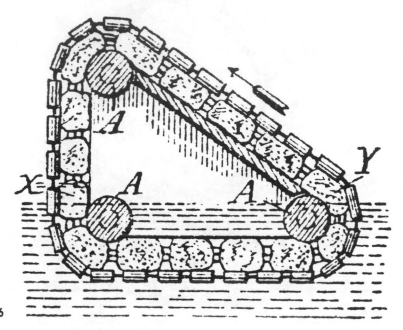

Figure 6

Office refuses to accept an application for a perpetual motion machine without a working model, a patent was granted in 1976 to David Diamond of Brooklyn, New York (figure 8). Yes, it is our familiar wheel, here in its underwater variation.

Doug Stewart, assigned to write an article on the subject of perpetual motion for *Smithsonian* magazine in 1986, found himself in Florida chatting with a seventy-six-year-old inventor named Edison Notestein, in front of a plastic wheel in which steel balls rolled back and forth in the hollow spokes. Notestein explained the operation: "Over here on the left side, the balls roll out toward the rim. They come down around here, then this cam pushes them toward the center. So it's always heavier on the left side. Always heavy." Something is wrong with the model, though; everytime Notestein starts it, it comes to a stop. "If I can once get it to run, then I can start refining it," he says, just as if his wheel had never before been seen by human eyes.

Stewart had advertised for perpetual motion devices in two magazines and found almost a subculture of inventors. A California man told

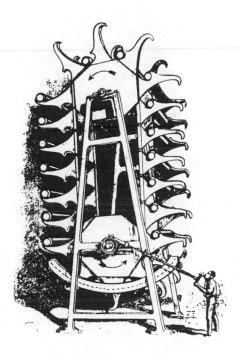

Figure 7

him his overbalanced wheel developed such speed on its own that one of its weights was hurled through a window. Success was also claimed for a machine built with magnets and a Lazy Susan table in Arkansas. According to the builder, "No professor can tell me it didn't work." A San Diego inventor assured Stewart that the only reason he had not built a working model using his design was that it would be twelve feet tall and too big for his backyard. "Besides," he said, "I know it will work, so why should I bother?"

What judgment should we pass on these perennial reinventors of de Honnecourt's wheel? How should they be graded? If they deserve high marks for their persistence, they surely fail in history. Most seem ignorant of the multitude of past efforts; those who are not simply reject the impossibility of the project.

The unbalanced wheel, however, is only one, if perhaps the most common, mechanical design for perpetual motion. Pneumatic power was the animating principle in the plan devised by Mark Antony Zimara (1460–1523), an Italian philosopher and physician. He proposed a huge

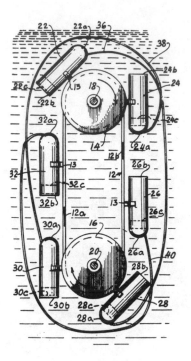

Figure 8

windmill juxtaposed with, and connected to, an equally huge bellows. The bellows forced air against the windmill's arms, turning them and creating the wind that supplied the bellows. The "instrument which will operate the bellows as the wheel itself turns," Zimara wrote, remained to be developed, but it "will be an honour to the ingenuity of the maker."

Figure 9 shows a device in which a vertically positioned Archimedes' screw carries balls to the top where they are deposited into cups attached to an endless chain. Their weight turns the chain and the screw.

More complicated yet is the device shown in figure 10 employing two spiral ball tracks. The rolling of heavy metal balls down the spiral track on the left actuates the track on the right, which raises the balls to restart the cycle.

A U.S. patent was issued around 1870 to Horace Wickham of Chicago for the oscillating beam machine shown in figure 11. A metal

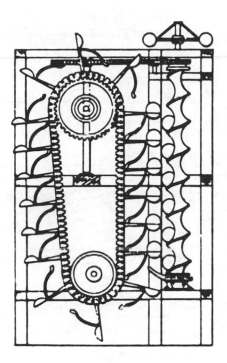

Figure 9

ball "charged with a necessary amount of quicksilver, for giving more weight to the same, and also for giving a much quicker momentum to the ball," rolls along the tube, which is hinged at the center, thereby depressing it. When the ball reaches the end of the tube it drops through a hole into the W-shaped tubes below, where it is returned to the starting point. The motion of the beam is translated into the rotation of a crankshaft, which drives a flywheel and a centrifugal governor.

A self-moving railway car is depicted in figure 12. The car is part of a double cone that rolls on a road made up of a series of inclined planes arranged in undulating fashion so that the cones will climb one hill and, when beyond the summit, descend the other, continuing in this alternating rise-and-fall method. The creator of this method of transportation early in the nineteenth century claimed that the greater the load of the car, the greater its speed, and if a path completely encircling the earth could be provided, the car would continue in its path until it

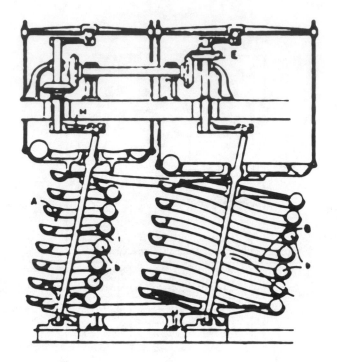

Figure 10

should "fall off the earth." Furthermore, if the car was stopped on any part of the road, the inventor claimed that "it will, when the cause of the stoppage is removed, proceed on its journey by mere power of gravity."

A tilting tray was the inspiration of Dr. Alois Drasch, an Austrian, whose invention received a patent in the United States in 1868 (figure 13). A metal ball in the tray continues in motion as the tray is tilted. The ball's motion is delivered to a shaft by a lever in the tray. In the drawing the motor is shown adapted to a wheeled vehicle, but the proud inventor pointed out that the motor "is applicable for the purpose of driving machinery of any kind, and it is particularly valuable in localities where the erection of a steam engine, or other motor, would be difficult and impracticable."

A separate chapter in the history of perpetual motion should be reserved for those who strove for the goal with water machines. Ord-Hume is perceptive in explaining why:

Figure 11

The use of water-power seems particularly prone to implant the idea [of perpetual motion] in the human mind. This is probably attributable to the assumption that water comes from nowhere in particular and costs Man nothing. This deludes the miller into assuming that his power costs him nothing by concealing the fact that his power is bought and paid for in terms of units of energy and that it can be delivered to him but once. In any event, it would seem that the proprietor of a water-mill—especially of one whose driving stream was subject to seasonal diminution of flow—was forever trying to make his water run back uphill and work for him again. . . .

Unfortunately, for the peace of the medieval mind, it knew of at least one highly plausible scheme for making water run uphill. If the end of a pipe, coiled like the thread of a screw, is immersed in water, and the whole pipe rotated like a screw, the water will climb up the pipe and keep on climbing as long as the pipe is kept turning. This strange but perfectly workable invention is called an Archimedean screw. . . . "What could be more simple," our ancestors asked, "than

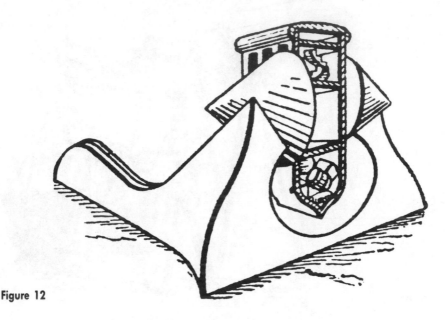

Figure 12

> to connect such an Archimedean screw with the water-wheel of a
> mill, and make the mill run the screw, and the screw run the mill?"

Robert Fludd (1574–1637) proposed a number of perpetual motion
water machines of which that shown in figure 14 is an example. In 1648
Bishop Wilkins of Chester, scientist and writer as well as clergyman,
analyzed the water-wheel-driven Archimedean screw, made a working
model, and concluded that it could not work. That discovery, however,
was no impediment to other inventors.

In Germany, Georg Andreas Bockler produced numerous schemes
for self-operating mills based on Archimedes's screw, which he described in a book published in 1686.

The marquis of Worcester, earlier mentioned in connection with
the overbalanced wheel, described "A Double Water-Screw" in his
Century of Inventions: "A double water-screw, the innermost to mount
the water, and the outermost for it to descend more in number of
threads, and consequently in quantity of water, though much shorter

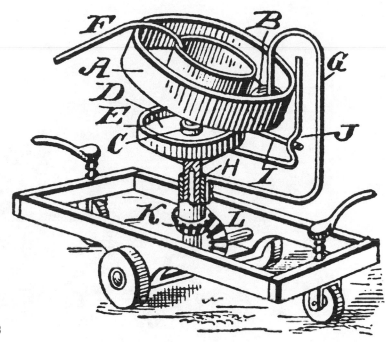

Figure 13

than the innermost screw by which the water ascendeth; a most extraordinary help for the turning of the screw to make the water rise."

Bishop Wilkins notwithstanding, more than two hundred years later the same machine was proposed to the *English Mechanic* (figure 15). Here mercury is substituted for water, and the Archimedean screw is enclosed, but the operation remains the same.

By 1871 an exasperated patent attorney in New York City was compelled to remark that one or another variation on Robert Fludd's closed-circuit water mill was submitted to him every year.

Hydraulic action of a different kind was incorporated into the motorized bicycle shown in figure 16. The rider's weight on the saddle forces water in the down-tube of the bicycle through nozzles and against a turbine wheel, thus propelling the bicycle and driving a pump, which sends the water back to the down-tube.

Working with fluids, some inventors either misunderstood their properties or misapplied them. Consider, for example, the scheme

Figure 14

shown in figure 17 where the glass receptacle features a hollow stem which permits the liquid to flow back into the main chamber. The assumption that the greater volume in the main chamber will force the liquid up, thereby creating a continuous movement, is dead wrong.

Even such a famous scientist, mathematician, and philosopher as Jean Bernoulli (1667–1748) could not resist entering the field. His creation, pictured in figure 18, involved mixing two liquids of different densities. The tube EF would have a filter, F, which would permit only the lighter liquid to pass. Since the lighter liquid would then rise in the tube, there would be a continuous flow. The assumption of a continuing replenishment of energy was as invalid here as it was in the case of the overbalanced wheel.

Buoyancy was also the animating principle in figure 19, where one half of the wheel is surrounded by water. It was claimed that the upward pressure on that surface would assist the wheel's rotation.

Somewhat similar, but involving capillary action again, is a device from the 1890s (figure 20). Here the absorption of water by the

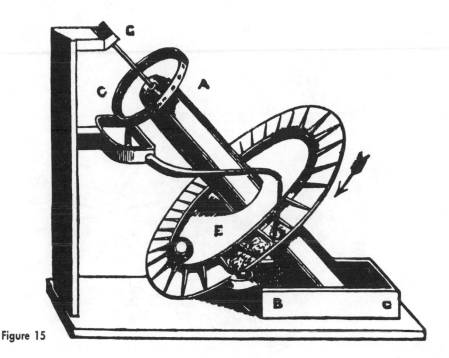

Figure 15

darkened areas of the wheels would make them heavier, creating the imbalance which would produce motion.

Even more startling is the idea shown in figure 21. The J-shaped glass tube is filled with water and contains a greased rope that passes through a watertight opening at the lower opening of the tube and continues around a pulley overhead. Motion is produced by the tendency of the greased rope to rise in the water and gravity's pull on that part of the rope that passes over the pulley.

The role of magnetism in perpetual motion may be as old as that of de Honnecourt's wheel. In 1269 Peregrinus proposed a gearlike metal wheel that would be drawn to a lodestone until a certain point in its revolution was reached, at which the lodestone then repelled the wheel, completing its cycle. No explanation of the method for the reversal was given.

Johannes Taisnerius, a Jesuit priest, published an illustration of magnetically induced perpetual motion around 1570 (figure 22). The lodestone on the top of the pillar draws a steel ball up the straight ramp

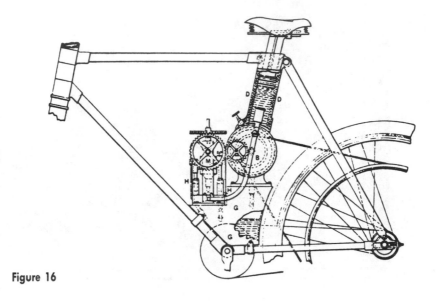

Figure 16

until it drops through a hole into the lower ramp, returning to the bottom where the lodestone starts attracting it again. Another Taisnerius scheme (figure 23) involved a crude gear which, when driven by the alternating attraction-repulsion of a lodestone, would spin a wheel. Bishop Wilkins, who had turned thumbs-down on Fludd's water wheel, came to a similar conclusion about Taisnerius's devices, although he ventured the opinion that magnetism seems "most conducible" to perpetual motion and perhaps "hereafter it may be contrived from" it.

Numerous wheels designed to operate though this force were proposed in the nineteenth century. In one variation, a plate made of a substance that would block the magnetic force was added to the assembly; by inserting and withdrawing the plate it was said that the wheel could be kept moving. A Scottish shoemaker named Spence claimed to have created two such machines. Although he was later exposed as a fraud, he succeeded in persuading Sir David Brewster, a noted physicist, that the machines "resolve the problem of perpetual motion."

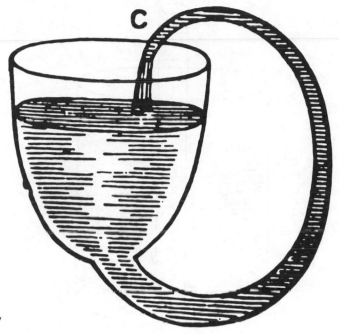

Figure 17

But if a material that blocks magnetism could be used, why not a material that blocks gravity? In its simplest form (figure 24), all that was needed was a piece of the magic stuff under one-half of a wheel. The intended result: Gravity would exert its pull only on the unblocked half.

With the development of electricity as a source of power, it was inevitable that the perpetual motionists would put it to use in their creations. The most common scheme involved coupling a motor with a generator in such a fashion that the motor drove the generator, which provided electricity for the motor.

Electromagnetism purported to energize a Kansas man's simple creation, shown in figure 25. The movement of the wheel produces electricity, which creates a magnetic field in the coil, C, attracting the core, G, forward, discharging the coil and turning the wheel to which it is attached by a crank.

*   *   *

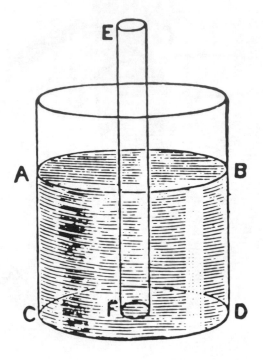

Figure 18

We pause here for a moment to ask a fundamental question: What is perpetual motion? Our first impulse is to say that it is endless motion. But we don't really mean that, or at least we don't need to go so far as to say "endless." Nothing in the universe is endless. Even the sun will come to an end. Besides, we are uncomfortable with the idea of eternity. We think of James Joyce's image of a tiny bird removing the largest of mountains by daily carrying away a grain of sand—when the mountain is completely removed that is the first moment of the dawn of the first day of eternity. But we need not struggle, for *perpetuum mobile* really refers to something else: Ultimately, it is a machine that produces more energy than it consumes. This is the important test, for everyone agrees that every machine will wear out. But this more precise test of producing more energy than the machine consumes leads us to the principle on which all the devices we have described so far founder: the first law of thermodynamics.

That law, in its most basic formulation, says simply that energy can be neither created nor destroyed—energy is always conserved.

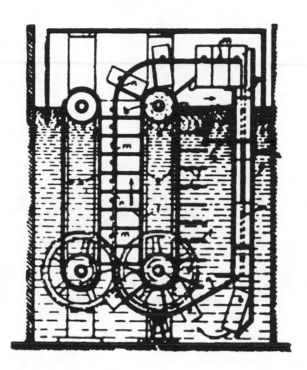

Figure 19

Therefore, for a machine to produce energy, energy must first be introduced from outside the machine. That outside energy source could be a human hand, gravity, wind, magnetism, electricity, etc. In the case of a water mill, energy in the form of gravity makes the water run downhill and pulls it over the mill, but in order to redeliver water back upstream, solar energy is needed to vaporize the water and return it as rain. Similarly, while a magnet may attract a piece of iron to it, an equal amount of force must be applied to separate the two. So, the devices we have been looking at all require *at least* as much energy to make them run as they can produce. However, nature has also created the equivalent of an energy leak in everything that "runs": friction—some energy is *always* lost to friction and this is why every perpetual motion machine will fail. In effect, a perpetual motion machine would be one that violates the first law of thermodynamics because, by definition, it must create new energy.

It may be ironic, then, but not surprising that the establishment of this law in the middle of the nineteenth century by James Joule, Julius

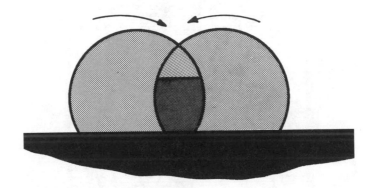

Figure 20

Robert von Mayer, and Hermann von Helmoltz derived, in part, from the observation that perpetual motion had never been achieved in spite of centuries of effort. If a machine that created energy out of nothing was impossible, the amount of energy in the world must be limited.

But if energy can't be created, perhaps it could be recaptured and used, over and over again. Stanley Angrist, writing in *Scientific American,* points out that while most perpetual motion machines violate the first law of thermodynamics, some do not: "Neither friction nor electrical resistance is a significant problem in their design. They are nonetheless impossibilities because they attempt instead to circumvent the second law of thermodynamics."

With the coming of the steam age, it was natural to ask whether, if a certain amount of mechanical energy could be transformed into the same amount of heat energy, was the reverse true? Could a certain amount of heat energy be transformed into the same amount of mechanical energy? That is a serious question, for if true, certain types of perpetual motion become possible. In heat engines, of which the steam

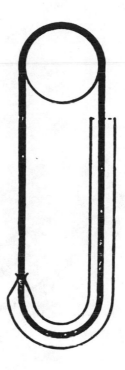

Figure 21

engine is the most common example, some of the heat put into the machine is lost in various ways, including losses to the surrounding areas. If it was possible to create such an engine that did not lose any heat, it would be a perpetual motion device. Since it had never been possible to create such a device, the second law of thermodynamics was formulated, which declares that in order to do work, heat always moves from a warmer body to a cooler body, or "runs downhill."

For a graphic proof of this proposition we need only look at the invention of John Gamgee's, which was the subject of intense interest in the 1880s. Gamgee was a Washington, D.C., inventor who had created a kind of steam engine in which liquid ammonia was used instead of water. He called it the zeromotor because it was designed to operate at zero degrees centigrade (figure 26). Liquid ammonia in the machine's boiler would be vaporized by heat from the environment. The vapor would be introduced into a cylinder where it would expand and drive a piston. Gamgee assumed the vapor would condense and return as a liquid to the boiler. In this he was mistaken, for the cooling

Figure 22

necessary to transform the vapor into a liquid would have required more energy than the zeromotor could produce.

Such a basic misconception did nothing to cool the enthusiasm with which official Washington received Gamgee's invention. In March 1881 B. F. Isherwood, the chief engineer of the U.S. Navy, reported favorably on the device to the secretary of the Navy:

> The purpose of the Department in ordering an examination of Professor Gamgee's . . . machine was . . . to obtain an opinion . . . as to whether his observations on the behavior of ammonia in the process were sufficiently accurate to warrant his inference of the practicability of constructing a successful zeromotor for industrial uses—a motor, in short, destined to supersede the steam engine. Accordingly, I have closely investigated the working of the apparatus. The facts of liquid ammonia gasifying at ordinary atmospheric temperature under very high pressures, and of that gas undergoing very great refrigeration

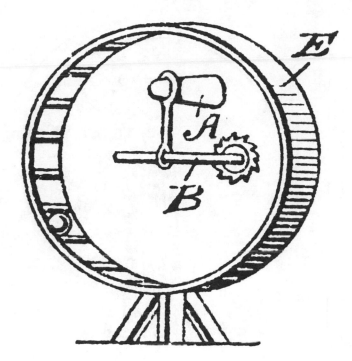

Figure 23

when used expansively in doing work, are not called in question by any one. Both are well-known phenomena. The special fact to be observed was whether any part of the ammonia which entered the cylinder as a gas left it as a liquid, and, so far as the form of the apparatus allowed any observation to be made, such appeared to be the case. The possibility of the invention of a new motor of incalculable utility would seem to be established, and in view of the immense importance of the subject for the Navy and to mankind at large, I strongly recommend it to the serious attention of the Department, suggesting further that whatever facilities the Department can, in its opinion, consistently extend, be allowed to Professor Gamgee for the continuance of his important experimental inquiries in the Washington Navy Yard. . . .

I have ventured these few remarks to show the nature and scope of Prof. Gamgee's invention, which is not that of a machine for the application of power, but for the immensely more important purpose of generating power itself, so that, strictly speaking, it includes as a basis all other machines.

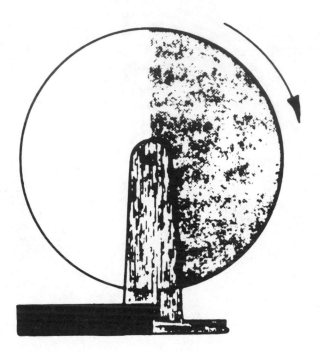

Figure 24

Models of the Gamgee motor were inspected by Cabinet members and even President Garfield, but no amount of official acknowledgment, even coupled with the enthusiastic endorsement of Chief Engineer Isherwood, could overcome a fundamental rule of physics, and the invention soon disappeared.

Among the follies of science, perpetual motion is not as old as alchemy or the quadrature of the circle, but the impossibility of creating such a machine was recognized at least as early as the late 1500s. In general, that conclusion derived not from an understanding of physical principles since the laws of thermodynamics would not be discovered for centuries, but from careful observation of each model and the detection of a flaw in each case that made the claimed operation impossible.

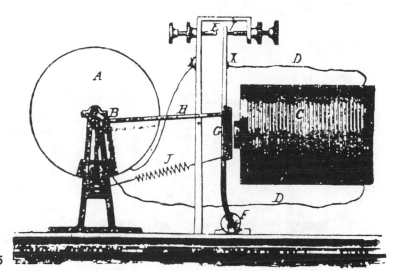

Figure 25

One of the earliest to reach that conclusion was the mathematician Simon Stevinus (1548–1620), who demonstrated principles of equilibrium on an inclined plane by showing that perpetual motion was impossible. The experiments of Galileo (1564–1642) comparing the motion of a freely falling body with that of one on an inclined plane evidenced a similar understanding. More explicitly, Marin Mersenne denied the possibility of perpetual motion in 1644 and likened those who sought it to the alchemists who searched for the Philosopher's Stone. By 1775 the Parisian Academy of Sciences closed its doors to those who dreamed up schemes for perpetual motion.

The experiences of patent offices provide some perspective on the history and intensity of this folly, for these were usually the focal points of the perpetual motionists' efforts. The patenting of inventions in England dates to 1623. The first perpetual motion machine was granted a patent in 1635. It described "engins, which being put in order, will cause and mainteyne their own mocions with continuance and without

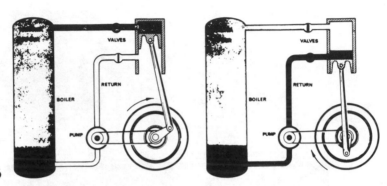

Figure 26

any borrowed force of man, horse, wind, river, or brooke, whereby many severall kinde of excellent rare worke may be pformed to the great good and benefitt of the common wealth, the like cause and means of which continuance of mocion hath not been heretofore brought to pfeccion." No drawing accompanied the patent.

By 1903 more than six hundred patents for this kind of device had been granted in Great Britain. Since only twenty-five had been issued in the period ending 1855, the tremendous surge of interest in the subject in the latter half of the nineteenth century becomes apparent. At the end of this period, the years 1901, 1902, and 1903 witnessed thirteen, ten, and nine applications for such patents respectively.

In America there were some ten patents for perpetual motion on file by 1836 in the United States Patent Office. For years, one commentator wrote, the Patent Office income was considerably augmented annually by the receipt of fees from inventors of perpetual motion machines. By 1911, however, the office had seen enough and began distributing the following advice:

The views of the Patent Office are in accord with those of the scientists who have investigated this subject and are to the effect that such devices are physical impossibilities. The position of the Office can be rebutted only by the exhibition of a working model. Were the application to be forwarded to the Examiner for consideration, he would make no examination as to the merits, but his first action would be the requirement that a working model be filed.

In view of all the circumstances, the Commissioner has instructed that applications for patent on Perpetual Motion, complete in all other particulars, shall be held in the Application Rooms as incomplete until a working model has been filed. Such model must be filed within one year from the date of application, or the application will become abandoned. The Office hesitates to accept the filing fees from applicants who believe they have discovered Perpetual Motion, and deems it only fair to give such applicants a word of warning that the fees paid cannot be recovered after the case has been considered by the Examiner. For these reasons it has been thought best to meet the inventor at the threshold of the Office, and give him an opportunity to recover the moneys paid into the Office, in the event of his failure to comply with the requirement

But even this did not turn away the creators of these machines, some of whom managed to get through anyway and finally secure a patent.

The British patent office takes a more forthright position, refusing any application that claims perpetual motion on the ground that it is obviously contrary to well-established physical laws.

Since *perpetuum mobile* occupied such a prominent place in the public consciousness, it is hardly surprising that there have been men who directed their efforts and energies not at solving the problem but at exploiting its commercial opportunities dishonestly. Orffyreus, with his secret wheel locked securely in the landgrave's castle, may have been one of the earliest of these.

In nineteenth-century Germany a man named Geiser exhibited his "successful" machine. Upon his death, the device was examined carefully and found to contain a clockwork, hidden in the supporting framework, which was powered by a hand-wound spring.

In London a machine was exhibited for some time on a pay-per-view basis until some in the audience lifted the device in such a way that the concealed spring motor unwound.

Philadelphia was the scene of a notable fraud in 1812. In that year Charles Redheffer set up a machine and charged admission to those interested in seeing it. It was soon a sensation and wagers were placed as to whether it was genuine. Interest was such that the promoter was able to charge men five dollars to view the device, although he admitted women free of charge.

Redheffer had applied to the Pennsylvania state legislature for a grant, and that body appointed a committee of experts to investigate. When the group came to examine the machine, they found that the door to the room containing it was locked and the key missing, so their inspection was limited to a viewing through a barred window. The son of one of the committee members astutely noted that the teeth of two gears in the assembly were worn in a manner inconsistent with the claimed motion, indicating that it was being driven by some concealed source of power.

The committee chose an ingenious method of exposing Redheffer. Isiah Lukens, a notable engineer and inventor, was engaged to make an exact model of the fraudulent machine. Although Lukens could work only from a verbal description furnished by the committee, he carried out his assignment so well that his model operated as well as Redheffer's—and it also contained a clockwork motor concealed in the hollow base of the machine. The whole contrivance was enclosed in a wood and glass case with four wooden knobs on top, apparently as ornaments. One of these knobs, however, was the winder for the clockwork motor which could be subtly wound by an attendant who seemed to be doing nothing more than polishing the case.

A demonstration of the Lukens model was arranged to which Redheffer was invited. When it appeared to work, Redheffer was so astounded that he privately offered a large amount of money to learn how it was done.

But the exposure of Redheffer as a fraud in Philadelphia was not the end of his career. The following year he opened a perpetual motion show in New York where crowds were soon flocking to pay his admission fee. Here he encountered Robert Fulton, the celebrated engineer, and experienced an even more dramatic debunking. Fulton had observed the machine for only a short time before he exclaimed, "Why, this is a crank motion!" He was perceptive enough to see the kind of irregularity in movement and hear the irregularity in sound that are characteristic of manual cranking. Fulton confronted Redheffer, denounced him as a fraud, and, with the approval of the crowd, began to demonstrate it. He took apart an apparently innocuous part of the machine located next to a wall and revealed a belt drive which passed through the wall. This eventually led Fulton to a back attic, where he found a long-bearded old man sitting on a stool eating a crust of bread with one hand and turning a crank with the other.

With this discovery the crowd became enraged, destroyed the perpetual motion machine, and forced Redheffer to flee, bringing his career at last to an end.

E. P. Willis, a Connecticut machinist, produced a machine in the 1850s that Stanley Angrist has called "perhaps the most elegant over-balanced wheel ever built." Willis first exhibited it in New Haven and then moved it to New York, charging admission in both places. Enclosed in a glass case, this contrivance features a tilting wheel that seemed to move by itself (figure 27). Sharp-eyed observers eventually focused on an apparently useless support which actually forced compressed air against a flywheel, thereby turning the overbalanced wheel.

In a factory building in Newark, New Jersey, in the 1870s, a demonstration of what was purported to be an electromagnetic perpetual motion machine for the purpose of raising money for its development seemed to be going well. Whenever the inventor hooked up the machine throughout the afternoon it appeared to produce more energy than its tiny electric batteries provided. After six o'clock, however, the machine would not function. It was revealed that power was being supplied from another source in the factory building, which closed down along with all the workshops at six.

The most famous of the perpetual motion frauds was probably John Worrell Keely. He came on the scene in Philadelphia in 1872 when he claimed to have discovered a new source of energy. Exhibitions in subsequent years in Philadelphia, New York, and Boston, of an appara-

Figure 27

tus which ran on a powerful force produced by the disintegration of a few drops of water, augmented his reputation, especially when some well-known scientists were unable to disprove his claims. By 1875 Keely had unveiled a combined generator and engine. The engine was a conventional steam engine, but the generator was a maze of metal globes, tubes, petcocks, nozzles, valves, and gauges. The inventor blew into a nozzle into which he then poured five gallons of water. After making a series of mysterious adjustments Keely would show visitors a pressure gauge indicating that the generator was full of a vapor, with a pressure of 10,000 pounds per square inch. "People have no idea of the power in water," he would say. "A bucket of water has enough of this vapor to produce a power sufficient to move the world out of its orbit."

A pseudotechnical language became part of the promotion. Keely referred to his "hydro-pneumatic-pulsating-vacu-engine," "sympathetic equilibrium," "etheric disintegration," "quadruple negative harmonics," and "atomic triplets."

Riding his rising star, he organized the Keely Motor Company, with a capital of $5 million to develop his motor, which he sometimes called the "Liberator." When the newspapers continued to report favorably and a number of scientists not only endorsed the motor but invested in the company, there was wild speculation in the stock.

By 1886, however, Keely had failed to develop a commercially feasible motor and the Keely Motor Company would no longer finance his activities. He probably would have disappeared had not Mrs. Bloomfield H. Moore, a wealthy widow, become a convert to his cause and a new source of financial assistance. In the years that followed Keely made new "discoveries" and was successful in avoiding exposure.

In 1895, however, Mrs. Moore invited Addison H. Burke, the president of the Spring Garden Institute, to investigate Keely's inventions. Burke, accompanied by E. Alexander Scott, an electrical engineer who was familiar with Keely, became convinced that the Keely devices were fake and reported that to Mrs. Moore. But the widow's faith in Keely was undiminished. In 1896 she engaged Professor W. Lascelles-Scott, an English physicist, to make an investigation. After a month of study the professor reported publicly that "Keely has demonstrated to me, in a way which is absolutely unquestionable, the existence of a force hitherto unknown." But when Mrs. Moore arranged for a final test before the professor and E. A. Scott, Keely refused and she discontinued most of her support.

Upon Keely's death in 1898, Scott and Burke proceeded to examine the inventor's house, and the Keely Motor Company took possession of his laboratory and arranged for the study of his engine by an electrician named T. Burton Kinraide.

The house was found to contain an elaborate arrangement whereby a motor in the cellar produced compressed air which was delivered through brass tubes hidden in a false wall and a false ceiling to the laboratory on the second floor where it was directed against the "motor's" wheel. Rubber bulbs concealed in the floor and responsive to foot pressure permitted Keely to start and stop the operation.

Kinraide, working separately with the Keely engine, soon found it to be fraudulent. "The new force he (Keely) introduced is bosh," said

Kinraide. "I have accomplished everything that we ever saw him do, and it is extraordinarily simple."

On January 29, 1899, the *New York Journal* headline proclaimed, "Keely, the Monumental Fraud of the Century!" The headline was ironic, for shortly before his death, Keely had confided to a close friend his choice of an epitaph in remarkably similar language: "Keely, the greatest humbug of the nineteenth century."

While Keely's career was coming to an end, J. M. Aldrich was exhibiting his version of a perpetual motion machine in Bradford, Pennsylvania, to prospective investors. The device worked so well that Aldrich was able to sell a number of interests in the enterprise— too many, it seemed, leading to his arrest. Escaping conviction, he continued to raise money with his invention until March 1899 when one of many investors who had purchased a half interest in the property somehow took possession of the apparatus and sent it to the patent office. There it was found that the source of the motive power was a spring hidden in the base. *Scientific American,* permitted to inspect it, could not resist an admiring remark: "The model, as it stands on our office table, is certainly a masterpiece of deception, and eminently calculated to deceive the unwary."

In 1928 Lester J. Hendershot announced in New York City that he had invented a motor that would run forever by tapping into the Earth's magnetic field. He had at least one impressive testimonial: the commandant of the U.S. Army's Selfridge Field in Detroit endorsed the machine and pictured a glorious future for it. A familiar denouement occurred, however, when it was discovered that a tiny battery hidden in the motor was the real source of power.

The deception that impostors like Keely practiced on the public should be considered in relation to the self-deception that seems at the heart of most perpetual motion schemes. The lonely inventor is convinced he is close to the breakthrough—so close, perhaps, that he believes he has really accomplished it. Such a transition requires considerable ego, a force which, if only slightly redirected, might produce the kind of charlatanry we have seen. Carleton Croyle, who heads the group in the U.S. Patent Office that deals with most perpetual motion submissions, finds this kind of elevated self-importance, often verging on arrogance, to be a common trait among these applicants.

No survey of perpetual motion would be complete without a consideration of how it has been intertwined with clockmaking. The skill with which these craftsmen dealt with the problem of friction and their ingenuity in harnessing external power sources made them natural confederates of the perpetual motionists. It is hardly surprising that many of the fake machines were actually driven by cleverly concealed clockworks. Orffyreus, whose wheel was celebrated in the early years of the eighteenth century and who was probably an impostor, had been a clockmaker. Beyond that, there are those who claim—incorrectly— that some of the clockmakers actually succeeded in the perpetual motion sweepstakes.

Most notable, perhaps, was James Cox, whose creation, aptly entitled "Perpetual Motion," was on display in London in 1774. This was a beautiful standing clock activated by variations in atmospheric pressure which, operating on a large reservoir of mercury, wound the timepiece's motor. Since the source of the power was perpetual in almost every sense, the Cox clock seemed to have attained the Holy Grail. While it no longer functions, this timepiece survives today and may still be seen in the Victoria and Albert Museum.

There have been other perpetual clocks. One observed in 1751 was said to wind itself "by alternating cold and heat." Temperature changes were also said to drive a perpetual clock exhibited in Paris about the time when the Cox clock was on display in London. A similar clock created in Sweden in 1934 utilized both changes in temperature and atmospheric pressure.

But do these clever mechanisms truly attain perpetual motion? In a vernacular sense they seem to pass the test, for they will operate forever, or as long as there are heat and air pressure fluctuations, subject, of course, to the limitation imposed by the durability of their moving parts. By the more rigorous test, however, they fail, for although they may be capable of movement over an indefinite period of time, they simply convert an external energy source and therefore do not produce more energy than that needed to operate. In other words, they leave intact the first law of thermodynamics.

The history of man's stubborn efforts over many centuries to create a machine that would never run down, in the face of consistent failure and the impossibility decreed by the scientific establishment, sometimes seems quixotic, sometimes incredibly wrongheaded, sometimes suggestive of some obscure moral meaning. It is no coincidence, perhaps, that this centuries-long effort overlapped a period of intensive searching for the secret of everlasting life, whether expressed as the Elixir of Life or the Fountain of Youth. The metaphor of the human motor discussed by Anson Rabinbach in his work with that title did not appear until the end of the nineteenth century, but whether the idea of the body as a piece of machinery that grew less efficient with age and finally ceased operation was influential or not, the search for physical immortality (as distinguished from the immortality of the soul) and the search for perpetual motion suggest parallel efforts driven by the same impulse. This commonalty has been expressed by Charles Gillispie, the science historian, who has shown that both energy and entropy "are highly sophisticated and abstract representations of certain elementary experiences of the world, certain serious intuitions: Energy, or the intuition that there is an activity, a 'force' in things beyond matter and motion that makes nature go," and entropy the "complementary experience of water seeking its own level, of hot bodies cooling, of springs untensing." To these images it would be easy to add that of the human body, with its growth and vitality gradually aging and subsiding into death.

It will be observed, quite properly, that the goal of perpetual motion held out enormous material promise, as self-sustaining machines would require neither muscle nor fuel. That is not to say, however, that in developing such a marvel the inventor would be simply adjusting a set of gears and reaping enormous profits in the business world. The concept amounted to nothing less than a miraculous act of creation, a fitting companion to the discovery of perpetual youth, as both involved a fundamental alteration of the divine order. Furthermore, the ever-running machine appeals powerfully as a symbol: If machine death can be overcome, perhaps the same can be done for human death. It was no accident, therefore, that when Jack Phin described *The Seven Follies of Science,* as recently as 1906, one chapter was devoted to perpetual motion and another to the Elixir of Life.

That we no longer have searchers for the fountain of youth, but an apparent abundance of perpetual motion inventors, may mean only that ours is a more technological age in which one branch of the same grand quest has withered while the other continues to grow.

MUSICAL MADNESS

10

"Have you ever seen," inquired Bernard Baruch, quoting an unidentified source in his forward to the 1932 edition of *Extraordinary Popular Delusions,* "in some wood, on a sunny quiet day, a cloud of flying midges—thousands of them—hovering apparently motionless, in a sunbeam? . . . Yes? . . . Well, did you ever see the whole flight—each mite apparently preserving its distance from all others—suddenly move, say three feet to one side or the other? Well, *What made them do that?* A breeze? I said a *quiet* day. But to recall—did you ever see them move directly back again in the same unison? Well, what made them do *that?* Great human mass movements are slower of inception but much more effective." Baruch's vivid image deserves further study, for it forces us to think about how crowd and delusional behavior come about.

Even before Gustave Le Bon showed that there was a separate crowd mind, there was some speculation about the way in which crowd behavior came about. J. F. C. Hecker, a doctor and professor in Berlin, writing in 1833, drew a parallel between such group behavior and the spread of disease in epidemics. In particular, he linked the Black Death and the medieval dancing manias. The theory that mental states are subject to infection just like the physical body has endured and has not only been studied by L. S. Penrose in his 1952 work *On the Objective Study of Crowd Behavior* but was sufficiently viable to have produced the bacillus metaphor that Gertrude Shelby used so effectively in reporting on the Florida land boom.

And yet there are cases where the epidemic theory of crowd behavior with its sequential character, almost like a line of dominoes collapsing one after another, seems incongruous with experience. Here we must question Baruch's observation that mass movements are slower of inception than the instantaneous flight of insects. An example, fictional, but no less persuasive for that reason, can be seen in one of the concluding episodes of *Perfume* by Patrick Suskind. It is the author's wonderful conceit in that novel that an ogre of a man who has committed a series of terrible crimes is suddenly transformed before a hostile crowd assembled to enjoy his torture and execution into a radiant, angelic being, if not the Messiah himself, only because he has scented himself with a powerful and irresistible perfume. If we are not accustomed to the creation of such delusions through the sense of smell, we are familiar with their production through the sense of sight, as only the briefest reflection on such matters as optical illusions, sleight of hand, and the potential of language to manipulate will affirm. Improbable as he may seem, however, it is Susskind's monster who carries with him the larger meaning that irrational behavior can be stimulated directly through the senses by way of powerful circuits in which all our carefully trained abilities to observe, compare, and deduce are bypassed. Perhaps there is no better example of this than the intoxicating character of music, which Diane Ackerman has called "the perfume of the senses" in her *A Natural History of the Senses*. In the right setting certain combinations of sounds can melt all our restraint, strip us of all our civilized character, inspire lunatic exhibitions, mindless prancing, fury, ecstasy, and more. This is the dark side of music, far removed from the pleasant reverie of the concert hall or the half-heard songs coming from the radio, but occupying a considerable tradition by itself in which we might find trance-inducing tribal dancing, the frenzy of the ancient Greek Corybantes, and the delirium of rock concerts. In our consideration of antic crowd behavior it has a special significance in that it tends to focus our attention on the stimulus for such behavior and thus sheds light on the manner in which it grows.

Rhythm, that basic element of music, is now beginning to be understood as a surprisingly profound and pervasive influence in the human makeup. Scientists studying synchrony have pondered how in the insect world crickets are able to chirp in time, and, even more dramatically, Southeast Asian fireflies in huge numbers can flash in perfect unison. The significance of the insect phenomena lies in what they might tell us about the way in which certain body cells fire together to control the human heartbeat and brain and other organ functions; how, for example, the menstrual cycles of women living together in prisons and dormitories tend toward conformity.

Partly subtle and not well understood, rhythm's intoxicating effects are nevertheless familiar to anyone who has been transported by the beat on a dance floor or exhilarated by the music of a marching band. A human analogue to the simultaneous chirping of crickets and illumination of fireflies may well be the unconscious tapping of thousands of feet to a rousing polka or the intense—and often puzzling—reaction of many young fans at popular music concerts during the last half century.

The time is October 12, 1944. The world is engulfed in war, but the tide of events has shifted in favor of the Allies. In Europe the invasion of Normandy in June led to the liberation of Paris two months later, and, in combination with the Russian drive west, was to produce the unconditional surrender of Germany the following May. In the Pacific theater, General Douglas MacArthur was returning to the Philippines and American military forces were moving closer to Japan, island by island. By the following August, in quick succession, Hiroshima and Nagasaki would have been destroyed by atomic bombs and, a few days later, Japan would have surrendered. In the White House Franklin Delano Roosevelt was about to win reelection to an unprecedented third term although he would be dead six months later, bereaved by a nation that was then dismayed to find that he had been succeeded by a little former haberdasher from Missouri who seemed devoid of any qualifications for the great office.

The place is the Paramount Theatre in New York's Times Square where a twenty-seven-year-old singer from Hoboken, New Jersey, is about to begin a three-week engagement of five shows a day that would create such an uproar that public attention would be briefly diverted from the momentous events in Europe and the Pacific. He had performed here before with great success in January 1943, but the sensation now would exceed everything that had gone before. A crowd of teen-agers estimated to number as many as 30,000 has formed trying to get in, but at 9:10 A.M. all 3,500 seats in the theater are filled and the crowd is out of control. Times Square is blocked; traffic cannot get through; agitated teen-age girls crash through store windows and stampede pedestrians. The injured are taken away by ambulance. An impressive police presence including 200 detectives, 70 patrolmen, 50 traffic cops, 421 police reserves, 12 mounted police, 20 radio cars, 2 emergency trucks, and 20 policewomen has proved incapable of controlling the throng.

Inside the ornate red and gold theater the fortunate 3,500 are rigid with attention, their pockets and purses filled with fruit and sandwiches, for most of them will stay on to see many shows. At the end of the first show only 250 leave the theater. Most in the audience are girls between the ages of twelve and sixteen, known as "bobby-soxers" for their white saddle shoes and low-cut socks, and they are already squealing and screaming although the object of their affections will not come on stage for another hour, not until the film is over. With the end of the film the stage is lit and the orchestra plays a few bars of music recognized as the entertainer's signature and the girls go crazy, their shrieks rising to a pitch that one observer said one hears but rarely in a lifetime. From one end of the stage appears the young Frank Sinatra dressed in an expensive brown sport coat and brown doeskin trousers. His movements and gestures are a little awkward and his somewhat scrawny physique and large ears hardly suggest the ideal of male beauty. Surrounded by curly black hair, his face was once described as that of a debauched faun. But all of that is unimportant. The bobby-soxers are on their feet now, applauding wildly while they continue to scream. Some are slumped in their seats, having fainted, or having decided to act as if they fainted. Others have rushed down the aisles to get as close as possible to the object of their adoration. When he blows a kiss to the audience the hysterical response it produces lasts for five minutes, subsiding only when he threatens to leave the stage. Sinatra's performance consists of some five or six songs interspersed with patter. There seems to be nothing unique in him or his renditions. To Bruce Bliven of *The New Republic,* his voice seemed "a pleasant, untrained light baritone—a weak one were it not boosted in power by the microphone." So intense is the energy level that the shrieking goes on even in the middle of the songs. When he sings, "I'll walk alone," plaintively, hundreds shout their willingness to accompany him. One girl shouts in anguish, "I'll walk wid ya, Frankie!" Later he modestly wonders aloud whether he is popular, whereupon the audience shouts, "Yes!" to his "No" over and over again. With his stint over, it requires a clever appeal to the audience's patriotism to get him off the stage. He can leave only when the orchestra starts playing "The Star-Spangled Banner" and spotlights illuminate American flags fluttering in an artificial breeze.

The Swoonatra Phenomenon, as some in the press labeled it, did not erupt suddenly at the Paramount Theatre in October 1944, but had been on the scene and growing for some time. While its appearance may have been natural, it was helped to expand mightily by shrewd publicity tactics. As early as May 1941 Sinatra was already an established performer with the band of Tommy Dorsey, and girls in the audience had begun to exhibit their curious reaction to his singing. When the girls groaned, Dorsey would stop the music and the band would groan back, creating a kind of dialogue in which the teenagers were encouraged to vent their feelings more and more boisterously.

Dorsey himself was amazed at the reaction: "You could almost feel the excitement comin' up out of the crowds when that kid stood up to sing. Remember, he was no matinee idol. He was a skinny kid with big ears. And yet what he did to women was something awful."

But after a contract dispute with Dorsey, Sinatra was an unattached singer at a time when the big band was the standard vehicle for such performers. Perhaps because he had caused some swooning in a performance the week before in a theater in Newark, New Jersey, the manager of the Paramount Theatre in New York City added him to the stage show for a run that was to commence on December 30, 1942. The program already seemed filled with attractions. In addition to a popular film, it featured Benny Goodman, known as the "King of Swing," singer Peggy Lee, and Jess Stacy on the piano. Benny Goodman himself, the country's top bandleader, could have packed the house. A serious musician who had never heard of Sinatra, Goodman played to a rapt audience for an hour, and then introduced Sinatra perfunctorily. When the singer stuck his head through the curtains, the girls in the audience screamed with such force that Goodman was startled. Looking over his shoulder the bandleader asked, "What was that?"

A few days into this first Paramount engagement Sinatra was introduced to George Evans, an energetic press agent who immediately began exploiting the swooning young fans in systematic fashion. He hired twelve girls to attend each show and, following a kind of script of their own, kick off a larger audience reaction. In the basement of the theater Evans rehearsed them to jump up and scream, "Oh, Frankie, oh, Frankie" when the singer began a certain song or hit a certain note. When Sinatra would sing, "I'm not much to look at, nothin' to see" from "She's Funny That Way," one of the girls was coached to yell, "Oh, Frankie, yes you are!" When he sang, "Come to Papa, come to Papa, do" from "Embraceable You," the girls were told to scream, "Oh, Daddy!" after which Sinatra would whisper into the microphone, "Gee, that's a lot of kids for one fellow." Two girls were to faint in the aisle and the others were to continue moaning loudly. Sinatra himself was instructed to carry out a role with gestures and remarks: He was to clutch the microphone in a certain way and spread his arms wide when singing a certain phrase. Evans then gave out hundreds of free tickets to schoolgirls on vacation, posted an ambulance conspicuously outside the theater, and passed out ammonia to the ushers to use with fans who fainted.

So successful were these strategies that the newspapers were soon showing pictures of girls being carried out of the theater after swooning over Sinatra. Although only twelve had been hired, thirty girls fainted. Within days the ticket line stretched around the block and the press was filled with stories of the sensational new crooner. To deal with the demand, the management of the Paramount held the show over for another four weeks, something that had not happened since 1929.

Encouraged by Evans, fan clubs sprang up around the country. Among them were the Moonlit Sinatra Club, the Slaves of Sinatra, the Flatbush Girls Who Would Lay Down Their Lives for Frank Sinatra Fan Club, the Sighing Society of Sinatra Swooners, and the Frank Sinatra Fan and Mahjong Club, the last consisting of forty middle-aged women who played the game while listening to Sinatra records.

Following his success at the Paramount, in April 1943 Sinatra was booked into the Riobamba, a New York City nightclub frequented by socialites. Although he was given a lower billing than the other entertainers and there was some doubt as to how this new audience would take to the singer, he was again a sensation. The following month he returned to the Paramount, where thousands of screaming teen-agers swirled around the theater, broke down doors, and brushed aside police and security men. One of the singer's associates said, "It was absolute pandemonium. This time they threw more than roses. They threw their panties and their brassieres. They went nuts, absolutely nuts."

The indefatigable Evans also arranged for Sinatra to sing around the country in concerts with various symphony orchestras. Although classical music fans were outraged, the performances were marked with the same delirious behavior by the singer's fans. At the Hollywood Bowl the audience, mostly teen-agers, waited through the first part of the program, in which the orchestra played a series of pieces by Russian composers, and then exploded when Sinatra came on stage. By the time he had sung a number of ballads the girls were out of control, and after his performance, which included encore after encore, many screamed, "Oh, Frankie, we love you so!"

The bizarre behavior of The Voice's fans was not restricted to the threaters and auditoriums where he performed. Some traveled to the Sinatra home in Hasbrouck Heights, New Jersey, where they worshiped the house for hours. The bolder among them rang the doorbell and talked to Sinatra's wife, asking about details of their idol's personal life, begging her for the clothespins that held Frankie's clothes on the line, and accompanying her as she shopped for food. In New York City one young lady followed Sinatra into a restaurant and, after he had finished his breakfast, gobbled up the cereal he had left in her passion to draw close to him.

What sense was to be made out of the phenomenon? Much of the public commentary was disapproving and even negative. The critic in the *Herald-Tribune* said, "The hysteria which accompanies his presence in public is in no way part of an artistic manifestation. It is a slightly disturbing spectacle to witness the almost synchronized screams that come from the audience as he closes his eyes or moves his body slightly sideways, because the spontaneous reaction corresponds to no common understanding relating to tradition or technique of performance, nor yet to the meaning of the sung text." Elsa Max-

well, the society columnist, derided both Sinatra and his fans, he for
"musical illiteracy," they for emotional instability, and suggested that
the girls be given "Sinatraceptives." In New York City the head of the
police department's missing persons bureau said the singer was
responsible for the problem of runaway girls, and a representative of
the board of education talked of pressing charges against him for
encouraging truancy, adding huffily, "We can't tolerate young people
making a public display of losing control of their emotions."

The search for an explanation was made difficult by the very
ordinariness of the performer. His appearance was unexceptional and
his few gestures modest. Neither was his voice or his song styling
remarkable. Faced with the blandness of what took place behind the
footlights, those who tried to understand what was happening turned to
the psyches of the teen-age fans and the social distortions of a country
at war. A sociologist called it "mass frustrated love without direction";
one doctor liked the phrase "mammary hyperesthesia," while another
said, "His voice is an authentic cry of starvation." *The New Yorker*
observed that the Sinatra fans were lonely girls from lower-middle-
class families whose love for their idol was more like worship than
anything else. Bruce Bliven, who attended one of the Paramount
shows in October 1944, also noted that the fans were mostly children
of the poor and speculated that to them Sinatra appeared both as a
father image and the possibility of what someone in their position in
society could become.

With the benefit of hindsight, Kitty Kelley, in her biography of the
singer, *His Way,* seems much closer to the truth. He had touched "the
innocent sexual buddings of adolescent America as no one else before
him," she pointed out, and "He made it a fad to scream hysterically and
to faint in the aisles, and by doing so the bobby-soxers became part of
the show."

Now, almost a half century later, equipped with a broader perspective and greater familiarity with it, we may have a better understanding
of such behavior. Not the least significant aspect of such a phenomenon
is the surprising frequency with which it was to appear in later years.
Bliven in the Paramount Theatre in 1944 surrounded by frantically
screaming bobby-soxers was so impressed that he decided he was

witnessing a rare event, "a phenomenon of mass hysteria that is seen only two or three times in a century," and that "to understand it you had to go all the way back in history to the dance madness that overtook some medieval German villages or the children's crusade." Like those analysts who had attributed the Swoonatra phenomenon to war conditions, however, Bliven was wrong, for it would not be many years before the phenomenon reappeared.

The first faint traces of the disturbance that was to become the next earthquake in popular music were recorded on the cultural Richter scale some time in the summer of 1954 in Memphis, Tennessee, when a nineteen-year-old truck driver, originally from Tupelo, Mississippi, went to a recording studio to make a record for his mother. He was disappointed with the performance; when he heard the record he said that he "sounded like somebody beatin' on a bucket lid or somethin'." But the head of the record company heard something special and a few months later called Elvis Presley in to sign a contract and make a commercial recording. Even then Elvis was doubtful. "I was a little leery of it," he said, and because he thought everyone would laugh, he hid out in a movie house when the record was first aired. But the new record was played over and over during the evening it was introduced as a result of forty-seven phone calls and seventeen telegrams requesting it. The next week it sold seven thousand copies in Memphis stores alone. Presley's early music became known as "rockabilly," an early form of rock 'n' roll that combined elements of blues, country, and gospel. To some he was the first white singer to sing with a black sound and feel.

Building on his local success, Presley began touring in the South and West with a backup trio and appeared regularly on the "Louisiana Hayride" radio show. A minor setback occurred when he performed at the Grand Ole Opry on September 25, 1954, and was advised by the show's talent coordinator to go back to driving trucks.

But the Presley mystique was growing rapidly and in less than two years he became a national figure. At first there was a measure of shock mixed in with the enthusiasm. One disc jockey said that Presley was so country he shouldn't be played after 5 A.M.; others said he was too black for them. One musician who saw the new nineteen-year-old singer playing in Kilgore, Texas, had this reaction:

> This cat came out in red pants and a green coat and a pink shirt and socks and he had this sneer on his face and he stood behind the mike for five minutes, I'll bet, before he made a move. Then he hit his guitar a lick, and he broke two strings. I'd been playing ten years, and I hadn't broken a *total* of two strings. So there he was, these two strings dangling, and he hadn't done anything yet, and these high school girls were screaming and fainting and running up to the stage, and then he started to move his hips real slow like he had a thing for his guitar. . . . He made chills run up my back, man, like when your hair starts grabbing at your collar. For the next nine days he played one-nighters around Kilgore, and after school every day me and my girl would get in the car and go wherever he was playing that night.

Jimmy Snow, son of singer Hank Snow, saw him in Lubbock, Texas, and was awed: " 'Elvis the Pelvis,' as he was already being called, sauntered onstage in black pants with pink stripes down the legs, topped off by a black jacket and pink shirt with the collar turned up to catch the ends of his hair. He grinned seductively at the girls in the front rows. Hips grinding and shaking, legs jerking and snapping, arms flailing the guitar to a fast drumbeat, he drove the women into hysterics."

Time magazine described his voice as a loud baritone "which goes raw and whining in the high notes, but down low it is rich and round. As he throws himself into one of his specialties . . . his throat seems full of desperate aspirates ('Hi want you, hi need you, hi luh-huh-huh-huv-yew-hew') or hiccupping glottis strokes."

At first he was known as the "Hillbilly Cat," or the "King of Western Bop" as the public struggled to identify him, but the crowd reaction was powerful. In May 1955 at Jacksonville, Florida, his performance caused a riot in which aroused fans ripped nearly all his clothes off. When he returned to that city in August 1956, a local juvenile court judge prepared for the event by readying warrants charging Presley with impairing the morals of minors and police, and Navy Shore Patrol were seated in the first rows of the orchestra to contain the fans who stormed the stage. By late 1955 RCA was also after the new singer and negotiated a contract for the then-astounding sum of $35,000 with his new manager, Colonel Tom Parker, a transplanted Dutchman who had become an experienced showbusiness promoter. Tours of the Far West followed and it seemed as if the intensity of fan reaction knew no limits. In the audience teen-age girls screamed, writhed on the floor, and fainted; others covered their mouths and looked as if they were experiencing unbearable pain. There were delirious mob scenes in San Antonio, Texas, in April 1956. In Fort Worth young girls carved his name into their forearms with knives, one doing it four times. In Oklahoma City a reporter who had interviewed him was mobbed by girls after Presley was escorted away by police, one shouting, "Touch him! Maybe he's touched Elvis." In Boston a disc jockey offered seven strands of Presley's sideburns and received 18,400 replies in a week. One distraught mother wrote, "If I had a strand of Elvis Presley's hair, I would cut it in three pieces, braid it, and hang myself to the tune of 'Hound Dog.' " An unconfirmed rumor described how young girls would themselves write part of Presley's signature on their brassiers to suggest that part of his autograph had been written on their breasts.

The powerful reaction was felt overseas. In 1956 the elderly senior mistress of a school in London came into the staff room one morning and said sternly, "I must speak to a boy called Elvis Presley because he has carved his name on every desk in the school."

Helen Beal Woodward, writing of "The Smitten Female" in *Mademoiselle*, cast a historical eye on the phenomenon from Lord Byron to 1957 and concluded that the current hero was Presley. "Whimpering, his worshipers hurl their firm young bodies against the police cordons that guard his passage. They scavenge barbershops for his hair clippings and collect the dust from his license plates (and sometimes the plates themselves). His name is emblazoned across their budding bosoms and down the thighs of their dungarees. They scoop up samplings from his swimming pool on the thrilling chance that said drops may have trickled off Elvis and they greet his every public appearance with a primitive, mindless screech of truly terrifying intensity."

Such a tidal wave of feeling necessarily produced parental concern, negative criticism, and even hostility among adults. Cries of alarm were sounded in letters-to-the-editor and psychologists expressed their concern publicly. An episcopal minister in New York City saw in the new idol a "revolt from the tried and true," but did not think youth really wanted it; it was the "result of the letdown that follows every war"; the teen-agers were just having a vicarious fling. Many, including some musicians, believed that Presley's performance was too blatantly sexual. Frank Sinatra, the idol of an earlier day, found Presley disgusting: "His kind of music is deplorable, a rancid-smelling aphrodisiac," he said; and in an article in the magazine *Western World,* he elaborated:

> My only deep sorrow is the unrelenting insistence of recording and motion picture companies upon purveying the most brutal, ugly, degenerate, vicious form of expression it has been my displeasure to hear and naturally I'm referring to the bulk of rock 'n' roll.
>
> It fosters almost totally negative and destructive reactions in young people. It smells phony and false. It is sung, played and written for the most part by cretinous goons and by means of its almost imbecilic reiterations and sly, lewd—in plain fact—dirty lyrics, it manages to be the martial music of every sideburned delinquent on the face of the earth.

In Texas a gas station gave away Presley records so that angry motorists could enjoy smashing them. One male reviewer thought Presley was "more of a male burlesque queen than anything else." When Adlai Stevenson, the 1956 Democratic presidential candidate, was endorsed by Presley, many in that party grumbled that it had been contrived by the opposition.

It was television, however, that elevated him from a regional sensation to a national idol. Although he had tried out and been rejected for Arthur Godfrey's "Talent Scouts" in early 1955, he began appearing regularly on television, first on the Dorsey Brothers' "Stage Show" and then on the Milton Berle, Steve Allen, and Ed Sullivan shows. When Presley last appeared on the Ed Sullivan show he was shown only from the waist up, a censorship that may now seem bizarre, but says a great deal about how shocking he seemed to many at the time and the way he divided opinion across the country.

These appearances plus the series of low-grade movies he starred in through the sixties raised Presley to the lofty celebrity he enjoys even now, many years after his death, and figured largely in the huge sales of many of his records. A hitch in the army starting in 1958, a gradual withdrawal from the public, and a decline in his music, interrupted in the opinion of many critics only by his 1968 Christmas television show, all failed to diminish the legend. When he died in 1977 in his Graceland mansion in Memphis he had become hugely overweight and drug-ridden, barely recognizable as the handsome young singer with the raw electric talent he had been some twenty years earlier.

The "King," as he had become known, affords an interesting comparison with Frank Sinatra, the teen-age idol of an earlier generation. Where The Voice sang standard ballads coolly and with a minimum of gesture, Elvis exploded in his performance of new, black-style music, leaping about, gyrating his hips, shouting and moaning. He poured vast amounts of energy out over his audiences and raised them to a similarly high-energy level of response. Handsome—"the pretty blue-eyed dream" in the words of one girl—he affected, and suggested, the young Marlon Brando and James Dean, the latter already a cult figure among disaffected youth, and added to the image of rebelliousness by wearing wild clothes. Sinatra clothed his skinny frame in the fashions of the day and laid no claim to beauty. But there was more. Where Sinatra was presented as a family man, Presley turned out to be surprisingly complicated and unconventional. His stage behavior may have been erotic, but he continuously insisted he did not do any "dirty body movements." To reporters he could be disarming. When asked if he would help combat juvenile delinquency, he observed that "juvenile delinquency isn't wearing long hair and a leather jacket." He denied that he had been autographing some unusual parts of the female anatomy, saying that he had written only on decent places where "you can take soap and wash it off," and "I don't want no daddy with a shotgun after me." But when asked what he did about the girls who threw themselves at him, he said, "I usually take them." Asked in his early years if he intended to marry, he queried, "Why buy a cow when you can get milk through the fence?"

But something else had happened since the Sinatra craze of the war years. The electronic age had dawned. Television sets were common and high fidelity sound systems were replacing the old phonographs. Quality sound systems, in particular, were being staked out as the preserve of the young, a change that would accelerate over the years. Youthful interest in records and the power of television spread the sound and image of Presley across the country in a short time, while the Sinatra phenomenon was largely confined to a few theaters, night-clubs, and auditoriums.

It is a curiosity that the word *mania,* which derives from the ancient Greek word for madness, in the frantic and often brutal world of latter-day popular music has been tied to a quartet that has now come to represent "soft" rock and even a civilizing influence.

The group that would become the Beatles traces its genesis back to the mid-fifties when John Lennon and Paul McCartney, both devoted to early American rock 'n' roll musicians, began playing together in an ensemble called the Quarrymen and writing songs for them. In the years that followed, the group played intensively in clubs in Liverpool, England, and Hamburg, Germany, and evolved by August 1962 into a quartet comprising Lennon, McCartney, George Harrison, and Ringo Starr. Along the way they changed their name to the Silver Beatles and then simply the Beatles. The name was chosen in response to Buddy Holly's group, the Crickets, the variant spelling attributed to Lennon's pun on beat music. They were a popular Liverpool band at this time, but that success was nothing compared to the rise that began when they recorded "Love Me Do" in September 1962.

By the following year the group's "She Loves You" was not only the number-one record in the British Isles, a position it sprang into upon its release, it was selling faster than any single record ever released and established a record for sales that would not be broken for

fifteen years. On tour the Beatles created mobs everywhere. On the
occasion of their first visit to Dublin there was a tremendous free-for-all
involving young fans. The police chief there said, "It was all right until
the mania degenerated into barbarism." In Birmingham, England, the
only way they could escape the raging crowd was by disguising themselves as police, complete with capes and helmets. At the London
airport a woman news reporter had her left hand kissed repeatedly
simply because the hand accidentally brushed the sleeve of a Beatle. In
October they appeared at the Palladium in London in a television show
seen by fifteen million viewers. Crowds at the theater and the excitement surrounding the group's arrival made them front-page news.
Suddenly, everyone knew about the Beatles, their music, their appearance (especially their odd hairdo), and the audience frenzy that greeted
their performances. When they appeared at the Royal Command Performance on November 5, 1963, their popularity may already have
surpassed that of the Royal family. While rehearsing for the show they
were effectively sequestered for thirteen hours because it was considered too dangerous for them to leave. Lennon's remark at the performance, "Will the people in the cheaper seats clap your hands, the rest
of you can just rattle your jewelry," brought the house down. The
following day the London *Daily Mirror* compressed the whole experience into one word: "BEATLEMANIA!"

First Great Britain, then America and the rest of the world. In mid
November 1963 the group's manager arranged for their appearance on
the Ed Sullivan television show and the release in America of their
newest single, "I Want to Hold Your Hand." It was a deal struck only
days before the calamity and piercing drama of the assassination of
President John F. Kennedy, timing that may have contributed to the
sensational introduction of the Beatles in this country. For months after
the death of the president the nation was in mourning trying to digest
the shocking events. Funeral music seemed to be heard everywhere as
millions watched images of the shooting, its immediate aftermath, and
the funeral over and over on their television screens. By February 9,
1964, the public may have been ready for lighter fare.

There was already evidence that an entertainment explosion was
about to occur. The new record "I Want to Hold Your Hand" was

released on December 26, 1963, and became number one a month later, having sold, in that short time, a staggering 1.5 million copies. Since a hit record was expected to sell about 200,000 copies, the experience was dizzying. When the Beatles arrived in New York City they were received like Charles Lindbergh had been after his solo trans-atlantic flight. The International Arrivals Building at Idlewild Airport was swarming with fans, and their screaming drowned out even the roar of the jet engines. Subjected to questions by a daunted press corps, the Beatles flashed their brand of wit, which was to become a part of their image:

> *Q:* What about the campaign in Detroit to stamp out the Beatles?
> *A:* We've got a campaign of our own to stamp out Detroit.
> *Q:* What do you do when you're cooped up in your rooms between shows?
> *A:* We ice skate.
> *Q:* What do you think of Beethoven?
> *A:* I like his poems.

Escorted by the police to the staid Plaza Hotel, the group encountered a throng there that grew throughout the day, again imprisoning them in their suite and requiring that traffic on Fifth Avenue be rerouted.

Ed Sullivan's brief introduction, delivered in his characteristically deadpan style, acknowledged that New York had never seen such excitement. When he announced the Beatles, the screaming started and continued throughout their performance. An estimated seventy-three million Americans watched the show, which received the highest rating in TV history. Beatlemania had come to the United States. In a press conference at the Plaza the following day representatives of more than 250 newspapers, TV and radio stations, and wire services showed up, including Dr. Joyce Brothers, the psychologist, who sought to explore the phenomenon's psychological implications, not the first and far from the last of the many who tried to rationalize the phenomenon. Three days later the Beatles gave two performances at Carnegie Hall, the first time that rock 'n' roll music had been heard in that sedate building. The predominantly teen-age audience all but drowned out the music with squealing. The arrival of this group of four young English musicians, the oldest only twenty-four, was the biggest news in the country.

It was the beginning of an empire. Continuing success with their records, concert tours on which only football stadiums were large enough to accommodate their audiences, and a series of successful movies, which expressed their whimsical spirit, all played large parts. So great was interest in the group that the merchandising of their celebrity became an enormous business itself. Early in their popular reign in this country the toy company that had bought the right to manufacture the trademark Beatle wig was turning them out at the rate of thirty-five thousand a day and even then could not meet the demand. The *Wall Street Journal* estimated that more than fifty million dollars' worth of Beatles products would be sold in the United States in the first year of their success.

By June of 1964 they were embarking on a global tour in which they would perform in fifty cities on four continents, including twenty-four cities in the United States. A tour of such magnitude may never have been accomplished before. The announcement of the tour produced riots at local ticket offices as fans scrambled for tickets. Wherever the Beatles went, screaming crowds besieged their hotels and followed their vehicles. In San Francisco two hundred sheriff's deputies were overrun by hysterical girls who came to greet the group; a mob of teen-agers captured the Beatles' limousine and crushed the roof while the four were inside; and fifty members of the local fan club jumped into the City Hall Plaza fountain fully clothed to protest the mayor's refusal to give the Beatles the key to the city. In Hollywood the towels with which they dried themselves after the concert were cut up into one-inch squares, mounted with certificates, and sold to Beatlemaniacs, a merchandising ploy later used in Kansas City with the hotel bed sheets on which they slept.

Their image and sound were perceived differently in various quarters. To *The New Republic* they were reminiscent of the Nairobi Trio, a television skit by comedian Ernie Kovacs in which three gorillas played a simple tune over and over again with one gorilla occasionally peering mindlessly at another. Frederick Lewis in the *New York Times* thought they looked "spectacularly demented" while playing and made Elvis Presley look like "an Edwardian tenor of considerable diffidence." Noting that they "apparently have their hair cut under a bowl," *Vogue* said, "They give out a deadpan realistic noise which has as its visual analogy their collective bloodhound expression." One naysayer likened them to the seven dwarfs of Snow White: three sweet, bright, furry ones, and then Ringo, the Dopey of the group, like the last duckling to get across the road in a cartoon film, squawking and hobbling to keep up. But such put-downs and criticisms were structures of sand overwhelmed and washed away by the oceanic tide that was Beatlemania.

Newsweek had a divided opinion: Visually, the group was "a nightmare" and musically "a near disaster," but "their gospel is fun. They shout, they stomp, they jump for joy, and their audiences respond in a way that makes an old-time revival meeting seem like a wake." The religious metaphor struck others. *The Reporter* referred to the Carnegie Hall concert as one of "a series of religious ceremonies . . . where the congregation is permitted to express its devotion directly through antiphonal responses that allow the Beatles themselves to conserve their own vocal chords for more demanding occasions, such as the Ed Sullivan Show."

Benny Goodman, the "King of Swing," a musical giant from another era, was taken to meet the new sensation at a performance in 1964 at the site of the world's fair in New York City. Goodman's daughter described the scene:

> Now they appeared. In the tidal wave of screams that greeted them, I thought this was what the end of the world must be like. The din went past the painful, too loud for the ear to register. It was precisely the sensation of being behind a jet plane taking off: the same pitch and intensity. Flashbulb after flashbulb made the whole stadium white, the points of brightness popping everywhere, but giving the impression of a constant unearthly glow.
>
> The Beatles sauntered to their place. . . . It was a physical impossibility to hear them. A girl in front of us kept clawing at the chicken wire in complete hysteria, ecstasy on her face. Policemen charged about shouting at the girls to get back to their seats, peeling them off the barrier. A girl near me would scream very

hard, as though in a contest, look quite pleased with herself and then glance sheepishly around her, unable to free herself from embarrassment. . . . There was something so apocalyptical about it, pure frenzy, an almost mystical atmosphere of heavens opening up.

After the concert Goodman was asked what he thought of the Beatles' music. They had a strong beat, he said, but he couldn't hear anything else because of the screaming.

The good fortune, excellent timing, or both that characterized the Beatles' career seemed not to allow for any reverses. When the hippie culture was developing in 1967 and the country was experiencing a "Summer of Love," the band produced, in *Sgt. Pepper's Lonely Hearts Club Band*, the perfect album for that time. One testimony to the epiphany created by the music is that of Langdon Winner in *Rock and Roll Will Stand:*

> For the closest that Western civilization has come to unity since the Congress of Vienna in 1815 was the week that the Sgt. Pepper album was released. In every city in Europe and America the stereo systems and radios played [Sgt. Pepper] and everyone listened. At the time I happened to be driving across country on Interstate 80. In each city where I stopped . . . the melodies wafted in from some far-off transistor radio or portable hi-fi. It was the most amazing thing I've ever heard. For a brief while the irreparably fragmented consciousness of the West was reunified, at least in the minds of the young. Every person listened to the record, pondered it, and discussed it with friends. While it is no doubt true that I have little in common with the gas station attendant in Cheyenne, Wyoming, we were able to come together to talk about the meaning of "A Day in the Life" during those few moments in which the oil in my VW was being changed.

Beatlemania provided a field day for analysts and commentators who tried to wrestle it into a rational category or at least connect it to tradition. One commentator reached all the way back to Greek mythology for a parallel: Orpheus, whose music was so charming that the trees and rocks followed him, was attacked by wild Bacchantes. He kept them at bay with his music until their screaming drowned it out and they then tore him to pieces. Closer to our time was the case of

Franz Liszt, the composer and pianist for whom women shrieked, fought, and fainted, a reaction the poet Heinrich Heine attributed vaguely and variously to "magnetism, galvanism, and electricity . . . of histrionic epilepsy, of the phenomenon of tickling of musical cantharides and other unmentionable matters."

The brigade of contemporary thinkers dug deeper. Jonathan Miller, doctor and theater director, saw the Beatles' appeal as consisting of the "incipient sensuality of the pre-pubic child." A New York psychiatrist also saw sexuality: The Beatles stirred sexual feelings in young girls that they were unable to control because they were new. It was said that the Beatles were phallic symbols, a view rejected, on the advice of his wife, by Alan Brien, a young English critic in *Mademoiselle* who observed that they no more suggested the image than any other human being. Sociologists saw a protest against the adult world. In one view the group filled deep religious needs not met by organized religion. A London doctor thought the girls' screaming was good because it made the pains of pregnancy and childbirth easier for them when they matured.

Explanation became such a cottage industry in itself that David Dempsey set out in the *New York Times Magazine* on February 23, 1964, to classify and evaluate the different kinds. In the anthropological explanation, jungle rhythms still beat deep within us ready to be brought to the surface by figures like the Beatles who are modern versions of ancient witch doctors. The psychological analysis, based on a 1941 study of jitterbugging, postulated two kinds of mass behavior toward popular music: rhythmic, obedient, and emotional. The latter is loving, but passive, while the former keeps time and is noisy. But while the rhythmic obedients crave louder and louder music they are really conformists at heart. In the socioeconomic interpretation the craze is seen as the product of an affluent society in which leisure makes such behavior possible. It was duly noted that many of the female Beatlemaniacs were rather homely and that their rabid group behavior made it easier for them to express feelings for boys that otherwise had to be repressed. Finally, the moral view is that Beatlemania is a teen-age protest against the hypocrisy of the adult world.

The demon was both common and complex, concluded Dempsey. "No wonder the jumpers can seldom explain what makes them jump. And no wonder that they have such a miserably happy time doing it."

"They don't gyrate around like Elvis," said one young girl in Britain of the Beatles in 1963, "they just send the joy out to you." "Joy" or energy, was now flowing out to the audience where it was amplified many times and sent back to the performers. What had been as restrained as the bobbing of Frank Sinatra's Adam's apple and his discreetly outstretched arms had become the copulationlike hip thrusts of Elvis Presley and the stamping and shaking of the Beatles. The electronic age had made it possible for the Paramount Theatre episode of October 1944 to become a global phenomenon by 1964. But while the audience reaction was broader, it could hardly become more intense. Later developments would bring even more manic behavior on the stage.

Typical were the Rolling Stones, who charted a course into violent waters. Avowedly striving for parental shock, sexuality, and hostility, they sought to become, in the words of their manager, Andrew Loog Oldham, "exactly opposite those nice, clean, tidy Beatles." Soon their concerts were regularly followed—and sometimes even preceded—by riots as a result of their high-energy message. According to Keith Richards, their lead guitarist, "There was a period of six months in England we couldn't play ballrooms anymore because we could never get through more than three or four songs every night, man. Chaos. Police and too many people in the places, fainting. We'd walk into some of those places and it was like they had the Battle of the Crimea going on, people gasping, tits hanging out, chicks choking, nurses running around with ambulances."

The soft rock of the Beatles was followed by hard rock, heavy-metal rock, and other variants, styles that were characterized by earsplitting volume, a deafening beat, and provocative lyrics. The musicians themselves continued patterns of drug and alcohol use that had become almost traditional, adopted lifestyles that took them to the fringes of society and beyond, and began to incorporate acts of violence into their performances to match the amplitude of their sound.

At the Who's debut in New York City the climax was reached when one member beat the microphone against the floor, another flailed his guitar against an amplifier, and the drummer ignited smoke bombs and then kicked over his ten drums. All but the smoke had become standard procedure for the group. The crowd was ecstatic.

Jimi Hendrix became famous for the sexual way in which he handled his guitar. He would fall to his knees with the instrument between his legs, pumping it, licking his lips, and howling as if in the throes of passion. To this he later added fire, ending a song by splashing lighter fluid over his guitar and setting it ablaze while still between his legs. Grace Slick of the Jefferson Airplane thought that was "an excellent visual image to accompany the incredible friction and volume of rock and roll."

Fire was also used by Jim Morrison and the Doors. At the end of his hit "Light My Fire," he began throwing lighted cigarettes out into the audience. Many fans responded by lighting matches and throwing them into the air, to the horror of the authorities.

At a concert in Miami, Morrison encouraged the crowd to storm the stage in spite of warnings by the security people over the public address system, then he exposed himself and simulated masturbation and fellatio. In the hubbub that followed, beer bottles cascaded onto the stage followed by a cloud of panties and brassieres.

The frenetic Janis Joplin also urged the audience to rush the stage, protesting when promoters began insisting that she stop. "My music's not supposed to make you riot," she said, "it's supposed to make you fuck."

When the Beatles played in Washington, D.C., in February 1964 Peter Brown, a friend who accompanied them, recalled the puny amplifiers that could not carry the sound throughout the coliseum. Later groups made ear-shattering volume their hallmark. At a typical Who concert there would be forty speakers, each as tall as a man. In London on May 31, 1976, the Who may have set a decibel record for rock concerts, recording a level of 120 at a distance of 50 yards, equivalent to a nearby jet engine or a loud thunderclap. The federal government has established the danger level for sound as beginning at 90, with anything over 115 as unsafe. Because rock bands are consistently in the danger zone, they and their audiences are exposed to the risks of irreversible damage, loss of hearing, and tinnitis, a constant ringing in the ears. A majority of musicians surveyed reported they could not play without severe pain. And yet, in the words of Grace Slick again, "Our eternal goal in life is to get louder." On the visual side, the ubiquitous use of strobe lighting helped sever whatever ties to reality remained.

The unleashing of so much manic energy regularly led to the storming of the stage and riots. Ultimately, national attention was focused on the violent side of rock music as a result of incidents at Altamont, California, and Cincinnati. Only four months after the peaceful love-in at Woodstock in August 1969, a crowd of 300,000 assembled in Altamont to hear the Rolling Stones, the Jefferson Airplane, and others. Security was provided by the Hell's Angels motorcycle gang who, drunk even before the concert began, randomly mauled an audience high on drugs. The atmosphere was malevolent and blood spattered the first aid tent and the stage. When it was finally over one man had been beaten to death, more than a hundred had been injured, and nearly a thousand required treatment for drug use.

A different sort of violence occurred at the Riverfront Coliseum in Cincinnati on December 3, 1979. In anticipation of a concert by the Who that evening, a huge crowd formed in the plaza in front of the building since "festival seating" was in effect, a euphemism for first-come-first-served. While the crowd appeared peaceful, something strange and deadly was actually going on. Moving back and forth rhythmically, the throng was gradually being compressed, crushing those nearest the entrances. Eleven people died, suffocated by the awful pressure.

The Cincinnati tragedy led John G. Fuller to examine violence in the rock world in his book *Are the Kids All Right?*. He concluded that the crowd had been conditioned to violence as a result of posthypnotic suggestion resulting from long hours of listening to hard rock on records. The long exposure created a trance state in which messages encouraging lawless and violent behavior were implanted in the young listeners. Blending new insights with Gustave Le Bon's concept of the disappearance of individual consciousness in a crowd and the appearance of a crowd mentality, Fuller concluded that even before they assembled on the plaza, Who fans had formed a technical "crowd" that was already primed for violence even though such thoughts were not in the minds of the individuals who composed it.

There was, then, violence not only on the stage and in the audience but in the unconscious group behavior of fans before the performance as well. Even that, however, was not the end of it as rumors spread that some rock music records had, buried in them, subliminal messages, usually of an evil character, exhorting the listeners to violence. "Backmasking," a technique whereby a record played backward will yield such a hidden lyric, achieved a special notoriety when the families of two boys in Reno, Nevada, sued the group Judas Priest, alleging that their sons' suicides were prompted by the backmasked lyrics "Do it!" in their record "Stained Class." In the summer of 1990 in a nonjury trial, the court dismissed the suit.

Scientific confirmation of the widespread view among parents that rock music was pernicious was produced by Dr. John Diamond, a New York City psychiatrist who also specialized in kinesiology. The latter discipline is based on the idea that the large muscles of the body indicate whether a given stimulus is beneficial or harmful to the entire organism. The tests are simple. In one, the subject holds an arm out and tries to maintain its position while the force required to press it down is recorded. Diamond discovered that the muscles tested well when classical, early rock and roll, jazz, ethnic, or country music were being played. When post-Beatle hard rock was played, however, the force required to depress the arm could diminish by as much as two-thirds. Expressed differently, a man who could normally bench press 120 pounds could barely press 40 pounds while listening to the Rolling Stones' "Satisfaction." To Diamond this meant that the music had a negative effect on the body. Analyzing this further, he found that one of the main causes of the negative effect was something he called the "stopped anapestic beat." This beat, common to rock music after the mid 1960s, conflicted with the body's natural rhythm and thus produced the weakening effect. Another cause was the high decibel level of the music. These, and other factors, meant that the new rock tended to destroy the body's life energy.

Extreme behavior often leads to extreme speculation about it.

As long ago as the sixth century, Boethius had pointed out that "music is part of us, and either ennobles or degrades our behavior." After reviewing the antic behavior of popular music audiences in our time we might agree with Boethius in part but reserve judgment as to the moral aspect of that behavior. As our understanding of the role of rhythm in the world increases we might incline to a less judgmental view. Like Baruch's cloud of flying midges or the synchronously flashing Asian fireflies we are powerfully involved in rhythms.

Charles Diserens, a professor of psychology who attempted a systematic investigation of these matters, saw music as producing four kinds of ecstasies—erotic, martial, fantastic, and melancholy. Where the audience hysteria we have examined fits into these categories is unclear. Erotic, certainly; fantastic and melancholy, perhaps; but even the martial ecstasy is relevant. In his 1939 work, *A Psychology of Music, the Influence of Music on Behavior,* he considered how music sometimes can induce a warlike spirit of great intensity producing abnormal states, enabling men to accomplish acts of valor of which they would otherwise be incapable. Diserens's martial "ecstasy" may be more easily understood as recklessness, and as such it is indeed not far from the wild and lawless behavior provoked in rock concert audiences by performers whose stage antics prove inflammatory. The joy of "letting go" experienced by thousands of teen-agers in a dark concert hall, their ears ringing from the noise, their eyes dazzled by strobe lights, their libidos stimulated by the lyrics and movements on the stage, may not be far removed from the mental and emotional state of the soldiers on the front lines whose caution melts away in a fighting frenzy.

JONESTOWN AND
OTHER CULTS

In the preface to the first edition of his book, Mackay declared, with commendable prudence, that he had purposely excluded religious manias. The avowed reason was that "a mere list of them would alone be sufficient to occupy a volume." Considering his was a time in which religion was considerably more of an influence in the world than it is now, his neat rationale may have concealed his unwillingness to deal with such controversial material. It is an attitude we should keep in mind as we turn to the subject of cults, for distinctions between these groups and those of more conventional religious persuasion are often elusive.

An early problem in this area is the myriad number and diversity of cults. So numerous and so varied are they that it becomes difficult to treat them in an orderly fashion. Disparate as they may be, however, each is the object of some measure of public disapproval. Disapproval may derive from such features as their exotic origins and novel procedures as well as allegations of brainwashing, violence, and illegal and immoral conduct, but it is also expressed in the word itself. *Cult* is a word that carries with it a negative burden. If not by strict definition then certainly by association and implication, a cult is a disliked organization. The disapprobation we express when we choose the word may involve elements of cultural condescension and parochialism: A cult suggests a more primitive group, perhaps *very* primitive, where horrors like cannibalism are practiced. Other unpleasant associations include satanism, witchcraft, voodoo, animal or even human sacrifices—a congeries of things evil. Secrecy, too, is an element. It rarely occurs to those who use it that the word may have an evolutionary dimension, for when the world's major religions first appeared, they were seen as cults by what was then the establishment. Perhaps there is no more convincing indication of the word's pejorative character than the obvious fact that no member of such a group would ever call himself or herself a cultist.

The proliferation of cults in the 1960s and 1970s eventually led to a public debate in which increasingly strident criticism of these groups was answered with legal and historical arguments. Those who were sympathetic to the new cults said this country was formed, in part, by a desire to achieve freedom to worship as one pleased, and although new forms of religious activity were not always received well here, the principle remained alive and important. As noted, also, the established religions of today were once regarded as cults. It could be said, in fact, that distinctions between the major religions and the new cults were little more than a simple matter of numbers. Religious or philosophical concepts had little to do with it. If its followers were sufficiently numerous, the organization somehow graduated from its disapproved cult status and became accredited.

With all of these problems we would be well advised to follow Mackay's advice and not join the debate, were there not, at the extreme edge of the world of cults, some unusual occurrences of delusional group behavior that cannot be ignored. Those cults examined are offered here merely as examples of such group behavior and are not representative of cult activity in general. In one instance an entire group of followers was led to give up their lives in a single, horrific event—the mass deaths at Jonestown. In others, more primitive people in the South Pacific were induced to surrender their cultural identity in a desperate effort to obtain wealth.

The People's Temple of the Disciples of Christ, as the organization led by the Reverend Jim Jones came to be known, was not always regarded as a cult. Throughout much of its history, in fact, it was surprisingly situated within the mainstream of enlightened social change in this country.

James Warren Jones seems to have come upon his vocation early in life, or perhaps even earlier. His mother was an unconventional woman who believed strongly in dreams and was convinced that she was the reincarnation of Mark Twain. In an early dream her dead mother called to her from the far side of a river that she would bear a son who would right the wrongs of the world. When she gave birth to her only child in 1931 she was convinced that James was the Messiah. The dream had a lasting influence on her and would often be incorporated into the Reverend Jones's sermons in later years.

Where other children pursued sports or the usual hobbies, young Jim Jones devoted himself to religion. Given to carrying a Bible around, he acted out the role of a minister, conducting mock sermons, baptisms, and other rituals. Especially memorable were the elaborate funerals he organized for dead pets. Even in these childish activities, however, Jones showed a predilection for stern discipline, and some of his little "parishioners" would receive a blow for a real or imagined mistake.

After graduation from high school in 1949 he sporadically attended several universities and then established the Christian Assembly of God, his first church. In a poor neighborhood of Indianapolis he built a congregation by distributing free food, providing nursing home care and secondhand clothes, and finding jobs for his members, although he did not become an ordained minister until 1964. Married with one son, he began adopting other children, ultimately seven in all, of which two were black and three Korean. This was his own "rainbow family," a microcosm of his racially diverse church membership. At the same time he was developing enough political influence in Indianapolis to lead to his appointment as the city's human rights commissioner in 1961. In part this was due to his reputation as a champion of the racially oppressed.

By 1961 Jones had emerged as a charismatic leader of a growing church that stressed service to the poor and railed frequently at racial inequalities, and also as a political figure capable or organizing crowds and demonstrations on short notice and delivering large blocs of votes. Although his organization was still nominally a church, the emphasis was increasingly on an agenda of social and political change. As the religious content of Jones's message faded it was replaced by a growing focus on Jones himself and often an outright attack on religious institutions. Among other things, he was known to urge his congregants to throw their Bibles away and to question the virgin birth. From his pulpit he would throw the Bible on the floor, spit upon it, and declare:

"Too many people are looking at this and not at *me.*" In his sermons there were few references to Christ, the inference being that Jones was then the living Christ. In time Jones would claim that in earlier incarnations he had been the Egyptian pharaoh Ikhnaton, Buddha, Jesus Christ, and Lenin.

But if he had moved away from traditional religion in most areas, he had embraced the faith healing side of evangelistic religion enthusiastically. In his own words Jones said, "I heard all these healers and I thought well if those sons of bitches can do it then I can do it too." He rapidly became renowned: The moribund were enlivened; the disabled became nimble; those with cancers miraculously sloughed off the malign growths.

The year 1961 was to be a fateful year for Jones, for that was the year he found a new model for his religious and entrepreneurial talents and also decided to move from Indianapolis. One weekend he traveled to Philadelphia to meet Father Divine, a black religious leader revered by some of Jones's older black members. For Jones it was a transforming experience. In 1961 Father Divine was in the last stages of an astounding career that had peaked in New York City in the decade of the Depression. Born somewhere in the South in the last quarter of the nineteenth century, the man who was to become Father Divine, and by his own proclamation God, was less grandly known in 1899 as George Baker. He worked seasonally in Baltimore clipping hedges and mowing lawns. Attending prayer meetings there, he came under the influence of Samuel Morris, a preacher whose interpretation of the New Testament convinced Morris that he was God.

By 1915 Baker was in New York, where he established a kind of meeting house and employment agency on Myrtle Avenue in Brooklyn. The disciples lived together in the same apartment, where prayer meetings were held every evening, and received both meals and shelter there. In return they turned over everything they earned to "The Messenger," one of the titles Baker adopted for himself. By 1919 the group had outgrown its New York City apartment and The Messenger purchased a house in Sayville in eastern Long Island. At this point The Messenger went through a change in title and emerged as Major J. Devine. That appellation may have been unsatisfactory, however, for in rapid succession the man became Rev. J. Divine (the vowel modification moving him closer to his ultimate destination) and then "Father Divine (God)."

For the next decade the Sayville commune grew slowly. Jobs for the original disciples were found nearby and new, more substantial disciples were attracted. Those who had accumulated property or cash were persuaded to turn these assets over to "God" and thereby become "Angels." Members were encouraged to regard Divine as "God" and call him "Father." To achieve a sublime state they were advised to relax their "conscious mentality." "Relaxation of the conscious mentality," Divine would say, "is the super-mental relaxativeness of mankind." Those who sat nearest to him at dinner had so relaxed their "conscious mentalities" that they had been reborn as Angels with new names like Hozanna Love, Frank Incense, Blessed Charity, and Onward Universe and had no memories of the past. Those who would enter the Kingdom of God, Divine also declared, must have nothing of their own. Property divestiture usually resulted in transfer to the church. Insurance was particularly evil for it meant that the beneficiary was, in his heart, a murderer. Since proper living meant a member would never die, there was no need for insurance; one who insured his property or his life had little faith. Members were told to cash out their policies and contribute the proceeds. And since there was everlasting life for true believers, there was no need for medical care. Consistent with this view, the death of a follower was barely acknowledged by the church.

Celibacy was also a strict rule, and even married couples were constrained to avoid intimate relations with each other whether they lived in "Heaven," as the Sayville house became known, or elsewhere. Basic to the program was the idea of the brotherhood of man, and words indicating racial classification like "Negro" were forbidden. Although the group was largely black, there were white members.

This combination of ideas, a charismatic leadership by a self-declared "God," and a highly organized communal life in which an individual surrendered both the need to make decisions and his or her responsibility for them and was completely cared for ("Father will provide" was a frequent chant) turned out to be powerfully attractive. By the late 1920s more affluent people from Harlem were coming out to Sayville on Sundays, white people were appearing among the followers, and money was pouring into Father Divine's coffers at a steady rate. In 1931 Divine bought other buildings in Sayville and set up an "Extension Heaven" in Harlem. His success, already considerable, was about to receive a giant boost from an extraordinary event that would make him a national figure.

In the fall of 1931 Divine was arrested on a charge that he was a public nuisance. At the trial the judge appeared to be racially biased and charged the jury in a manner that virtually required a guilty verdict. Upon conviction the judge sentenced Divine to a $500 fine and one year in jail. Four days later the judge, a healthy man aged fifty-five, suddenly died. Many people across the country who read the newspaper accounts were convinced that Father Divine, who was in jail at the time, had struck the judge dead. When Divine's conviction was overturned on appeal, it was seen as further evidence of the man's divinity. Scores chose to join the commune in Sayville, which now numbered some three hundred. On the crest of this wave of publicity Divine established new headquarters in New York City.

By 1936 his following had grown and he had many business interests. In Harlem he was the leading keeper of lodging houses in which sleeping quarters were provided for about fifteen hundred people. In the windows of each of these "Extension Heavens" were signs proclaiming "Peace!" and "Father Divine is God Almighty." His followers fell into two classes: "Angels" and "Children." The former either worked for or turned their wages over to Divine and received free room and board if they lived in an Extension Heaven, while the latter were not that committed—they did not turn everything over to "God," but paid weekly room rent if they lived in an Extension Heaven and purchased their meals there. The class of Children was an innovation created when Divine moved to Harlem. Where new followers had come in twos and threes to Sayville, the publicity now brought in hundreds. Angels now were created only in exceptional cases, and the path of belief began when one became a Child.

Each of the Extension Heavens was run efficiently as a profit-making enterprise. If it failed to make money, it was dropped. Meetings were held at each Extension Heaven throughout the day and into the evening. Conducted in an informal fashion, and whether or not Divine was present, they were marked by testimonials of cures and other miracles, and frequent shouts of "Thank you, Father!" and "It is so wonderful!" were interspersed with rhythmic stomping.

In addition to these boarding houses, Divine established twenty-five restaurants, about six groceries, ten cleaning and pressing shops, a coal business, two weekly newspapers, twenty or thirty peddler wagons selling clams, oysters, and fresh vegetables, a group of shoeshine men, and other businesses and acquired substantial farmland in upper New York State. The restaurants served modest fare at competitive prices, displayed signs that said, "Peace! It's wonderful!", and featured waiters and waitresses who murmured "Peace!" as they served customers and "Thank you, Father!" when they were paid. Each of these enterprises was run on a profit-making basis, an operation that was greatly facilitated by the absence of labor costs.

Now perhaps in his sixties, Divine was a short, dignified man with soft eyes, unprepossessing in figure and in dress. He was mostly bald and one could see what looked like an old scar on the back of his head. When he appeared at a prayer meeting the assembly would sing, "He's God, He's God. Father Divine is God" to the tune of "Marching Through Georgia." Not an eloquent speaker, he managed to rouse his followers nevertheless, and his sermons were characterized by some unusual word forms. In a typical speech he declared, "Remember, we are not representing Heaven as a place geographically, but a State of Consciousness wherein all men can arise to, and recognize God's Presence as Real, as Tangibleatable, and as practical as the principles of Mathematics. It is indeed wonderful! Not only tangibleated but as tangibleatable. It has been tangibleated, and it can be retangibleated; it can and will continue to materialize, and repersonify, rematerialize, and repersonify, for the great materializing process is going on!" In another routine Divine would chant

> One million blessings
> Blessings flowing free;
> Blessings flowing free.
> There are so many blessings,
> Blessings flowing free for you.

The next verse would raise the ante to a billion blessings, and in succeeding verses the number would rise to a trillion, quadrillion, quintillion, sextillion, septillion, octillion, and so on.

Divine began to show an interest in and aptitude for politics. He cultivated the press so assiduously that by the fall of 1936 Henry Lee Moon in *The New Republic* remarked that hardly a week went by without his appearance in the daily news. He publicly denounced the unions, but sent his followers to parade with the Communists on May Day, a position that disturbed Henry Lee Moon, who saw it as an impediment to better wages and working conditions for blacks.

Divine was destined to live until 1965 and his wife, "Mother Divine," would carry on after him. If his movement faded somewhat after the glory days of the 1930s, his blending of a communal lifestyle and an efficient organization active in business and politics remained as an impressive model when a young pastor from Indianapolis came to visit in 1961. It would have been simple to dismiss Father Divine as an anachronism, to attribute his earlier success to the economic hardship and social dislocation of the Depression and the growing fears of war against the background of which his chants of "Peace, it's wonderful!" sounded like a tonic. But if some thought his formula for success had become obsolete, Jim Jones thought otherwise and henceforth patterned himself on Father Divine.

After his return from Philadelphia, Jones became increasingly concerned with his personal power. Where he had been "Jim" to his followers, now he demanded to be called "Father" or "Dad." He made organizational and other changes designed to suppress criticism and insulate his followers from the outside world. Like Divine he required followers to turn over their wealth to him and even designated as "Angels" those closest to him in the temple.

Some differences between Jones and Divine are worth noting. While Divine sought the Brotherhood of Man by refusing to acknowledge words of racial distinction, Jones, although he may have contemplated the same ideal, took the opposite route, stressing such distinctions, challenging racial prejudice, and flaunting his rainbow family. A much more eloquent and powerful speaker, Jones also eventually led his followers away from religion. The concept of revolutionary suicide, which Jones adopted from Black Panther leader Huey Newton, would undoubtedly have been incredible to Divine.

It was in 1961, too, that Jones decided to move the People's Temple from Indianapolis. The catalyst, ostensibly, was an article in *Esquire* magazine that listed the safest places in the world in a nuclear war. In 1962 Jones traveled to one of them—Belo Horizonte, Brazil—but was unable to establish himself there, and after a stay in Rio de Janeiro and a brief visit to Guyana, returned to the United States toward the end of 1963.

Whether he was impelled by fears of a nuclear holocaust, or, as some believed, was anxious to remove himself from the increasing scrutiny the temple was receiving from the authorities in Indianapolis, Jones now chose another location rated safe by *Esquire,* and in June 1965, with some 150 of his followers, moved to the hamlet of Redwood Valley near Ukiah in northern California. Here the temple blossomed and by 1972 it claimed an active membership of about 4,000. Temple activities were not restricted to Redwood Valley, however; for a time the temple in Indianapolis continued to function, and the group made long bus trips to Washington, Florida, and elsewhere. In particular, evangelistic roots were set down in San Francisco, where the temple eventually acquired a building in the run-down Fillmore district, and in Los Angeles.

The success of the temple in California was based on the same formula that had worked in Indianapolis. Through public service pro-

grams the community and the press eventually came to see the temple
as a socially active organization that would help people in trouble, care
for stray animals, and even assist travelers stranded in the area. Jones
himself was active in the political sphere, using the votes of his followers adroitly and, as far as possible, maintaining good relations with all
political parties. By 1967 Jones was appointed foreman of the Mendoci-
no County Grand Jury. He also served on the Juvenile Justice and
Delinquency Prevention Board and taught government and history in
night school.

In San Francisco the temple experienced an even greater success.
These were the years of civil unrest and Jones positioned the temple
effectively with respect to the black community and the demand for
equality. Jones enlisted the support of the leading black publisher,
established himself in the NAACP, soon becoming a member of the
board of directors, and so outdistanced the other inner-city black
ministers in the civil rights struggle that by 1977 he was chosen to host
a testimonial dinner commemorating Martin Luther King, Jr.

On the larger political scene Jones became an influential player in
city, state, and national matters. In the 1975 election he helped elect
George Moscone mayor of San Francisco and was rewarded with the
chairmanship of the city's Housing Authority. Among other activities,
Jones contributed to the California gubernatorial campaign in 1974 and
the Carter presidential campaign in 1976. Temple members turned out
to help Walter Mondale when he visited San Francisco, and Jones dined
with Rosalynn Carter.

But there were more and more stories of frightening events within
the Temple. Defectors gave accounts of Jones's bizarre sexual behavior in which he publicly complained of the "burden" of his huge
penis, how he had sexual relations with female and male followers, and
how he variously forced followers to have relations with each other,
banned any sexual relations except with him, and forced men to admit
publicly that they were homosexuals. Nor was that all. Fraudulent faith
healing episodes were staged in which chicken gizzards and other foul
and strange things were triumphantly produced as the malignant
growths removed by Jones's miraculous powers from the believer's

body. On one occasion Jones staggered on stage apparently bleeding and claiming to have been shot. He disappeared briefly to return unwounded in a further demonstration of his healing powers. Public beatings were administered to followers, sometimes for the slightest infraction, sometimes for an imagined reason. Those punished included babies only months old. From some Jones extracted confessions of horrible acts, whether real or not, intended to keep them under his control. The man's megalomania seemed boundless. Where he once called himself the reincarnation of Jesus Christ, he now called himself God, the actual God who made the heavens and the earth. He ordered the temple members to buy and to sell to the public small pictures of him to ward off evil. The defections which increased as a result were the bane of Jones's life. Unlike Father Divine who seemed completely untroubled when one of his Angels woke up and left Heaven, Jones experienced intense paranoid spasms at such a development. Increasingly he interpreted these departures as personal defeats and looked upon the defectors as parties to a conspiracy directed by the establishment and the government to destroy him and the temple. In this period his growing use of drugs no doubt contributed to the paranoia.

A crisis was now approaching, if only in Jones's mind, for he had learned that a major magazine article was soon to appear exposing some of the more unpleasant facts of the People's Temple. Marshall Kilduff, a young investigative reporter for the *San Francisco Chronicle*, felt there was a good story, but was unable to sell it to the paper's city editor, who admired Jones. Kilduff then approached the magazine *New West* and was assigned to do the story. In the months that followed a powerful campaign was launched to kill the story in which hundreds of calls and letters poured in to the offices of the magazine, important local personalities spoke up on behalf of the temple, and even the American Civil Liberties Union sought to prevent publication. The story appeared nevertheless in August 1977 and described such ugly matters as fake healings, violence, the extortion of life savings from temple members, and the misuse of funds. Even after publication, pillars of the San Francisco community spoke out for Jones and Mayor Moscone took a passive position. But by the time the magazine with its damning piece appeared, Jones and the temple had left California and taken up their next, and last, position in a jungle setting in Guyana near the Venezuelan border. The first group, numbering almost 400, arrived in May, but by September nearly 1,000 had come. The move had been accomplished in secrecy, and, in a kind of foreshadowing of what was to happen little more than a year later, Jones persuaded his followers to go by telling them lurid stories of how the blacks who stayed behind would be put in concentration camps and that whites were on the CIA's "enemies" list.

While the temple sought to clear the jungle and turn it into productive farmland, back home in California the group of temple defectors had organized effectively and now had a sympathetic hearing from Congressman Leo Ryan. Many of the defectors were driven by the desire to rescue family members from the temple. Chief among these and leaders in the defector group were Timothy and Grace Stoen, who had joined the temple in Redwood Valley and had been close and trusted assistants of Jones's. Now the object of the Stoens' efforts was John Stoen, aged seven, who Jones had taken with him to Guyana. While still in the temple, Timothy Stoen had signed a document at Jones's behest acknowledging that he had asked Jones to father a child with Grace Stoen and that John was Jones's natural child. Whether this was true or was just another instance of Jones humiliating and extending control over his followers is unclear, but little John-John, as he was called, became a central piece in the deadly game that now began to be played. As the Stoens made efforts to regain custody of John-John, Jones declared that if he lost the boy, the entire temple would die. Although the Stoens obtained a custody order from a California court, Jones's political connections in Guyana were already such that he was able to stall the case in the local courts.

Such is where matters stood in 1978 when Congressman Ryan decided he would personally visit Jonestown and speak to the temple members himself. In this he was motivated by a desire to help out those constituents who were trying to rescue loved ones, but he was also mindful that such a foray might enhance his political standing.

Ambitious to move up to the Senate, he sensed that he was about to uncover a sensational story of human rights violations, and referred to it as essentially the hijacking of a thousand people.

From Jones's point of view the coming of Ryan must have seemed like the final assault. Already his paranoia had converted the defectors' group into an evil conspiracy directed by the government. Dealing through two lawyers—Charles Garry and Mark Lane—who had become well known for their representation of radical groups, Jones first sought to avoid Ryan but then attached rigid conditions to his visit. Lane apparently contributed to Jones's paranoid theory of a governmental conspiracy by advising temple members over the Jonestown public address system that the FBI and the CIA were their enemies and that they would be tortured by those agencies if the members ever talked to them. As late as September 19, 1978, Lane told a press conference in Georgetown, Guyana, that he had concluded "there is a conspiracy to destroy the People's Temple, Jonestown, and Jim Jones," and recommended civil action against agencies in the United States. As one of the conditions of the Ryan visit Jones demanded that there be no press present, a demand Ryan ignored, possibly seeing press coverage as a protective shield, or else as a certain way of generating the publicity he was looking for.

In the period before the Ryan delegation arrived, conditions in Jonestown had become more and more repressive. Since publications and radio were forbidden, news from the outside world was unavailable except as it was announced by Jones, in distorted fashion, over the public address system. Jones's version of events in the United States featured accounts of racial conflict, Ku Klux Klan marches in major cities, and the desertion of Los Angeles because of a drought. In the pavilion, theme plays were acted out embodying Jones's ideas. In one popular piece a black man would be lynched by men in white hoods, but most gripping of all were the "White Nights," dress rehearsals for mass suicide, which occurred at least twice a month. These horrifying events would begin with rifle fire in the middle of the night and a loudspeaker would announce that the temple was under attack. When everyone assembled in the pavilion, a grim-looking Jones would declare that there were CIA mercenaries out in the jungle waiting to destroy them, and, since the situation was hopeless, they must all die. A tub of "poison" was brought out and everyone lined up to take a drink. Only later did it develop that the tub's contents were not lethal.

New security units were established to maintain an ever-tighter discipline with stern punishment. Members who tried to escape were either shackled eighteen hours a day for three weeks while assigned to chopping wood, or confined in solitary to a tiny wooden box for a week. Those who tried to return to the United States were sedated with Thorazine until pronounced "cured."

At first the Ryan entourage was well received and a festive spirit prevailed. Like others before him, Ryan was impressed by the accomplishment of the temple in this wild setting and the high spirits of the members. After dinner there was entertainment in the pavilion; a band played for dancing and there seemed no evidence of the ugly things the defectors had reported. Nor did any of the members seem interested in leaving. At the close of the evening Ryan stood up and said, "From what I've seen, there are a lot of people here who think this is the best thing that has happened in their whole lives." Everyone applauded loudly.

But the next day Ryan and other members of his group began receiving secret pleas for help in leaving Jonestown. Jones at first said anyone was free to leave, but then complained, "They will try to destroy us." As Ryan was conferring with Jones about those who wanted to leave, temple member Don Sly seized Ryan from behind and brandished a knife. Although Sly was quickly disarmed, Ryan was shaken. Fourteen defectors accompanied Ryan and his group as they were driven to the nearby air strip to board the planes that would take them back to Georgetown. As they waited apprehensively, a truck appeared towing a trailer with armed men. When the vehicle neared the planes the men opened fire, killing Ryan and killing and wounding others in the party.

Back in Jonestown the final act was now ready. Jones gathered all his followers together in the pavilion just as he had done before on the White Nights, but this was to be the real performance. Sitting on his special chair beneath a sign that read "Those who do not remember the past are condemned to repeat it," he told the group that he had arranged for an aide to insinuate himself into the Ryan plane and kill the pilot. The plane would then crash in the jungle, killing everyone on board. That would lead inevitably to an attack on the temple and the torture of their children and older members. It was time, therefore, for their act of revolutionary suicide. Among his first words were these: "I want my babies first. Take my babies and children first." Arrangements went smoothly. Guards armed with rifles and crossbows ranged the perimeter ensuring that no one would leave.

Attorneys Garry and Lane had been warned by Jones that there was resentment against them. Now they were astonished to meet two young men they knew, armed, smiling, and happy, who said they were all going to die for the battle against racism and fascism. The lawyers wanted no part of this, but were trapped until Lane told the guards he and Garry should leave to write the history of the event. This pleased the guards, who permitted them to flee into the jungle.

In a particularly macabre addition to a gruesome event, Jones recorded most of the final minutes in the pavilion, thereby leaving a taped suicide note to the world. Jones addressed his followers:

> I've tried to give you a good life, but in spite of all that I've tried, a handful of our people, with their lies, have made our lives impossible. There's no way to detach ourselves from what's happened today. We're sitting on a powder keg . . . and to sit here and wait for the catastrophe that's going to happen on that airplane . . . and it's going to be a catastrophe—it almost happened here. Almost happened, the Congressman was nearly killed here. . . . We've been so betrayed . . . . We've been so terribly betrayed. What's going to happen here in a matter of a few minutes is that one of the people on that plane is going to shoot the pilot. I know that; I didn't plan it, but I know it's going to happen . . . and down comes that plane into the jungle and we had better not have any of our children left when it's over because they'll parachute in here on us. I'm saying it just as plain as I know how to tell you. I've never lied to you. I never have lied to you—I know what's going to happen. That's what he intends to do, and

he will do it. God can see, I'm so bewildered with many, many pressures on my brain, seeing these people behave so treasonous. It's just too much for me to put together, but I now know what he was telling me. . . . So my opinion is that we be kind to children, and be kind to seniors, and take the potion like they used to take in ancient Greece. Step over quietly because we are not committing suicide— it's a revolutionary act. We can't go back. They won't leave us alone; they're going back to tell more lies, which means more Congressmen; and there's no way—no way we can survive.

When someone suggested fighting back, Jones explained that they could not fight the Guyanese military composed of black, socialist soldiers: "We can do it, but if our children are left we are going to have them butchered. We can make a stand, but we'll be striking against people we don't want to strike against."

When it seemed as if the entire group was persuaded, Christine Miller, a heavyset black woman in her mid-forties, stood up to ask why they could not seek refuge in Russia, a subject Jones had discussed often. No, said Jones, it was too late for that, but under pressure from Miller he agreed "to check on that, check with the Russians to see if they'll take us immediately. Otherwise we die. . . . You know, to me death is not the fearful thing. It's living that's treacherous. I have never, never, never, never seen anything like this in my life. I'm telling you, it's not *worth* living like this. *It is not worth living like this!*"

Miller went on: "I think that there were too few who left for twelve hundred people to give up their lives for those people who left."

When Jones reiterated his certainty that Ryan's death would result in an attack on the temple, Miller returned again to the idea of an airlift to Russia.

> *Jones:* To Russia? You think the Russians are going to want us with all this stigma? Maybe we had some value before, but now we don't have any value.
> *Miller:* Well, I don't see it like that. I mean, I feel like that as long as there's life there's hope. That's my faith.

Jones: Then how come everybody's dying? . . . Some place that hope runs out. Because everybody dies. I haven't yet seen anybody that didn't die. And I'd like to choose my own kind of death for a change. I'm tired of being tormented to hell—that's what I'm tired of. Tired of it!

Now the crowd began to shout at Miller to sit down and let matters proceed.

Jones: I'm going to tell you, Christine. Without me, life has no meaning. I'm the best friend you'll ever have. I've always taken your troubles right on my shoulders. And I'm not going to change that now. It's too late! I've been running too long—I'm not going to change now. [The crowd cheered.] Maybe next time you'll get Russia. The next time around. What I'm talking about now is the dispensation of justice. This is a revolutionary suicide council. I'm not talking about self-destruction—I'm talking about that we have no other road. . . .

Miller: But I look at all the babies and I think *they* deserve to live. You know?

Jones: I agree. But they deserve much more. They deserve peace. We all came here for peace. But have we had it? ["No!" roared the crowd.] I tried to give it to you. I laid down my life practically, I practically died every day to give you peace. And you're still not having any peace. You look better than I've seen you in a long while, but it's still not the kind of peace I wanted to give you. A person's a fool to say you're winning when you're losing.

Miller: When we destroy ourselves . . . we've let them, the enemies, defeat us.

Jones: No. We win. We win when we go down.

Miller: What I think, what I feel and think is that we all have our right to our own destiny as individuals. And I think I have a right to choose mine—and everybody else has a right to choose theirs.

With the crowd now beginning to show its anger at Miller, one of Jones's aides, Jim McIlvaine, entered the argument on Jones's side.

McIlvaine: Christine, you're only standing here because *he* is here! So I don't know what you're talking about, having an individual life. Your life has been extended to the day you're standing here— because of *him.*

Miller [appealing to Jones's omnipotence]: Can't you save so many people?

Jones: I have saved them. I *have* saved them. I made my expression, I made my manifestation—and the world was not ready for me. Paul says there are men born out of due season. *I've* been born out of due season. I've been born out of due season—just like we all are. And the best testimony we can make, the best testimony we can make is to leave this goddamned world!

Miller's brave persistence had angered many in the audience, who began to scream at her. Some struggled to reach her, and one woman was restrained from trying to scratch her eyes out.

Miller now asked Jones directly if he wanted to see John-John die. Stunned at first, Jones declared the boy to be no different to him than any of his children.

A young woman in the crowd shouted: "Dad, we're all ready to go. If you tell us we have to give our lives now, we're ready. All the children and the brothers are with me."

Jones replied, "For a month I've tried to keep this thing from happening, but now I see it's the will of the sovereign being that this happened to us. Now we lay our lives down in protest against what's been done . . . the criminality of the people, the cruelty of the people . . . . And I don't think we should sit here and take any more time for our children to be endangered. . . ." The crowd cheered.

At this point Jones received word about the killing of Ryan and the others.

It's all over. It's all over, all over. What a legacy, what a legacy. . . . They invaded our privacy, they came into our homes. They followed us six thousand miles away. . . . Well, the Red Brigade showed them justice. The Congressman's dead. Please get the medication. It's simple, it's simple. There's no convulsions with it—it's simple. Just, please, get it before it's too late. The GDF [Guyanese Defense Force] will be here soon. I tell you—get moving, get moving, get moving. . . . Don't be afraid to die. You'll see, if these people land out there, they'll torture some of our children here. They'll torture some of our people—they'll torture our seniors. . . . Now, please, please, can we hasten? Can we hasten our medication? You don't know what you've done. . . . Are you gonna get that medication here? You got to move. Marceline [Jones's wife], we got forty minutes.

Two nurses brought out a large tub containing a mixture of cyanide, valium, and Fla-Vor-Aid. In the first row a young mother holding her infant child rose, unbidden, and walked to the stage. Taking a cup of poison, she poured half of it down the baby's throat, drank the rest herself, and walked outside. Another young mother with a baby came up and did the same thing.

Then Jones said, "The people that are standing there in the aisle go stand in regular lines. Everybody get back behind the table and back this way, okay? There's nothing to worry about. Everybody keep calm and try to keep your children calm. Older children can help lead the little children and reassure them. They're not crying from pain. It's just a little bitter tasting, but they're not crying out of any pain."

The line that formed was led by mothers with small children. As they approached the tub, the nurses would squirt poison into the children's mouths with syringes while the mothers took paper cups of the liquid. Together with the frightening order there was a lot of noise and confusion. Some people were screaming, others were searching for family members, others were hugging and saying goodbye.

Jim McIlvaine took the microphone to reassure the community. They would all meet on the other side, he told them; death was nothing but "a little rest—it feels good, it never felt so good, family. I'll tell you, you've never felt so good as how that feels."

But those who had taken the poison were having a different experience, convulsing violently and foaming at the mouth. Expressions of horror and screams were heard. At this point Irene Edwards, an elderly black woman, took the microphone to calm everyone:

Edwards: I just want to say something to everyone that I see is standing around crying. This is nothing to cry about. This is something we should rejoice about. You should be happy about this. They always told us that we should cry when we're coming into the world. But when we're leaving it, and we're leaving it peaceful, I think we should be, you should be happy about this. I was just thinking about Jim Jones. He has just suffered and suffered and suffered. I've been here about one year and nine months and I never felt better in my life, not in San Francisco but in a town called Jonestown. I don't want this life—I had a beautiful life—and I don't see nothing I should be crying about. We should be *happy*.

Jones: Please, for God's sake, let's get on with it. We've lived—we've lived as no other people have lived—and loved. We've had as much of this world as you're going to get. Let's just be done with it—let's be done with the agony of it. It's far, far harder to have to watch you everyday die slowly . . . and this, this is a revolutionary suicide, because none of us self-destructed . . . so they'll pay for this. . . . They brought this on us, and they'll pay for that. I leave that destiny to them.

Many others followed Irene Edwards to the microphone to give their testimonials, thanking Jones for bringing them to "this land of freedom" and for the "chance to die with our brothers and sisters." From time to time Jones returned to the microphone. Once he said

We tried to find a new beginning, but it's too late now. . . . You can't separate yourself from your brothers and sisters. . . . Now I would expect us to die with a degree of dignity. Don't lay down with tears and agony. . . . Don't be this way. Stop this hysterics. This is not the way for people who are socialistic-communists to die. No way for us to die. We *must* die with dignity. . . . Oh God! Mother, mother, mother, mother—please, please, please don't do this. Don't do this. Lay down your life with your child, but don't do this. . . . Free. . . . Free at last. Free at last. . . . You say it's never been done before? It's been done by every tribe in history, every tribe facing annihilation. All of the Indians of the Amazon are doing it right now. They refuse to bring any babies into the world—they kill every baby that comes into the world. They don't want to live in this kind of world. So be patient, be patient. . . . I don't care how many screams I hear, I don't care how many anguished cries, death is a million times preferable to ten more days of this life. . . . Adults, adults, adults, I call on you to stop this nonsense. I call on you to stop exciting your children when all they're doing is going to a quiet rest. Are we black and socialist, or what are we? Now stop this nonsense. It's all over and it's good. . . . Hurry, hurry, hurry, my children. All I say, let's not fall into the hands of the enemy . . . quickly, quickly, quickly. . . . No more pain now. No more pain, I said. No more pain. We're not letting them take our lives. We're laying down our lives.

A young woman began playing a funeral march on an electric organ over the loudspeaker. Over the music Jones could be heard: "We've stepped over, one thousand people who said we don't like the way the world is. Nobody takes our lives from us. We laid it down. We got tired. We didn't commit suicide; we committed an act of revolutionary suicide protesting the conditions of an inhumane world."

Many took the poison and wandered into the fields surrounding the pavilion where they convulsed and died, mostly facedown, often in groups with arms around each other. In some areas the dying fell on the dead leaving layers of corpses, which led the authorities to an erroneous initial count of some four hundred bodies. An indeterminate number of people may not have taken the poison voluntarily, including Christine Miller, whose body showed evidence of an injection on the upper arm. Jones and his chief nurse died of gunshots. It was never determined who fired the shots.

Not everyone died. Two young black men, Odell Rhodes and Stanley Clayton, determined to live and managed independently to escape into the jungle. Two others in the compound survived because they were not noticed. At temple headquarters in Georgetown, Sharon Amos, a trusted Jones aide, and her three daughters were found with their throats cut. Although another temple member was charged with their murders, many believed that Amos wielded the knife herself.

News of the events in Jonestown electrified the world. The *New York Times* reported the story under headlines reserved for the most momentous developments and pondered it editorially as an evocation of Joseph Conrad's *Heart of Darkness*. An enormous outpouring of magazine articles and books followed. If one of the goals of Jones's "revolutionary suicide" was a thunderclap of publicity and memories burned into the world's consciousness, he may have succeeded.

In the torrent of news the world learned a great deal about Guyana, a hitherto forgotten corner of South America. Among other things the country seemed to abound in cults of the broadest variety. Most prominent of all, after the People's Temple, was the House of Israel, a black supremacist Jewish group led by Rabbi Edward Emmanuel Washington. Formerly known as David Hill in the United States, where he had been convicted of larceny and corporate blackmail, Washington was a self-proclaimed rabbi who came to Guyana in 1972 and eventually developed a large following. Blacks, he preached, were the original Jews, and Christianity historically oppressed black people. There were some striking similarities with the People's Temple. Like Jones and Father Divine, Washington preached that he was God. "If I'm not God," he asserted in a sermon to his congregation, "you send a message to the other one and tell Him to come prove I'm not." The rabbi was customarily greeted by his adherents with a curious blend of black power and Judaism—a raised, clenched fist, and the salutation "Shalom, master." House of Israel followers were also required to turn over all of their possessions and pledge allegiance to Washington, and were put to work in the House's small factories or farm. Like Jones, too, Washington was the arbiter of every aspect of his followers' lives, approving dating, marriage, and outside employment. In sermons denouncing whites and Christians he exhorted members to prepare for the "Battle of Armageddon," a race war which would begin in Guyana in 1981. Mass suicide was not in his ideology, but followers had to be prepared to die for the cult. Washington saw the Jonestown tragedy as a blessing for him since it gave him publicity and swelled his congregation to more than 8,700.

The rabbi was also politically astute, but seemed even more accommodating to political power than Jones. To many, the House of Israel was almost a paramilitary arm of the government. Its members wore distinctive dashikis with the black, red, and green colors of the party in power. A force of 125 young men known as the Israel Royal Cadets, led by a former Guyanese army officer, and a group of 300 teen-aged boys made up the group's military. Not only did the House of Israel regularly turn out at government rallies and parades and generally support the government's policies, they also broke up the meetings of other parties. More than that, they had gone out into the cane fields to help break a strike in the country's important sugar industry in 1977, and in the summer of 1979 helped break up other strikes at the request of the government. With the death of Prime Minister Forbes Burnham in 1982, however, the House of Israel fell out of favor with the Guyanese government.

After the initial shock of the Jonestown catastrophe, commentators began sifting through the ashes to extract some meaning from the horror. Efforts to identify historical antecedents were not satisfactory. The suicide of the defenders at Massada was different since they faced certain death or slavery at the hands of the besieging Romans. The suicides of the Old Believers in Russia during the seventeenth to nineteenth centuries seemed closer to what happened at Jonestown since the self-inflicted deaths were intended to protest changes in ritual, but ultimately that, too, was seen as different. At last it became evident that Jonestown was truly unique in history. As to how it could happen, it was relatively easy to blame Jones's slide into madness, the way stations of which temple detectors were ready to describe in detail.

Psychiatrist Marc Galanter saw a special significance in the way Congressman Ryan forced his way into Jonestown, a violation of a system's boundary with explosive consequences. He compared it to an incident in Philadelphia in 1985 when the authorities' attempt to oust from their fortified building a violent cult called "MOVE" had disastrous consequences, including the destruction by fire of sixty-one homes and the death of all but two MOVE members.

A recurring theme, sounded in comments by the world's press, was that the event was a symptom of the failure of American culture in general, and in particular of the lunacies of life in California.

In a vein similar to the *New York Times*'s evocation of Conrad's *Heart of Darkness,* Meg Greenfield in *Newsweek* wrote that the images of Jonestown suggested "the dark impulses that lurk in every private psyche" and that "what made the Jonestown affair such a disturbing metaphor . . . was its reminder that the jungle is only a few yards away." Midge Decter's conclusion in *Commentary* that the event was really an outgrowth of 1960s radicalism was certainly a minority view, for the overwhelming tenor of published analysis targeted cults in general. Linking the People's Temple with "SLA, est, the Process, Hare Krishna, Synanon, Manson's extended Family, and many others—differing one from the other but in some ways similar," the *National Review* expressed the popular anticult sentiment, and picking out the Reverend Moon's Unification Church for special mention, urged a full-scale investigation of "the religions and cults," concluding with an exercise in circular reasoning: "If it looks like a cult, walks like a cult, and quacks like a cult, then the chances are that it's a cult." For his part, the Reverend Moon protested the media's comparisons of his Unification Church to the People's Temple, labeling them "outrageous accusations."

It seemed as if guilt by association was an inevitable fallout of the Jonestown tragedy to be borne by most groups no matter how "cult" was to be defined. The event was seen by many as a vindication of their critical view of cults in general and a powerful moral lesson concerning such aberrant groups. Extreme as it was, it suggested to hostile observers the ultimate destination toward which the new cults—with their exotic rituals, peculiar ideas, and abrasive encounters with society and the law—were all tending and generally provided an evil perspective for viewing them. In some quarters, an anticult hysteria was expected that would lead to restrictive legislation.

But whether the People's Temple was a cult still proves to be an elusive question, partly because of the term's uncertain meaning and partly because of the career of the group. Acknowledging both the tendency to use the word imprecisely and its derogatory connotation, we might consider the approach of psychologists such as Rodney Stark and William Sims Bainbridge who distinguish among religious organizations on the basis of the relation of their beliefs to the religious mainstream of the culture in question and the degree of tension they generate with society. This scheme begins at one end with a church that is at peace with society, moves to a sect that has broken off from an established church with some resulting tension, and arrives, finally, at the cult that has no prior church affiliation, is in greatest tension with society, and is based on the most radical set of beliefs. Although such definitions seem rather artificial, are meaningful only in the context of religious institutions, and may have some other failings, they also shed some light.

Applying such a formula, it might be said that the People's Temple began as a sect and evolved into a cult. As Jones moved away from the parent body, the Disciples of Christ, rejected the Bible and what he called the "Sky-God," and began to proclaim his own divinity, he also generated the increasing tension with society that led to the flight to Guyana and its awful conclusion. At the same time he began instituting those practices of total control over temple members and exhibiting the irrational behavior that led to increasing defections and the beginning of adverse publicity.

But if the temple became a cult, it was not always so, and if its later years were marked by the rising frequency of its collisions with society, its earlier years and the positive services it provided should not be overlooked. For many of the members who were drawn from the ranks of the disadvantaged and the oppressed—poor blacks, drug addicts, habitual criminals, and the like—the temple worked very well indeed. In exhibiting these two features, the temple might even serve as an example for other cults and cultlike organizations that combine programs that are either socially useful or individually beneficial with repugnant elements of mind control, deviant behavior, violence, and megalomania.

It is when we come to the events of November 18, 1978, however, that the temple seems to outdistance all other cults. What had been merely erratic or irrational, here rises to an entirely different plane, escaping all efforts at classification. If we were plotting a curve on some graph to show the rise and fall of each group's aberrations, the event in Jonestown would take the temple's curve off the chart completely. The group death there seems so unique and so riveting that it becomes unfair to attribute to other groups, whether sects or cults, the same characteristics. When the anticultists pointed to Jonestown and said, in effect, "I told you so," the plain horror of the event weakened their argument, for if the mass suicide of so many people in one cult was incredible, the recurrence of such an event could hardly be more plausible.

The exact nature of the horror may somehow have fallen through the thousands of lines of comment and analysis. The *Heart of Darkness* perception was partly right, enhanced no doubt by the fact that the tragedy occurred in the jungle. Beyond the photographs of bodies, shocked readers imagined the wild flora of an equatorial forest inhabited by fierce animals. But this was ornamental only and by no means at the core of the matter. Two other elements seem much more central: the identity of the victims and the darkly mysterious way in which they had been led to give up their lives.

Although it occurred in a jungle clearing in a South American country many had never heard of, the tragedy was definitely an American event. It was not only that the victims were Americans, their organization was American, and its roots and the roots of the tragedy were American. Some passing attention was given to the Guyanese government, but never with a view to exporting the catastrophe to another culture. Here it becomes interesting to speculate about what reactions might have been if the victims were not Americans or if the event had occurred in the United States. News of such calamities occurring around the world are regularly digested with one's breakfast with little real feeling for the actuality of the event. The death of thousands by tidal wave in Bangladesh, earthquake in China, or famine in Ethiopia is acknowledged on these shores, halfway around the world, without much emotion. Indeed the daily news is too often filled with that kind of report, to which, in time, the reader becomes desensitized. But should the event involve one's countrymen, it immediately takes on an infinitely more poignant meaning. Obvious and elusive at the same time, the full meaning of the principle might be understood by asking ourselves whether we would have experienced the Jonestown tragedy in the same way if those involved had been Pakistanis or

Hungarians. At work here is a process of identification which does not function well across oceans or national boundaries.

Even more important, however, was the suggestion of sorcery in the readiness with which so many temple members took the poison. Publicity concerning the new religions had sufficiently alerted the public to their idiosyncratic features. Such peculiarities as shaved heads, exotic dress, and oriental chants had become well known, and there was a general awareness of deviant sexual behavior, trouble with the law, and even episodes of violence. But nothing that had gone before could have prepared the public for what happened at Jonestown. Suicide is among the most dramatic and incomprehensible of acts. Multiply it by some figure in the hundreds, after giving due consideration to the children and those who were coerced, and the incident takes on the most extraordinary character. *Sorcery* seems the appropriate term, suggesting both the astonishing influence Jones had over the group and a mysterious, even otherworldly cause.

In listening to the tape or reading the transcript of the temple's final minutes, one begins to feel separated from reality and wonders whether the individuals who cheered Jones's plan for revolutionary suicide and then lined up in orderly fashion to die had not been taken over by some mysterious, alien influence. Perhaps more apposite than the image of Kurtz in *Heart of Darkness* surrendering to his savage self is the sinister method by which people's souls were stolen in *The Invasion of the Body Snatchers*. In that film classic the horror was heightened by the silent and invisible process by which plantlike beings from another world invaded and took over human beings. In some mysterious fashion an individual's very soul was destroyed and he continued to exist only as a robot. A similar feeling can be detected in the shocked reaction to the Jonestown deaths. How, we ask, could all of those people somehow be transformed into mechanical beings who, when directed by their master, would not only agree to kill themselves, but do it enthusiastically. How could mothers, insensible of the powerful urges of motherhood, poison the infants in their arms? Somehow the souls of these people, or their very identities—the most fundamental, private and cherished parts of their being—had been surreptitiously stolen. Only words were needed and the process was completed while the victims went about their daily tasks.

Mingled with the horror, which involves, among other things, our identification with the victims, is our conviction that it could never have happened to us. We are with Christine Miller or Odell Rhodes rather than the majority who willingly drank. In this we may deceive ourselves. The failure of our imagination to bring home to us fully the charismatic influence of Jones and the dynamics of the temple should now be familiar. It is very much like our certainty that we would never have given money to Charles Ponzi, bought land in Florida during the boom, or speculated in Dutch tulip bulbs. This distancing may even be salutary, protecting us from too intimate, and therefore traumatic, an experiencing of the event, but it certainly reveals an inability to understand group forces. This psychological "push-pull"—our identification with the victims drawing us close to the scene, fascinated by its horror; and our refusal to understand how we, too, could become victims setting us apart from it—is worth further investigation. The intensity of our feelings at each pole suggests that Jonestown may be one of the major moral lessons of our time.

In the years after World War II, when civilized nations were still shocked by the policies and deeds of the Nazis and struggled to understand how such evil could have taken root in the cultured soil of Germany, psychologists showed rather conclusively through experiments that anyone could be conditioned to treat his fellow humans in the most bestial fashion. To the revelation that we are all potential Nazis, Jonestown now appears to add the awful truth that each of us is vulnerable to having his or her precious individuality stolen. Perhaps we only think we are strong individuals, self-reliant, and rational at all times.

The members of Jones's People's Temple fell into two groups, the disadvantaged blacks who constituted by far the largest number, and educated, affluent whites, many of whom, like Timothy Stoen, were determined to correct the evils they saw in society. Common to both was a disaffection with society, which is one of the broadest characteristics of those who join cults. The flourishing of such organizations in the United States in the 1960s is usually explained in terms of such discontent, or of rapid social change. The existing institutions of society are perceived as unfair or inadequate and new beliefs are developed to improve society or lead to greater individual fulfillment.

Willa Appel, for example, in *Cults in America,* has pointed out how "The Vietnam war challenged cherished beliefs about the basic goodness of America and democratic ideas. That challenge, however, extended beyond the war. Social institutions and values had been changing since World War II. Sexual mores, the structure of the family, and the role of the schools and churches in the socialization of the young had all been in a prolonged process of transformation. Cults were yet another response to those changes."

But while such an explanation seems plausible to many, to others for whom America has always been the best of places, it only highlights the bizarre nature of cults and their disturbing role. In this view, life here continues to be the best it has ever been; the rantings about an illegal and unjust war, a tyrannical government controlled by big business and the wealthy, and the oppression of racial minorities and the poor are contrived and, at bottom, untrue. This is an attitude indicated, if not fully argued, in the angry observation, "If you don't like it here, leave!" And since our world is really not that imperfect, these fringe groups make no sense. At one extreme, such an attitude spawned the anticult movement which, in the zeal of its advocacy, may have painted cults in more sinister tones than they deserved; in a broader fashion, that attitude also became an impediment to an understanding of cults by less partisan observers. At work here is a kind of territorial prejudice: pride of place and position within the culture make it more difficult to perceive clearly those movements that challenge the culture. One way to remove that cloud might be to examine cult activity elsewhere in the world, cleansed of the emotional attachments we have developed for our own cultural situation. The juxtaposition with local cult activity might be most instructive were we to search for similar behavior among the most exotic societies.

In rejecting the American way of life, many of those who became cult members were moved by a revulsion for the country's obsession with material goods. If this is a frequently heard indictment of America, it may have been heard to greater effect by young people. Ironically, many of those who were drawn into cults came from affluent families. Having received the benefits of prosperity, including higher education, they now found the continuing prospect of a life of material well-being so distasteful that they elected a group style that simulated poverty. A notable example is the Society of Krishna Consciousness, but all communal groups represent a turning away from materialism.

While the children of prosperous families were rejecting the materialistic American way of life by joining certain cults in this country, on the other side of the world cult activity continued to flourish among other people in Melanesia, specifically for the purpose of realizing that same American material way of life. And if the disavowal of wealth by America's sons and daughters was accomplished briskly by joining a cult, the expectation at the heart of the Cargo cults was that American wealth, in the form of houses, refrigerators, stoves, radios, tools, weapons, and the like, would appear in a glorious moment from the hold of a ship or the belly of an airplane.

Melanesia (the "black islands") consists of a group of islands in the South Pacific to the north of Australia, covering a large area bounded on the east by the islands of Polynesia, on the west by Indonesia, and on the north by the coral atolls of Micronesia. The group includes New Guinea, the second largest island in the world, the New Hebrides, and the Solomon and Fiji islands.

Cargo cults have had a fairly long and diverse history in Melanesia, but it was the coming of American military forces during World War II that gave the movement a new focus on the United States. In their earlier relations with Europeans, the natives had been impressed by the white man's goods, but that paled by comparison with the staggering abundance that the Americans brought. The full panoply of military equipment was dazzling; furthermore, the Americans were generous in a way that their white predecessors had not been, and possessed such an excess of material that they threw or gave away a great deal of it.

Cargo cults were aptly named, for they viewed the products of an industrialized world only as they were unloaded from ships or planes. To the native mind, the long process by which ore is excavated, turned into metal, and then transformed into a kitchen appliance, for example, was inconceivable. Their knowledge was limited to what they saw. The whites came to their islands with superior things; they never worked and yet wonderful material was delivered to them. It seemed only natural that if the natives concentrated on the means of delivery, they, too, could enjoy this fabulous wealth.

The Cargo cults were essentially millennial, believing that on the great day when the mythical ship arrived the dead would arise, the old would be rejuvenated, and, most importantly, the whites would be driven into the sea. In some versions the millennium would also be the occasion for a change in skin color: the natives would then become white since it seemed obvious the gods preferred white people.

The fascination with America was expressed in curious ways. The island of Tanna was home to the John Frum movement—named for an imaginary messiah whose role was assumed over the years by various men. In 1943 a native named Neloiag proclaimed himself John Frum, king of America and of Tanna, and organized a force of two hundred men who set to work building an airfield to receive planes carrying the wealth from John Frum's father in America. Two years earlier, Joe Nalpin, another self-proclaimed reincarnation of John Frum, had announced that John Frum was king of America, that his sons were going there to seek him, and frequently spoke of "Rusefel" (Roosevelt). Still another Tannese who claimed to be John Frum went about with a piece of copper wire around his waist, through which he said he was receiving news from America. On the islands of Malekula and Pentecost land was cleared for roads and an airfield for the expected trucks and planes. In the Madang area of New Guinea, the natives built large imitation camps on sites where the United States had established real camps and simulated the routine of daily military life. In the morning they would "fall in" with their "commanders," and they designated "paymasters," "sergeants," and "guards." Elsewhere special Cargo houses were built in cemeteries, and, imitating the American troops, the people built "hospitals" staffed by "doctors" and "nurses." From underneath the earth a factory was expected to rise.

Driven by memories of American military abundance, Solomon Islanders fully expected the Americans to return with LSTs and Liberty ships that would disgorge huge stores for the people. In preparation they built large numbers of storehouses which were, by 1946, all sited and completed with military precision, and all empty.

The thought of America as a cornucopia of goods has continued unabated and taken some even more unusual turns: On the island of Neu-Hannover, in 1964, the natives tried to vote for President Lyndon B. Johnson in local elections. When it was explained to them that he was not a candidate for the local council, they raised money to "buy" him. A visiting United Nations mission was presented with a petition, addressed to Washington, D.C., seeking the annexation of the island by the United States.

What must have looked like the millennium itself from the native side, but more like a practical joke on the white side, occurred at Tanna in April 1957. The most recent epiphany of the John Frum movement had begun when the *Yankee,* a white-colored sailing ship from America, showed up. Irving Johnson, the ship's owner, was in the area writing articles for *National Geographic* magazine when he became interested in John Frum. Johnson's radio message announcing his coming, delivered in a recognizably American accent, was received by the native operator in Tanna with great excitement and passed on to the local population. The ship arrived in a storm, and although it was under power, Johnson put up the sails. With the entire Tannese population watching, the dream ship from America appeared out of the fog. When Johnson went ashore with his crew he was greeted with presents in the company of some two hundred natives and taken to the local volcano, a place of great magic. That the whites were equipped with binoculars, cameras, and other gadgets seemed only fitting to the natives. At the volcano a crewman made a speech advising the natives that goods could be obtained only by work, a message that may not have survived the translation. People lined the road back to the ship offering gifts of food and drink. With the crew back aboard the *Yankee,* the natives surrounded the ship in their canoes and threw letters aboard listing the kinds of goods they wanted.

The first appearance of the Cargo cults occurred in the Fiji Islands in the closing decades of the nineteenth century. Known as the Tuka movement, it combined elements of traditional magic, the Bible, and military procedure. Believers, with blackened faces and long robes, carried out military drills. High officers were called "destroying angels," but there were also "sergeants" and "scribes" issuing commands to the rank and file, who were known as "soldiers." The leader predicted the coming of the millennium—when stores would be jammed with goods, there would be eternal life and pleasure, the old lands and independence would return, and the whites would be driven into the sea. To join the movement and thereby obtain a bottle of holy water from the Fountain of Life which conferred immortality, one was charged a fee. Miracles were performed in temples and a cult house of sleep and pleasant dreams was built to provide the faithful with a taste of the paradise to come. Viewed by the whites as a dangerous conspiracy, the movement was suppressed by the government, but traces lasted well into the next century.

The most celebrated of the Cargo cults produced the Vailala Madness in the Gulf Division of Papua, New Guinea, beginning around 1919. The leader was an old man named Evara, described at the time as an outstanding personality, heavily influenced by European customs, and given to wearing a coat of white duck while displaying a 1919 Victory Medal. As a result of revelations he experienced, Evara prophesied the coming of a steamer containing both the spirits of the ancestors and the "Cargo," goods that would be allotted to villages by signs of identification on the crates. To obtain these goods, however, it was necessary to drive out the whites and observe new ceremonies and rules of conduct.

The Vailala Madness was unusual for the intensity of the feeling it produced, its group dynamics, the odd behavior to which it gave rise, and its violent break with tribal traditions. Under the direction of Evara and other leaders known as "big men," whose authority seemed to supersede even that of the village chiefs, the old religious customs were disavowed; all the masks and other paraphernalia used in the old rituals were publicly burned, and the rituals prohibited. To white observers this abandonment of ages-old traditions in favor of the absurdities of the new cult seemed deplorable. Ironically, those "absurdities" were features of European life that the natives sought to copy in order to achieve the whites' superior status.

In the villages affected, ornamental flag poles, dining tables, and "offices" appeared. The painted flagpoles were believed to permit communication with ancestors or spirits. A "big man" would station himself at the foot of the pole and act as if he was receiving a message which came down the pole into his stomach. He would relate the message to his followers in the form of meaningless songs, which they repeated. Some poles had details suggesting antenna used for wireless transmission—a pumpkin at the top, "wires" made of braided cane, and an "operator cabin." Dining tables, decorated with flower-filled bottles and surrounded by benches, were set up in the center of the village. The men would sit at the tables in their best clothes holding feasts in what they believed to be the correct European style. Since the offices of white people were seen as places of white power, they, too, were imitated, but what the cults referred to as "offices" functioned more like ceremonial temples. Cult followers would sit on the verandas, just as they saw the whites sit on their verandas, and attempt to communicate with "Goss" (God).

In some villages large poles were kept in the cult temples hidden from Europeans and used for divinatory purposes. Carried by at least two men, they were believed to move under their own power, much like dowsing rods. In cases of theft or other offense, the pole would be brought out, and, on the shoulders of the men, point to the guilty party, who would then confess. Even innocent people would accept the pole's verdict.

Military and religious activities were also imitated, as leaders required their followers to "fall in" and salute them, flags were raised, and there was regular drilling. A nine o'clock curfew was established in some places even though no one could tell time, and rifles were expected to be included in the Cargo. Sunday "prayers" were conducted, "reading" from books was common even though the natives were illiterate, and confession of sins was a regular event. Aspects of Christian theology surfaced in oddly distorted ways: Jehovah became the younger brother of Jesus, heaven was confused with Yesu, and a martial portrait of King George V was displayed as Ihova Yesu-nu-ovaki. Heaven was pictured in European, and not Melanesian, terms without a forest and with stone houses. Some natives dressed in long robes in mimicry of the robes worn by missionaries.

The old morality was discarded and new ethical rules adopted which required the people, among other things, to keep the village tidy, to be clean in eating, and to wash their hands. Frequently heard commandments forbade stealing, adultery, and breaking the Sabbath. The old personal ornaments were banned, the ears and noses of children were no longer perforated, and hair was cut short. The Madness even had its own language—"Djaman." The natives admired the sound of German, which they had heard in Rabaul, German territory before 1914, and imported it into the cult even though they could not understand it. It was the "big men" who spoke in this unintelligible tongue as further evidence of their special relationship with the spirits. Nominally "Djaman" (German), it mainly consisted of corrupted English words and phrases.

Those seized by the Madness were sometimes referred to as "Jesus Christ men," but more frequently as "Head-he-go-round-Men." Other epithets were "Belly don't know," "giddy," "crazy," and "whirl-wind." In order to perform the rituals necessary to deal with the dead, "heat" was required, which was produced by eating large amounts of ginger. This not only created the feeling of heat in the stomach but also acted as a stimulant that may have accounted for the peculiar behavior of many of the natives.

As the movement spread with great rapidity from village to village, one early observer quoted in Peter Worsley's *The Trumpet Shall Sound,* was startled to come into a village and see "the natives . . . taking a few quick steps in front of them, and . . . then stand, jabber and gesticulate, at the same time swaying the head from side to side; also bending the body from side to side from the hips, the legs appearing to hold firm. Others would take . . . quick steps forward and stop, placing the hands on the hips, jabbering continuously, swaying the head from side to side, and moving the trunk backwards and forwards, remaining in this position for approximately a minute. . . ."

The Madness moved rapidly both east and west, even though the government took it seriously and arrested and punished cult leaders. In spite of official predictions of its decline, there were fresh outbreaks, as on the occasion of the sighting of the first airplane in the region, but by 1923 the peak had passed and some villages were reviving the ancient ceremonies. The movement was dead by 1931, but so vivid were the memories it left that some people insisted they had seen the wash of the great Cargo ship, heard its engines, the rattle of its anchor chain, and the sounds of its dinghy being lowered. Others claimed to have seen the ship's great red funnel, its three masts, and its lights. Evara's Victory Medal had been thrown into his canoe by a ghostly passenger on the ship as the prophet paddled alongside.

In the great number of cults that developed in these islands the simulation of military and religious procedures and ideas appears again and again. The Taro cults in New Guinea required its followers to "fall in" and commands such as "A shun, man!" were given. The "German Wislin" (Wesleyan?) movement was led by "generals" and "captains" who were distinctly stated not to be "King George's Men." During the Japanese occupation of New Guinea in World War II even more elaborate military details were taken up. Not only were leaders designated as military officers, but "doctors" and "ministers" were appointed as well as "radio telegraphists" for the "radio stations." Homemade uniforms were worn and leaders displayed cloth badges of rank. The troops were armed with wooden rifles and knives which would become real weapons at the Coming. A holy-water drink would make one invulnerable, turning to water bullets that struck the user's body.

About 1956 a Tanna Army was in existence as part of the John Frum movement. They drilled energetically with wooden rifles and bayonets said to be excellent copies of United States military equipment, many of the men wearing American-type uniforms. When ready, they marched off across the island, but disappeared in confusion before the government sent real troops with real weapons to deal with them. A local trader inspecting the Tanna Army's base later found their "radio"—a cast-iron boiler with one side missing from which a rope "antenna" went up out of the house to a tree—with which they tuned in America.

Elsewhere, Christ was expected to arrive with the Cargo ship. Mission services were imitated, with one cult leader performing a "Holy Communion" service using coconut milk for wine and reciting a garbled prayer-book service. Biblical place names were adopted: villages were renamed "Galillee," "Jericho," "Bethlehem" and the like, an islet became "Judea" and a small river "Jordan," and one leader who called himself "Mozes" received his inspiration on a local mountain he renamed "Mount Karmel." In one new ritual the natives piled their traditional clothes besides two graves; the cult leader stood in each grave, crucifix in hand, and made the sign of the cross over the crucifix and each pile. After he jumped out of the grave the clothes were buried, perhaps to symbolize a repudiation of the old ways and an affirmance of the new style represented by the European-style clothes the people now wore. In another village a daily ritual called "school" merged the classroom with church services. An empty box would be placed in the center of the village and the leader would walk about it incanting with a stick in his hand, looking toward Heaven. Another leader would kneel with his head on the box and, with all the followers joining in, repeat the incantation. After further incantations and speaking in tongues those assembled were chided for their ignorance and wickedness.

But the natives' search for the right symbols of white power was not limited to these matters. One cult specialized in making small bamboo buildings throughout the jungle to represent "banks," complete even down to "tellers' windows" through which they expected money to be delivered. When one prophet predicted the coming of a factory together with the Cargo ship, large crowds came to visit him from as far as 150 miles away. In the eastern highlands of New Guinea, several large "wireless houses" made of bamboo were found during the war through which the natives expected advance notice of the coming of Jesus. As the population learned of airplanes, landing fields and airports were built and even airplanes were constructed of bamboo, perhaps to encourage the coming of Cargo from the sky.

The Melanesian view of the world relied on magic and placed great importance on the role of ancestors. Given these facts, it is not surprising that these people hoped to rid themselves of the whites and acquire white power in the way they did. It has been pointed out that the Cargo response is actually quite plausible given the background of these people. When their efforts failed, the natives began to attribute failure to the malicious whites. Previously it was believed that the whites made their goods in some mysterious way, but now it was said that the goods were actually made for the people by their ancestors, who lived in a volcano or on an island, but that the evil whites intercepted the Cargo before it could reach its correct destination. Others claimed that the goods were sent by the spirits but stolen by the whites. When a prophecy was unfulfilled, the government was said to have prevented it, and the true meaning of the Bible was supposedly kept hidden by the whites by tearing out the first page. In fact, Jesus was said to be a Papuan. People set about learning English and other white languages so that they could learn the Cargo secrets buried in the Bible.

One native response to the activities of missionaries was motivated by a desire to obtain material goods. The people believed that by converting to Christianity they would learn the secret of Cargo. When this failed to occur, some cult groups turned hostile to mission Christianity.

Edward Rice, who lived on Tanna, explored the John Frum movement from the natives' point of view, and wrote a sympathetic account of it, has pointed out that what we perceive to be the absurdities of Cargo cults may not be so far removed from our more sophisticated lives after all:

Within our own world, such expectations as winnings from sweepstakes, numbers, lotteries and sports pools, or foundation grants,
welfare, marrying an heiress or a Rockefeller, a meteoric rise in some
exotic career (being discovered by a movie or TV talent scout), or
even in ordinary business, the discovery of a new miracle stock (a
new IBM or Xerox), the reliance on cult works like I Ching or on
astrology—these are all notably crass expressions of white Cargo
yearnings. The fact that certain gratuitous rewards are bestowed
from time to time (a few people do win sweepstake lotteries, or
refrigerators on "The Price is Right") serves to confirm such hopes
for western Cargo. Religion easily becomes a form of Cargo: people
pray before a statue of the Holy Infant of Prague for success in
business, and there are numerous other devotions among Christians
of all sects which will bring health, wealth and happiness. To say
nothing of the gypsy, who *knows*. Even in the New Hebrides a kind of
white Cargo runs rampant. The white occupation forces have gone all
out for tourism in two centers (Vila and Santo), despite the fact that
ordinary services such as electricity, water, sewage, hotel space and
telephones are in extremely short supply and cannot even meet the
current demand. This kind of white man's "Cargo" expectation runs
throughout many parts of the world.

Rice may not have gone far enough in searching for parallels. It
does not require the most strenuous effort of the imagination to see in
some of the groups that have appeared in the United States in the
1960s and 1970s similarities with some features of the Melanesian
Cargo cults. In those movements that arrived on these shores from the
East, the chanting in languages incomprehensible to their devotees is
no different from the "Djaman" recited in New Guinea or the speaking
in tongues by Cargo adherents. Is there really much difference between the ritual utterances of the Papuans on the one hand, and on the
other those of the International Society of Krishna Consciousness,
Rajneeshism, or the Nichiren Shoshu Society when they are all spoken
not for their meaning but just for their sound? In the last group a direct
connection is made between the number of times the chant ("Nam-
myoho-renge-kyo") is repeated and the size or value of that sought,
suggesting an equation between wealth and ritual blunt even by Cargo
standards.

We smile condescendingly at Cargo believers who try to simulate the dress of missionaries or the military, perhaps failing to remember that those who become Hare Krishnas don diaphanous orange wraps, the followers of the Bhagwan Shree Rajneesh are committed to wear red or orange and a necklace of 108 beads with a picture of the guru, and those of the "I Am" movement eschew the colors red and black.

From time to time on Tanna someone appears to declare himself John Frum, and other Cargo leaders have identified themselves as Jesus and "Mozes." But then David Berg, the founder and leader of the Children of God, has also announced that he was Moses, Jim Jones claimed to be Jesus, the Reverend Sun Myung Moon has taken the title "Lord of the Second Advent" indicating his completion of Jesus' work on earth, and Father Divine said he was God.

The use of ginger to generate "heat" and kava, the Melanesian hallucinogenic drink, as part of Cargo seems characteristically primitive until we remind ourselves of the close relationship between the drug culture in this country and certain counterculture groups.

Certainly, the idea of the millennium is not peculiar to Cargo. The notion of a great catastrophe followed by a return to paradise may be embellished in their own ways by the Melanesians, but it is basic in the teaching of the Unification Church of the Reverend Sun Myung Moon, where it involves a battle with Communism and accounted for the peregrination of the People's Temple.

The regimentation that Cargo leaders imposed on their followers resembles that found in the communal life common to many cults and similar groups in the United States.

Even the attempts to evoke white power in Melanesia by building simulated white structures—airfields, stores, radio stations, planes, and banks—may have its counterpart in the use by the believers in Scientology of a "scientific" apparatus consisting of tin cans and a galvanometer to clear one's consciousness of "engrams," the mental images produced by the painful experiences of one's prior lives.

The detection of parallels between the primitive Cargo cults and our modern groups is interesting and useful because it holds up a mirror to the latter groups in which we may see them more clearly, but it has its limits. Nothing in Melanesia, no matter how bizarre, can compare with the mass suicide of hundreds of believers of Jones's People's Temple in the jungles of Guyana in November 1978, an event that may have seemed more incomprehensible to the natives than anything in Cargo seems to us.

Taking It The Hard Way

JAPAN TIMES & ADVERTISER

THE NEW YORK TIMES

WAR:
THE ULTIMATE DELUSION

If we were to consider the subjects dealt with in Mackay's linked themes of delusion and crowd madness in ascending order of magnitude, there can be no question that war would occupy the ultimate place. The honor of this dishonor is made secure by the very numbers of lives affected, war's severity and unparalleled intensity, and its lasting consequences. Mackay ventured no further into this subject than the Crusades, which he described as "the most extraordinary instance upon record of the extent to which popular enthusiasm can be carried," because they seemed to him to combine most of the causes of folly, including those of a political and religious nature. It is their religious dimension, however, that tends to disqualify the Crusades from representing the subject of war, a circumstance magnified by their remoteness in time. So huge is the subject, however, that it threatens to overwhelm: the bloodless recitation of the facts from centuries of war still constitutes the largest part of traditional historical works, and library shelves are filled with books dealing with the conflicts of this century alone. And yet no sampling of follies supplementing Mackay's original miscellany could be complete without attending, in some fashion, to the madness of war.

It is in the soil of nationalism that much of the wartime spirit is rooted, and it is, therefore, no accident that territorial disputes are usually the precipitating cause. Until recently this spirit was commonly cloaked in an attitude of moral righteousness, but the United States' involvement in Vietnam, and, to a lesser degree, years before in Korea, has seemed to signal an end to the kind of phenomenon that Studs Terkel has called the "Good War." The Vietnam experience may represent many things, but it certainly was not an example of the kind of powerful national unity and unanimous moral outrage that marked some earlier wars.

A more promising candidate is to be found in that portion of World War II which pitted Japan against the United States in the Pacific. In that global conflict each of the principal nations was convinced of the moral strength of its position, but there were other aspects that raised the war to a higher level of moral intensity. Even before the commencement of hostilities with the surprise Japanese attack on Pearl Harbor on December 7, 1941, the relations between the two countries were marked by derogatory racial attitudes, which made a peaceful resolution of issues difficult. It was not surprising that with the war those attitudes were brought out into the open, magnified, and used publicly by each side to attack the other and to bolster popular sympathy for the war effort. But that is not all, for the Japanese-American war involved issues that transcended even those of race. Principally as the result of Japanese foreign policy in which a massive readjustment was to be accomplished in east Asia under Japanese hegemony, with a consequent diminution of European and American influence, the war became a struggle between East and West, the confrontation of polarized cultures on the largest of scales.

In historical terms that war is also not far removed in time. Still alive in the memory of many, its influence remains strong although nearing the half-century mark, and some of the circumstances that led to the war and the attitudes exhibited during that time foreshadowed problems that even now trouble the relationship between this country and Japan.

Since war is mankind at its maddest, there would seem to be no part of the subject inappropriate for examination. The unique racial and cultural elements of the Japanese-American conflict, however, point to a more specific topic. From the beginning the powerfully felt moral positions were conceived of in graphic terms, and the press gave vivid expression to those feelings through editorial cartoons in which racial hostility and cultural superiority were regular themes. Those cartoons, together with such other graphic materials as magazine illustrations, posters, and comic books, afford something more than the simple advantage in impact that the visual enjoys over the textual. It was in this wartime iconography that the deepest and strongest prejudices were brought to the surface and some of the ideas that were the real moral engines of the war received their most forthright expression.

The limited study of the Japanese-American war through cartoons serves other purposes. Even at a remove of some five decades, the way in which the war began reverberates in the American mind as an unforgettable episode of treachery and assassination, and other elements of the war produced memories that make difficult, if not impossible, a dispassionate review. If it is too much to say that a direct view will turn one to stone like viewing Medusa's head, or blind one like looking at an atomic explosion, it remains true that for those who experienced the events of the war a calm reconsideration may not be possible. By wandering through this gallery of images we seek to avoid such risks by approaching the subject obliquely, and if the technique does not convey the reality of warfare or allocate ultimate responsibility, it may promise, by arranging the gallery in such a way that each side's images of the enemy is juxtaposed with the other's, a more balanced perspective.

Examining the war through cartoons may strike some as a frivolous exercise, an almost perverse scaling down of the field of vision so that we end up looking at the most tragic of subjects in the most lighthearted way. This is not the case. It is not simply that these cartoons offer an insight into powerful attitudes that were at work in both countries during those years, for they reveal, at the most fundamental level, the self-hypnotic folly that enters into the decision to make war.

The pattern of symbols that begins to take shape upon reviewing these cartoons is plain and familiar. There is almost one great, unifying theme behind many of them even though they were produced by a large number of artists over a period of years and were tailored for different publications. Even more astonishing is the similarity between many Japanese and American cartoons. That predominant theme is a reduction of the war to the image of a barehanded fight between two men. As a first approach to this idea we might look at several cartoons from both sides.

The December 10, 1941, issue of the English-language *Japan Times and Advertiser* contained a cartoon specially drawn by Eturo Kato entitled "Taking It the Hard Way" and intended to depict the Japanese attack on Pearl Harbor and coordinated thrusts against China and British military positions. A huge, dark-colored fist labeled "Japan" delivers a crushing blow to the face of Uncle Sam who is driven back against John Bull who, in turn, falls against Chiang Kai-shek. Stars appear over the stunned enemy figures as they fall domino-fashion.

Some months pass and a series of United States defeats gives way to some successes. On August 12, 1942, the *New York Times* published a cartoon representing the American invasion of the Japanese-held Solomon Islands. Here a clean-cut figure bearing "U.S. Marines" on his chest is seen landing a similarly crushing punch to the jaw of a Japanese soldier. The latter sees stars and the enormous dagger he held drops to the ground.

In *The Nashville Tennessean* a cartoon dealt with the same Solomon Islands battle in like fashion except that the combatants were equipped with boxing gloves and the fight took place in a ring labeled "The Solomons." Both the disproportionately large gloved arm representing the U.S. Marines and the caption ("Coming Back for More") left little doubt about the outcome.

The war coincided with the golden age of comic books, and after Pearl Harbor many of the comic book heroes, some with superpowers and others merely human, turned away from their usual foes to deal with the Axis powers. The cover of the April 1942 issue of *Captain America,* for example, shows the costumed hero delivering a thunderous blow to the jaw of a Japanese soldier as he says, in the manner of John Wayne in his prime, "You started it! Now—we'll finish it!"

The Black Terror, "Nemesis of Crime," another superhero, administers a similar blow on the cover of the December 1944 issue of *Exciting Comics.* Even though the enemy position seems well armed and the hero is supported by armed American soldiers, it was somehow deemed necessary for him to close with the Japanese and duke it out. That detail, it will turn out, signifies something considerably more profound than the fact that the publication's readership consisted mainly of young boys.

Joe Palooka was a non-superhero of the times, a heavyweight boxing champion with a big heart and strong patriotic feelings. After enlisting in the army he is shown on the cover of the January 1943 issue of *Big Shot* casually dealing with an armed Japanese soldier while apparently jogging, this time with a gloved left hook. Joe is not even looking at the enemy here for he has turned away to address a grizzled soldier with a machine gun at his side: "Y'see, sargint, these boxing gloves are as deadly as a tommy gun!"

It would be easy to multiply these examples since the instances are so numerous on both sides. In one sequence of Japanese cartoons that takes place in a boxing ring, a defeated Chiang Kai-shek is replaced by two pudgy fighters, one representing America, one Great Britain, who are both promptly knocked out by a trim Japanese wearing a rising sun headband.

In another Japanese cartoon, distributed in China to show initial Japanese victories, a Japanese airman is shown simultaneously punching President Roosevelt head over heels while kicking Churchill to similar effect.

A punch to the jaw is a symbol with special meaning. Not only is it more easily grasped by the average man than the more intricate and horrifying realistic images of war, it also carries with it a subtle moral message. The punch to the jaw is a more righteous act than a bullet in the stomach or dismemberment by explosion. It implies a vindication in which one establishes his superiority and debases his opponent. For these purposes, showing the reality of warfare with all its grisly detail may—paradoxically—be too abstract.

That the cartoons we have been looking at seem unexceptional may be due to the durability and influence of the metaphor upon which they are founded. To depict warfare in these terms is presently no novelty and may even be deemed a convention. It is our familiarity with the convention that may have dulled our perception of how pervasive the metaphor is, how powerfully it moves us, and how wrong it is.

These cartoons show only one aspect of the metaphor—the punch to the jaw. But other aspects of a fistfight are also routinely incorporated into cartoons by way of expressing ideas of what is fair and what is not and the invective that usually accompanies such fights.

How appropriate is this Fistfight Metaphor? Faced with the idea of representing warfare in this fashion, some unsophisticated people might wonder at the propriety of the images, a problem we don't encounter today because they are so familiar to us. If we were to test the imagery by any standard of fidelity or accuracy, it would fail completely. What, after all, is the relation between a fistfight between two angry, but unarmed, boys in a schoolyard, perhaps, or two men behind a bar on Saturday night, and armed combat, the systematic, planned murdering of thousands, in which men are shot, blown up, incinerated, drowned, gassed, and maimed in the most horrible of fashions? The equation is, of course, wholly wrong, even if it continues to prevail—an observation that does not require the more refined conscience of an Albert Einstein, who believed that "to kill in war is not a whit better than to commit ordinary murder."

The operation of the Fistfight Metaphor in the worlds of editorial cartoons and comic books is not to be thought of as an idiosyncrasy of those publications and the groups of their readers who are juvenile or "low-brow." Rather, these images of the metaphor faithfully reflect attitudes that are expressed in the media and by members of the intellectual community and—most frighteningly—by government officials responsible for deciding whether military force is to be used. It is not simply that the comments of the man in the street about war will be shaped by the metaphor. Consider, for example, the case of the famous Japanese novelist Dazai Osamu who, upon hearing the news of Pearl Harbor, burst out that he was "itching to beat the bestial insensitive Americans to a pulp." And the analogy seems also at work in the thinking at the highest levels of government. Such phrases as "a knockout blow," "bringing the adversary to his knees," and "punching through enemy lines," or references to an enemy that received "a bloody nose," was "stunned," or "turned tail and fled" suggest that the same shallow and misleading analysis is still prevalent in public debates over the use of international force and in discussions of wartime events. Random examples from official comments based on the metaphor include Secretary of State Dean Rusk who, on the occasion of the 1962 Cuban missile crisis, when it seemed that the United States and the Soviet Union were on the brink of nuclear war, said, "We were face to face and the other guy blinked"; President George Bush who, after sending more than four hundred thousand men and women to Saudi Arabia to force Saddam Hussein of Iraq to withdraw from Kuwait, warned that "if we get into an armed situation, he's going to get his ass kicked"; Brent Scowcroft, the president's national security adviser, who followed Bush's remark the next day by reaching back to Dean Rusk's image to comment that "we haven't blinked so far, we're not blinking now, and we will not blink," and President Harry Truman who stated that he "was not brought up to run from a fight."

This is vivid talk, immediately understood by ordinary people. It derives from the menacing rhetoric that precedes a scrap between two men, and except for the startling fact that it issues from the mouths of well-educated, thoroughly experienced, mature men, some of them charged with the responsibility of running our country, preserving our society, and maintaining the peace, it might be followed by the kind of threats, dares, and questions about the sexual virtue of the opponent's leader's mother more commonly heard in the street. The approach to international hostilities by way of memories of personal physical encounters should be recognized for what it is—international machismo.

Newspapers and other organs of the media as well as government officials contentedly indulge in the same defective thinking. Witness this passage from a piece by R. W. Apple, Jr., in the *New York Times* on January 27, 1991, reviewing the Persian Gulf War. The reference is to Iraq's attacks on Israeli cities, the use of American POWs for political purposes, and the release of oil into the Gulf by the Iraqis: "President Bush, a *Marquess of Queensbury man* all the way, said that the Iraqi dictator had a sick mind. American generals huffed and puffed and said none of his actions had military significance. But each of the things that Westerners consider *dirty tricks or low blows* make life harder, in one way or another, for Mr. Bush and his commanders, and they all make Saddam Hussein look like a *dukes-up guy*, unafraid of *the American bully.*" (Emphasis added.)

In trying to understand how such an inappropriate metaphor could come to dominate our thinking about war we might consider how decision making turns on visualization. Even nonnuclear war is unthinkable in the sense that most of us cannot visualize what actually happens. As we search for a way to understand it, memory serves up the few images of conflict it has in storage, usually of a personal encounter. Those images and the conventions that have sprouted from the Fistfight Metaphor have produced a situation in which gray-haired, portly men occupying the seats of power reach decisions about war while recollecting a bloodied nose either given or received after school some fifty years earlier.

The surprise Japanese attack on Pearl Harbor on December 7, 1941, instantly gave the United States an invaluable moral setting for the war. It seemed as if the country had been victimized in the most perfidious fashion and the villainous character of the Japanese was firmly and dramatically established. What first appeared to be an overwhelming Japanese victory carried out with exceptional military skill, however, would turn out to have incalculable moral advantages for the United States and lead to the destruction and defeat of Japan. The grand Japanese strategy envisioned the crippling of the American fleet in the Pacific, a rapid military expansion on the mainland and in the South Pacific, and then the swift negotiation of peace when the Americans, believed by the Japanese to be soft, declined to embark on the kind of war of attrition necessary to roll back Japan's newly established perimeter. It was a strategy that backfired completely when American sentiment, previously divided over intervention in the European war, now united powerfully behind the government's declaration of war.

Across the country, editorial cartoonists went to work to produce the graphic side of President Franklin D. Roosevelt's observation to Congress that December 7, 1941, would be a "day that would live in infamy." In St. Louis, the *Post-Dispatch* artist Fitzpatrick heard the news at home on Sunday afternoon and went immediately to the nearly deserted newspaper office where he drew a cartoon for Monday's paper showing a stealthy Japanese hand appearing through an opening, a bloody dagger in its grasp. The caption read, "The assassin strikes."

The dagger was a frequently used symbol. Werner of the Chicago *Sun* drew a bestial Japanese soldier with a shredded United States flag in his left hand and a dagger dripping blood in the other. Hearst papers carried a more realistic tableau by sports cartoonist Jenkins using the same theme. A grim Uncle Sam kneels over a man knifed in the back while a small dark figure seen in the distance flees toward the rising sun. In a cartoon by Knox in the *Memphis Commercial Appeal*, reprinted in the *New York Times* on January 4, 1942, the bloody dagger became a writing implement. A huge Japanese figure, scowling and drooling, uses it to write the names of Pearl Harbor and Manila in the book of history.

As a symbol of treachery, the bloody dagger was often invoked in this country, but it was also used in Japan to attack America. The *Japan Times and Advertiser* featured a cartoon by S. Kawasaki on December 21, 1942, captioned "Neutrality-Killer," showing President Roosevelt attempting, by sweet talk and bags of money, to insinuate himself with the neutral countries represented as a number of dogs, while behind his back he conceals a dagger that drips blood.

As a symbol of treachery the dagger seems obvious, but its greater significance here lies in its relation to the Fistfight Metaphor. Showing the weapon with which one is stabbed in the back implies a situation in which rules of fairness apply. The dagger's representation in these cartoons indicates a violation of those rules. A detailed explanation of those rules is not necessary for it's clear that they contemplate a personal, barehanded fight without weapons. In this connection it is worth reflecting on modern war as the organized use of increasingly deadly weaponry, a trend that seems to have had no effect at all in making the dagger symbol obsolete. The ease with which cartoonists resorted to the Fistfight Metaphor suggests that there is some vestige of the idea that war is a sporting enterprise in which fair play must somehow be observed. That idea was presumed dead after World War I, but continues to show surprising signs of life.

The cartoon survey shows how frequently both sides resorted to the image of a blow to the jaw to signify some victory on land or at sea, but just as a punch in the face seems a miserably inadequate symbol for a ferocious battle in which tens of thousands are killed and wounded, so, too, does the bloody dagger fail to communicate the vast destruction that occurred at Pearl Harbor. It is a terrible irony that in the cartoon world extreme outrage at an act that would touch off four years of bloody fighting and the death of millions and culminate in the emergence of atomic warfare could be symbolized only by a knife.

*   *   *

So far the exploration of the Fistfight Metaphor has yielded images of the blow to the jaw and the dagger, with the latter's implication of rules of fairness. We know, however, that the kind of fight we are talking about involves something more than just the physical acts observed, and is usually preceded and accompanied by heated invective, the human variation on the kind of screaming with which animals menace each other. Typical of this behavior are those scenes in Stanley Kubrick's film *2001: A Space Odyssey,* where the ape-men groups confront each other at the water hole with frantic screams and threatening gestures. When one of the groups discovers tools through the intervention of some extraterrestrial influence, they take control at the next water-hole confrontation. After an initial period of the usual screaming and menacing, one unarmed ape-man is swiftly clubbed to death. If we choose to think of war as group aggression with tools, that could have been the way in which it first appeared in the affairs of men.

Whether the opposing forces are armed only with bones or equipped with rifles, planes, tanks, cannon, and ships, however, the exchange of invective is still very much a part of warfare. In the Japanese-American conflict that invective was abundantly in evidence in cartoons on both sides. In the United States these illustrations regularly vilified the Japanese as little yellow men with goggles and protruding teeth and as monkeys and apes. Japanese artists tended to caricature Allied leaders as demons with horns and fangs. On both sides the motive seemed the same—to picture the enemy in as demeaning a fashion as possible. If schoolchildren recite, "Sticks and stone may break my bones, but words will never hurt me," the adult world seems to know otherwise and in time of war strives mightily to inflict as much harm as possible through words and their illustrations.

Life magazine, which collected editorial cartoons responding to the Pearl Harbor attack, described how the artists "stabbed at their drawing boards in cold, bitter anger." Where the prewar image of the Japanese had been that of "an oily little man, amiable but untrustworthy, more funny than dangerous," now he was "swarthy, evil, and ominous. He had small weak eyes that glinted with a kind of crazy lust and were usually set off by big goggles. His toothy mouth was filled with oversized incisors. They stretched all across the front of his mouth as it opened wide in a hypocritical grin." There were variations on the theme. Johnstone in the New York *World-Telegram,* for example, depicted a huge snake with a "peace-talk" flag on its tail, its head Japanese, toothy and be-goggled, with the observation that "Even a Rattlesnake Gives Warning," and Arthur Szyk reached into the supernatural to create a *Collier's* cover featuring a vampire with a fanged Japanese face clutching a huge bomb as it soars over Pearl Harbor. But it was the image of the toothy little yellow man with heavy glasses that would reappear for years in newspapers, magazines, comic books, and posters until the end of the war. The nation's rage at the treacherous attack was such that it even produced a new addition to the vernacular; henceforth "Jap" would be used as a verb signifying the act of betrayal.

In the factories of the Douglas Aircraft Company and its suppliers the image was sharpened and put to use to reduce tool breakage and waste. The company distributed posters featuring a character called the "Tokio Kid" who started out with the usual distinctive ethnic facial features but went through a rapid evolutionary change. Later posters showed him with progressively longer and sharper claws, a brow more and more ape-like, and more pointed ears. One poster featuring a worm crawling out of a huge front tooth was withdrawn as a little too gruesome.

Comic books took to the image readily. On the cover of the June 1942 issue of *Big Shot Comics* Joe Palooka is seen hitting a little Japanese soldier with a baseball bat and pronouncing it a foul ball as Uncle Sam looks on as the umpire. The cover of a 1943 edition of a comic book entitled *The United States Marines* has a diminutive Japanese soldier with extraordinary buckteeth fleeing from a Marine bayonet in the direction of Tokyo.

The caricature implies a comparison with the ideal American image of a tall, clean-cut, well-muscled hero, a figure frequently in view in editorial cartoons, and in comic books, the ever-present hero of the story. This ideal American image was hardly representative of many in the military and could not have been an inspiring sight to our nonwhite personnel. But its deficiency in representation is less troubling here than its provenance, for this conception also owes its formulation to the Fistfight Metaphor. Our tall, well-built American hero seems to have been designed to excel in barehanded single combat or in the boxing ring. It is easy to see him delivering those tremendous punches which, in the vernacular of the cartoons (and too often in the minds of government decision makers) are the equivalent of a military triumph. Forty-some years later we find Sylvester Stallone in the *Rambo* films—a cinematic descendant of the comic book heroes—flaunting his muscles and fixing everyone with a baleful eye in a face of stone, all intended to signal his ability and readiness, even in this time of sophisticated weaponry, to land the all-important, symbolically mighty (if militarily insignificant), blow to the jaw. In this fantasy world in World War II it was irrelevant that the slighter Japanese proved to be hardier, better able to survive under extreme conditions, and altogether redoubtable as fighters.

In his splendid book *War Without Mercy: Race and Power in the Pacific War*, John Dower has shown how racial attitudes shaped the war on the battlefield, at home, and in the government. Hostility toward the Japanese and ignorance of their culture by America was matched by Japanese thinking about the Western barbarians. He has explained how the behavior of Japanese on the battlefield led to an American determination to kill every "Jap," and how charges of atrocities by each side "justified" like acts by the other.

To demonstrate these ideas, Dower has drawn on a wide variety of sources including cartoons by American and Japanese artists. We have reference to cartoons for another purpose—to show how the war was commonly viewed in terms of personal combat, a prismatic rendering that imports its own inaccuracies and evils without regard to the compelling observations Dower makes about race.

The powerful current of outrage that pulsed through the country at Japan's treacherous attack must have startled some officials in Washington who had been certain that Japan would take military action and even more certain that it would occur when it did. While the consensus was that the target would be the Philippines, information became available during the days when the Japanese striking force was steaming across the northern Pacific that the true target was farther east.

The failure to act on this information contributed to the catastrophe at Pearl Harbor but was part of an overall casual attitude in which Japanese military capabilities were dismissed as a joke.

Much of this attitude was grounded in racial stereotypes, as Dower has pointed out. Japanese were believed to have inner ear defects which, together with their myopia, made them poor aviators; their belief in Bushido led them to accept death cheerfully to the detriment of effective military action; they were stupid, incapable of logical thinking, and had little mechanical training. The British shared these views. In Malaya, commanders regretted the prospect of meeting such an unworthy foe in battle, and when the colonial governor of Singapore was informed of the Japanese invasion to the north he calmly observed, "Well, I suppose you'll shove the little men off." In this country *Time* took a similar view, reporting at the end of December 1941 that "the little men," barefoot or wearing rubber sneakers, were advancing down Malaya "on a miniature scale," using "tiny one-man tanks and two-man gun carriers. The British even said that their doctors cut miniature Japanese bullets out of miniature British wounds." The attitude was pervasive. Even Secretary of the Navy Frank Knox confided to friends as late as December 4 that a war with Japan would only last about six months.

But there was also a sound assessment that Japan's military capacity was far exceeded by that of the United States. The more considered opinion was that Japan's decision to go to war was, as Churchill put it, "difficult to reconcile . . . with prudence, or even sanity." In Congress, the day after Pearl Harbor, Hamilton Fish declared that the Japanese "have gone stark, raving mad, and have by their unprovoked attack committed military, naval, and national suicide." Fish, an ardent isolationist, then voted for a declaration of war.

In the public view, however, it was treachery, pure and simple. At the time it would have been unthinkable to ask the question, but in what, exactly, did the treachery consist? The Hague agreement of 1911, to which both Japan and the United States were parties, required an official declaration of war prior to the commencement of hostilities. Japan had certainly not given such notice, and in fact, its representatives were still negotiating a mutual accommodation in Washington while its naval force was approaching Pearl Harbor. A desire on the part of the Japanese government to break off those negotiations prior to the attack was frustrated as a result of a communication failure. In our time, at least, the rules for war have become, increasingly, no rules at all. Even before the advent of the atomic bomb, modern weaponry had developed such destructive power that it was folly to think of warfare in any terms other than the most ferocious. Against such a background, the notion of a formal notice of intention to make war seems peculiarly antique, sounding more like a formal announcement of marriage than what it really is. But these distinctions mattered not at all to the American public for whom the facts of the debacle and the scale of the defeat blotted out all other considerations in a tide of rage.

Images of treachery were soon to be joined by a different kind of image as the war progressed. After a series of Japanese victories it seemed as if the enemy was unstoppable. Moving swiftly down the Malay peninsula, on February 15, 1942, a Japanese army captured the fortified city of Singapore (believed impregnable until its artillery was discovered to be able to fire only seaward) from a much larger British defending force. Two mighty British warships, the *Prince of Wales* and the *Repulse,* were sent to the bottom by the Imperial Fleet. In the Philippines, despite resistance on Bataan, American forces withdrew to Corregidor, the fortified island facing the Bataan peninsula, where they were forced to surrender on May 6, 1942, after a siege of twelve hours. Three years later when American forces recaptured the island, the Japanese defended it with such ferocity for eleven days that out of a force of 5,000 only 20 Japanese survived.

The image of the grinning little yellow men with goggles and big teeth who waged war barefoot or in rubber shoes on a miniature scale was abruptly replaced by that of the superman. The Japanese fighting man, it now turned out, was tough, disciplined, well trained, and willing to fight to the death. His leaders were efficient and imaginative. Suddenly the Japanese became formidable opponents and what had been smugly predicted to be unequal combat against a puny foe now seemed a hopeless task.

If news of Japanese fighting capability had a sobering effect, reports of Japanese brutality later produced a different response. Information about the Bataan death march in which more than 7,000 Filipino and American soldiers who had earlier surrendered died of sickness, starvation, beatings, and execution created a sensation when it was released, as did reports of battlefield atrocities by Japanese soldiers, the bayoneting of captives in Hong King, Singapore, and elsewhere, and the execution in Japan of some of the captured airmen shot down in General Doolittle's bombing raid of Tokyo.

The transformation of the Japanese into formidable opponents and news of atrocities encouraged American cartoonists to portray the enemy in simian form. This style, in which Japan and its fighting men were regularly drawn as monkeys, chimpanzees, gorillas, and orangutans was not an American innovation and had some recent antecedents. David Low, the famous British cartoonist, in July 1941 had shown a monkey called "Jap" swinging from a tree by its tail, a knife in one hand, trying to decide which of three soldiers representing the United States, Great Britain, and the Soviet Union to stab in the back, and later used three monkeys to represent initial Japanese successes in Malaya. *Punch*, in January 1942 showed the Japanese advancing through the Malay jungle toward Singapore as armed monkeys swinging through the trees.

In this genre, Lawson Wood's elaborate cover for the April 18, 1942, issue of *Collier's* showing a chimpanzee parachuting onto cactus while clasping a toy gun is really an exception, evoking almost a feeling of affection for the hapless animal while most artists used similar images to convey more malicious feelings. The following year Wood moved closer to the mainstream with his May 8, 1943, *Collier's* cover depicting two monkey airmen in goggles paddling away from a downed Zero. In spite of the rising sun decals on their helmets, however, they engendered feelings one might have at the zoo as well as hatred for the enemy.

More typical was Hutton in the *Philadelphia Inquirer* who tended to represent the Japanese military as a gorilla with huge teeth and a hat, as in cartoons in which the enemy is seen threatening Australia and the Aleutians. Here the foe was large and powerful, quite different from Lawson's cute monkeys, and also different from the bespectacled, bucktoothed little yellow men seen elsewhere.

In the *New York Times* a monkey was shown looking at himself in a mirror, the image in the glass being that of a Japanese face. Even the sedate *New Yorker* joined in with a cartoon in which an attack is about to be made in the jungle on Japanese soldiers high up in trees in which monkeys are also seen. The caption: "Careful, now—only those in uniform."

And the protesting of atrocities, such as the execution of some of Doolittle's airmen after the United States' daring carrier-based bombing of Tokyo in 1942, took simian form. Sy Moyer's famous drawing of a bloody Tojo crouched over a body labeled "Murdered American Airmen" powerfully evokes the killer ape. The *New York Times* over the caption "Let the punishment fit the crime" showed a powerful, malevolent gorilla with the words "Murderers of American Fliers" on its chest facing a cocked revolver held by the mighty hand of civilization.

It became common to picture individual Japanese soldiers as monkeys or monkeylike. In a six-panel cartoon appearing in the Marine Corps' *Leatherneck,* a veteran marine, annoyed when his drink is shot out of his hand, plunges into the jungle and returns with four Japanese soldiers he refers to as "slant-eyed Jerks" and "jaundiced baboons" slung over his shoulders by their tails.

The *American Legion Magazine* portrayed caged monkeys in a zoo erecting a sign that read, "Any similarity between us and the Japs is purely coincidental."

Common as the depiction of Japanese as simians was, it will be noted that this was almost wholly the work of those who drew for newspapers and adult periodicals. The artists who worked on comic books could not venture into this style, but generally had to content themselves with the little yellow men stereotype because their product required story form with a hero, villain, and plot. It is some irony that the more venomous racial invective poured out of the adult newspapers and magazines rather than the comic books produced for and read by children.

Portraying the Japanese as simians communicated a number of powerful messages. On one level it struck the right note of racial condescension. By portraying the Japanese as monkeys they were placed in an inferior position, and, by implication, Americans were elevated. It was both comforting and disturbing to think of the enemy in this way. If he was only an animal, then he could be dealt with more easily; but as an animal he was also capable of wild and savage acts.

In the frequency with which American cartoonists adopted these images, we can see how widespread the notion that we were embroiled in a stupendous fistfight was. Drawing the Japanese as simians is the graphic manifestation of the racial invective that is so often heard in such fights. Such insults are regularly exchanged before, during, and after the incident together with other comments, sometimes sexual, of a similarly insulting nature. To resort to this kind of invective in a physical confrontation is not surprising. That it was used so extensively and to such effect to express public opinion toward the enemy during wartime was probably to be expected, but offers yet another glimpse of that dangerous and shifting border where rational response becomes uncontrolled emotion.

Dower has quoted, to great effect, the exhortation of General Sir Thomas Blamey to his Australian troops in early 1943, when they were just beginning to gain control over the Japanese on New Guinea: "Your enemy is a curious race—a cross between the human being and the ape. And like the ape, when he is cornered he knows how to die. But he is inferior to you, and you know it, and that knowledge will help you to victory."

When and how simians came to stand for a lesser position in the hierarchy of groups of people is not known, but it was certainly not pioneered by American cartoonists in the 1940s. In the middle of the nineteenth century English cartoonists in comic weeklies were drawing Irishmen as anthropoid apes, a radical change from the previous image of Paddy as an amusing and innocent character.

Frederick B. Opper's drawing in the February 15, 1882, issue of *Puck* showed an Irish couple by their shanty. Their heavy facial features are strongly simian and the caption, "The King of A-Shantee," puns on the word for a native of west Africa. "An Irish Jig" by James A. Wales in the *Punch* issue of November 3, 1880, featured a corpulent

Irishman with a similarly apelike face dancing ponderously in the fore-
ground while in the rear John Bull and Uncle Sam despair of bringing
him under control.

The hairy ape-man was a product of the times in which physiog-
nomy was widely accepted as a valid technique for determining character. Since the face was the key, it was not surprising that in the new
scientific world the Dutch anatomist and naturalist Pieter Camper could
postulate in the eighteenth century a formula for ordering the intelligence of monkeys, orangutans, Negroes, and Kalmucks
physiognomically. It was very simple. A "facial angle" was constructed
by running two lines, one from the forehead down to the foremost point
of the teeth, the other from the ear opening to the nostrils. The angle
created by the intersection of those lines revealed the subject's intelligence, there being a direct relationship between the size of the
angle and intelligence. So, for example, Camper found a facial angle of
only 42 degrees for a tailed monkey, 58 degrees for an orangutan, 70
degrees for a Negro and a Kalmuck, and 80 degrees for Europeans.
Grecian and Roman busts exhibited facial angles of 90 and 95 degrees.
In effect, Camper's facial angle said a sloping forehead and a prominent
jaw were signs of stupidity.

Preposterous as Camper's facial angle may seem, it became an
influential notion, and, while submerged, continues to color our thinking even now. In the apelike Irishmen of the Victorian period the small
facial angle is obvious, as it is in the simianlike Japanese of World
War II.

The technique did not simply establish inferior intelligence, it also
meant that the people portrayed in this fashion were lower down in the
great evolutionary scheme, that they had been retarded in development. Whether such a calumny would have been effective before
Darwin's time is unclear, but this particular kind of ethnic vilification
owes something to his theory of evolution.

By the end of the nineteenth century the simian invective was
sufficiently established so that the Irish cartoonists were using it to
strike back at their English oppressors, and American cartoonists were
familiar enough with it to use it not only to depict certain Irish people,
but turned to it on the occasion of the sinking of the *Maine* to protest

Spanish atrocities. Cartoonist Grant Hamilton drew Spain as a power-ful, angry gorilla, dressed in rough clothing, a bloody sword in one hand, the other resting on a gravestone bearing the legend "Maine Sailors Murdered by Spain." Hamilton's conception of a huge gorilla seems to be an ancestor of the apes summoned up by artists in 1942 to protest the execution of Doolittle's airmen by the Japanese. A Spanish artist responded with a drawing of Uncle Sam as a huge pig standing erect on its hind legs wearing a hat and puttees decorated with the stars and stripes.

The word *gorilla* has had an interesting, circular history according to Stuart Berg Flexner, the linguist, author, and editor. The word comes from the Greek *gorillai,* which was derived in the fifth century B.C. from the local name for a tribe of hairy African natives, possibly women. The Greeks used it to mean any savage. The word *gorilla* appeared in the English language in 1799 to mean a hairy aborigine, but did not become the name of the largest of the anthropoid apes until Thomas S. Savage, an American missionary and naturalist, used it in this way upon his return from Africa in 1847. This etymological nicety, that the ape got its name from man and not the other way around, seems not to soften the impact when the word or its image are used for purposes of insult.

As the Lawson Wood covers for *Collier's* indicate, it was not just any simian image that would do in striking back at the Japanese. Many monkeys are cute, the chimpanzee is capable of charming, humanlike behavior, and the orangutan can seem amusingly absentminded. To ensure that the right message was conveyed, many artists doctored their simians by addings fangs to signify their evil character. This touch may have derived from the Dracula legend so enduringly fascinating in Western culture, but in any event it proved effective.

In shuffling through these images, which derive from the Fistfight Metaphor, it is important to keep in mind that the phenomenon is still very much alive. Now, almost half a century after the Japanese-American war, when American artists regularly caricatured the enemy as inferior humans and animals, there is no lack of evidence that the same kind of invective is still invoked in time of war. David Levine, in the *New York Times* of February 1, 1991, has gone even further than the World War II artists in his drawing of an evolutionary structure in which the current foe, Saddam Hussein of Iraq, occupies a place lower than gorillas, monkeys, and snakes. Entitled "The Descent of Man," the illustration shows a regression beginning at the left with a civilized gentleman who looks very much like Clark Gable, moving on to a gorilla, a chimpanzee, and a cobra, and ending with the figure of Saddam Hussein, reduced in size and surrounded by flies. No doubt at the same time artists were also hard at work in Baghdad doing their best to vilify George Bush and the American enemy.

We have already seen evidence that the Fistfight Metaphor was at work in Japan in the form of cartoons of Japanese figures delivering stunning blows to Uncle Sam, President Roosevelt, and Prime Minister Churchill. Just as in the United States, however, that was only the core image, and other, derivative effects appeared as well. While American cartoonists tended to a pictorial invective that degraded Japanese into monkeys, apes, or little yellow men, in Japan cartoonists drew on a different cultural background to vilify the enemy.

Dower has shown how these artists portrayed Americans and British primarily as demons or devils, images powerfully evocative of evil to the Japanese although they were also rendered as beasts in the form of alligators, serpents, fish, frogs, octopuses, and whales. To convey the demonic persona, horns, claws, and fangs were commonly added.

The cover of a 1943 edition of *Manga,* Japan's premier humor magazine, showing a caricatured President Roosevelt, is representative. The figure's grasping hands, baleful stare, and protruding teeth breathe evil. It will fall to others to determine whether these details add up to a composite image of villainy commensurate, in Japanese eyes, with the villainous caricatures of Japanese as little yellow men and apes that were common in this country. Where American artists preferred the long upper incisors to create the evil Dracula effect, in Japan cartoonists used the fangs of the lower jaw to identify their demons, as in the case of the *Manga* cover showing Roosevelt.

When the war had begun to go badly for Japan and the homeland had experienced bombing, another artist drew the deadly figure of a huge Roosevelt looming over the countryside dealing out death and destruction through hands with cannonlike fingers. Here the fangs are not in evidence, but the prominent horns leave no doubt as to the figure's character.

An October 1944 magazine entry added some text to a ferocious drawing in which an ogre is shown removing a mask with the smiling face of Roosevelt to reveal a beastly visage replete with massive horns. An awful necklace of human skulls is around the creature's neck. The cartoon is titled "Naming the Western Barbarians," for which the text offered this explanation:

> It has gradually become clear that the American enemy, driven by its ambition to conquer the world, is coming to attack us, and as the breath and body odor of the beast approach, it may be of some use if we draw the demon's features here.
>
> Our ancestors called them Ebisu or savages long ago, and labeled the very first Westerners who came to our country the Southern Barbarians. To the hostile eyes of the Japanese of former times they were "red hairs" and "hair foreigners," and perceived as being of about as much worth as a foreign ear of corn. We in our times should manifest a comparable spirit. Since the barbaric tribe of Americans are devils in human skin who come from the West, we should call them *Saibanki*, or Western Barbarian Demons.

In still another rendition of a demonic Roosevelt, fangs and a pair of horns have given way to a single horn rising from the top of his head. This more complex cartoon, entitled "Grieving Statue of Liberty," shows Roosevelt perched on the head of the statue waving a banner that says "Democracy" while holding a club that says "Dictatorship." Among the figures on the statue's crown are a Jew inflating the balloon of profits disguised as the American flag.

Churchill was a favorite target as well as Roosevelt. In a cartoon that appeared in the February 1942 issue of *Osaka Puck* he is shown as a corpulent figure with telltale horns, recoiling from a Japanese bayonet thrust while native figures lie shackled in the background. The heading reads, "India! Now is the time to rise!"

The demon image had a number of sides, as Dower has pointed out. While it primarily represented an evil enemy it had two additional aspects. One was the possibility of a conversion to benevolent purposes, a transformation made familiar to Japanese by fairy tales and folklore. Another was the ferocity of Japanese resistance. In this last evocation, the image was that of the protective demon gods of the country. That is the role in which we see the demonic figure in a cartoon from the magazine *Hinode* captioned "The demon who took off his mask." Featured in a text describing the battlefield atrocities committed by the Americans, it shows an angry, horned demon who has taken off his placid Japanese face before dealing with a seated and bound Westerner.

The demonization of Allied leaders was not the only technique used in railing at the enemy, for Japanese cartoonists also gave bestial form to enemy figures as part of the invective. Picturing the enemy as simians never became the widely accepted mode as in the United States, although there were isolated instances. In one cartoon a huge ape representing both the United States and Great Britain leads the poorly armed Chiang Kai-shek to advance toward bayonets by dangling a bait in front of him with one hand while holding a whip ready in the other.

More common was the depiction of Roosevelt and Churchill with some features of other animals intended to signify their clever and lying nature. In a cartoon that appeared in Japan in 1942, both leaders are revealed to have animal hindquarters, Roosevelt those of a horse, Churchill those of a badger, while their upper bodies are clothed in death and money. The badger signified cunning and the horse's rear evil, while the disguises were intended to communicate the duplicitous nature of the two men. The revelation is effected by Japanese planes that pull away the figures' lower garments, showing in the case of Churchill a pattern of skulls and crossbones. A religious variation on this theme of hypocisy shows Roosevelt grasping a cross as if it were a dagger.

Roosevelt and Churchill are again paired with animal features in a cartoon from the magazine *Kodanska Kurabu,* where they are seen using treachery to lure a symbolic horse into a pit. Their deceitful character is indicated by the bushy tails of animals that are only partly concealed by their coats.

Japanese caricatures could sometimes employ more realistic images in commenting upon American history or morals. One cartoon narrative consists of a virtual negative history of the United States represented by a ponderous, armed, gangsterlike figure initially seen with a slavering wolf gazing rapaciously across the sea to Japan where children huddle innocently beneath Mount Fuji. The history begins with the gangster driving Great Britain off in a shooting spree in the Revolution, then discovering great wealth, which he uses aggressively to expand into the West, murdering those who refuse to bend to his will. By the fifth panel he has become a rich man, although his criminal nature is still evident as he extends his grasp into the Pacific, represented by his abduction of a native dancing girl. At the end he is again drooling over Japan. The title indicates that the United States has been planning such a move for 150 years.

Another multipanel cartoon is a small catalog of the ways in which the American people show their cruelty. On the right they are seen enjoying a bloody prizefight and stoning a black child while swimming; in the center they amuse themselves at a bar by throwing eggs at black men. Only those American films dealing with lynching, murder, and mystery will be well received in such a bloodthirsty land, the cartoon claims. In the last panel an American plane drops bombs on a hospital ship. The concluding text expresses wonder that such a race can be so haughty.

As artists in the United States pressed comic book superheroes such as Captain America into service against the foe, so did their Japanese counterparts reach for their superheroes. One result was the appearance of cartoons featuring Momotaro, the "Peach Boy," a figure from Japanese folklore. Momotaro was born out of a peach found floating in a river by an old couple. Gifted with prodigious strength, he assumed responsibility for ridding the country of evil demons, a task in which he was assisted by three friends: a dog, a monkey, and a pheasant. The Momotaro legend was one of the best known of all folk tales and was easily adapted for use in World War II in view of the identification of the Allies as demons. In a typical cartoon of the time,

Momotaro wields a sword threateningly while his monkey and pheasant subdue Roosevelt and Churchill, shown as hairy, horned demons with long claws on hands and feet.

Having shown how both sides were influenced by the Fistfight Metaphor at the start of the war and used racial and other invective throughout the conflict in order to menace and vilify the other much as the combatants do in a personal fight, we also find that the same imagery played a part in shaping the conclusion of the war. The idea of an unconditional surrender, insisted upon by the United States as Japan's defeat drew near, may have seemed morally justified at the time, but ultimately derives from the same doubtful metaphor that has filled so much of our gallery of images. At the Potsdam Conference near the end of the war, when the United States was already in possession of the atomic bomb, Churchill expressed his concern to President Truman, suggesting that insistence on unconditional surrender could lead to a tremendous loss of American lives. Churchill raised the possibility that the Japanese should be given assurances of military honor and continued national existence, but Truman replied that he did not think the Japanese had any honor after Pearl Harbor.

Fiercely proud and never defeated, Japan was nevertheless faced with the inevitable Allied victory. Some sense of the national feeling may be gained from a cartoon that appeared in a popular magazine of that period, which again makes use of a demon as the evil enemy. Illustrating a text that speculates about the agony of defeat and the cruel conditions under which defeated people must exist, the cartoon shows the burdened and exhausted figure of a defeated nation being beaten on the ground by the victors.

If the idea of unconditional surrender has a familiar ring to many, it is not surprising. Behind this more elaborate phrase lurks yet another facet of the Fistfight Metaphor—forcing the other fellow to admit his complete defeat and your victory. An experience that began with a figurative stab in the back, was marked by strident racial and other invective, and was pictured in terms of a pugilistic encounter could only end when the winner forced his beaten foe to cry "Uncle!"

It would serve no purpose here to speculate as to whether insistence on unconditional surrender actually cost lives. Since the war was in its final weeks and would soon be ended with the bombing of Hiroshima and Nagasaki, it might be argued with force that the policy had little or no actual effect. More to our point, however, is the observation that in its conclusion, as well as in its earlier phases, the war gave rise to thinking that was controlled by imagery of the most inappropriate kind, and that thinking took place even at the highest levels of government.

Among the many changes that have occurred since World War II, the effort to raise our consciousness has led many people to an increased awareness of habits of thought and expression that are inaccurate and injurious. The acknowledgment of subtle gender prejudices, for example, has led to revisions in the manner in which we address others; with respect to racial prejudices, the revisions have made us properly sensitive about using a whole series of coded slurs. At a time when many thinking people are careful enough to address an official as a "Chairperson," and would be shocked by a public reference to a black man as "boy," it would seem opportune to encourage the process, already begun, of ending our habit of viewing war as a matter essentially involving nothing more than two teen-agers swinging at each other in the schoolyard.

Two events may have combined to launch the process. The first of these was the divisive Vietnam war, in which the Fistfight Metaphor seemed particularly inapplicable. If the enemy was, in fact, similar in some respects to the Japanese enemy in World War II, his evil character was by no means clearly established, and the role of the United States was morally ambiguous. The second was the appearance of television cameras at the battlefront. With pictures of actual warfare and its terrible consequences coming back into the living room it became more difficult to think of the event merely as an exercise in pugilism.

Powerful as these developments may be, however, they have yet to make the Fistfight Metaphor obsolete, as events in the war between the United States and Iraq made clear. The verbal and pictorial evidence that the metaphor is still in use is not the most troubling aspect of the matter. Of greater concern is the possibility that crucial policy decisions remain irreversible for fear that they will amount to a loss of face. Driven by the most incongruous notions of machismo, leaders who bring their nations to war find it extremely difficult to withdraw by negotiation—the equivalent in metaphor terms, of dropping one's hands and ending the fight to talk it over.

The mighty events of the Pacific War produced many memorable images. The raising of the flag on Iwo Jima, MacArthur wading ashore on his promised return to the Philippines, the surrender on the deck of the U.S.S. *Missouri* in Tokyo Bay are but a few. Some, like the remains of bombed ships at Pearl Harbor, have been turned into a museum, perhaps to immortalize the event which brought the United States into World War II, perhaps as a reminder to be more vigilant in the future.

From these and like images we construct a national reputation for military prowess, valor, and honor. It might be observed that such a reputation may tilt us in the direction of war in the future for while we keep these memories alive in order to honor those who served and died, we are also warning potential aggressors how we will react should they turn on us.

The cartoon images we have looked at have not survived in similar fashion. At least publicly, we no longer vilify the Japanese or strive to land a punch on the Japanese jaw. But if those particular images have become obsolete, their basic premise that international warfare is only a fistfight on a larger scale has not. "War," Clemenceau said, "is much too serious to be left to the military." We might add that, no matter who is in charge, it is also much too serious to be thought of in such juvenile terms as an unarmed encounter between a hero and a villain.

SOURCES

INTRODUCTION

Baruch, Bernard M. *Baruch: My Own Story.* New York: Holt, 1957.

Galbraith, John K. [Mark Epernay]. *The McLandress Dimension.* Boston: Houghton Mifflin, 1963.

Schwarz, Jordan A. *The Speculator: Bernard M. Baruch in Washington, 1917–1965.* Chapel Hill, NC: University of North Carolina Press, 1981.

1 PONZI AND COMPANY

"Are Chain-Letters a Hopeless Evil?" *The Christian Century* (May 15, 1935).

Allen, Frederick Lewis. *Only Yesterday; An Informal History of the Nineteen-Twenties.* New York: Harper & Brothers, 1931.

———. *Since Yesterday; The Nineteen-Thirties in America.* New York: Harper & Brothers, 1940.

Boston Post (various front-page stories: July 4, 1920–September 11, 1920).

"Bursting of the Ponzi Bubble." *The Literary Digest* (August 28, 1920).

"Chain-Letter Prosperity-by-Mail." *The Literary Digest* (May 18, 1935).

"Cracking Down on 'Pyramid Plans'; The Problem: No Workers at the Bottom." *Business Week* (December 11, 1971).

Cross, Wilbur. *Investor Alert! How to Protech Your Money from Schemes,* *Scams, and Frauds.* Kansas City: Andres and McMeel, 1988.

Dunn, Donald H. *Ponzi! The Boston Swindler.* New York: McGraw-Hill, 1975.

du Von, Jay. "Chain-Letter Madness." *The Nation* (June 12, 1935).

"For Exposing Ponzi—a Gold Medal and $2,000." *The Literary Digest* (June 25, 1921).

Klores, Dan. "The Pyramid Scam Hits Town." *New York* (June 23, 1980).

McClintick, David. "The Biggest Ponzi Scheme, A Reporter's Journal." In *Swindled! Classic Business Frauds of the Seventies,* Donald Moffitt, ed. New York: Dow Jones, 1976.

Maxa, Rudy. *Dare to be Great.* New York: Morrow, 1977.

Mehling, Harold. *The Scandalous Scamps.* New York: Holt, 1959.

"Mr. Ponzi and His 'Ponzied Finance.' " *The Literary Digest* (August 21, 1920).

Nelson, Ben. "The Greatest Hoax of the Century." *Coronet* (March 1952).

Olson, Ted. "Brother Can You Spare a Dime." *The New Republic* (May 22, 1935).

Perret, Geoffrey. *America in the Twenties.* New York: Simon & Schuster, 1983.

Ponzi, Charles. *The Rise of Mr. Ponzi.* New York: Charles Ponzi, 1935.

"Ponzi's Dupes." *The New Republic* (September 8, 1920).

"The Pyramid King Gets Sandbagged." *Business Week* (June 24, 1972).

419

"Quick Riches: Chain-Letters Sucker Food Until Postman Gets Tired and Calls on Courts." *The Literary Digest* (April 24, 1937).

Reeve, Arthur B. "New and Old South Sea Bubbles." *The World's Work* (March 1920).

Richman, Eleanor. "On the Road to Riches." *Harper's* (February 1975).

Robinson, Kenneth M. *The Great American Mail Fraud Trial.* Plainview, NY: Nash Publishing, 1976.

Russell, Francis. "Bubble, Bubble—no Toil, no Trouble." *American Heritage,* 24 (February 1973).

Tobias, Andrew. "The Great Chain Robbery." *Esquire* (August 1977).

"Where Are They Now?" (byline: J. B. C.). *The New Yorker* (May 8, 1937).

2 THE FLORIDA LAND BOOM

Allen, Frederick Lewis. *Only Yesterday; An Informal History of the Nineteen-Twenties.* New York: Harper & Brothers, 1931.

Buzzell, J. W. "The Florida Land Rush." *Stone & Webster Journal* (March 1926).

Crossley, Stella. "Florida Cashes in Her Chips." *The Nation* (July 7, 1926).

Daniels, Jonathan. *The Time Between the Wars.* Garden City, NY: Doubleday, 1966.

Essary, J. Frederick. "Have Faith in Florida." *The New Republic* (October 14, 1925).

"Florida Boom's Effect on Shipping." *The Literary Digest* (November 28, 1925).

"The Florida Madness." *The New Republic* (January 27, 1926).

Hecht, Ben. *A Child of the Century.* New York: Simon & Schuster, 1954.

Holbrook, Stewart H. *The Age of the Moguls.* Garden City, NY: Doubleday, 1953.

Isman, Felix. "Florida Land Boom." *The Saturday Evening Post* (August 22, 1925).

Miller, J. Leroy. "In the Land of the Realtor." *The Outlook* (January 13, 1926).

Payne, Will. "Capturing the Simple Life; or The Boom in Florida," *The Saturday Evening Post* (June 20, 1925).

Roberts, Kenneth. *Florida.* New York: Harper & Brothers, 1926.

Russell, C. P. "The Pneumatic Hegira." *The Outlook* (December 9, 1925).

Sakolski, Aaron. *The Great American Land Bubbles.* New York: Harper & Brothers, 1932.

Shelby, Gertrude Matthews. "Florida Frenzy." *Harper's* (January 1926).

Sloan, Laurence H. "Making Money in Florida." Two parts of a 10-part special supplement. *Standard Daily Trade Service* (November 6, 1925, to December 15, 1925).

Stockbridge, Frank Parker. "The Florida Rush of 1925." *The Current History Magazine* (November 1925).

"The 20th Century Lodestone." *Southern Banker* (December 1925).

Vanderblue, Homer B. "The Florida Land Boom." *The Journal of Land and Public Utility Economics* (May and August 1927).

Villard, Oswald Garrison. "Florida Aftermath." *The Nation* (June 6, 1928).

3 THE TULIPMANIA REVISITED

Anderson, W. *How We Got Our Flowers.* New York: Dover Publications, 1966.

Blunt, Wilfrid. *Tulipomania*. Harmonsworth, Middlesex: Penguin Books, 1950.

Braudel, Fernand. *Civilization and Capitalism, 15th–18th Century*. Vol. 2, The Wheels of Commerce. New York: Harper & Row, 1982.

Coats, Peter. *Flowers in History*. New York: Viking Press, 1970.

Cotterell, Geoffrey. *Amsterdam, The Life of a City*. Boston: Little, Brown, 1972.

Garber, Peter M. "Digging for the Roots of Tulipmania." *The Wall Street Journal* (January 4, 1988).

———. "Tulipmania." *Journal of Political Economy*, 97:3 (June 1989).

Geyl, Pieter. *The Netherlands in the Seventeeth Century, Part One*. London: Ernest Benn; New York: Barnes & Noble, 1961.

Huizinga, J. H. *Dutch Civilization in the Seventeenth Century*. London: Collins, 1968.

Krelage, Ernst H. *Bloemenspeculatie in Nederland*. Amsterdam: Van Kampen, 1942.

Montias, John Michael. *Artists and Artisan in Delft, A Socio-Econonic Study of the Seventeenth Century*. Princeton: Princeton University Press, 1982.

Murray, John J. *Amsterdam in the Age of Rembrandt*. Norman, OK: University of Oklahoma Press, 1967.

Murray, W. S. "The Introduction of the Tulip, and the Tulipomania." *Journal of the Royal Horticultural Society* (1909).

Penso de la Vega, Josef. *Confusione de Confusiones*. N.P.: Amsterdam, 1688.

Posthumus, N. W. "The Tulip Mania in Holland in the Years 1636 and 1637." *Journal of Economic and Business History* (May 1929).

———. *Inquiry Into the History of Prices in Holland*. Leiden: Brill, 1964.

Regin, Deric. *Traders, Artists, Burghers*. Assen, The Netherlands: Van Corcum, 1976.

Schama, Simon. *The Embarrassment of Riches: An Interpretation of Dutch Culture in the Golden Age*. New York: Knopf, 1987.

Shapiro, Max. "Trading in Tulips?" *Barron's* (August 26, 1968).

Tergit, Gabriele. *Flowers Through the Ages*. London: Oswald Wolff, 1961.

Tuchman, Barbara. *A Distant Mirror*. New York: Knopf, 1984.

Wilson, Charles H. *The Dutch Republic and the Civilization of the Seventeenth Century*. New York: McGraw-Hill, 1968.

Wirth, Max. *Geschichte der Handelskrisen*. 1890. Reprint. New York: Burt Franklin, 1968.

4 INVADERS FROM MARS AND BAT-MEN ON THE MOON

Broun, Heywood. "It Seems to Me." *New York World-Telegram* (November 2, 1938).

Cantrill, Hadley. *The Invasion from Mars*. Princeton: Princeton University Press, 1982.

Fedler, Fred. *Media Hoaxes*. Ames, Iowa: Iowa State University Press, 1989.

Griggs, William N. *The Celebrated "Moon Story."* New York: Bunnell and Price, 1852.

Klass, Philip. "Wells, Welles and The Martians." *New York Times Book Review* (October 30, 1988).

Koch, Howard. *The Panic Broadcast*. Boston: Little, Brown, 1970.

Leaming, Barbara. *Orson Welles.* New York: Viking, 1985.

Locke, Richard Adams. *The Moon Hoax.* New York: William Gowans, 1859.

"The Night the Martians Landed." *New York Daily News Magazine Section* (October 30, 1988).

Oxford, Edward. "Night of the Martians." *American History Illustrated.* October 1988.

Price, George R. "The Day They Discovered Men on the Moon." *Popular Science Monthly* (July 1958).

Swanson, Glen E. "The War That Never Was." *Starlog* (December 1988).

Thompson, Dorothy. "Mr. Welles and Mass Delusion." *New York Herald Tribune* (November 2, 1938).

Wells, H. G. *The War of the Worlds.* New York: New American Library, 1986.

5 THE DESTRUCTION OF THE XHOSAS

Brownlee, Charles. *Reminiscences of Kafir Life and History.* Pietermaritzburg: University of Natal Press; Durben: Killie Campbell Africana Library, 1977.

Burton, A. W. *Sparks from the Border Anvil.* King Williams Town: Provincial Publishing Company, 1950.

Canetti, Elias. *Crowds and Power.* New York: Viking Press, 1962.

Chalmers, John A. *Tiyo Soga: A Page of South African Mission Work.* Edinburgh: A. Elliott, 1878.

Hammond-Tooke, W. D., ed. *The Bantu-Speaking Peoples of Southern Africa.* London and Boston: Routledge & Kegan Paul, 1974.

Meintjes, Johannes. *Sandile, The Fall of the Xhosa Nation.* Cape Town, South Africa: T. V. Bulpin, 1971.

Mooney, James. "The Ghost-Dance Religion and the Sioux Outbreak of 1890." In *Fourteenth Annual Report of the Bureau of Ethnology to the Secretary of the Smithsonian Institution, 1892–93.* J. W. Powell, director. Part 2. Washington, D.C.: Government Printing Office, 1896.

Peires, J. B. *The Dead Will Arise,* Johannesburg, South Africa: Ravan Press, 1989.

Thompson, Leonard. *A History of South Africa.* New Haven and London: Yale University Press, 1990.

The Times, London (various news stories, March 4, 9, 10, 14, 15, 17, 1842).

Wilson, Monica, and Leonard Thompson, eds. *A History of South Africa to 1870.* Boulder, CO: Westview Press, 1983.

6 SOCCER

Allen, Glen. "The Deadly Reality of a Soccer Game." *Maclean's* (June 10, 1985).

Blank, Joseph P. "Twenty Minutes of Horror." *Reader's Digest* (April 1965).

"Blood in the Stands." *Time* (June 10, 1985).

Canter, David, Miriam Comber, and David L. Uzzell. *Football in Its Place, An Environmental Psychology of Football Grounds.* London and New York: Routledge, 1989.

"Central America: The 'Soccer War' " *Newsweek* (July 28, 1969).

Chyzowych, Walter. *The Official Soccer Book of the United States Soccer Federation.* Chicago: Rand-McNally, 1958.

Cort, David. "Soccer: The Rabble Game." *The Nation* (August 30, 1965).

Durham, William H. *Scarcity and Survival in Central America: Ecological Origins of the Soccer War.* Stanford, CA: Stanford University Press, 1979.

"Football Fanimals." *Time* (April 17, 1978).

Gammon, Clive. "Those Thugs Again." *Sports Illustrated* (June 27, 1988).

Golesworthy, Maurice. *The Encyclopedia of Association Football.* London: R. Haley, 1967.

Hazleton, Lesley. "The Deadly Game." *New York Times Magazine* (May 7, 1989).

Hollander, Zander. *The American Encycopedia of Soccer.* New York: Everest House, 1980.

Kapuscinski, Ryszard. *The Soccer War.* New York: Knopf, 1991.

LeBon, Gustave. *The Crowd: A Study of the Popular Mind.* New York: Viking Penguin, 1960.

Lever, Janet. *Soccer Madness.* Chicago: The University of Chicago Press, 1983.

Menke, Frank G. *The Encyclopedia of Sports.* New York: A. S. Barnes, 1944.

Orwell, George. "The Sporting Spirit." *Shooting an Elephant and Other Essays.* London: Secker and Warburg, 1950.

Pringle, Peter. "Why Britain produces Thugs, Wogs and Louts." *The New Republic* (July 1, 1985).

Reed, J. D., *et al.* "A Disgrace to Civilized Society." *Time* (June 27, 1988).

Walvin, James. *Football and the Decline of Britain.* London: Macmillan, 1986.

Watson, Russell, *et al.* "Britain's Shame." *Newsweek* (June 10, 1985).

"Why Are Soccer Fans So Violent?" *Discover* (August 1985).

Williams, John, Eric Dunning, and Patrick Murphy. "Football's Fighting Traditions." *History Today* (March 1988).

7 LOTTERIES

Asbury, Herbert. *Sucker's Progress, An Informal History of Gambling in America from the Colonies to Canfield.* New York: Dodd, Mead, 1938.

Bayer, Amy. "Are Lotteries a Ripoff?" *Consumer's Research* (January 1990).

Beck, Melinda, *et al.* "The Lottery Craze." *Newsweek* (September 2, 1985).

Clotfelter, Charles T., and Philip J. Cook. *Selling Hope, State Lotteries in America.* Cambridge, MA: Harvard University Press, 1989.

Cook, James. "Lottomania." *Forbes* (March 6, 1989).

Ezell, John Samuel. *"Fortune's Merry Wheel, The Lottery in America.* Cambridge, MA: Harvard University Press, 1960.

Karcher, Alan J. *Lotteries.* New Brunswick, NJ: Rutgers-The State University, Transaction Publishers, 1989.

Lemaire, Jean. "After 553,058 Years, a Win!" *New York Times* (May 6, 1989).

Peirce, Neal R. "State Lotteries Are a Sucker Bet." *Reader's Digest* (September 1978).

Robbins, Peggy. "Louisiana Lottery Was So Big It Didn't Have to Be Rigged." *Smithsonian* (January, 1980).

Sarasohn, David. "The Bookie State." *The New Republic* (February 7, 1983).

"State Lotteries: A Legal Sucker Bet." *Consumer Reports* (February 1974).

Suplee, Curt. "Lotto Baloney." *Harper's* (July 1983).

Weinstein, David, and Lillian Deitch. *The Impact of Legalized Gambling, the Socioeconomic Consequences of Lotteries and Off-Track Betting.* New York: Praeger Publishers, 1974.

Will, George F. "In the Grip of Gambling." *Newsweek* (May 8, 1989).

8 DOWSING

Baring-Gould, Sabine. *Curious Myths of the Middle Ages.* London: Rivingtons, 1869. Reprint, New Hyde Park, NY: University Books, 1967.

Barrett, Sir William, and Theodore Besterman. *The Divining Rod: An Experimental and Psychological Investigation.* New Hyde Park, NY: University Books, 1968.

Bird, Christopher. *The Divining Hand: The 500-Year-Old Mystery of Dowsing.* New York: Dutton, 1979.

Ellis, Arthur J. *The Divining Rod, A History of Water Witching.* Washington, DC: Government Printing Office, 1917.

de France, Le Vicomte Henry. *The Elements of Dowsing.* London: G. Bell & Sons, 1948.

Hester, Ben G. *Dowsing: An Exposé of Hidden Occult Forces.* Arlington, CA: B. G. Hester, 1984.

Roberts, Kenneth. *Henry Gross and His Dowsing Rod.* Garden City, NY: Doubleday, 1951.

———. *The Seventh Sense.* Garden City, NY: Doubleday, 1953.

———. *Water Unlimited.* Garden City, NY: Doubleday, 1957.

Vogt, Evon Z., and Ray Hyman. *Water Witching U.S.A.* Chicago: University of Chicago Press, 1979.

9 PERPETUAL MOTION

Angrist, Stanley. "Perpetual Motion Machine." *Scientific American* (January 1968).

Dieterich, Fred G. *The Inventor's Universal Educator.* Washington, DC: 1899–1906.

Dircks, Henry. *Perpetuum Mobile; or A History of the Search for Self-Motive Power from the 13th to the 19th Century.* N.P.: Amsterdam, 1968; London, 1870.

Gardner, Martin. "Perpetual Motion, The Quest for Machines That Power Themselves." *Science Digest* (October 1985).

Heppenheimer, T. A. "Perpetual Motion, Earth." *Omni* (December 1985).

Hering, D. W. *Foibles and Fallacies of Science.* New York: D. Van Nostrand, 1924.

Ord-Hume, Arthur W. J. G. *Perpetual Motion: The History of an Obsession.* New York: St. Martin's Press, 1977.

Phin, J. *The Seven Follies of Science.* London: A. Constable, 1906.

Smedile, S. R. *Perpetual Motion and Modern Research for Cheap Power.* Boston: Science Publications of Boston, 1962.

Stewart, Doug. "Wheels Go Round and Round, but always run down." *Smithsonian* (November 1986).

10 MUSICAL MADNESS

Ackerman, Diane. *A Natural History of the Senses.* New York: Random House, 1990.

"The Beatles' Secret." *The Reporter* (February 27, 1964).

Bliven, Bruce. "The Voice and the Kids." *The New Republic* (November 6, 1944).

Brien, Alan. "The '64 Beat: After-thoughts on the Beatles." *Mademoiselle* (August 1964).

Brown, Carlton. "A Craze Called Elvis." *Coronet* (September 1956).

Clarke, Donald, ed. *The Pengiun Encycopedia of Popular Music.* London/New York: Viking Penguin, 1989).

Dempsey, David. "Why the Girls Scream, Weep, Flip." *New York Times Magazine* (February 23, 1964).

Diserens, Charles M., and Harry Fine. *A Psychology of Music, the Influence of Music on Behavior.* Cincinnati: College of Music, 1939.

"Elvis—A Different Kind of Idol." *Life* (August 27, 1956).

"The Feeling of Youth" (byline: J. R.). *The New Republic* (February 22, 1964).

Fuller, John G. *Are the Kids All Right?* New York: Times Books, 1981.

"George, Paul, Ringo, and John." *Newsweek* (February 24, 1964).

Goodman, Rachel. "The Day the King of Swing Met the Beatles." *Esquire* (July 1965).

"Hillbilly on a Pedestal." *Newsweek* (May 14, 1956).

"Inextinguishable." *Newsweek* (August 27, 1956).

Kelly, Kitty. *His Way.* New York: Bantam Books, 1986.

Lewis, Frederick. "Britons Succumb to Beatlemania." *New York Times Magazine* (December 1, 1963).

Miller, Jim, ed. *The Rolling Stone Illustrated History of Rock & Roll.* New York: Random House, 1980.

Penrose, L. S. *On the Objective Study of Crowd Behavior.* London: II. K. Lewis, 1952.

"People Are Talking About . . . the Beatles, Four Parody Singers, Now the Passion of British Youth." *Vogue* (January 1, 1964).

Rouget, Gilbert. *Music and Trance.* Chicago and London: The University of Chicago Press, 1985.

"Teeners' Hero." *Time* (May 14, 1956).

Woodward, Helen Beal. "The Smitten Female." *Mademoiselle* (July 1957).

11 JONESTOWN AND OTHER CULTS

Appel, Willa. *Cults in America.* New York: Holt, Rinehart and Winston, 1983.

Axthelm, Pete, *el al.* "The Emperor Jones." *Newsweek* (December 4, 1978).

"By Death Possessed" (editorial). *New York Times* (November 26, 1978).

Cochrane, Glynn. *Big Men and Cargo Cults.* Clarendon Press: Oxford, 1970.

"Cult Taxonomy." *The National Review* (December 22, 1978).

Decter, Midge. "The Politics of Jonestown." *Commentary* (May 1979).

Galanter, Marc. *Cults, Faith, Healing and Coercion.* New York: Oxford University Press, 1989.

"Hurry, My Children, Hurry." *Time* (March 26, 1979).

Kondracke, Morton. "My Belongs to Dad." *The New Republic* (December 9, 1978).

McKelway, St. Clair, and A. J. Liebling. "Profiles, Who Is This King of Glory?" *New Yorker* (June 13, 20, 27, 1936).

Mathews, Tom, *et al.* "The Cult of Death." *Newsweek* (December 4, 1978).

Merton, Thomas. "Cargo Cults of the South Pacific." *América* (September 3, 1977).

Moon, Henry Lee. " 'Thank You, Father, So Sweet.' " *The New Republic* (September 16, 1936).

Moore, Rebecca, and Fielding McGehee III, eds. *New Religious Movements, Mass Suicide, and Peoples Temple.* Lewiston, NY: The Edwin Mellen Press, 1989.

Naipaul, Shiva. *Journey to Nowhere.* New York: Penguin Books, 1982.

"Nightmare in Jonestown" and "Messiah from the Midwest." *Time* (December 4, 1978).

Rice, Edward. *John Frum, He Come.* Garden City, NY: Doubleday, 1974.

Tucker, Carll. "The Back Door, A Monster's Bill of Rights." *The Saturday Review* (February 17, 1979).

Worsley, Peter. *The Trumpet Shall Sound, A Study of "Cargo" Cults in Melanesia.* New York: Schocken Books, 1968.

12 WAR: THE ULTIMATE DELUSION

Dower, John W. *War Without Mercy.* New York: Pantheon Books, 1986.

Gerber, Ernst. *The Photo Journal Guide to Comic Books,* Minden, NY: Gerber Publishing Company, 1989.

Hess, Stephen, and Milton Kaplan. *The Ungentlemanly Art, A History of American Political Cartoons.* New York: Macmillan, 1975.

Keen, Sam. *Faces of the Enemy.* San Francisco: Harper San Francisco, 1991.

Perry, L. Curtis, Jr. *Apes and Angels, The Irishman in Victorian Caricature.* Washington, DC: Smithsonian Institution Press, 1971.

Rhodes, Anthony. *Propaganda, The Art of Persuasion: World War II.* Secaucus, NJ: Wellfleet Press, 1987.

Toland, John. *The Rising Sun.* New York: Random House, 1970.

INDEX

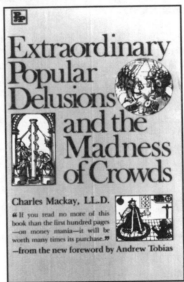